ROCK ON™

The Illustrated Encyclopedia of Rock n' Roll

THE VIDEO REVOLUTION
1978–Present

VOLUME 3

NORM N. NITE
with
CHARLES CRESPO

Special introductions by

**NINA BLACKWOOD, MARK GOODMAN,
ALAN HUNTER, J. J. JACKSON,
AND MARTHA C. QUINN**

1817

HARPER & ROW, PUBLISHERS, New York
Cambridge, Philadelphia, San Francisco, London
Mexico City, São Paulo, Singapore, Sydney

Photo credits appear on page 443.

 For information address Harper & Row, Publishers, Inc., 10 East 53rd Street, New York, N.Y. 10022. Published simultaneously in Canada by Fitzhenry & Whiteside Limited, Toronto.

FIRST EDITION

Library of Congress Cataloging in Publication Data

(Revised for volume 3)

Nite, Norm N.
Rock on.

Vol. 3 by Norm N. Nite with Charles Crespo.
Includes index.
Contents: v. 1. The solid gold years—v. 2. The years of change 1964–1978—v. 3. The video revolution, 1978–present.
1. Rock music—Bio-bibliography. I. Crespo, Charles. II. Title.
ML105.N49 1985 784.5'4'00922 [B] 85-42723
ISBN 0-06-181644-2 (v. 3)

85 86 87 88 89 RRD 10 9 8 7 6 5 4 3 2 1

This book is dedicated to both my mother, Jean,
and to the loving memory of my late father, Jim,
whose love and inspiration enabled me
to develop my interest in music,
which eventually led to my first two books
and now this one becoming reality.

CONTENTS

ACKNOWLEDGMENTS

It would have been extremely difficult to gather the enormous amount of information needed for this book had it not been for my assistant on this project, Charlie Crespo. He, along with diligent workers like Ursula Kadziela, Richard Lorenzo and Renée Casis made my job in putting this book together a lot easier.

Special thanks go to Dorene Lauer, Carole Robinson, and Buzz Brindle of MTV as well as all the MTV VJs; Arthur Levy of Columbia Records; Dick and Kari Clark, Wolfman Jack, Don Kelly, Rick Newman, and Rich Fields.

Also, thanks to Little Steven, Jane Scott, Steve Popovich, Joe Senkiewicz, Joe McCoy, and Bob VanDerheyden. Heartfelt appreciation to Bob Shannon; Hank LoConti; Bruce Morrow; Donald, Rich and Barb Durma; Tony DeLauro; Dick Fox; Adam Berg; Carolyn and Joe Lascko; Andy Hotz, Jr.; Suzy Phalin; Suzy Baldwin; Marc Wiener; Frank Lanziano; Joe Contorno; Michel Landron; Tom Jones; Jay Riggio; Chuck Lester; Rick Durma; Linda Lascko; Charles Scimeca; Dr. Arch; Byron N. Rowland; Nancy Clifford Widmann; Rod Calarco; Steve Piazza; Bobby Leszczak; Brian Williams; Suzan Evans; Jack Soden; Barb Temple; Richard Turk; Ken Zychowski; Jimmy "JP" Pullis; Stan Snyder; Don Imus; Sanford Fisher; Tony Durma; Geoffrey Schuhkraft; Dan Fritz; Paula Szeigis; Lindsay Scott; Lynn Feiner; Jeffi Powell; Terri Rodgers; Chris Kable; George Ghiz; Denise Marder; Sandy Pearlman; Natalie Ripp; Max Rubinowitz; Ron Weisner; Freddy DeMann; Susan Rubio; Joe Corace; Donna Mathers; Steve Petryszyn; Tom Long; Claude Blevins; Kevin G. McCoy; Peter DePeitro; Michael Dainard; Anita Webb; Ken Adamany; Elliot Roberts; Ronda Espy; Jody Miller; Julie Foley; Andrea Starr; Cary Baker; Kathy Gangwisch; Janabai Gayle Tuvil; Mary Smith; Bruce Allen; Patrick J. Armstrong; Terri Lynn Engelsher; Lorie, Chris and Jeannie Zychowski; Kid Leo; John Gorman; Gail Gavert; and especially to my editor Lucy Adelman O'Brien.

My deepest gratitude to Ahmet Ertgun, chairman, Atlantic Records; Michael Klenfner, Brighton Records; Pat Blanks, Geffen Records; Caroline

Pressman, EMI-America; Shirley Divers, Sire Records; Jerri Humbles, Polygram Records; Patrice Pinder, Motown Records; Julie Hooker, Chrysalis Records; Perry Cooper, Atlantic Records; Mary Jo Myszelow, RCA Records; Annette Monaco, A & M Records; Katie Valk and Juanita Stephens, MCA Records; Gigi Hara, Arista Records; Jack Hopke, Warner Bros. Records; Eliot Hubbard, Epic Records; Carol Tatarian, Capitol Records; and Ann Carli, Jive Records.

Without hundreds of long hours and much dedication to this project this book would never have come to pass. Everyone gave of themselves so that this could be the most comprehensive book on today's rock n' roll. I am indebted to them for that.

INTRODUCTIONS

NINA BLACKWOOD

Born: September 12
Hometown: Springfield, Massachusetts

A large part of my work as a VJ requires extensive knowledge of music and the artists who create it. *Rock On,* Volumes 1 and 2, have been essential tools in my day-to-day research (except when they are locked in Martha's dressing room and I can't get to them). The books are factual, accurate and, on top of that, fun to read. Any fan of rock n' roll music will surely find *Rock On,* Volume 3 a delight as well. Norm—thanks for doing all the hard work involved in putting together this series.

MARK GOODMAN

Born: October 11
Hometown: Philadelphia, Pennsylvania

Even before I became a VJ, I was a DJ. (Remember them? Norm's one.) Every air studio I ever worked in had to have copies of *Rock On* Volumes 1 and 2. They were always in terrible condition from overuse. (Rock n' roll DJs are notoriously irresponsible with station property.)

Well, times have changed—now we watch music and some of what you'll find in this third volume of *Rock On* can be seen as well as heard, a fact that has changed the face of rock music. Now more than ever musicians must decide how they wish to be perceived visually, and this latest evolution in music has revealed talent in artists we'll be hearing from for years to come. Years ago we wanted to know the facts behind Paul Anka or Little Richard, and then Crosby, Stills & Nash or Traffic; today we want to know about the artists on both our stereos and screens. Once again, Norm Nite tries to answer all our questions.

With the video stage being added to the concert stage (as well as LPs and cassettes) as performance outlets, the next thirty years of rock n' roll will bear only one similarity to the first thirty. It will not go away, no matter what critics, politicians, or parents say. Rock n' roll isn't just music, it's a way of life—and life is so much sweeter when you Rock On!

ALAN HUNTER

Born: February 14
Hometown: Birmingham, Alabama

Rock On—a great phrase, but how do you use it? What does it mean? Some people say it to be cool—you know, in place of "right on." Others perhaps use it to terminate a battle of words with some intellectual type. Frustrated for lack of a good comeback, they spew out the only thing that comes to mind: "Well . . . rock on, you creep!" (wonderfully inappropriate—but end of conversation). Philosophically speaking, maybe it means "Who cares? Let's have a good time."

However we use it, or whatever it means, rock on we do, because Alan Freed was right. He said something about having "rocks in your head, dad" if you think rock is just a passing fad. Over the years the fads have certainly come and gone, but rock itself is not a fad and it ain't passing. We know this because people continue to write books on the subject—like this one. And it's a good thing they do, because I wasn't alive when rock was born—when Muddy Waters had his "Mojo Workin'," when Bill Haley was "Rockin' Around the Clock," or when Chuck Berry told Beethoven to roll over. And since I was hatched, music has certainly kept up with technology in terms of its proliferation. Therefore it's hard to keep up with all the different groups of today (and a couple of days ago). So I'm humming a tune, can't remember who or when, and I look it up. I'm pleased. I can continue to Rock On—with the facts in my head.

J. J. JACKSON

Born: November 25
Hometown: Boston, Massachusetts

One of the most accurately detailed rock encyclopedias ever. A must for the rock enthusiast.

MARTHA C. QUINN

Born: May 11
Hometown: Ossining, New York

As a VJ on MTV, I'm often asked if I think video music will bring an end to music on the radio. Absolutely not! Morning drive-time would be *disastrous* if everyone were watching MTV in their cars—not to mention the tangled cables!

While the video age has ushered in a new way for music to be heard and seen, the music fans are the same as they've been in every generation. We've always wanted to know more about the people in the grooves: Did David Bowie really work in an advertising agency? What is Phil Phillips doing today? Norm Nite answers these questions in *Rock On*, Volumes 1 and 2. And now people are asking "What is Madonna's last name?" "What about Boy George? and Sting?" Well, needless to say, Mr. Music has come to the rescue once again, with *Rock On*, Volume 3.

Thanks, Norm, you've made my job a lot easier. Now I can go on MTV, use all your research, and maybe people will call me Ms Music!

AUTHOR'S FOREWORD

Since 1969, when I began putting together information for my first *Rock On* book, I have been deeply involved with tracing the history of rock music and its artists. *Rock On* Volume 1 was published in 1974 (and revised in 1982). *Rock On* Volume 2 came out in 1978 (and revised in 1984). I have compiled information on over 2,500 artists who have recorded over 16,000 national chart singles. I have watched this industry grow into the most exciting, influential, and talked-about entertainment medium in the world. From the simple tunes of the fifties to the complex melodies of the sixties and seventies to the video revolution of the eighties: What was once just listened to has now evolved into visual art as well.

It began so simply in the fifties with disc jockeys like Alan Freed (the man who popularized the words "rock n' roll") playing songs by Little Richard, Fats Domino, Chuck Berry, and Frankie Lymon and the Teenagers. Elvis took the music to a new level that changed the course of rock n' roll forever.

Rock expanded in the sixties thanks to The Beatles, The Rolling Stones, Bob Dylan, The Beach Boys, The Four Seasons, Motown, Phil Spector, Chubby Checker, and hundreds of others.

Then came the seventies and Elton John, Disco, The Bee Gees and the hit soundtrack from *Saturday Night Fever*. Rock n' roll became a $3 billion a year business and everyone thought the ceiling had been reached. Well, then came the eighties and MTV astounded us with its video revolution and a sixties singer named Michael Jackson pushed rock n' roll to heights never before dreamed of. I am, along with millions of others, awaiting the exciting developments that each new year brings.

I well remember the work that went into the first two *Rock On* books, and I thought this third volume would be relatively easy to pull together because most of the artists are alive and well. I was wrong. This book was the most difficult. The fifties and sixties performers didn't worry about telling people their ages, birth dates, hometowns, or things about their personal lives. This was probably due in part to the fact that when my first book, covering 1950 to 1963, came out, about 70 percent of the acts were no longer performing or recording. In Volume 2 (1964 to 1978), only about 50 percent were active. However, in this volume, almost 90 percent are pursuing recording/performing careers. Some are concerned about their images in this youth-oriented business. Some do not want their astrological charts done. Therefore, personal information is closely guarded or unavailable. The record companies have limited biographical material; in fact, some companies had no information whatsoever.

As for getting photos of the rock stars, suffice it to say that's a lot more complicated now too. I'm grateful to the record companies who were able to cut through the red tape and to the individual photographers who allowed me to use their photos.

Even with the pitfalls, I welcomed the challenge to put together the most comprehensive book on today's rock n' roll stars. My assistant Charlie Crespo and I forged ahead. I spent literally hundreds of hours on the phone calling managers all over the country to gather this material. In most cases they opened up their personal files to me so that this book could stand with the other volumes as the music industry's "bibles." I thank them for their helpfulness and their trust in my books.

The people at MTV, the company that changed the art of rock n' roll forever with their presentations of music videos, were most cooperative about lending their support to this project, especially the VJs (video-jocks) who expressed their kind words in their introductions.

I feel quite pleased with this book and know you will find it to be a great source of information. I intend to continue to bring you these quality rock encyclopedias and in some small way make my contribution to rock n' roll.

To the thousands of recording artists, the thousands of disc jockeys past and present, the people in the recording industry, and especially to the millions of fans, I hope we continue to Rock On forever with the world's greatest music: "rock n' roll."

Norm N. Nite

ROCK ON™

*The symbol ★ indicates
the song was number one on the charts.*

A

ABC

Members:
- Martin Fry—vocals
- David Palmer—drums
- Steve Singleton—sax
- Mark White—guitar, keyboards

Hometown: Sheffield, England

ABC came together in Sheffield, England, when Martin Fry interviewed a local band called Vice Versa for a fanzine he was editing. Steve Singleton and Mark White, who were in Vice Versa, wound up asking Fry to join them in the band as lead singer.

The three then recruited drummer David Palmer and formed a new group, ABC. The group's debut album, *The Lexicon of Love*, was an international hit, and so for their first world concert tour, the colorful pop music quartet donned gold lamé suits and hired an 18-piece orchestra. Soon after, ABC starred in *Mantrap*, a 60-minute espionage thriller that premiered in America on MTV in 1983. Less than a year later, however, the group became a trio when Palmer left.

September	1982	THE LOOK OF LOVE	Mercury
January	1983	POISON ARROW	Mercury
February	1984	THAT WAS THEN BUT THIS IS NOW	Mercury

AC/DC

Members:
- Bon Scott—vocals—born: July 9, 1946—died: February 19, 1980—replaced (1980) by Brian Johnson
- Angus Young—guitar—born: March 31, 1959
- Malcolm Young—guitar—born: January 6, 1953
- Cliff Williams—bass—born: December 14, 1949
- Simon Wright—drums

Hard-rock fans revere AC/DC more than just about any other rock band. Brothers Angus and Malcolm Young formed the group in their native Australia in 1974 and quickly became a top attraction on the rock-club circuit. The overflow crowds were attracted not only to the quintet's hard and heavy rock, but they also came to see Angus dressed like a schoolkid—

AC/DC. *Left to right:* Cliff Williams, Malcolm Young, Simon Wright, Angus Young, Brian Johnson.

in short pants, knee socks, matching blazer and cap, with a schoolbag on his back—and playing his guitar as if it were a machine gun.

In February 1980, just as *Highway To Hell* became AC/DC's first million-selling album in America, 33-year-old lead singer Bon Scott was found in his car in London after one of his infamous boozing binges, dead from alcohol poisoning. True to its hard-working nature, AC/DC quickly hired a 27-year-old Englishman, Brian Johnson, as its lead singer. Bon is remembered, however, through the group's feature-length concert film, *Let There Be Rock.* Today, the Young brothers are the only members of AC/DC from the original line-up.

October	1979	1. HIGHWAY TO HELL	Atlantic
September	1980	2. YOU SHOOK ME ALL NIGHT LONG	Atlantic
December	1980	3. BACK IN BLACK	Atlantic
January	1982	4. LET'S GET IT UP	Atlantic
October	1983	5. GUNS FOR HIRE	Atlantic

BRYAN ADAMS

Born: November 5, 1959
Hometown: Vancouver, British Columbia, Canada

In 1977, Bryan Adams met fellow musician Jim Vallance by chance in a Vancouver music store, unaware that they would quickly form a writing partnership. Before long, B.T.O., Prism, and Ian Lloyd were recording Adams-Vallance songs.

The lack of attention Adams received on his self-titled debut album tempted him to title his second album *Bryan Adams Hasn't Heard of You*

Bryan Adams

Either, but ultimately it was titled *You Want It—You Got It.* That album produced his first big hit, "Lonely Nights." Adams still calls Vancouver, British Columbia, his home. "Run To You" and "Somebody" are from his latest album, *Restless.*

March	1982	1. LONELY NIGHTS	A & M
March	1983	2. STRAIGHT FROM THE HEART	A & M
June	1983	3. CUTS LIKE A KNIFE	A & M
September	1983	4. THIS TIME	A & M
November	1984	5. RUN TO YOU	A & M
February	1985	6. SOMEBODY	A & M
May	1985	7. HEAVEN	A & M

AFRIKA BAMBAATAA AND THE SOULSONIC FORCE

Members:
Afrika Bambaataa—D.J.
Mr. Biggs—rapper
Emcee G.L.O.B.E.—rapper
Pow Wow—dancer
Hometown: Bronx, New York

Afrika Bambaataa was already a legend in New York when he formed the colorful, wildly costumed Soulsonic Force. He came to fame in the midseventies as one of the first disc jockeys to incorporate rappers into his live performances. He also pioneered a style of spinning known as "quickcutting," in which the turntable is used as a musical instrument itself. Bambaataa, whose name means "affectionate leader," is also a founder of the Zulu Nation, a large New York area youth organization.

| July | 1982 | PLANET ROCK | Tommy Boy |

THE AFTERNOON DELIGHTS

Members:
    Rebecca Hall—vocals
    Suzanne Boucher—vocals
    Janet Powell—vocals
    Robalee Barnes—vocals
Hometown: Boston, Massachusetts

The Boston-based Afternoon Delights were created in a recording studio and scored with "General Hospi-tale," a novelty song that chronicled the entanglements of the popular daytime drama "General Hospital." Lead vocalist on the tune was Rebecca Hall, who at one time was named Top Female Vocalist by *Singout* magazine.

July   1981   GENERAL HOSPI-TALE   MCA

AFTER THE FIRE

Members:
    Andy Piercy—vocals, bass, guitar
    John Russell—guitar
    Memory Banks—synthesizer
    Pete King—drums
Hometown: London, England

After The Fire's biggest hit, "Der Kommissar," was also an international success in a version sung by an Austrian named Falco in his native German. While both versions were available in America simultaneously, After The Fire's English version proved to be the bigger hit here.

February   1983   DER KOMMISSAR   Epic
     May   1983   DANCING IN THE SHADOWS   Epic

AIR SUPPLY

Members:
    Russell Hitchcock—born: June 15, 1949
    Graham Russell—born: June 1, 1950
Hometown: Melbourne, Australia

Soon after Graham Russell moved to Australia from England as a teenager he met Russell Hitchcock and formed Air Supply. But when the duo came to America in 1977 for a tour with Rod Stewart, the Australian fans turned their backs, accusing the group of abandoning them and "selling out" for glamour. Air Supply tried to counteract this viewpoint on their next American tour, in 1982, by taking along stage props and a backdrop resembling an Australian landscape. They chose the name Air Supply because they felt they brought a bit of fresh air to the music industry.

Air Supply. Graham Russell (*left*), Russell Hitchcock.

February	1980	1. LOST IN LOVE	Arista
June	1980	2. ALL OUT OF LOVE	Arista
October	1980	3. EVERY WOMAN IN THE WORLD	Arista
May	1981	★ 4. THE ONE THAT YOU LOVE	Arista
September	1981	5. HERE I AM	Arista
December	1981	6. SWEET DREAMS	Arista
June	1982	7. EVEN THE NIGHTS ARE BETTER	Arista
September	1982	8. YOUNG LOVE	Arista
November	1982	9. TWO LESS LONELY PEOPLE IN THE WORLD	Arista
July	1983	10. MAKING LOVE OUT OF NOTHING AT ALL	Arista

ALABAMA

Members:
Randy Owen—vocals, guitar—born: December 13, 1949
Jeff Cook—guitar, keyboards, fiddle, vocals—born: August 27, 1949
Teddy Gentry—bass, vocals—born: January 22, 1952
Mark Herndon—drums, vocals—born: May 11, 1955
Hometown: Fort Payne, Alabama

Although Randy Owen, Jeff Cook, and Teddy Gentry have known each other all their lives (they're cousins), they met musically in 1969. Randy

Alabama. *Left to right:* Mark Herndon, Jeff Cook, Teddy Gentry, Randy Owen.

and Teddy grew up on adjacent farms, teaching each other guitar chords and the like, while Jeff was a well-known local player. Around Christmastime that year, the three jammed for the first time, and though they repeated the experience a few times, it took a job offer as a backup band at a nearby tourist attraction, Canyonland, to really turn them into a working unit. The cousins' musical career was stop and go until March 1973, when they gave up their day jobs and headed for Myrtle Beach, South Carolina, where they played clubs six nights a week for tips. The group began incorporating original songs into their repertoire, which led to recording and pressing their own records. These records were personally distributed to regional radio stations and all the record companies in Nashville.

Alabama went on to record for two small record companies and by early 1980, the group (with new drummer Mark Herndon) hit the country music top 20 with "My Home's In Alabama." In April 1980, Alabama signed with RCA Records, which quickly released an album called *My Home's In Alabama.* The quartet has gone on to become one of the most popular country/pop acts in the world.

June	1981	1. FEELS SO RIGHT	RCA
November	1981	2. LOVE IN THE FIRST DEGREE	RCA
May	1982	3. TAKE ME DOWN	RCA
September	1982	4. CLOSE ENOUGH TO PERFECT	RCA
May	1983	5. THE CLOSER YOU GET	RCA
October	1983	6. LADY DOWN ON LOVE	RCA
May	1984	7. WHEN WE MAKE LOVE	RCA

ALESSI

Members:
    Bobby Alessi—guitar, bass, vocals
    Billy Alessi—keyboards, synthesizer, vocals
Hometown: West Hempstead, New York

Known both as Alessi and the Alessi Brothers, these identical twins specialized in pop harmonies. As songwriters, the brothers have had their tunes covered by Olivia Newton-John, Richie Havens, Benny Mardones, and Frankie Valli. As vocalists, they have appeared on recordings by Barbra Streisand, Art Garfunkel, and Samantha Sang. Their songs have been translated and recorded in France and Japan.

May	1982	PUT AWAY YOUR LOVE	Qwest

DEBORAH ALLEN

Born: September 30, 1953
Hometown: Memphis, Tennessee

Following high school graduation, Deborah made an attempt at becoming a star in her own hometown. After playing local clubs she realized that

Deborah Allen

the success she was looking for could only be found in Nashville, so in 1973 she moved there looking for stardom.

Her first big break came when she met Roy Orbison, who eventually hired her to sing background vocals on one of his sessions. Later she got a job at Opryland Amusement Park as a singer, whereupon she met Jim Stafford, who asked her to come out to California to be on his television show. She spent two years there working on Stafford's summer program and doing local concert dates. It was at this time that Allen developed her songwriting talents, writing songs that were influenced by her idol, Patsy Cline.

Allen returned to Nashville, and was signed by a publishing company as a songwriter. It was at this time that she met Rafe Van Hoy, another songwriter, the man she would marry.

In 1983, while recording for RCA, she had a major chart single called "Baby I Lied," a song that showed she could sing as well as write.

| October | 1983 | BABY I LIED | RCA |

PETER ALLEN

Born: February 10, 1944
Hometown: Tenterfield, Australia

Judy Garland discovered an act called Chris and Peter Allen at the Hong Kong Hilton and was reportedly so impressed that she asked the duo to open for her in Miami, Las Vegas, and other cities.

Peter Allen eventually married Garland's daughter, Liza Minnelli. At the same time this marriage broke up, so did Allen's professional arrangement with Chris Bell. However, it was Minnelli who had first encouraged Allen to write and perform his own music, and so he did. In addition to his own hits, Allen has cowritten the Grammy-winning "I Honestly Love You" for fellow Australian Olivia Newton-John, "Don't Cry Out Loud" for Melissa Manchester, "You and Me" for Frank Sinatra, and the Oscar-winning "Arthur's Theme" for Christopher Cross.

| January | 1981 | FLY AWAY | A & M |

ALL SPORTS BAND

Members:
    Michael John Toste—vocals
    Cy Sulack—guitar, vocals
    Chuck Kentis—keyboards, vocals
    Alfonso Carey—bass, vocals
    Jimmy Clark (The Boxer)—drums

Manager Tracy Coats created the All Sports Band as a gimmick—a group whose members dressed as athletes—designed to appeal to a young audience. After spending a year and a half listening to demo tapes and auditioning musicians, Coats selected five people to portray a martial arts expert, a baseball player, a football player, a race car driver, and a boxer. The group appeared on the "Solid Gold" and "American Bandstand" TV shows, and charted two singles from one album.

| November | 1981 | I'M YOUR SUPERMAN | Radio Records |
| February | 1982 | OPPOSITES DO ATTRACT | Radio Records |

AMBROSIA

Members:
    David Pack—guitar, vocals
    Joe Puerta—bass, vocals
    Burleigh Drummond—drums, percussion, vocals
Hometown: Los Angeles, California

When Zubin Mehta, the conductor of the Los Angeles Philharmonic, discovered Ambrosia, he was so impressed with the trio's potential that he featured the one-year-old L.A.-based group in his 1971 "All American Dream Concert." Author Kurt Vonnegut, Jr. also proved to be an unlikely but valuable resource; the lyrics to a song called "Nice, Nice, Very Nice" were inspired by one of his works. Ambrosia has been nominated twice for a Grammy Award.

June	1975	1. HOLDIN' ON TO YESTERDAY	20th Century
November	1975	2. NICE, NICE, VERY NICE	20th Century
February	1977	3. MAGICAL MYSTERY TOUR	20th Century
September	1978	4. HOW MUCH I FEEL	Warner Bros.
April	1980	5. BIGGEST PART OF ME	Warner Bros.
July	1980	6. YOU'RE THE ONLY WOMAN	Warner Bros.
June	1982	7. HOW CAN YOU LOVE ME	Warner Bros.

JOHN ANDERSON

Born: December 13, 1954
Hometown: Apopka, Florida

When John Anderson's first album hit the streets in early 1980, the young singer was instantly hailed as the heir to the honky-tonk kingdom of George Jones, Buck Owens, and Webb Pierce. His wonderfully inventive note-curling, phrase-bending singing style delighted country music fans and led critics to compare him to the likes of Lefty Frizzell and Merle Haggard.

John Anderson

John grew up in a small town in the flat country northwest of Orlando, Florida, one of six children whose father was a retired marine and landscaping superintendant at the University of Central Florida. He began playing guitar at age seven, and as an adolescent he led a rock 'n' roll band called the Living End. After John graduated from high school, he moved to Smithville, just outside of Nashville, to sing with his sister Donna. For the next eight years, he worked as a plumber's helper, a carpenter's helper, and a grocery packer. Step by step, he made his way up the country-music ladder of success so that by 1983, he dominated the Country Music Awards with five nominations. "Swingin' " is the best-selling country single in Warner Brothers' history to date. Today, Anderson resides with his wife in "a little house in the woods" some 70 miles east of Nashville, where he enjoys hunting and fishing for smallmouth bass in his spare time.

March   1983   SWINGIN'   Warner Bros.

ANGEL

Members:
    Frank DiMino—vocals—born: October 15, 1951
    Punky Meadows—guitar—born: February 6, 1950
    Felix Robinson—bass
    Barry Brandt—drums—born: November 14, 1951
    Greg Guiffria—keyboards—born: July 28, 1951
Hometown: Washington, D.C.

Angel started in a bar in Washington, D.C., in March 1975, when the remnants of two popular local rock bands met. Most of the musicians who became Angel had several years of experience as rock performers behind them. Gene Simmons of Kiss saw potential in Angel, and helped persuade his record company, Casablanca Records, to sign the group. Angel recorded many albums and did the title song to the film *Foxes*.

Unfortunately for the group, Angel was better known for its image than for its music. The quintet always performed in elaborately designed white satin costumes—even Frank's mike stand was white. Performances began with the members seeming to magically appear on stage one by one and ended with them just as mysteriously disappearing, thanks in large part to illusions crafted by the fellow who creates illusions for Doug Henning. Despite all the visuals, however, Angel failed to sell many records, and broke up in 1980.

April	1977	THAT MAGIC TOUCH	Casablanca
April	1978	AIN'T GONNA EAT OUT MY HEART ANYMORE	Casablanca

ADAM ANT

Real Name: Stuart Goddard
Born: November 3, 1954
Hometown: London, England

Stuart Goddard formed the original Adam and the Ants in 1976 while he was finishing art school. In a short time Goddard, renamed Adam Ant, captured a sizable audience with his colorful look, a combination of pirate fashions and Native American-style feathers and warpaint. He called his music "antmusic for sexpeople" and saw each of his early records become instant hits in his homeland. Later on, he altered his image to that of a Prince Charming and toured with a lavish show he called the Prince Charming Revue. The concert became so talked about that it was even staged for Princess Margaret at the London Palladium.

American FM radio played selected cuts from the Adam and the Ants albums, but it wasn't until Adam Ant went solo that he saw his first big American hit, "Goody Two Shoes." Members of the original Adam and the Ants have since gone on to form Culture Club (Jon Moss) and Bowwowwow (Dave Barbarossa and Matthew Ashman).

November	1982	GOODY TWO SHOES	Epic
March	1983	DESPERATE BUT NOT SERIOUS	Epic
February	1984	STRIP	Epic

APRIL WINE

Members:
  Myles Goodwyn—vocals, guitar—born: June 23, 1948
  Gary Moffet—guitar—born: June 22, 1949 (replaced David Henman in 1973)
  Brian Greenway—guitar—born: October 1, 1951—added in 1977
  Steve Lang—bass—born: March 24, 1949 (replaced Jim Clench in 1975)
  Jerry Mercer—drums—born: April 27, 1939 (replaced Richard Henman in 1973)
Hometown: Montreal, Canada

While April Wine has struggled for recognition in the United States, they have been a supergroup attraction in the province of Quebec since forming in 1969. The band's fourth album became Canada's first English-language album to go platinum and the next album became the first to *ship* platinum.

Miles Goodwyn is the group's only original member. He first hit the rock 'n' roll trail at age 13, when he began organizing dances and playing with bands in his hometown. At age 18, he and three friends formed April Wine, left Halifax for Montreal, and talked their way into a record contract. Some of the group's early work was produced by Gene Cornish and Dino Danielli, formerly of the Rascals, but later music was produced by April Wine itself. The group has won numerous Juno Awards, Canada's equivalent of the Grammy.

March	1972	1. YOU COULD HAVE BEEN A LADY	Big Tree
March	1979	2. ROLLER	Capitol
February	1980	3. I LIKE TO ROCK	Capitol
February	1981	4. JUST BETWEEN YOU AND ME	Capitol
May	1981	5. SIGN OF THE GYPSY QUEEN	Capitol
July	1982	6. ENOUGH IS ENOUGH	Capitol
February	1984	7. THIS COULD BE THE RIGHT ONE	Capitol

JOAN ARMATRADING

Born: December 9, 1950
Hometown: St. Kitts, British West Indies

When Joan Armatrading was seven, her family, which included six children, moved from the Carribean island of St. Kitts to the industrial city of Birmingham, England. Her father worked as a bus driver and carpenter by day and played guitar and bass in a band at night. Still, he opposed Joan's interest in music, and hid his guitar on a closet shelf where she couldn't reach it. One day, her mother bought a piano and Joan was given the task of cleaning it. It wasn't long before the youngster taught herself to play it as well.

Joan traded two baby carriages that were sitting around the house for her own guitar and taught herself to play. She wrote her first song at age 14, and while she saw herself becoming a lawyer and a songwriter, not an entertainer, her friends convinced her to perform locally. By 1984, she had ten critically lauded albums and had sold over 7 million records around the world. Nevertheless, she still prefers street clothes onstage, and her only jewelry is her house key, which dangles from her neck. Armatrading now lives in the English countryside, where she collects British comic books, antique autos, and clocks.

May   1983   DROP THE PILOT   A & M

ASIA

Members:
John Wetton—vocals, bass—born: July 12, 1949—replaced (1983) by Greg
    Lake—born: November 10, 1948
Steve Howe—guitar—born: April 8, 1947
Geoff Downes—keyboards
Carl Palmer—drums—born: March 20, 1947
Hometown: Birmingham, England

Asia was formed in early 1981 as an outgrowth of a series of jam sessions

Asia. *Left to right:* Steve Howe, Carl Palmer, John Wetton, Geoff Downes.

between John Wetton and Steve Howe. Wetton—who had been in King Crimson, Uriah Heep, Roxy Music, and U.K.—and Howe, formerly with Yes, sought to pick up where the great progressive bands of the seventies left off. They recruited Geoff Downes, who'd played in the Buggles and Yes, and Carl Palmer, formerly with Atomic Rooster and Emerson, Lake & Palmer. Together the quartet was a supergroup, featuring the talents of some of the best rock musicians England ever produced.

After two successful albums, Wetton and the group split. Wetton wanted to take Asia in a more pop-oriented direction, while the others opted for a hard rock/progressive format. Ironically, he was replaced by Greg Lake, whom Wetton himself had replaced in King Crimson 10 years earlier. Lake was now reunited with Carl Palmer, his onetime comrade in Emerson, Lake & Palmer.

April	1982	1. HEAT OF THE MOMENT	Geffen
July	1982	2. ONLY TIME WILL TELL	Geffen
July	1983	3. DON'T CRY	Geffen
October	1983	4. THE SMILE HAS LEFT YOUR EYES	Geffen

A TASTE OF HONEY

Members:
  Janice Marie Johnson—bass, vocals (contralto through second soprano)
  Hazel Pearl Payne—guitar, vocals (alto through first soprano) (replaced Carlita Dorhan in 1976)
  Perry L. Kimble—piano, vocals (left group in 1980)
  Donald R. Johnson—drums, vocals (left group in 1980)
  Gregory Walker—vocals (left group in 1976)
Hometown: Los Angeles, California

The genesis of this female lead band was in 1972, when the band in which Janice Johnson was singing and Perry Kimble was playing bass suddenly broke up. Janice and Perry took on the name A Taste of Honey, and Janice switched to bass and Perry to piano. They added a guitarist, Carlita Dorhan, who was later replaced by Hazel Payne, and a drummer, Don Johnson, and began playing the L.A. club circuit. Additional members, including vocalist Gregory Walker, came and went. A Taste of Honey soon toured for the U.S.O., and in 1974 represented the United States at the Fifth World Popular Song Festival in Tokyo, Japan.

Fonce and Larry Mizell, who had worked with the Jackson Five, discovered A Taste of Honey in a Hollywood club called the Etc., and began guiding the group's writing and performing talents. In short time, the group secured a recording contract, and their first single, "Boogie, Oogie Oogie," from the self-titled debut album, was a number-one hit. The song and the album both achieved platinum certification for selling 2 million and 1 million units, respectively, and the group was named Best

New Artist of the Year at the 21st Annual Grammy Awards presentation in 1979, becoming the first black group ever to receive that award.

Janice and Hazel had been the nucleus of the group since 1976, and A Taste of Honey became a duo in 1980. After achieving great popularity in Japan, the duo recorded a remake of Kyu Sakamoto's 1962 hit "Sukiyaki," with Janice writing English lyrics; the song also went to number one and sold over a million copies.

Janice and Hazel split amicably in 1984. Janice released a solo album later that year cleverly titled *One Taste of Honey*.

June	1978	★ 1. BOOGIE OOGIE OOGIE	Capitol
August	1979	2. DO IT GOOD	Capitol
March	1981	3. SUKIYAKI	Capitol
March	1982	4. I'LL TRY SOMETHING NEW	Capitol

ATLANTIC STARR

Members:
  Sharon Bryant—vocals—born: August 14, 1956—replaced in 1984 by Barbara
    Weathers—born: December 7, 1963
  David Lewis—guitar, vocals—born: September 8, 1958
  Wayne Lewis—keyboards, vocals—born: April 13, 1957
  Clifford Archer—bass—born: May 25, 1951
  Porter Carroll, Jr.—drums, vocals—born: April 24, 1953
  Joey Phillips—percussion—born: May 2, 1949
  Jonathan Lewis—trombone—born: December 5, 1953
  Bill Sudderth III—trumpet—born: April 18, 1950
  Koran Daniels—saxophone—born: June 18, 1958
Hometown: White Plains, New York

Atlantic Starr was formed in 1976 as a merger of three local bands. Koran Daniels joined after the second album in 1979. According to Wayne Lewis, "It's a simple matter of friendship that keeps us going." In 1984, the band was regrouped and now consists of Barbara Weathers, David, Wayne, Joey, and Jonathan.

| March | 1982 | CIRCLES | A & M |
| December | 1983 | TOUCH A FOUR-LEAF CLOVER | A & M |

PATTI AUSTIN

Born: August 10, 1948
Hometown: New York, N.Y.

Patti Austin made her debut performance at New York's Apollo Theater. Upon meeting the star of the show, Dinah Washington, she quipped, "Hi, I'm Patti Austin, and I'm a singer, too." After a brief tryout in the dressing room, Dinah brought her out to do her own selection, "Teach Me

Tonight," in the key of B-flat. The band began to play, but not in the key of B-flat, and Patti brought the band to an immediate halt. Patti brought the house down: After all, not many three-year-olds can tell 12 adult musicians they're not in the right key! Sammy Davis, Jr. was backstage and quickly signed the showstopper to appear in his show.

A year later Dinah introduced Patti to Quincy Jones at a recording session. When the session was over, Patti repeated note for note every take that Dinah had sung, as well as each of the additional parts played by the musicians. Quincy was amazed and promised he'd record her one day. While Patti's childhood was spent on TV soundstages and under Broadway lights, she eventually sang on commercials as well as on albums for Michael Jackson, Paul Simon, Billy Joel, Frankie Valli, Roberta Flack, and Steely Dan. She now records her own albums for Qwest Records, Quincy Jones's record company.

December	1981	1. EVERY HOME SHOULD HAVE ONE	Qwest
April	1982	2. BABY, COME TO ME (with James Ingram)	Qwest
October	1982	★ 3. BABY, COME TO ME (with James Ingram)	Qwest
March	1983	4. EVERY HOME SHOULD HAVE ONE	Qwest
May	1983	5. HOW DO YOU KEEP THE MUSIC PLAYING (with James Ingram)	Qwest
February	1984	6. IT'S GONNA BE SPECIAL	Qwest

AXE

Members:
    Bobby Barth—vocals, guitar—born: December 5, 1952
    Michael Osborne—guitar, vocals—born: December 22, 1949—died: July 21, 1984

Axe. *Left to right:* Michael Osborne, Wayne Haner, Bobby Barth, Ted Mueller, Edgar Riley, Jr.

Edgar Riley, Jr.—keyboards, vocals—born: May 11, 1954
Wayne Haner—bass (replaced Michael Turpin in 1978)—born: July 2, 1952
Ted Mueller—drums—born: September 13, 1954
Hometown: Gainesville, Florida

While Axe formed in 1978, the group's roots date back to nearly a decade earlier, when Bobby Barth and Michael Osborne were playing the Boulder, Colorado club scene in local bands. In the early seventies, the two musicians headed for Los Angeles, hoping to join up with like-minded musicians. They found Edgar Riley and Ted Mueller, formed a band called Baby Face, and moved to Wisconsin to break in the music and avoid the high costs of living in L.A. That band broke up in the mid-seventies, but reunited in Gainesville, Florida in 1978, when they added Haner to the group and called themselves Axe.

Michael and Bobby were involved in an auto crash on July 21, 1984, in which Michael was killed. Bobby survived; however, the group disbanded shortly thereafter.

| July | 1982 | NOW OR NEVER | Atco |
| October | 1983 | I THINK YOU'LL REMEMBER TONIGHT | Atco |

B

PHILLIP BAILEY

Born: May 8, 1951
Hometown: Denver, Colorado

Phillip, a percussionist and vocalist who shared the lead vocals with Maurice White of Earth, Wind & Fire, has been with the group since its beginning in 1971. In late 1984, Bailey decided to try it as a soloist and recorded "Easy Lover" which became a big hit for him. Although he still remains with Earth, Wind & Fire, his newfound success may force him to choose between the group or his solo career.

See *EARTH, WIND & FIRE, Rock On: The Years of Change.*

| November | 1984 | EASY LOVER (with Phil Collins) | Columbia |
| April | 1985 | WALKING ON THE CHINESE WALL | Columbia |

BALANCE

Members:
    Peppy Castro (Emil Thielhelm)—vocals—born: June 16, 1949
    Chuck Burgi—drums—added in 1982
    Dennis Feldman—bass—added in 1982
    Bob Kulick—guitar
    Doug Katsaros—keyboards
Hometown: New York, New York

According to Peppy Castro, the name Balance indicated the backgrounds of the group's original members: Doug Katsaros came from theater, Bob Kulick came from rock, and Castro himself came from both. Castro's career began in New York's Greenwich Village, when at age 14 he formed the Blues Magoos of "We Ain't Got Nothin' Yet" fame (1967). When the Blue Magoos disbanded in 1970, Castro moved into theater, playing the roles of Berger and Woof in the original production of Hair. He continued writing songs, and these tunes were recorded by Kiss, Cher, England Dan, and Melanie. Kulick, meanwhile, was playing guitar for Lou Reed, Alice Cooper, Meat Loaf, LaBelle, Mark Farner, Tim Curry, and Rex Smith. Katsaros played in the Broadway revival of "Hair" and served as the orchestra conductor with the touring companies of "Jesus Christ Superstar," "Godspell," and "Man of La Mancha."

| July | 1981 | BREAKING AWAY | Portrait |
| November | 1981 | FALLING IN LOVE | Portrait |

18

MARTY BALIN

Born: January 30, 1942
Hometown: San Francisco, California

A former member of Jefferson Airplane/Starship, Marty Balin has had several hit songs as a solo performer.

See *JEFFERSON AIRPLANE/STARSHIP, Rock On: The Years of Change.*

May	1981	HEARTS	EMI-America
September	1981	ATLANTA LADY	EMI-America
February	1983	WHAT LOVE IS	EMI-America

RUSS BALLARD

Born: October 31, 1947
Hometown: Waltham Cross, Hertfordshire, England

Russ Ballard is best known as a writer for others. His hits include "Winning" for Santana, "Since You've Been Gone" for Rainbow, "Free Me" for the Who's Roger Daltrey, "Hold Your Head Up" for Argent, and "Liar" for Three Dog Night. In the sixties, he was in a British pop band called Unit 4 + 2, and in the early seventies he performed with Argent, led by former Zombie Rod Argent. Ballard left Argent in 1975 and has since pursued a solo career.

June   1980   ON THE REBOUND   Epic

BAMA

Members:
    Jerry Wallace—guitar
    Kenneth Bell—guitar
    Terry Skinner—guitar
Hometown: Muscle Shoals, Alabama

The members of Bama are three session musicians and writers, who have given songs to country greats Narvel Felts, Sammi Smith, the Amazing Rhythm Aces, Mac Davis, and others.

October   1979   TOUCH ME WHEN WE'RE DANCING   Free Flight

Bananarama. *Left to right:* Keren Woodward, Siobhan Fahey, Sarah Dallin.

BANANARAMA

Members:
    Siobhan Fahey—vocals
    Sarah Dallin—vocals
    Keren Woodward—vocals
Hometown: London, England

The three members of Bananarama were roommates living over the rehearsal studio of the Professionals, an offshoot band of the legendary Sex Pistols. One day in 1981, drummer and ex-Pistol Paul Cook asked them to sing with his band. He liked what he heard and asked if he could coproduce a single for them. According to Siobhan, the name Bananarama came about because they wanted a silly name. They thought tropical and came up with "banana," and added "rama" because it sounded silly. Bananarama occasionally worked with its British male counterparts, Fun Boy Three.

July	1983	1. SHY BOY	London
May	1984	2. ROBERT DENIRO'S WAITING	London
July	1984	3. CRUEL SUMMER	London
November	1984	4. THE WILD LIFE	London

CLAUDJA BARRY

Hometown: Jamaica

The youngest of eight children, Claudja Barry was born in Jamaica, but left at age six when her parents moved to Toronto, Canada. She made her television debut at age 17, then took acting and voice lessons. Claudja has recorded several albums since her first record in 1976, but her biggest hit was "Boogie Woogie Dancin' Shoes," which reportedly sold 1.5 million copies worldwide. She has also appeared in theatrical productions of *AC/DC*, *Hair*, and *Catch My Soul*.

| February | 1978 | DANCIN' FEVER | Salsoul |
| April | 1979 | BOOGIE WOOGIE DANCIN' SHOES | Chrysalis |

TONI BASIL

Born: 1950
Hometown: Los Angeles, California

Toni Basil was known worldwide as a singer, dancer, choreographer, and video director before she ever recorded her own records. She choreographed some of the sixties TV shows like "Shindig" and "Hullabaloo," and also worked on the film *American Grafitti*. Her debut single, "Mickey," reportedly sold more than 2 million copies. This colorful performer is

Toni Basil

usually seen wearing outrageous outfits designed by her boyfriend, Spazz Attack.

September	1982	★ MICKEY	Chrysalis
February	1983	SHOPPIN' FROM A TO Z	Chrysalis
January	1984	OVER MY HEAD	Chrysalis

BELL & JAMES

Members:
    Leroy Bell—Hometown: Florida
    Casey James—Hometown: Portland, Oregon

Leroy Bell (nephew of famed producer Thom Bell) and Casey James had already written songs for the Spinners and the O'Jays when they recorded a self-produced tape of new songs on which they sang all the vocals and played all the instruments. Looking for jobs as songwriters, they sent the demo to the publishing division of A & M Records, but the talent division heard it and signed the duo as recording artists instead. While working on their careers as artists, though, they also found the time to write "Mama Can't Buy Your Love" and other tunes for Elton John. Freda

Payne, L.T.D., Maxine Nightingale, and MFSB have also recorded songs written by Bell & James.

January   1979   LIVIN' IT UP   A & M

BELLE EPOQUE

Hometown: Paris, France

Belle Epoque was a trio of female singers from Paris, France, who had a major disco hit in Europe in 1978 called "Miss Broadway." The song was first released on the French label Carrere Records; it was then acquired by Shadybrook Records, and then again by Doug Morris of Big Tree Records. It was the trio's only hit in America.

March   1978   MISS BROADWAY   Big Tree

THE BELLE STARS

Members:
> Jennie McKeown—vocals
> Sarah-Jane Owen—guitar
> Stella Barker—guitar
> Miranda Joyce—sax
> Clare Hirst—sax, keyboards
> Lesley Shone—bass
> Judy Parsons—drums

Until 1980, the British Belle Stars were known as the Bodysnatchers, and they played the ska and "two-tone" music that was the rage in England. After a personnel shake-up and a change in musical direction, the Belle Stars were born. The all-female septet has opened concerts for the Police, Pretenders, Madness, Clash, Elvis Costello, and Joe Jackson.

May   1983   SIGN OF THE TIMES   Warner Bros.

JOHN BELUSHI

Real Name: John Adam Belushi
Born: January 24, 1949   Died: March 5, 1982
Hometown: Wheaton, Illinois

"Saturday Night Live" stars John Belushi and Dan Aykroyd formed the popular duo known as the Blues Brothers, turning out four chart singles between 1978 and 1980. John had one solo hit in 1978, with his version of the 1963 Kingsman's hit, "Louie, Louie."

On March 5, 1982, Belushi was found dead of an apparent drug overdose in bungalow 3 of the Chateau Marmont Hotel in Los Angeles.

September   1978   LOUIE, LOUIE   MCA

PAT BENATAR

Born: January 10, 1953
Hometown: Brooklyn, New York

At only five feet tall and 90 pounds, Pat Benatar has become a powerhouse of rock. Although she studied opera while growing up on Long Island, she eventually dropped it, saying she found opera boring. Nevertheless, this training taught her how to sing rough without hurting her voice box.

Pat majored in health education at the State University of New York at Stony Brook. Before completing her studies, she married Dennis Benatar and moved to Richmond, Virginia, where she worked as a bank teller and as a singing waitress. In 1975, she divorced Dennis and returned to her native New York. There she was discovered in a showcase club, Catch a Rising Star, by owner Rick Newman, who became her manager.

Now the most prominent woman in rock and roll, Pat insists she is still a rocker and not a pop singer. "Low key or laid-back I'm not," she once said. "A lot of women singers today seem to be saying 'If you love me and then hurt me, I'll die.' I say, 'If you love me and then leave me, I'll kick your ass.' "

The Pat Benatar Band consists of guitarist Neil Geraldo, keyboardist Charlie Giordano (who replaced guitarist Scott St. Clair Sheets), bassist Roger Capp, and drummer Myron Grombacher. Pat eloped with Geraldo to Hawaii, and the two now reside in southern California's San Fernando Valley.

December	1979	1. HEARTBREAKER	Chrysalis
April	1980	2. WE LIVE FOR LOVE	Chrysalis
July	1980	3. YOU BETTER RUN	Chrysalis

October	1980	4. HIT ME WITH YOUR BEST SHOT	Chrysalis
January	1981	5. TREAT ME RIGHT	Chrysalis
July	1981	6. FIRE AND ICE	Chrysalis
October	1981	7. PROMISES IN THE DARK	Chrysalis
October	1982	8. SHADOWS OF THE NIGHT	Chrysalis
February	1983	9. LITTLE TOO LATE	Chrysalis
April	1983	10. LOOKING FOR A STRANGER	Chrysalis
September	1983	11. LOVE IS A BATTLEFIELD	Chrysalis
October	1984	12. WE BELONG	Chrysalis
January	1985	13. OOH OOH SONG	Chrysalis

BERLIN

Members:
Terri Nunn—vocals—born: June 6, 1951
John Crawford—bass, synthesizer—born: January 17, 1960
David Diamond—synthesizer—left the group in 1984
Rick Olsen—guitar—born: August 20, 1956
Rod Learned—drums—left the group in 1983—replaced by Rob Brill—
born: January 21, 1956
Matt Reid—keyboards—born: April 15, 1958
Hometown: Los Angeles, California

John Crawford originally formed Berlin in the summer of 1979, but for
two years the line-up altered periodically. By mid-1981, Terri Nunn and
David Diamond became permanent members, and in the spring of 1982,

Berlin. *Left to right:* John Crawford, Terri Nunn, Rob Brill, David Diamond, Matt Reid,
Rick Olsen.

the other three members were added. "Sex (I'm A . . .)," the group's first single, was controversial and earned Berlin national attention.

March	1983	1. SEX (I'M A . . .)	Geffen
May	1983	2. THE METRO	ɩ effen
September	1983	3. MASQUERADE	Ueffen
March	1984	4. NO MORE WORDS	Geffen
June	1984	5. NOW ITS MY TURN	Geffen

B-52's

Members:
  Fred Schneider III—vocals, organ, guitar—born: July 1, 1951
  Kate Pierson—vocals, organ, guitar—born: April 27, 1948
  Cindy Wilson—vocals, percussion, guitar—born: February 28, 1957
  Ricky Wilson—guitar—born: March 19, 1953
  Julian Keith Stickland—drums—born: October 26, 1953
Hometown: Athens, Georgia

According to the band members, the B-52's formed in October 1976 when, after some tropical drinks at a Chinese restaurant, they went to a friend's house and jammed. The quintet took its name from a southern slang term for a high bouffant hairdo, and the two women in the group adopted the namesake look. After a few showcases in New York, the five

The B-52's. *Left to right:* Cindy Wilson, Ricky Wilson, Kate Pierson, Fred Schneider III, Julian Keith Strickland.

musicians were able to quit their jobs as waiters, bus-station porters, and pasteup artists for a life of new-wave dance music.

The B-52's received early acclaim with a self-released single called "Rock Lobster," which was later rereleased by Warner Brothers. The quintet continues to be known for their novelty songs and striking appearance.

April	1980	ROCK LOBSTER	Warner Bros.
October	1980	PRIVATE IDAHO	Warner Bros.
July	1983	LEGAL TENDER	Warner Bros.

BIG COUNTRY

Members:
    Stuart Adamson—guitar
    Bruce Watson—guitar
    Tony Butler—bass
    Mark Brzezicki—drums
Hometown: Dunfermline, Scotland

When Stuart Adamson quit a British punk band called the Skids, he left London and returned to his wife and family in Dunfermline, Scotland.

Big Country. *Left to right:* Tony Butler, Bruce Watson, Stuart Adamson, Mark Brzezicki.

There, he laid the groundwork for a band that would be called Big Country. His first recruit was Bruce Watson, who needed little encouragement to leave a job scrubbing out nuclear submarines. Together, they worked on Big Country's unique guitar sound. They then picked up Tony Butler and Mark Brzezicki, who'd worked as a rhythm section for the Who's Peter Townshend and for the Pretenders. The group received broad attention in the United States when it performed on the Grammy Awards telecast in 1984.

October	1983	IN A BIG COUNTRY	Mercury
February	1984	FIELDS OF FIRE	Mercury
June	1984	WONDERLAND	Mercury

Big Ric

BIG RIC

Members:
> Joel Porter—vocals
> John Pondel—guitar
> Kevin DiSimone—vocals, keyboards
> Bud Harner—drums

Hometown: Los Angeles, California

All from different parts of the United States (Joel comes from Cincinnati, John from Chicago, Bud from Washington, D.C., and Kevin from Canton, Ohio) the members of Big Ric all met in Los Angeles in early 1982 and formed their group, intending to blend rock and pop music and create a new danceable sound.

The four musicians got together with producers John D'Andrea and Carmine Rubino, who had worked on arrangements for the Beach Boys and Diana Ross, and at Santa Monica Sound Recorders in California recorded their first album for Scotti Brothers Records, resulting in the hit "Take Away."

September   1983   TAKE AWAY   Scotti Bros.

BILLY & THE BEATERS

Members:
> Billy Vera—vocals, guitar—born: May 28, 1944
> Jeff "Skunk" Baxter—guitar
> Bryan Cumming—saxophone
> Jim Elringer—piano
> Chuck Fiore—bass
> George Marinelli, Jr.—guitar
> Jerry Peterson—saxophone
> Lon Price—saxophone
> Beau Segal—drums
> Ron Viola—saxophone

Hometown: Los Angeles, California

Billy & The Beaters were born on stage at Los Angeles' famed Troubadour one Monday night/Tuesday morning, and immediately the group was booked for six weeks of return engagements. The band's drummer said he came up with the name because the group started playing together to meet girls but found themselves going home alone. The Beaters are all L.A.-based session musicians, led by Jeff "Skunk" Baxter, formerly of the Doobie Brothers and Steely Dan.

Two decades before this ensemble formed, Vera hit with "With Pen In Hand" and, with Judy Clay, "Storybook Children," the latter becoming

top 40 radio's first interracial duet. Vera has had songs recorded by Rick
Nelson and Dolly Parton.

| April | 1981 | I CAN TAKE CARE OF MYSELF | Alfa |
| September | 1981 | AT THIS MOMENT | Alfa |

BLACKFOOT

Members:

     Rick Medlocke—guitar, vocals—born: February 17, 1950

     Jakson Spires—drums—born: April 12, 1951

     Greg T. Walker—bass—born: July 8, 1951

     Charlie Hargrett—guitar (left in 1984)—born: February 11, 1949

     Ken Hensley—keyboards—added in 1983—born: August 24, 1945

Hometown: Jacksonville, Florida

Ricky Medlocke was brought up by his grandfather, the late Shorty
Medlocke. The former sharecropper was a well-known local musician, and

Blackfoot. *Left to right:* Jakson Spires, Charlie Hargrett, Rick Medlocke, Ken Hensley,
Greg T. Walker.

he had Ricky playing banjo when he was only three years old. Together, they appeared regularly on a local TV show, "The Toby Doddy Show." At eight years of age, Ricky began playing drums, and at 10 he played guitar. It was at age 10 that Ricky put together a combo with two neighborhood buddies, Jakson Spires and Greg Walker. Years later, Charlie Hargrett joined the band, then called Fresh Garbage.

In 1971, Fresh Garbage became Blackfoot and moved to New Jersey, where a lucrative club scene was flourishing. For a brief period, Ricky and Greg left Blackfoot to join Lynyrd Skynyrd, but returned in 1972. The group has since moved back to Jacksonville.

Ken Hensley, a 10-year veteran of the British hard rock band Uriah Heep, joined Blackfoot in January 1983.

June	1979	HIGHWAY SONG	Atco
October	1979	TRAIN, TRAIN	Atco
June	1981	FLY AWAY	Atco

J. BLACKFOOT

Hometown: Memphis, Tennessee

J. Blackfoot first got involved in music by hanging around Stax Records. He became the lead vocalist for the Soul Children, who had a moderate hit in the early seventies with "I'll Understand." When Stax Records dissolved in 1975, so did the Soul Children. Blackfoot was then out of the spotlight until he launched his solo career in 1984.

| March | 1984 | TAXI | Sound Town |

BLACKJACK

Members:
    Michael Bolton–vocals
    Bruce Kulick—guitar
    Jimmy Haslip—bass
    Sandy Gennaro—drums
Hometown: New York, New York

Michael Bolton and Bruce Kulick met in 1977 while playing the Connecticut bar circuit, in and around Bolton's hometown of New Haven. (See *Michael BOLTON.*) With Haslip and Gennaro, they formed Blackjack. After securing an album deal, Blackjack performed important club dates nationally and opened concerts for choice headliners, but the group broke up in 1980. Bolton has since resumed a career as a solo artist, and Gennaro has joined Pat Travers's hard rock band.

| July | 1979 | LOVE ME TONIGHT | Polydor |

Blondie. *Left to right:* Deborah Harry, Clem Burke, Frank Infante, Jimmy Destri, Nigel Harrison, Chris Stein.

BLONDIE

Members:
    Deborah Harry—vocals—born: July 1, 1945
    Chris Stein—guitar—born: January 5, 1950
    Jimmy Destri—keyboards—born: April 13, 1954
    Nigel Harrison—bass (replaced Gary Valentine 1977)
    Clement Burke—drums—born: November 24, 1955
    Frank Infante—guitar—added in 1977
Hometown: New York, New York

Deborah Harry had sung in Wind In The Willows, Stilleto, and Snake, and had worked as a waitress, beautician, and Playboy Club "bunny" before forming a band with her boyfriend, Chris Stein. The group's early personnel changed many times, but solidified as Blondie by the summer of 1976. Harry claims the name of the band came from truck drivers and bums who often called out to her, "Hey, Blondie."

Blondie became the forerunner of the original punk rock scene in 1976, headlining New York clubs like CBGB's and Max's Kansas City. Several record companies were beginning to take an interest in these bands, but the great moment came when Frankie Valli, who then owned a large chunk of Private Stock Records, came to CBGB's, saw a performance, and okayed the signing of Blondie. The group recorded a self-titled debut album, but quickly became disenchanted with the small record firm. Blondie was wooed away by a larger company, Chrysalis Records, and in an unprecedented deal, the group bought the Private Stock contract and album.

Harry quickly became rock's sex kitten, and after only two major hits, signed a million-dollar-deal to write and appear in a Murjani Jeans commercial. With this, she became the first punk star to cross over to the corporate world outside the music business.

Blondie has appeared in the films *Roadie, Blank Generation,* and *Naked Lunch,* and performed "Call Me," the title song to the film *American Gigolo.* Harry has recorded under her own name as well, and has appeared in the films *Unmade Beds, Union City* (with Pat Benatar), and *Videodrome.* Blondie broke up in 1982, but the group's history has been chronicled in Harry and Stein's own tome, *Making Tracks: The Rise of Blondie.*

February	1979	★ 1. HEART OF GLASS	Chrysalis
June	1979	2. ONE WAY OR ANOTHER	Chrysalis
September	1979	3. DREAMING	Chrysalis
February	1980	4. THE HARDEST PART	Chrysalis
February	1980	★ 5. CALL ME	Chrysalis
May	1980	6. ATOMIC	Chrysalis
November	1980	★ 7. THE TIDE IS HIGH	Chrysalis
January	1981	★ 8. RAPTURE	Chrysalis
May	1982	9. ISLAND OF LOST SOULS	Chrysalis

KURTIS BLOW

Born: August 9, 1959
Hometown: New York, New York

Though Harlem-born Kurtis Blow attended New York's High School of Music & Art, where he majored in voice, and City College of New York,

Kurtis Blow

where he studied communication, he learned rapping on the streets and in the uptown clubs. After tagging along with a neighborhood dj, Kurtis tried rapping on his own for the first time in late 1976 at the Charles Gallery in Harlem, and later at Small's Paradise, the club where the Commodores got their start. When rapping found a place in the recording industry, Kurtis Blow was its first full-fledged star.

| September | 1980 | THE BREAKS | Mercury |
| May | 1985 | BASKETBALL | Mercury |

BLUE ÖYSTER CULT

Members:
- Donald "Buck Dharma" Roeser—guitar, vocals—born: November 12, 1947
- Eric Bloom—vocals, guitar—born: December 1, 1944
- Allen Lanier—keyboards, guitar, vocals—born: June 25, 1946
- Albert Bouchard—drums, vocals—replaced (1981) by Rick Downey—born: August 29, 1953
- Joe Bouchard—bass, vocals—born: November 9, 1948

Hometown: Stony Brook, Long Island, New York

First known as Soft White Underbelly, then as Stalk Forrest Group, Blue Öyster Cult was born circa 1970. The group has recorded over a dozen

Blue Öyster Cult. *Left to right:* Allen Lanier, Albert Bouchard, Joe Bouchard, Donald "Buck Dharma" Roeser, Eric Bloom.

hard-rock albums and has toured the States many times. One show on a 1980 tour with Black Sabbath was filmed and released as *Black and Blue.* Donald Roeser has also released a solo album as Buck Dharma.

Blue Öyster Cult single-handedly revived Steppenwolf's "Born To Be Wild" and the Doors' "Roadhouse Blues" as standards in live sets.

July	1976	1. (DON'T FEAR) THE REAPER	Columbia
September	1979	2. IN THEE	Columbia
August	1981	3. BURNIN' FOR YOU	Columbia
February	1984	4. SHOOTING SHARK	Columbia

BLUES BROTHERS

Members:
Joliet Jake Blues (John Belushi)—vocals—born: January 24, 1949—Wheaton, Illinois—died: March 5, 1982
Elwood Blues (Dan Aykroyd)—harmonica, vocals—born: July 1, 1952— Ottowa, Ontario, Canada

The Blues Brothers debuted on NBC-TV's "Saturday Night Live" series in a skit by two of the show's regulars, John Belushi and Dan Aykroyd. (See *John BELUSHI.*) The skit, which featured two blues singers dressed in identical dark suits, hats, glasses, and skinny ties, was received so well that Belushi and Aykroyd negotiated a record contract. The comedy/ singing duo and its band played their first concerts at the Universal Amphitheater in Los Angeles in 1978; these performances were recorded for the debut album, *Briefcase Full Of Blues.*

According to their self-made legend, the Blues Brothers grew up in Calumet City, Illinois, where they were adopted at a very early age by black parents. By age eight, they were playing the blues in Chicago-area clubs. Their musical career survived numerous near-disastrous interruptions, including Jake's three-month stint at Joliet Prison for armed robbery, as well as Elwood's careers in the industrial diamond and window-washing trades. They travelled the country in their 1967 Dodge Polara, looking for gigs and paying their dues in after-hours clubs and black-light bars across the steel belt.

Belushi also released a solo single, "Louie, Louie," in late 1978. The Blues Brothers filmed their fictitious adventures in the 1980 comedy, *The Blues Brothers.* In addition to this film, Belushi starred in *Animal House, Girlfriends, Neighbors, 1941,* and *Continental Divide;* Aykroyd starred in *Neighbors, 1941, Stripes,* and *Ghostbusters.* Belushi was found dead of a drug overdose in a Los Angeles motel room on March 5, 1982.

December	1978	1. SOUL MAN	Atlantic
March	1979	2. RUBBER BISCUIT	Atlantic
May	1980	3. GIMME SOME LOVIN'	Atlantic
December	1980	4. WHO'S MAKING LOVE	Atlantic

Blues Brothers. Elwood (*left*), Jake.

MICHAEL BOLTON

Born: February 26, 1954
Hometown: New Haven, Connecticut

Michael Bolton organized his first rock band at age 13, and even though he wasn't yet old enough to drink, he soon got steady gigs playing in bars. At age 15, his mother cosigned his first record contract. After two unsuccessful albums, he fronted Blackjack for another two albums, but then left to resume his pursuit of a solo career. Bolton's tunes have been recorded by the Pointer Sisters, Bill Medley of the Righteous Brothers, Laura Branigan, Larry Graham, and France Joli.

| May | 1983 | FOOLS GAME | Columbia |

BONEY M.

Members:
 Liz Mitchell—vocals—born: July 12
 Maizie Williams—vocals—born: March 25
 Marcia Barrett—vocals—born: October 14
 Bobby Farrell—vocals—born: October 6
Hometown: Hamburg, West Germany

In 1975, an ex-performer named Frank Farian used studio musicians to record a single called "Baby Do The Bump" under the name Boney M. The record became a smash in Holland, and Farian began to receive offers to appear on Dutch television. There was only one problem—he had no band to perform the song. Farian found four singers in various parts of West Germany (coincidentally, the three women were originally from the Carribean) and hired them to be Boney M. The packaging clicked, and the new Boney M. became an international success, eventually selling more than 50 million records worldwide in two and a half years. A highlight was a rare extended engagement by this western group in Moscow.

January	1977	1. DADDY COOL	Atco
August	1977	2. MA BAKER	Atlantic
June	1978	3. RIVERS OF BABYLON	Sire
December	1978	4. MARY'S BOY CHILD	Sire

Boney M. *Left to right:* Bobby Farrell, Liz Mitchell, Marcia Barrett, Maizie Williams.

Bon Jovi. *Left to right:* David Rashbaum, Alec John Such, Jon Bon Jovi, Tico Torres, Richie Sambora.

BON JOVI

Members:
Jon Bon Jovi (John Bongiovi)—vocals—born: March 2, 1962
Richie Sambora—guitar—born: July 11, 1959
David Rashbaum—keyboards—born: February 7, 1962
Alec John Such—bass—born: November 14, 1956
Tico Torres—drums—born: October 7, 1953
Hometown: Sayreville, New Jersey

As teenagers, Jon and David played many local clubs, doing material of Led Zeppelin and Judas Priest. In March of 1983, the five-man group known as Bon Jovi came together, and shortly thereafter signed with Mercury. Their debut album later that year was *Bon Jovi*, from which came the hit single "Runaway."

February	1984	RUNAWAY	Mercury
May	1984	SHE DON'T KNOW ME	Polygram
May	1985	ONLY LONELY	Mercury

KARLA BONOFF

Born: Dec. 27, 1952
Hometown: Los Angeles, California

Karla Bonoff initially took piano lessons as a child; she then tried violin and clarinet, and finally switched to guitar while in her teens. When she was 16, she and her sister Lisa formed a duo and began playing the Troubadour's famed Monday-night hootenannies. Around that time (1969), Karla met bassist Kenny Edwards, who was between gigs with Linda Ronstadt. He suggested that Karla join forces with him, Andrew Gold (who later became Ronstadt's lead guitarist), and Wendy Waldman in an acoustic vocal group that became known as Bryndle. That group played around town, but eventually broke up and landed Karla back at the Troubadour's hootenannies, where she was discovered by a talent scout and given her own record contract. When Ronstadt recorded three songs written by Bonoff on one album in 1976, there was little doubt that Bonoff herself would see her career take off. Bonoff's songs have also been recorded by Bonnie Raitt and Lynn Anderson.

February	1978	1. I CAN'T HOLD ON	Columbia
March	1980	2. BABY DON'T GO	Columbia
May	1982	3. PERSONALLY	Columbia
September	1982	4. PLEASE BE THE ONE	Columbia

Karla Bonoff

Boomtown Rats. Bob Geldof (*third from left*).

BOOMTOWN RATS

Members:
    Bob Geldof—vocals—born: October 5, 1954
    Garry Roberts—guitar (left group in 1983)
    Gerry Cott—guitar (left group in 1983)
    Johnny Fingers—keyboards
    Pete Briquette—bass
    Simon Crowe—drums
Hometown: Dun Laoghaire, Ireland

In 1975, when seven friends in Dublin were collecting unemployment, the six who played instruments formed a band, and the seventh became their manager. On Halloween night, halfway through their first gig, the group changed their name from the Nightlife Thugs to the Boomtown Rats, the new moniker taken from a youth gang in Woody Guthrie's autobiography, *Bound For Glory.*

According to the group's leader and chief songwriter, Bob Geldof, Ireland's established music scene in the mid-seventies consisted largely of show bands playing top 40 hits in ballrooms. But the Boomtown Rats started an alternative system, playing in any little pub that would have a live band, and in the process created a rock circuit for other acts to utilize. The enthusiasm of the Rats's Irish audience spread to England and, eventually, to rock markets around the world. Geldof may be best known for his role as Pink in the film *The Wall*. The group's best-known song, "I Don't Like Mondays," was about 17-year-old Brenda Spencer, who was convicted of murdering two people and wounding one police officer and eight children at San Diego's Cleveland Elementary School in January, 1978; the schoolgirl had explained her homicides with a shrug and a single statement: "I don't like Mondays."

In 1984, Geldof was the driving force behind Band Aid and the single, "Do They Know It's Christmas," for the relief of the Ethiopian famine victims.

February   1980   I DON'T LIKE MONDAYS   Columbia

RICK BOWLES

Hometown: Shelby, North Carolina

Rick Bowles once led a double life, teaching high school students with learning and reading disabilities by day and pursuing a music career by night in the Charlotte, North Carolina, area. Bowles and a local keyboardist, Richard Putnam, became a duo and started writing songs together, which led to Bowles landing a record contract.

July   1982   TOO GOOD TO TURN BACK NOW   Polydor

BOWWOWWOW

Members:
    Annabella Lwin (Myant Myant Aye)—vocals (left group in 1983)—born:
        October 31, 1965
    Matthew Ashman—guitar
    Leroy Gorman—bass
    Dave Barbarossa—drums
Hometown: London, England

Matthew Ashman, Leroy Gorman, and Dave Barbarossa played together behind Adam Ant as the original Ants, but jumped ship in 1980 when, according to the mutineers, Adam opted for visual flash over solid musicianship. Bowwowwow's original manager, Malcolm McLaren, united the trio with a 14-year-old Burmese girl he said he met in a London launderette, and she became the group's lead singer.

Throughout its history, Bowwowwow has met with controversy. "Your Cassette Pet," the group's first project, preached that "records are obsolete, cassettes are the future." To emphasize the message, the group's debut recording was released in Great Britain only on tape, with one side left blank for home taping, much to the record industry's dismay. Then Bowwowwow's first American concert tour was nearly cancelled when Annabella's mother sought to prevent her underage daughter from coming to the United States. A press conference in New York turned into a barroom brawl. Meanwhile, the group's *The Last of the Mohicans* EP jacket raised some ire because it depicted a nude Annabella sitting with her three fully-dressed bandmates in a pastoral setting.

Bowwowwow appeared in the film *Scandalous*. Annabella is now pursuing a solo career, and Bowwowwow continues without her.

May	1982	I WANT CANDY	RCA
April	1983	DO YOU WANNA HOLD ME?	RCA

THE BOYS BAND

Members:
  Greg Gordon—vocals—born: November 30, 1950
  Rusty Golden—keyboards, vocals—born: January 3, 1959
  B. James Lowry—guitars, vocals—born: January 26, 1958
Hometown: Hendersonville, Tennessee

Greg Gordon is the son of Howard and Anne Gordon of the Chuck Wagon Gang, and he performed in that group at age six. Rusty Golden is the son of William Lee Golden of the Oak Ridge Boys. Gordon, Golden, and Lowry backed the Oak Ridge Boys, where they were first christened the Boys Band in 1981. All three are veterans of the music industry, with lengthy track records as both sessionists and touring artists.

March	1982	DON'T STOP ME BABY (I'M ON FIRE)	Elektra

BILL BRANDON

Born: 1944
Hometown: Huntsville, Alabama

As a youngster, Brandon learned to play the trumpet, bass, and drums. In the late sixties he recorded a soul single, "Self Preservation," for Quincy Records out of Muscle Shoals, Alabama. In 1972, he had another soul hit, "Stop This Merry-Go-Round," on Moonsong Records. This was followed by "The Streets Got My Lady" on the Piedmont label. In late 1977, Brandon signed with Nashville-based Prelude Records, the only black-owned and -operated music company doing business in the country-music capital. A few months later he recorded his only chart entry to date, "We Fell In Love While Dancing."

February	1978	WE FELL IN LOVE WHILE DANCING	Prelude

LAURA BRANIGAN

Born: July 3, 1957
Hometown: Brewster, New York

Raised in upstate New York, Laura Branigan came to New York City to study drama before Canadian folksinger Leonard Bernstein asked her to tour Europe as his backing vocalist. Upon her return to New York, Laura began to build a solo repertoire. Her first major hit, the Grammy-nominated "Gloria," however, sounds remarkably similar to Elton John's "Saturday Night's All Right for Fighting." Branigan has since sung the theme songs to two feature films, *Kiss Me Goodbye* and *Some Sunny Days*, and appeared in an episode of the television series "CHiPs."

March	1982	1. ALL NIGHT WITH ME	Atlantic
July	1982	2. GLORIA	Atlantic
March	1983	3. SOLITAIRE	Atlantic
July	1983	4. HOW AM I SUPPOSED TO LIVE WITHOUT YOU	Atlantic
April	1984	5. SELF CONTROL	Atlantic
August	1984	6. THE LUCKY ONE	Atlantic
November	1984	7. TI AMO	Atlantic

ALICIA BRIDGES

Hometown: Lawndale, North Carolina

Alicia Bridges started playing guitar at age 10, and at 13 she persuaded the station manager at WADA in Shelby, North Carolina, to let her do her own radio show one summer. After working at a bank and at a Sears store, Bridges began working as a singer; her first professional date was singing for strippers in burlesque houses. She earned a Grammy nomination for her first record, "I Love The Nightlife (Disco Round)." Alicia now lives in Atlanta, Georgia.

| July | 1978 | I LOVE THE NIGHTLIFE (Disco Round) | Polydor |
| April | 1979 | BODY HEAT | Polydor |

MARTIN BRILEY

Hometown: London, England

Martin Briley was a session musician in the late sixties and early seventies, playing in the orchestra for British TV's "Top of the Pops" and "The Cliff Richard Show." Some days he would do as many as five sessions, ranging from commercial jingles to backing vocals for *The Rocky Horror Picture Show*. In 1975, Briley came to America, and by 1977, he had settled in New York City for good. Since then, he's worked as musical director for Ellen Foley and bassist for Ian Hunter and Mick Ronson. Barry Manilow, Pat Benatar, and Karla DeVito have recorded Briley's songs.

May   1983   THE SALT IN MY TEARS   Mercury

BRITISH LIONS

Members:
    John Fiddler—vocals, guitar—born: September 25, 1947
    Ray Major—guitar—born: July 16, 1949
    Morgan Fisher—keyboards—born: January 1, 1950
    Overend Watts—bass—born: May 13, 1949
    Terry Buffin—drums—born: October 24, 1950
Hometown: Birmingham, England

When Ian Hunter left Mott The Hoople in 1976, Overend Watts, Morgan Fisher, and Terry Buffin stayed together and, with Ray Major, formed a short-lived group called Mott. In 1977, with the addition of John Fiddler, who had once played in Medicine Head with Fisher, the group became British Lions, only to break up after one unsuccessful album and concert tour. The group's only charted single was an interpretation of Garland Jeffreys's youth anthem, "Wild In The Streets."

July   1978   WILD IN THE STREETS   RSO

BROOKLYN DREAMS

Members:
    Joe "Bean" Esposito—vocals, guitar
    Eddie Hokenson—vocals, percussion
    Bruce Sudano—vocals, guitar, keyboards
Hometown: Brooklyn, New York

Though lots of kids sang at the candy store owned by Eddie Hokenson's mother in the Flatbush section of Brooklyn, Eddie and his friend Joe "Bean" Esposito were serious; they eventually graduated to the Brooklyn club circuit as the Movements. Bruce Sudano, meanwhile, had formed a group called Constant Changes, which at one point backed up The

Movements. (Sudano later became a member of Alive and Kicking, which had one hit, "Tighter, Tighter," and then quickly disappeared.) In the mid-seventies, Hokenson and Esposito headed to Los Angeles, and after being mugged by three hoods one night, Sudano followed.

Although each singer worked separately as a studio vocalist behind Donna Summer and Ringo Starr, they one day found themselves together at a Bobby Womack date. The three musicians found they had something and formed Brooklyn Dreams. The group later appeared as a fifties doowop group, the Planotones, in the film *American Hot Wax* and were also featured in *Hollywood Knights*. Sudano is Donna Summer's husband.

November	1977	1. SAD EYES	Millenium
March	1978	2. MUSIC, HARMONY & RHYTHM	Millenium
January	1979	3. HEAVEN KNOWS (with Donna Summer)	Casablanca
February	1979	4. MAKE IT LAST	Casablanca

HERMAN BROOD & HIS WILD ROMANCE

Members:
Herman Brood—vocals, keyboard—born: 1946
Danny Lademacher—guitars
Freddie Cavalli—bass
Ani Meerman—drums
Hometown: the Netherlands

Herman Brood, who has stated that he is known in the Netherlands as "a junkie, a professional burglar, a crook, and a psychiatric patient," spent a large part of his life in reform school, prison, hospitals, and other institutions. He has also bared himself in German hardcore porno films, and is known for leading what was at one time Holland's biggest native act. Brood starred as a bank robber turned rock star in a European film, *Cha Cha*, with rock vocalists Lene Lovitch and Nina Hagen.

| July | 1979 | SATURDAY NIGHT | Ariola |

DON BROWN

Born: 1949
Hometown: Seattle, Washington

Don Brown was born in Minneapolis, and lived there until he was 17. He then moved to Seattle, where he got involved in the music business. In 1974, Brown recorded an album at Seattle's Kaye-Smith Productions, a studio launched by comedian Danny Kaye and businessman Lester Smith. (The studios were eventually taken over by producer Thom Bell of Philadelphia.)

In early 1978, Brown recorded an album for Seattle-based First

American records called *I Can't Say No* from which came the single "Sitting In Limbo." The song was a pop version of the Jimmy Cliff tune from the album *The Harder They Come.*

| March | 1978 | SITTING IN LIMBO | First American |

PETER BROWN

Born: December 25, 1940
Hometown: Chicago, Illinois

Peter Brown was one of the hottest acts to come on the scene during 1977–1978. In November of 1977, Brown made music history when "Do You Wanna Get Funky with Me" became the first 12-inch disco-disc to sell a million copies. Even though he had played with many bands—as keyboardist, drummer, and singer—he had thought of music as a hobby, never as a career. Being talented in painting and sculpture, he attended the prestigious Art Institute of Chicago but, disenchanted with the school, he returned to music. While negotiating the sale of a painting to record producer Cory Wade, Brown asked Wade to listen to a demo; soon afterwards Peter Brown was brought to T.K. Records (distributors of the Drive label that Peter was signed to) in Florida.

September	1977	1. DO YOU WANNA GET FUNKY WITH ME	Drive
March	1978	2. DANCE WITH ME	Drive
September	1978	3. YOU SHOULD DO IT	Drive
August	1979	4. CRANK IT UP	Drive
December	1979	5. STARGAZER	Drive

PEABO BRYSON

Real Name: Robert Peabo Bryson
Born: April 13, 1951
Hometown: Greenville, South Carolina

By the age of five, Peabo Bryson was attending concerts with his mother. His first experience on stage himself was in a high school talent show at age 12, when he sang Sam Cooke's "Another Saturday Night" and won the contest. By age 14, Peabo was paying his dues in local bands such as Al Freeman & the Upsetters. After studying accounting in college for a couple of years, Peabo gave up formal education for a career as a singer/songwriter, playing and writing in Moses Dillard & the Tex-Town Display, with which he toured the world for five years.

Peabo has since become the king of the black love ballad. He has dueted with Natalie Cole, Melissa Manchester, Minnie Ripperton, and Roberta Flack. His song, "Feel The Fire," was recorded by Stanley

Turrentine and Stephanie Mills (Mills did both a solo and duet version, the latter with Teddy Pendergrass). Peabo also recorded the title theme to the film, *D.C. Cab.* His first dramatic role was in an episode of TV's "Fame." He now lives in a palatial home in Atlanta, Georgia.

January	1982	1. LET THE FEELING FLOW	Capitol
July	1983	2. TONIGHT I CELEBRATE MY LOVE (with Roberta Flack)	Capitol
December	1983	3. YOU'RE LOOKING LIKE LOVE TO ME (with Roberta Flack)	Capitol
March	1984	4. YOU'RE LOOKING LIKE LOVE TO ME (with Roberta Flack)	Capitol
May	1984	5. IF EVER YOU'RE IN MY ARMS AGAIN	Elektra
September	1984	6. SLOW DANCIN'	Elektra

LINDSEY BUCKINGHAM

Born: October 3, 1947
Hometown: Palo Alto, California

Lindsey Buckingham took up the guitar at age seven, strumming along to his older brother's collection of Elvis Presley, Buddy Holly, and Everly Brothers records. Later, he switched from those rockabilly sounds to folk, before playing rock in local bands.

After the breakup of their popular Bay Area rock band called Fritz, Lindsey and his girlfriend Stevie (then Stephanie) Nicks recorded an album called *Buckingham Nicks.* The album's producer, Keith Olsen, sent a tape of that music to Fleetwood Mac's drummer and manager, Mick Fleetwood, hoping to get a production gig. Fleetwood was so impressed that he did hire Olsen, and when Bob Welch announced he was leaving Fleetwood Mac to go solo, Fleetwood also hired Buckingham and Nicks. The new Fleetwood Mac became a supergroup, allowing its five members to pursue individual projects in addition to their work with the group. Buckingham began a solo career, and produced albums for John Stewart and Walter Egan.

See *FLEETWOOD MAC, Rock On: The Years of Change.*

October	1981	TROUBLE	Asylum
August	1983	HOLIDAY ROAD	Warner Bros.
July	1984	GO INSANE	Elektra

BUCKNER AND GARCIA

Members:
    Jerry Buckner—keyboards, vocals
    Gary Garcia—vocals

Jerry Buckner and Gary Garcia tapped in on the video game craze, and had a hit in 1982 with "Pac-Man Fever."

January	1982	PAC-MAN FEVER	Columbia

THE BUGGLES

Members:
   Trevor Horn—vocals, guitar
   Geoff Downes—keyboards
Hometown: Birmingham, England

After a stint as the Buggles, both Horn and Downes joined Yes. Geoff Downes later joined the group Asia, and Trevor Horn became a sought-after record producer. (See *ASIA*.) Trivia buffs will be interested to know that when MTV went on the air, August 1, 1981, the Buggles's "Video Killed the Radio Star" was the first video seen on the music channel.

November   1979   VIDEO KILLED THE RADIO STAR   Island

CINDY BULLENS

Hometown: Boston, Massachusetts

A chance encounter with Elton John at a party led to Cindy Bullens's singing background vocals for him on one album, *Blue Moves,* and in three concert tours. In between these duties, she contributed vocals to Rod Stewart's *Atlantic Crossing* album and Bob Dylan's touring Rolling Thunder Revue. Bullens came into her own with three tunes on the *Grease* soundtrack, after which she recorded her own albums. Bullens has been nominated twice for Grammy Awards.

February   1979   SURVIVOR   United Artists
January   1980   TRUST ME   Casablanca

BILLY BURNETTE

Real Name: Dorsey William Burnette III
Born: May 8, 1953
Hometown: Memphis, Tennessee

Billy Burnette is a true second-generation rock and roller; he is the son of Dorsey Burnette and the nephew of Johnny Burnette, two rock 'n' roll pioneers. Dorsey moved the family to Los Angeles in 1959 and had Billy recording a year later, when Dorsey wrote and produced for him a Christmas 45, "Hey Daddy" b/w "Santa's Coffee." At age 11, Billy did a Dr. Seuss record, "Just Because We're Kids," for a then-fledgling producer named Herb Alpert. At 13, he was leading Brenda Lee's band on a tour through the Far East, something he continued to do in subsequent summers. He learned to play guitar at 16, and began organizing his father's band for concerts, only to return to Memphis as a session musician. When he later went back to Los Angeles, Billy played in many local bands

Billy Burnette

including Jawbone and Froglegs; the latter included actor Gary Busey on drums. Although Billy fashions himself a rock and roller, his songs have been recorded by a dozen or more country artists.

November   1980   DON'T SAY NO   Columbia

ROCKY BURNETTE

Born: June 12, 1953
Hometown: Memphis, Tennessee

Rocky Burnette, cousin of Billy Burnette and son of legendary rock 'n' roll pioneer Johnny Burnette, grew up in a house where Elvis Presley came to visit, Eddie Cochran stopped in for dinner, and Gene Vincent dropped by just to hang out. Rocky moved out to Los Angeles with his dad when he was a teenager, and eventually gave up a budding career in football to write and record his own music.

May   1980   TIRED OF TOEIN' THE LINE   EMI-America

Jenny Burton

GEORGE BURNS

Real Name: Nathan Birnbaum
Born: January 20, 1896
Hometown: New York City

The star of such films as *Oh God!*, *Going in Style*, and *Oh, God! You Devil*, and of "The George Burns and Gracie Allen Show" (with his late wife), as well as countless TV specials, George Burns had his only pop hit in 1980. That song was about how much he wished he were eighteen again.

January   1980   I WISH I WAS EIGHTEEN AGAIN   Mercury

JENNY BURTON

Born: November 18, 1957
Hometown: New York, New York

Jenny Burton was raised as a foster child, living in several different homes between the ages of 18 months and 18 years. Right after high school, she began singing gospel in churches throughout the New York area. Her first break in the music business came when she was working as a receptionist at Bell Records; a vocalist was needed at the last minute for a demo session, and Jenny was asked to fill in. This led to her first single, "Nobody Loves Me Like You Do." In 1983, she found herself singing to a track again, this time "One More Shot," which was a hit for an anonymous entity called C-Bank. Later that year, she resumed her solo career, while still singing gospel in a church in the Bronx.

| January | 1984 | REMEMBER WHAT YOU LIKE | Atlantic |
| June | 1984 | STRANGERS IN A STRANGE WORLD (with Patrick Jude) | Atlantic |

KATE BUSH

Born: July 30, 1958
Hometown: Lewisham, England

Kate Bush's songwriting career took off when a tape of her songs found its way to Pink Floyd's guitarist, David Gilmour. Gilmour was so impressed that he let her record three of the songs in his recording studio and, though she was only 16 and still in school, helped her get a record contract. In a short time, Bush formed a three-piece band, the KT Bush Band, and began performing locally. By the time her first single, "Wuthering Heights," became an international hit in 1978, Bush had perfected a unique stage presentation that combined song, dance, and theater. The show was videotaped and became a best-selling videocassette.

| February | 1979 | MAN WITH THE CHILD IN HIS EYES | EMI |

C

JOHN CAFFERTY AND THE BEAVER BROWN BAND

Members:
    John Cafferty—vocals, guitar—born: 1951
    Gary Gramolini—guitar
    Robert Cotoia—keyboards
    Pat Lupo—bass
    Michael "Tunes" Antunes—saxophone
    Kenny Jo Silva—drums
Hometown: Narragansett, Rhode Island

In 1972, John, Gary, Robert, Pat, and Kenny formed The Beaver Brown Band in Narragansett, a beach town across the bay from Newport, and began playing local colleges in the area doing a repertoire of Elvis, Wilson Pickett, Chuck Berry and Mitch Ryder songs. (The name Beaver Brown was the name of the paint color they used in their rehearsal studio.) As their popularity grew they started branching out to Cape Cod and Boston. In 1977, Michael Antunes joined the group and travelled with the band throughout the New England area.

In 1980, the Beaver Brown Band recorded a single, "Wild Summer Nights," b/w "Tender Years." They got some airplay throughout the East, and eventually did live shows at New York's Bottom Line club.

In 1981, veteran producer Kenny Vance, who sang with Jay & the Americans during the sixties, took movie director Martin Davidson to see one of their shows. Davidson was so impressed that he offered Cafferty the job of writing the music for the film *Eddie and the Cruisers*. "Wild Summer Nights" and "Tender Years" were put into the movie.

When the movie came out during the late summer of 1983, not much happened at the box office. However, when it was showcased on HBO during the summer of 1984, the soundtrack began selling in large quantities. This resulted in a renewed interest in the band that recorded the sound track but did not appear in the movie itself. John Cafferty and the Beaver Brown Band came to the forefront of the pop music scene, eclipsing the actors who starred as Eddie and the Cruisers.

January	1984	TENDER YEARS	Scotti Bros.
August	1984	ON THE DARK SIDE	Scotti Bros.
November	1984	TENDER YEARS (rereleased)	Scotti Bros

BOBBY CALDWELL

Born: August 15, 1951
Hometown: New York City, New York

Bobby Caldwell hails from a family of singers, musicians, and actors. At age 10, Bobby received a guitar from his father and promptly taught himself to play it. He formed his first group, the Rooftops, and played teen-age parties and "sock hops." In the next few years, Caldwell learned to play saxophone, bass, steel guitar, and piano, and studied music theory, writing, and arranging. Meanwhile, following in the family tradition, he also appeared in print ads and television commercials, and later did more than 100 soundtracks for Walt Disney's *New Mickey Mouse Club* TV show, playing his vast collection of instruments. By the time Caldwell began recording his own songs, he'd become a virtual one-man band. His songs have been recorded by Roberta Flack, Dionne Warwick, Toni Tennille, Cheryl Lynn, Roy Ayers, Natalie Cole, and Peabo Bryson.

Bobby now lives in Miami, Florida.

December	1978	WHAT YOU WON'T DO FOR LOVE	Clouds
April	1980	COMING DOWN FROM LOVE	Clouds
September	1982	ALL OF MY LOVE	Polydor

IRENE CARA

Born: March 18, 1959
Hometown: New York, New York

Irene Cara's show business achievements seem endless. Born to Puerto Rican and Cuban parents in New York's South Bronx, Irene's mother encouraged her five-year-old daughter's interest in playing the piano. Soon Irene was also studying dancing and singing. At age seven, she began performing at benefits and on local New York Spanish-language TV and radio shows. A year later, she made her Broadway debut as one of the orphans in the Jack Cassidy–Shirley Jones musical, *Maggie Flynn*. At age 10, Cara appeared at a tribute to Duke Ellington at New York's Madison Square Garden, sharing the stage with such luminaries as Sammy Davis, Jr. and Roberta Flack. The following year, she starred in another musical, *The Me Nobody Knows*, for which she won a prestigious Obie award. The show then moved to Broadway. When she was 12, Irene began a year-long stint on "The Electric Company" TV show for children, as a member of the Short Circus, a rock 'n' roll band that delivered grammar lessons in song. She used some of those earnings to put herself through Lincoln Square Academy, a private school in New York City. Meanwhile, she continued to guest-star on many TV shows, including "Kojak," "What's Happening?," and "The Tonight Show," and appeared on talk shows hosted by Mike Douglas, Merv Griffin, and Dinah Shore.

Irene Cara

Cara made her feature film debut at age 16, starring as Angela in *Aaron Loves Angela*. A year later she starred in *Sparkle*, in which she also got to sing and dance. At age 19, she appeared in the ABC-TV miniseries, "Roots: The Next Generation," portraying the young woman who would later give birth to *Roots* author Alex Haley, Jr. In *Fame*, she played Coco Hernandez, and the movie's title song, sung by Cara, was an international hit. Although she sang the hit "Flashdance," she did not appear in that film; she did make a cameo appearance in the film *D.C. Cab*, from which came another hit, "The Dream." As a result of all these hits from soundtracks, Cara is invited every year to perform at both the Grammy and Academy Awards presentations. In late 1984, she appeared in the movie, *The Cotton Club*.

June	1980	1. FAME	RSO
August	1980	2. OUT HERE ON MY OWN	RSO
November	1981	3. ANYONE CAN SEE	Network
January	1982	4. ANYONE CAN SEE	Network
April	1983	★ 5. FLASHDANCE . . . WHAT A FEELING	Casablanca
October	1983	6. WHY ME?	Geffen
December	1983	7. THE DREAM	Geffen/Network
March	1984	8. BREAKDANCE	Geffen/Network
July	1984	9. YOU WERE MADE FOR ME	Geffen/Network

TONY CAREY

Born: October 16, 1953
Hometown: Fresno, California

Tony Carey moved to the East Coast for high school, and once he opted for music over college, he never looked back. In 1978, after a three-year

Tony Carey

stint with Ritchie Blackmore's Rainbow, he accepted an offer to go to
Frankfort, Germany, for a two-week recording session. Tony wound up
settling in Germany. He also records under the name Planet P, with which
he had a hit in "Why Me."

March	1983	1. I WON'T BE HOME TONIGHT	Rocshire
July	1983	2. WEST COAST SUMMER NIGHTS	Rocshire
March	1984	3. A FINE FINE DAY	MCA
June	1984	4. THE FIRST DAY OF SUMMER	MCA

STEVE CARLISLE

Although Steve Carlisle started out playing in rock bands while in high
school and college, even touring with Melissa Manchester, he decided to
work the technical end and become an audio engineer. One day, during
a recording session, a background vocalist was needed; Carlisle fit the slot
and he has been singing ever since. Carlisle's career isn't limited to
singing the theme for the TV series "WKRP in Cincinnati." He can be
heard daily on numerous radio jingles for Coca-Cola, Fresca, Orkin, and
other products.

| November | 1981 | WKRP IN CINCINNATI | MCA/Sweet City |

LARRY CARLTON

Hometown: Torrance, California

Larry Carlton started playing guitar at age 6 and by age 15 had formed
his own working group. In 1968 he toured with the Fifth Dimension and

recorded his first solo LP. Within two years, Carlton was a top session musician, working on commercials and TV and film scores. He joined the jazz supergroup the Crusaders in 1974 and stayed for four years, establishing his guitar sound in the jazz community. Always in demand, he played on albums recorded by over 120 different acts, including John Lennon, Linda Ronstadt, Ray Charles, Joni Mitchell, and Steely Dan, and began producing and arranging for Barbra Streisand and other performers, often working from his 24-track home studio. Carlton also conducts guitar seminars.

February   1982   SLEEPWALK   Warner Bros.

KIM CARNES

Born: July 20, 1946
Hometown: Hollywood, California

Kim Carnes blames "a lifetime of too many late nights and far too many wine spritzers" for her deep, raw singing voice. At a mere five feet four inches and 100 pounds, the Pasadena-raised daughter of a corporate attorney was destined to use her big voice in a big way.

When Carnes was 14, she and a girlfriend formed a singing duo and tried selling their music along Sunset Boulevard. Finally, they met a producer who said he'd make them a demo tape for $200. Each girl hit her parents for $100, and they recorded three songs. The next thing they

Kim Carnes

knew, however, the producer vanished to Australia and the recording studio became a travel agency.

Upon graduation from high school Kim started college. She quit after one semester, however, when she decided that she was going to make a living in music, and that the only way to do that would be to just go out and do it. She wrote some songs and passed tapes around, finding work singing jingles and in demo sessions for other writers. Her first big break came when she joined the New Christy Minstrels for an extensive tour. It was on the road with the Minstrels that she met Kenny Rogers (then a minstrel himself) and her future husband and cowriter, Dave Ellingson. Upon their return to Los Angeles, Kim worked as a staff writer for producer Jimmy Bowen, composing alongside Glenn Frey (later of the Eagles) and J. D. Souther.

With her husband, Carnes composed many songs, including "Love Comes From Unexpected Places," which won both the American and Tokyo Song Festivals in 1977. She remained on the edge of fame with critically lauded albums, but didn't have a substantial hit until she dueted with Kenny Rogers on "Don't Fall In Love With A Dreamer," which she cowrote. A year later, "Bette Davis Eyes" established Kim as a major artist. Ironically, that song was written not by Carnes but by Jackie DeShannon and Donna Weiss, in 1974; Kim's interpretation held the number-one spot for nine weeks.

Kim once joked that after she got her first hit, she'd release albums by her alter egos, Latin singer Connie Con Carne and country singer Connie Crawford. Con Carne actually had a regional hit in Ellingson's home territory of Oregon when a disc jockey there got ahold of a joke demo Carnes and Ellingson recorded in their small home studio.

Frank Sinatra, Barbra Streisand, Anne Murray, Rita Coolidge, and Andy Williams have all recorded Carnes songs. Ellingson and Carnes have one son, Collin.

June	1978	1. YOU'RE A PART OF ME (with Gene Cotton)	Airola
February	1979	2. IT HURTS SO BAD	EMI-America
March	1980	3. DON'T FALL IN LOVE WITH A DREAMER (with Kenny Rogers)	United Artists
May	1980	4. MORE LOVE	EMI-America
October	1980	5. CRY LIKE A BABY	EMI-America
March	1981	★ 6. BETTE DAVIS EYES	EMI-America
August	1981	7. DRAW OF THE CARDS	EMI-America
October	1981	8. MISTAKEN IDENTITY	EMI-America
August	1982	9. VOYEUR	EMI-America
November	1982	10. DOES IT MAKE YOU REMEMBER	EMI-America
October	1983	11. INVISIBLE HANDS	EMI-America
January	1984	12. YOU MAKE MY HEART BEAT FASTER	EMI-America
May	1984	13. I PRETEND	EMI-America
September	1984	14. WHAT ABOUT ME (with Kenny Rogers and James Ingram)	RCA
December	1984	15. MAKE NO MISTAKE, HE'S MINE (with Barbra Streisand)	Columbia
January	1985	16. INVITATION TO DANCE	EMI-America

PAUL CARRACK

Born: April 22, 1951
Hometown: Sheffield, England

Paul Carrack's father had a large record collection and a drum set. Not surprisingly, Paul began his musical career thrashing about on the drums in his school group before switching to keyboards. Eventually, he played in several British bands, and saw his first hit, "How Long," with a band called Ace. Later, Carrack joined Squeeze, with whom he had another hit, "Tempted." He has since also played in a band fronted by Carlene Carter (Johnny Cash's stepdaughter) and coheaded Noise To Go with British pop singer Nick Lowe.

September   1982   I NEED YOU   Epic

THE CARS

Members:
    Ric Ocasek (Richard Otcasek)—vocals, guitar
    Benjamin Orr (Benjamin Orzechowski)—vocals, bass
    Elliot Easton—guitar, vocals
    Greg Hawkes—keyboards, percussion, saxophone, vocals
    David Robinson—drums, percussion, vocals
Hometown: Boston, Massachusetts

The Cars's origins may be traced to 1972, when Baltimore-born Ric Ocasek met Cleveland-born Benjamin Orr while both were working at a now-defunct booking agency in Columbus, Ohio. They had an all-night jam session, and Ocasek was impressed with Orr's vocal ability, especially on songs Ocasek wrote where he himself couldn't hit the high notes. They moved to Boston hoping for an environment more conducive to their music, and put together a series of bands, picking up New York-born left-handed guitarist Elliot Easton when they played as Cap'n Swing. Next to join was Greg Hawkes, who had moved to Boston after going through several bands in his hometown of Baltimore, and had quickly landed brief stints with Orphan and Martin Mull; Hawkes was creating electronic soundtracks for experimental films shown on public television when he accepted an invitation to join Cap'n Swing. Last to join (1976) was David Robinson, who had played drums in Jonathan Richard's Modern Lovers, a Los Angeles band called Pop!, and the Boston-based DMZ; he became Cap'n Swing's only true Bostonian, and suggested the name The Cars.

The Cars officially debuted December 31, 1976, at Pease Air Force Base in New Hampshire. The band graduated to become the most popular group on the local circuit by working the Rat and other clubs, and via a demo tape that got considerable local air play. Ultimately, The Cars won a record deal, and received a Grammy nomination for best new group.

The Cars. *Left to right:* (*top*) Ben Orr, Ric Ocasek, Greg Hawkes; (*bottom*) David Robinson, Elliot Easton.

The Cars continued to be successful, and launched solo careers for Ric Ocasek and Greg Hawkes. Ocasek has also produced a variety of striving artists, including Suicide, Bad Brains, the Fast, the New Models, the Peter Dayton Band, Romeo Void, Bebe Buell, and the Dark. Dave Robinson produced tracks for Boy's Life and the Vinny Band.

CARS

June	1978	JUST WHAT I NEEDED	Elektra
October	1978	MY BEST FRIEND'S GIRL	Elektra
March	1979	GOOD TIMES ROLL	Elektra

THE CARS

June	1979	1. LET'S GO	Elektra
October	1979	2. IT'S ALL I CAN DO	Elektra
September	1980	3. TOUCH AND GO	Elektra
November	1981	4. SHAKE IT UP	Elektra
March	1982	5. SINCE YOU'RE GONE	Elektra
March	1984	6. YOU MIGHT THINK	Elektra
May	1984	7. MAGIC	Elektra
August	1984	8. DRIVE	Elektra
October	1984	9. HELLO AGAIN	Elektra
January	1985	10. WHY CAN'T I HAVE YOU	Elektra

ROSANNE CASH

Born: May 24, 1955
Hometown: Memphis, Tennessee

When Rosanne Cash was four years old, her father Johnny Cash was making a big name for himself in country & western music, and moved the family to California. Despite the breakup of her parents when she was 11 years old, Rosanne led a normal life with her mother in Ventura, California. The day after her high school graduation, she went on the road working wardrobe for the Johnny Cash Show. Within a month, Rosanne and two half-sisters were in the show doing a couple of tunes and adding background vocals. After three years with the show, she began plotting her own career as a singer and actress, but her efforts met with little success. By early 1979, she was singing three and four sets a night in beer joints. On April 7, 1979, she married Rodney Crowell, who later became a leader in the country music field; they now live a few miles outside Nashville with their two daughters, Chelsea Jane and Caitlin, and Rodney's daughter from a previous marriage, Hannah.

| April | 1981 | SEVEN YEAR ACHE | Columbia |

FELIX CAVALIERE

Born: November 29, 1943
Hometown: Pelham, New York

In 1965, Felix Cavaliere, Gene Cornish, and Eddie Brigati made a momentous decision. Then active members of Joey Dee & the Starlighters, they broke away to form the Young Rascals with Dino Danelli.

After many hits, the Rascals broke up and Felix recorded his own album. He has not yet matched his success with the Rascals.

| March | 1980 | ONLY A LONELY HEART SEES | Epic |

CAZZ

Real Name: Robert C. Lewis
Hometown: Wolf City, Texas

Although Cazz, a black singer from a small Texas town midway between Dallas and Shreveport, recorded a few r&b hits during the early seventies, they were just local hits. In 1977, he met fifties rocker Dale Hawkins, who in 1957 had a major pop hit called "Susie-Q." Hawkins, based in Shreveport, started working with Cazz and produced the single "Let's Live Together" which was eventually sold to Dallas-based Number One Records. The song became Cazz's only chart entry.

| February | 1978 | LET'S LIVE TOGETHER | Number One |

CELEBRATION

Celebration had themselves one hit single, "Almost Summer," which featured Mike Love of the Beach Boys.

April   1978   ALMOST SUMMER   MCA

CENTRAL LINE

Members:
 Linton Beckles—vocals, percussion
 Henry Defoe—guitars
 Camelle Hinds—bass, vocals
 Lipson Francis—keyboards
Hometown: London, England

Originally a six-piece unit in 1978, the British-based Central Line found itself inspired by American pop and funk groups like Kool & the Gang, the O'Jays, and Cameo. Streamlined into a quartet, Central Line became a leader in London's East End funk scene.

November   1981   WALKING INTO SUNSHINE   Mercury

CERRONE

Real Name: Jean-Marc Cerrone
Born: 1952
Hometown: France

Jean-Marc Cerrone is the youngest of three children of a small shoe manufacturer. In school, Cerrone angered teachers by tapping his desk

Cerrone

with a ruler to the beat of the music in his head. At home, he tapped the same rhythms with a fork at the dinner table. His father initially opposed his son's musical ambition, but finally relented and bought Jean-Marc a drum set.

At 12, Jean-Marc was making music; at 14, he was playing in groups; and at 18, after passing his certification exams for a hairdressing career, he decided to become a full-time musician, earning a living by hawking street-scene sketches to tourists in the St. Michel district of Paris.

Cerrone's musical efforts went unnoticed until 1976, when he recorded the album that would change his life. Although many people assured him the public wasn't ready for this definitive disco album, *Love In "C" Minor* sold over five million copies in Europe alone.

| February | 1977 | LOVE IN "C" MINOR | Cotillion |
| January | 1978 | SUPERNATURE | Cotillion |

CHAMPAIGN

Members:
    Paulie Carmen—vocals—born: September 5, 1953
    Rena Jones—vocals—born: March 17, 1954

Champaign. *Left to right: (top)* Leon Reeder, Rocky Maffit, Dana Walden; *(bottom)* Michael Day, Paulie Carmen, Rena Jones.

Michael Day—guitar, keyboards—born: January 28, 1953
Howard ("Leon") Reeder—guitar—born: April 26, 1950
Dana Walden—keyboards—born: March 12, 1948
Michael Reed—bass (left group in 1982)
Rocky Maffit—percussion—born: March 27, 1952
Hometown: Champaign, Illinois

Named after Champaign the city, not champagne the drink, this group originated in Creative Audio, a busy recording studio owned and operated by a partnership consisting of Michael Day, Leon Reeder, Dana Walden, and Michael Reed. All musicians, they often ended up contributing production and musical backup to projects recorded in their studio. The next logical step was to form a band, which they did.

| February | 1981 | HOW 'BOUT US | Columbia |
| April | 1983 | TRY AGAIN | Columbia |

BILL CHAMPLIN

Born: May 21, 1947
Hometown: Oakland, California

After leading a San Francisco Bay area-based band called the Sons of Champlin through 13 years and seven albums, Bill Champlin moved to Los Angeles and went solo in 1978. As a session singer, he sang background for Elton John, Donna Summer, Barbra Streisand, Boz Scaggs, Barry Manilow, Nancy Wilson, Earth, Wind & Fire, the Tubes, and others. Earth, Wind & Fire, George Benson, Herbie Hancock, Lee Ritenour, and the Pointer Sisters have all recorded Champlin songs. He is married to singer Tamara Matosian and has two children from a previous marriage.

| December | 1981 | TONIGHT TONIGHT | Elektra |
| July | 1982 | SARA | Elektra |

CHANGE

Members:
    James "Crab" Robinson—vocals
    Debora Cooper—vocals
    Rick Brennen—vocals, percussion—added in 1983
    Mike Campbell—guitar
    Vincent Henry—saxophone, guitars
    Jeff Bova—keyboards
    Timmy Allen—bass, vocals
    Rick Gallwey—percussion—replaced (1983) by Toby Johnson
Hometown: New York, New York

Change was originally the name of a makeshift group designed by Italian-based producers Jacques Fred Petrus and Mauro Malavaso, who brought

Change. *Left to right:* Timmy Allen, Mike Campbell, Jeff Bova, Debora Cooper, James Robinson, Vincent Henry, Rick Brennen, Toby Johnson.

together top session musicians and singers from Europe and America for an album. The highlights on that album, *The Glow Of Love*, were two lead vocals by a then up-and-coming vocalist, Luther Vandross. When the album became a top seller, a permanent group was constructed for a tour, on which Vandross was a featured vocalist. A more stable group was formed later to work under the name Change.

May	1980	1. A LOVER'S HOLIDAY	RFC
June	1981	2. PARADISE	Atlantic/RFC
August	1981	3. HOLD TIGHT	Atlantic/RFC
May	1982	4. THE VERY BEST IN YOU	RFC/Atlantic

CHARLENE

Real Name: Charlene Duncan
Hometown: Los Angeles, California

Charlene had some successes on Prodigal Records in the late seventies. Eventually, she signed with Motown and had several hits, including one with Stevie Wonder.

March	1982	I'VE NEVER BEEN TO ME	Motown
October	1982	USED TO BE (with Stevie Wonder)	Motown

CHARLIE

Members:
    Terry Slesser—vocals—added in 1980
    Terry Thomas—vocals, guitar

Martin Smith—guitar—replaced (1977) by Eugene Organ (Organ left group
   in 1979–80)
Julian Colbeck—keyboards (left group in 1979–80)
John Anderson—vocals, bass
Steve Gadd—drums
Shep Lonsdale—drums—added in 1978—replaced (1981) by Robert Henrit

Terry Thomas was a member of a North London band with Simon Kirke
(Free, Bad Company) when he auditioned for and was accepted into a
group called Axe, which was led by John Anderson. Shortly thereafter,
Terry left London to work for a communications firm in Portugal. In his
absence, Axe recruited another guitarist, Martin Smith. Once Thomas was
back in London, he, Anderson, Smith, and Steve Gadd began jamming
together, and formed a new group, Charlie. One night while on a tour of
the United States with the Doobie Brothers, Gadd's hand was broken by
"a drunk security guard" (according to Thomas), and Shep Lonsdale, who
was mixing sound for the Doobies, filled in on drums for the remainder
of the tour, ultimately joining Charlie alongside Gadd. The band has
changed its line-up several times.

August	1977	1. TURNING TO YOU	Janus
August	1978	2. SHE LOVES TO BE IN LOVE	Janus
September	1979	3. KILLER CUT	Arista
June	1983	4. IT'S INEVITABLE	Mirage

Charlie. *Left to right:* Robert Henrit, Terry Thomas, Terry Slesser, Steve Gadd,
John Anderson.

Cheap Trick. *Left to right:* Bun E. Carlos, Robin Zander, Rick Nielson, Jon Brant.

CHEAP TRICK

Members:
    Robin Zander—vocals—born: January 23, 1955
    Rick Nielsen—guitar—born: December 22, 1950
    Tom Petersson—bass—replaced (1980) by Pete Comita—Comita replaced
       (1982) by Jon Brant—born: February 20, 1954
    Bun E. Carlos—drums—born: June 12, 1953
Hometown: Rockford, Illinois

The members of Cheap Trick reveal very little about anything but band facts, and even these are subject to change periodically. The furthest back Cheap Trick can be traced is to 1966–67, when Chicago-born Rick Nielsen and Swedish-born Tom Petersson played in a midwest band called the Grim Reaper, later called Fuse. Although Fuse recorded, Nielsen and Petersson left the group, and in 1969, between trips to Europe, they formed another band with a short future, Honey Boy Williamson & the

Manchurian Blues Band. In Germany they met Venezuelan-born Bun E. (short for Bunezuela) Carlos and American-born Robin Zander, who'd been singing in Scotland. Another version of the story has a Panama-born Brad Carlson and American-born Robin Zander joining Cheap Trick in Rockford, Illinois. In any case, the new band began playing midwest bars in 1974.

Cheap Trick was immediately recognizable. Zander was the handsome, long-haired blond dressed in a white three-piece suit. Nielsen wore a cardigan sweater, baseball cap, bow tie, and old-fashioned black sneakers. Petersson wore pirate-style shirts, leather pants, and boots. A slightly portly Carlos sported short hair, glasses, fifties clothes, and a perennial cigarette on his lower lip.

While still virtually unknown in the United States, Cheap Trick became one of the biggest attractions ever in Japan. While on tours there, extensive press coverage reported that the four band members were mobbed anywhere they went by hundreds of chasing, screeching, grabbing teenage fans. While Cheap Trick ultimately became popular in the United States, upon the release of the *Live At Budokan* album recorded in Japan, fan reaction stateside was never as intense as in Japan.

Along with many albums, Cheap Trick also contributed to the soundtrack of the film *Roadie*, most notably the single "Everything Works If You Let It." Rick Nielsen has also played on recordings by John Lennon and Yoko Ono, Daryl Hall & John Oates, and Kiss's Gene Simmons.

July	1978	1. SURRENDER	Epic
April	1979	2. I WANT YOU TO WANT ME	Epic
August	1979	3. AIN'T THAT A SHAME	Epic
October	1979	4. DREAM POLICE	Epic
December	1979	5. VOICES	Epic
May	1980	6. EVERYTHING WORKS IF YOU LET IT	Epic
November	1980	7. STOP THIS GAME	Epic
June	1982	8. IF YOU WANT MY LOVE	Epic
October	1982	9. SHE'S TIGHT	Epic

JUDY CHEEKS

Hometown: Miami, Florida

The first person to expose Judy Cheeks to the music world was her father, the Reverend Julius Cheeks, gospel singer and preacher. Three days after graduating from high school, Judy set out for Los Angeles, where she met Ike and Tina Turner. That duo was so impressed with their "discovery" that they produced Judy's debut album. Shortly thereafter, she began writing songs for the Jackson Five, Diana Ross, and the Miracles. Eventually, Cheeks moved to Munich, Germany, where she became a professional singer and actress.

October	1978	MELLOW LOVIN'	Salsoul

CHERI

Members:
   Rosalind Milligan Hunt
   Amy Roslyn
Hometown: Montreal, Canada

When disco diva Geraldine Hunt needed a vocal duo for a song she'd written, she hardly thought one of the voices she needed was right under her own roof. Her daughter, Rosalind Milligan Hunt, had done background vocals on her mother's records, but Roz wanted to be a lawyer, not a singer. On a whim, Geraldine asked her daughter to sing her new song, and before anyone knew it, Roz and a friend had recorded the song, "Murphy's Law." The two friends called themselves Cheri, although they were not a permanent act. Following the success of "Murphy's Law," Roz joined up with New York-born vocalist Amy Roslyn, and Cheri became a professional duo.

April   1982   MURPHY'S LAW   Venture

DESMOND CHILD & ROUGE

Members:
   Desmond Child—lead vocals
   Diana Grasselli—backup vocals
   Myriam Valle—backup vocals
   Maria Vidal—backup vocals
Hometown: New York, New York

Desmond Child formed Rouge in 1975 when he met Myriam Valley in Woodstock, New York, and Diana Grasselli and Maria Vidal in music classes at Dade Community College in Florida.
   Their only chart song, "Our Love Is Insane," was inspired by r&b.

January   1979   OUR LOVE IS INSANE   Capitol

CHILLIWACK

Members:
   Bill Henderson—vocals, guitar, keyboards—born: November 6, 1944
   Brian MacLeod—guitar, keyboards, drums, vocals—born: June 25, 1952
   Ab Bryant—bass, vocals—born: November 15, 1954
Hometown: Vancouver, British Columbia, Canada

The original members of Chilliwack were Bill Henderson, Clair Lawrence, Glenn Miller, and Ross Turney, who originally played in an adventurous psychedelic jazz-rock band, the Collectors, along with Howie Vickers. When Vickers left the group after three years, in mid-1969, the remaining four members became Chilliwack, named after a small town in British Columbia and meaning "valley of many streams." The pop/rock band became very popular in its native Canada. After many personnel changes in the mid-seventies, Chilliwack became a trio, with only Bill Henderson remaining from the original line-up.

February	1972	1. LONESOME MARY	A & M
December	1974	2. CRAZY TALK	Sire
April	1977	3. FLY AT NIGHT	Mushroom
August	1978	4. ARMS OF MARY	Mushroom
September	1981	5. MY GIRL	Millennium
January	1982	6. I BELIEVE	Millennium
October	1982	7. WHATCHA GONNA DO	Millennium

CITY BOY

Members:
    Lol Mason—vocals
    Steve Broughton—vocals, guitar (left group in 1980)
    Mike Slamer—guitar, mandolin, bass
    Max Thomas—piano, organ, synthesizer, harmonium
    Chris Dunn—bass, guitar (left group in 1980)
    Roy Ward—drums, vocals—replaced Roger "Barley" Kent in 1977
Hometown: Birmingham, England

Lol Mason, Steve Broughton, Max Thomas, and Chris Dunn formed a folk-oriented quartet in September 1972. By March 1974, they incorporated Mike Slamer and Roger "Barley" Kent and became an electric rock band called Back-In-The-Band. In January 1975 the band members adopted the name City Boy, quit their day jobs, and turned professional. Many European countries embraced the new act immediately. Roger Kent left in 1977, and was replaced by Roy Ward.

City Boy had only one hit and, ironically, that song brought people trouble: the digits in the song title referred to a fictitious telephone number, leading to crank calls to virtually anyone whose telephone number ended in "5705." The group broke up in 1981 after moving to America.

August	1978	5-7-0-5	Mercury

ALLAN CLARKE

Born: April 5, 1942
Hometown: Sulford, Lancashire, England

When World War II ended, the Clarke family moved across Sulford to live with Allan's grandmother. At his new school, a teacher had seven-year-old Allan stand in front of the class and asked "Who would like to sit next to this little boy?" Another seven-year-old, Graham Nash, said, "You can sit next to me if you want."

The two childhood buddies loved to sing, and later began playing guitars as well. They formed groups called the Guytones (modelled after the Everly Brothers), the Deltas, and the Dominators of Rhythm before forming the Hollies in 1962. The Hollies went on to have many international hits. Clarke has been in and out of the Hollies since the early seventies, and has had two solo hits.

| March | 1978 | SHADOW IN THE STREET | Atlantic |
| May | 1980 | SLIPSTREAM | Elektra/Curb |

STANLEY CLARKE

Born: June 30, 1951
Hometown: Philadelphia, Pennsylvania

Stanley Clarke's mother, an accomplished opera and church singer (and painter), encouraged young Stanley to study violin and cello in elementary school. Stanley played in various bands (he switched to electric bass at age 16) and continued studying music right through college, attending the Philadelphia Academy of Music. In 1970, Clarke moved to New York City and played in mainstream jazz bands led by Horace Silver, Stan Getz, Art Blakey, Dexter Gordon, Thad Jones & Mel Lewis, Gil Evans,

Stanley Clarke

and others, and played on albums by Aretha Franklin, Quincy Jones, Santana, Deodato, and Gato Barbieri. A year later, he met Chick Corea, and together they formed Return To Forever, which in its five-year existence became a prototype for jazz-rock fusion bands to come. More recently, Clarke played in the New Barbarians alongside the Rolling Stones' Keith Richards and Ron Wood. He has collaborated and toured with guitarist Jeff Beck and has teamed up with George Duke in the Clarke/Duke Project. Clarke has produced records for Natalie Cole, Ramsey Lewis, Roy Buchanan, Rodney Franklin, and Dee Dee Bridgewater, and has written or cowritten songs for Cole, Shalamar, and Paul McCartney, while still maintaining his solo career. Clarke is recognized as one of the best bassists in the world.

May   1981   SWEET BABY (with George Duke)   Epic

THE CLASH

Members:
    Joe Strummer (John Mellors)—vocals, guitar—born: 1953
    Mick Jones—vocals, guitar—replaced (1983) by Nick Shepherd and Vince White
    Paul Simonon—bass
    Pete Howard—drums (replaced Terry Chimes in 1983)—(Chimes replaced Nicky "Topper" Headon in 1982)—(Headon replaced Chimes himself in 1977)
Hometown: London, England

Brixton-born Paul Simonon was attending art school on a scholarship and had been playing bass for only six weeks when a friend and fellow art student, Mick Jones, asked him to form a group. At the same time, Joe Strummer was singing with a pub band, the 101-ers, which he had formed in order to pass the time and pay the rent. As soon as he was asked, Strummer quit his group and joined the prototype Clash. Guitarist Keith Levine (later of Public Image Ltd.) was also a founding member, but left the band early on, saying he had some urgent business to take care of in North London.

In May 1976, the drummerless group began rehearsing in a small flat near Shepherd's Bush Green in London. Three months later, they began refurbishing an abandoned warehouse in the district of Camden Town. When it was finished, drummer Terry Chimes was enlisted, and every day the warehouse shook with the sound of hard practice.

Yet, the Clash had nowhere to perform. The manager of London's famous Marquee Club, for example, reportedly told the group, "Sorry mates; no punk rock in here." As a result, Bernard Rhodes, the group's manager, created gigs.

One day, during a particularly nasty gig, when bottles and cans were coming down like rain, a wine bottle smashed into little pieces on Chimes' high hat, and he quit the band. Auditions were held for a replacement, and Nicky "Topper" Headon was selected from over 200 candidates.

Meanwhile, British punk rock, spearheaded by the Sex Pistols and the Clash, was becoming big news. The Clash received favorable attention from its fans (who religiously tagged the band "the only band that really matters"), but unfavorable attention from the daily newspapers and the police all over Europe, which culminated in a bust of two Clash members, performed by armed police on top of the group's warehouses. The two were charged with various gun offenses and the shooting of some valuable racing pigeons.

The Clash's popularity grew gradually. In 1982, the band played before 150,000 appreciative fans while opening two concerts for The Who in New York's Shea Stadium. In 1983, the Clash performed at the US Festival.

The Clash is featured in the 1980 film, *Rude Boy*, and has a cameo in the 1983 *The King of Comedy*.

March	1980	1. TRAIN IN VAIN	Epic
July	1982	2. SHOULD I STAY OR SHOULD I GO	Epic
October	1982	3. ROCK THE CASBAH	Epic
February	1983	4. SHOULD I STAY OR SHOULD I GO	Epic

LINDA CLIFFORD

Hometown: Brooklyn, New York

Linda Clifford has been in show business since she was a tot. At the age of four, she was a serious student of ballet, jazz, and tap dance. By age seven, she had already appeared as an actress on the TV shows *Startime* and *The Merry Mailman*. At 10, she appeared with Harry Belafonte and Sidney Poitier on an NAACP television special. At 17, Clifford won several beauty contests, including Miss New York State.

Clifford's first professional engagement as a singer was in the Catskills. After winning the Miss New York State contest, she left New York for Chicago to try a professional singing career with a ten-piece band. That didn't work out, but she later managed to land several recording deals as a solo singer. Clifford, who says she can sing in five different languges, has a daughter, Gina.

June	1978	1. RUNAWAY LOVE	Curtom
August	1978	2. IF MY FRIENDS COULD SEE ME NOW	Curtom
March	1979	3. BRIDGE OVER TROUBLED WATER	Curtom
August	1980	4. RED LIGHT	RSO

CLOCKS

Members:
    Jerry Sumner—vocals, bass
    Lance Threat—guitar
    Gerald "Rod" Graves—keyboards, vocals
    Steve Swain—drums, vocals
Hometown: Wichita, Kansas

Clocks formed in 1979; they soon built a strong following in Manhattan, home of Kansas State University, and later expanded their tour market to Missouri and New Mexico. Even before Clocks' debut LP was released, the quartet was asked to open concerts for Rick Springfield in St. Louis, Kansas City, and Joplin, Missouri. At the other end of the spectrum, Clocks has also opened for Dave Edmunds and Black Sabbath.

| August | 1982 | SHE LOOKS A LOT LIKE YOU | Boulevard |

CLOUT

Members:
    Cindi Alter—vocals, guitar
    Sandie Robbie—guitar, vocals
    Jennie Garson—piano, guitar, vocals
    Bones Brettell—keyboards, vocals
    Lee Tomlinson—bass, flute, vocals
    Ingi Herbst—drums, vocals
Hometown: Johannesburg, South Africa

Formed in 1977 by Lee Tomlinson and Ingi Herbst, Clout quickly collected practically every accolade in its home country, including Saarie Awards for best vocal group, best pop music group, and top 20 artists of the year. Clout consists of four women and two men.

| September | 1978 | SUBSTITUTE | Epic |
| November | 1978 | SUBSTITUTE | Epic |

BRUCE COCKBURN

Born: May 27, 1945
Hometown: Ottawa, Canada

Bruce Cockburn (pronounced CO-burn) first discovered the guitar in 1959, while listening to Elvis Presley, Buddy Holly, and Gabor Szabo. He found an old guitar in his grandmother's attic, and banged away on it trying to play rock 'n' roll. A year later, Cockburn joined his first band, which had two or three guitarists, depending on how many people showed up. In 1963, he entered the famous Berklee College of Music in Boston as a guitar composition major. He was also trained in clarinet, piano, and trumpet.

A year later, after bumming his way from Norway to France by freighter, Cockburn found himself playing simplified international Dixieland in Paris with a French trumpet player and an American clarinetist. That trio was arrested for unlawful begging.

Back in Canada, Cockburn released his self-titled debut album in 1971. Although not all of his albums have been made available in the United States, Cockburn is revered in Canada, where he received gold album awards and numerous Juno Awards. His songs have been recorded by Anne Murray, Tom Rush, Mary Hopkins, and others. To coincide with the stateside success of his "Wondering Where The Lions Are," Cockburn performed a benefit concert at the Philadelphia Zoo.

March   1980   WONDERING WHERE THE LIONS ARE   Millennium

PHIL COLLINS

Born: January 30, 1951
Hometown: Chiswick, England

Phil Collins began playing a toy drum at age five and the instrument has been a focus of his energies ever since. Collins was also a child actor— one of his first professional roles was as a screaming fan in the concert scene of the Beatles' first film, *A Hard Day's Night.* At 14, he starred as the Artful Dodger in the London production of *Oliver.*

Collins played drums in a series of bands, and in 1970, at the age of 19, he won an audition to be in Genesis. Five years later, when Peter

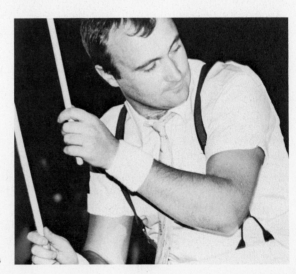

Phil Collins

Gabriel quit Genesis, Collins moved into Gabriel's vacated spot as lead vocalist and frontman. For a time, Collins also led a jazz fusion band called Brand X whenever he had time off from Genesis, but that group eventually split up. Later, he drummed on a Robert Plant album and produced albums for John Martyn and Abba's Frida. Collins now juggles a solo career with his commitments to Genesis.

March	1981	1. I MISSED AGAIN	Atlantic
May	1981	2. IN THE AIR TONIGHT	Atlantic
November	1982	3. YOU CAN'T HURRY LOVE	Atlantic
February	1983	4. I DON'T CARE ANYMORE	Atlantic
May	1983	5. I CANNOT BELIEVE IT'S TRUE	Atlantic
February	1984	★ 6. AGAINST ALL ODDS (Take A Look At Me Now)	Atlantic
February	1985	★ 7. ONE MORE NIGHT	Atlantic

CON FUNK SHUN

Members:
  Michael Vernon Cooper—guitar, sitar, synthesizer, vocals
  Karl "Deacon" Fuller—trumpet, flugelhorn, percussion, vocals
  Paul "Maceo" Harrell—saxophone, flute, percussion, vocals
  Cedric A. Martin—bass, vocals
  Louis "Tony" McCall—drums, percussion, vocals

Con Funk Shun

Felton Pilate II—trombone, guitar, piano, synthesizer, vocoder, vocals
Danny "Sweet Man" Thomas—piano, synthesizer, clavinet, organ, vocoder,
     vocals
Hometown: Vallejo, California

Michael Cooper and Louis McCall decided to form a group when they
were tenth graders at Vallejo High School. Within a year, the rest of the
group was enlisted and, as Project Soul, they became one of the premier
bands in the San Francisco area. Project Soul then moved to Memphis,
changed its name to Con Funk Shun (taken from a song title by the Night
Lighters) and became the backup group for the Soul Children, as featured
in the film *Wattstax*. The band began recording its own music in 1976.

December	1977	1. FFUN	Mercury
August	1978	2. SHAKE AND DANCE WITH ME	Mercury
January	1981	3. TOO TIGHT	Mercury
January	1983	4. BABY I'M HOOKED	Mercury

CONTINENTAL MINIATURES

Members:
     Kevin McCarthy—vocals, keyboards
     Rich Bytnar—guitar
     Eric Ramon—guitar
     Matt Walker—bass
     David Kendrick—drums
Hometown: Los Angeles, California

Matt Walker and Eric Ramon met in San Francisco in 1973. In 1975 they
went to Los Angeles, where they met Kevin, Rich, and David. Eventually
the musicians met producer Michael Lloyd, the king of the youth-oriented
remakes who produced hits for Shaun Cassidy, Leif Garrett, and Donny
& Marie Osmond. Lloyd had them record two songs—the Dave Clark
Five's first hit, "Glad All Over," and Dusty Springfield's second hit, "Stay
Awhile," both from 1964. The songs were sold to London Records and
released as a single in 1978; only "Stay Awhile" reached the national
charts.

| May | 1978 | STAY AWHILE | London |

ELVIS COSTELLO

Real Name: Declan Patrick McManus
Born: August 25, 1955
Hometown: London, England

Declan Patrick McManus was the only child of a marriage that ended
when his father, a jazz trumpeter and cabaret singer, hit the road for
good. The young boy had no fantasies of following in his dad's footsteps
as a musician until his late teens, when he took up the guitar. After high

Elvis Costello

school, he began writing prolifically and tried peddling his songs to record companies, all the time working full-time as a computer technician.

In the summer of 1977, the confident but frustrated songwriter took his guitar into the streets, and sang his songs outside the Hilton Hotel in London, where CBS Records executives were attending their annual convention. He was arrested for causing a public disturbance, but the angry young man did get his record contract. Renamed Elvis Costello (*Elvis* from the king of rock and roll, *Costello* from a surname in his mother's family), he recorded his debut album, and then formed his band, the Attractions. Over the years, Costello evolved from the abrasive punker to a fairly mainstream but engaging singer/songwriter, as evidenced by his concert with the 92-piece Royal Philharmonic Orchestra at London's Royal Albert Hall, his pure country & western album, *Almost Blue*, and a never-televised guest appearance with Tony Bennett on a pilot for a Count Basie TV show.

In 1979, Costello made news when in a Columbus, Ohio, hotel bar, he made racial slurs regarding Ray Charles and James Brown to singers Stephen Stills and Bonnie Bramlett. This led to a minor barroom brawl and a press conference in New York, where Costello publicly apologized and insisted, "I'm not a racist."

| August | 1983 | EVERYDAY I WRITE THE BOOK (with the Attractions) | Columbia |
| July | 1984 | THE ONLY FLAME IN TOWN (with the Attractions) | Columbia |

GENE COTTON

Hometown: Columbus, Ohio

Gene Cotton grew up one of nine children of an Ohio Highways Department employee, and attended Ohio State University as a political science major in the mid-sixties. Opting for music, he began playing small clubs and colleges in the midwest. Cotton later moved around between Ohio, New York, Nashville, and Los Angeles. He recorded his first album in 1972 and formed his band, American Ace, in 1979.

November	1974	1. SUNSHINE ROSES	Myrrh
May	1975	2. DAMN IT ALL	ABC
December	1976	3. YOU'VE GOT ME RUNNIN'	ABC
February	1978	4. BEFORE MY HEART FINDS OUT	Ariola America
June	1978	5. YOU'RE A PART OF ME (with Kim Carnes)	Ariola
September	1978	6. LIKE A SUNDAY IN SALEM	Ariola
March	1982	7. IF I COULD GET YOU	Knoll

JOSIE COTTON

Hometown: Dallas, Texas

Josie Cotton studied voice and music theory in school as a teenager and gained experience singing everything from complex Latin jazz to authentic Gypsy love songs. About that time, she and a girlfriend had a comedy show on a local radio station.

Cotton eventually moved to California to pursue a pop singing career. While in a recording studio someone needed a singer for a demo of "Johnny, Are You Queer?" Josie volunteered. By the end of 1981, she was signed to a recording contract.

| August | 1982 | HE COULD BE THE ONE | Elektra |
| April | 1984 | JIMMY LOVES MARYANN | Elektra |

JOHN COUGAR

See *John Cougar MELLENCAMP.*

THE CRETONES

Members:
    Mark Goldenberg—vocals, guitar
    Peter Bernstein—bass, vocals

Steve Leonard—keyboards, vocals
Steve Beers—drums
Hometown: Los Angeles, California

Mark Goldenberg was in Al Stewart's touring band when Stewart's opening act was Wendy Waldman, who featured the talents of Peter Bernstein and Steve Beers in her band. Goldenberg, Bernstein, and Beers became good friends, and all three later backed Waldman again before officially debuting the Cretones in 1978 as the house band at Mike's Munchies, a submarine sandwich shop near the University of Southern California. Steve Leonard had played in a high school band with Goldenberg and was invited by him to join the Cretones. The group's biggest claim to fame is that Linda Rondstadt recorded three of their songs on her *Mad Love* LP, when she opted for a harder rock 'n' roll sound. Bernstein and Goldenberg played guitars on that album.

May   1980   REAL LOVE   Planet

CHRISTOPHER CROSS

Real Name: Christopher Geppert
Born: May 3, 1951
Hometown: Austin, Texas

Christopher Cross, the son of an army physician and professional musician, was inspired in his early teens by the music of Buddy Holly, the Beach Boys, and the Beatles. He started playing drums and later switched to

Christopher Cross

guitar as he began writing songs. Throughout high school, Cross formed and fronted rock bands. In 1972, he and a few buddies quit college and moved to Austin, where they formed the nucleus of Cross's present band. Cross's self-titled debut album in 1979 won him a trunkload of Grammy Awards. He also won an Academy Award for "Arthur's Theme," written for the film *Arthur*.

February	1980	1. RIDE LIKE THE WIND	Warner Bros.
June	1980	★ 2. SAILING	Warner Bros.
October	1980	3. NEVER BE THE SAME	Warner Bros.
March	1981	4. SAY YOU'LL BE MINE	Warner Bros.
August	1981	★ 5. ARTHUR'S THEME	Warner Bros.
January	1983	6. ALL RIGHT	Warner Bros.
May	1983	7. NO TIME FOR TALK	Warner Bros.
December	1983	8. THINK OF LAURA	Warner Bros.
June	1984	9. A CHANCE FOR HEAVEN	Columbia

RODNEY CROWELL

Born: August 7, 1950
Hometown: Houston, Texas

Rodney Crowell's family is made up of working people who played music for enjoyment. One of Rodney's grandfathers was a church choir leader, the other a bluegrass banjo player. His grandmother played guitar and his father performed in bars and honky tonks in a semiprofessional capacity. Rodney began playing drums at age 11, eventually playing in teen rock bands. When the songwriter/guitarist boom arrived in the early 1970s, Rodney moved to Nashville to try his chances, and was given work by Jerry Reed.

When Rodney met Emmylou Harris's husband and producer, Bruce Ahern, things began to click. There was an instant creative affinity between Rodney and Emmylou; as a result, many of his songs appear on her albums, and he toured with her for two and a half years, before stopping in 1977 to record his first solo album.

Crowell's songs have also been recorded by John Denver, Willie Nelson, Bob Seger, Waylon Jennings, Jerry Jeff Walker, the Oak Ridge Boys, Bobby Bare, the Dirt Band, Nana Mouskouri, his wife Rosanne Cash, sister-in-law Carlene Carter, and father-in-law Johnny Cash. Crowell has produced Rosanne Cash's albums. The couple lives with their two daughters and Crowell's daughter from a previous marriage.

May	1980	ASHES BY NOW	Warner Bros.

CULTURE CLUB

Members:
    Boy George (George O'Dowd)—vocals—born: June 14, 1961
    Helen Terry—vocals—added in 1983—left in 1984

Culture Club. *Clockwise from top:* Roy Hay, Mikey Craig, Boy George, Jon Moss.

Roy Hay—guitars, keyboards, sitar—born: August 12, 1961
Michael Craig—bass—born: February 15, 1960
Jon Moss—drums, percussion—born: October 11, 1957
Hometown: Bexleyheath, Kent, England

Culture Club's Boy George is a mix of contradictions—a man who mimics a woman, a Catholic who demonstrates his love of Hebrew, a white man who sings black soul music—yet he has become a teen idol and media star. The origins of Culture Club go back to 1981 when, in a music paper, Mikey Craig spotted a photograph of George (then Lieutenant Lush) and Annabella Lwin, both of whom were singing in Bowwowwow at the time. The article under the photograph suggested that the group's manager, Malcolm McLaren, wanted to form a separate band for George. Mikey and George met, and formed a band with guitarist John Suede and drummer Jon Moss. About the time Roy Hay replaced John Suede, the group became Culture Club and established its unique look.

December	1982	1. DO YOU REALLY WANT TO HURT ME	Virgin/Epic
April	1983	2. TIME	Virgin/Epic
July	1983	3. I'LL TUMBLE 4 YA	Virgin/Epic
October	1983	4. CHURCH OF THE POISONED MIND	Virgin/Epic
December	1983	★ 5. KARMA CHAMELEON	Virgin/Epic
March	1984	6. MISS ME BLIND	Virgin/Epic
May	1984	7. IT'S A MIRACLE	Virgin/Epic
October	1984	8. THE WAR SONG	Virgin/Epic
December	1984	9. MISTAKE NO. 3	Virgin/Epic

CHERIE & MARIE CURRIE

Hometown: Los Angeles, California

Cherie Currie was a member of the all-female hard-rock band called the Runaways, and appeared in the film *Foxes*. She later teamed up with her sister Marie for one album.

October	1979	SINCE YOU'VE BEEN GONE	Capitol

TIM CURRY

Hometown: England

Since his appearance as a crazed transvestite, Dr. Frank N. Further, in the cult film *The Rocky Horror Picture Show*, Tim Curry has been trying to establish another image—*any* other image. Although he appeared in both the London and Broadway productions of *Travesties*, starred as Mozart on Broadway in *Amadeus*, played the roles of a disc jockey in the film *Times Square* and a thirties gangster in the film *Annie*, portrayed William Shakespeare in a six-hour BBC-TV miniseries, "The Life of Shakespeare," and co-starred in a 1984 film, *The Ploughman's Lunch*, his fans still remember him from the cult film.

Raised on the south coast of England, the son of a Navy Methodist chaplain, Curry attended private school from the age of 10, which is when he first discovered his interest in singing and theater. He attended the University of Birmingham, where he spent the bulk of his time acting and singing in a swing band. From 1978 to 1981, he recorded three rock albums.

November	1979	I DO THE ROCK	A & M

D

STEVE DAHL

Born: November 20, 1954
Hometown: La Canada, California

Chicago disc jockey Steve Dahl created a furor when he talked about how he disliked disco music and in 1979, at Chicago's Comiskey Park, he held a rally to burn and destroy all disco records. His fame may have contributed to his only hit, in 1979. Today Dahl works afternoons on WLS-FM in Chicago.

September   1979   DO YOU THINK I'M DISCO   Ovation

RODNEY DANGERFIELD

Real Name: Jack Roy
Born: 1921
Hometown: Babylon, Long Island, New York

The man we've come to know as Rodney Dangerfield started out in comedy at age 19 as Jack Roy, working the small-club circuit for nine years before retiring to a more stable life of marriage and business. Twelve

Rodney Dangerfield

years later, he tried comedy again, working small clubs on weekends for four years while maintaining an office job during the week. At age 44, he started all over again full-time, this time working on TV shows, including "The Ed Sullivan Show." At 45 he opened his own club in New York City, Dangerfields, where he could do his own act without touring, as well as book other top comedians. He has starred in two films, *Caddyshack* and *Easy Money.* For "Rappin' Rodney," Dangerfield delivered his trademark one-liners to the beat of dance music.

December   1983   RAPPIN' RODNEY   RCA

SARAH DASH

Born: August 18, 1943
Hometown: Trenton, New Jersey

Born the seventh child in a family of 13, Sarah Dash began singing in a Pentecostal church where her father was a minister. She enjoyed singing so much that she and her friends formed a group called the Del Capris, which later merged with the Ordettes to become the Bluebelles— consisting of Patti LaBelle, Nona Hendryx, Sarah Dash, and Cindy Birdsong

Sarah Dash

(who went on to join the Supremes). Sarah sang lead on the Bluebelles' biggest hit, "I Sold My Heart To The Junkman." Sarah sang with Patti and Nona for 16 years, first with the Bluebelles and later as one-third of LaBelle, whose biggest hit was "Lady Marmalade."

While Sarah's mother, a nurse, had approved of her daughter's interest in music ever since Sarah was in high school, her father disapproved of secular singing and never saw Sarah perform until LaBelle became the first group to headline New York's prestigious Metropolitan Opera House. Sarah took full advantage of her four-and-a-half-octave voice when, after LaBelle's break-up, she embarked on a solo career in 1979.

February   1979   SINNER MAN   Kirshner

F. R. DAVID

Born: January 1, 1954
Hometown: Paris, France

F. R. David was born in Tunisia but moved to Paris with his parents when he was 10 years old. Five years later, he began singing and learned to play both bass and guitar. He recorded a few singles in the early seventies, but his first real success was as a producer on "Superman Superman," which was a hit in France in 1972. Later, he played rhythm guitar and percussion in Vangelis' band, performing at the Paris Olympia and London's Queen Elizabeth Hall. David also played in a French/Moroccan rock band called Les Variations and a band called Café De Paris. "Words," however, became an international hit for him as a solo artist.

July   1983   WORDS   Carrere

JOHN DAVIS

John Davis was a serious jazz musician while attending the Philadelphia Academy of Music with Stanley Clarke and other contemporary figures. He had studied clarinet and saxophone as a child and even played in the naval academy band while in the armed forces. After getting his degree, however, Davis began arranging and producing r&b numbers for several local acts. Before long, a record label asked him to orchestrate disco instrumentals. That's how John Davis and the Monster Orchestra was born. Since then, John Davis has written, produced and arranged music for Grace Jones, Diana Ross, Ashford & Simpson, John Travolta, Joey Travolta, Arthur Prysock, Charo, the Silver Convention, Lou Rawls, MFSB, the O'Jays, the Stylistics, Johnny Mathis, Billy Paul, the Three Degrees, Harold Melvin & the Blue Notes, Carol Douglas, the Intruders, and Arthur Fiedler & the Boston Pops Symphony Orchestra.

December   1978   AIN'T THAT ENOUGH FOR YOU   Sam

ARLAN DAY

Hometown: Manchester, England

Arlan Day showed an early inclination for music, especially jazz, which his father played all the time on the radio. When Arlan was 11, his parents bought him a piano and paid for a few lessons. Then his father handed him a book of Fats Waller improvisations, and Arlan mastered them all in a matter of weeks. At seventeen, Day entered the prestigious Royal Northern College of Music, but promptly bolted because the school's dedication to classical music precluded jazz. He then played in jazz combos which toured other parts of the world, and began writing songs. Sometime later, Day wound up as musical director for fellow Britisher and ex-Monkee Davy Jones, touring America and England. In 1981, Day got his own record contract and embarked on a solo career.

October   1981   I SURRENDER   Pasha

CORY DAYE

Born: April 25, 1952
Hometown: Bronx, New York

Cory Daye was lead vocalist of Dr. Buzzard's Original Savannah Band. She had a solo hit in 1979 and is currently the lead singer of the new Dr. Buzzard's Savannah Band.
See DR. BUZZARD'S ORIGINAL SAVANNAH BAND, Rock On: The Years of Change.

October   1979   POW WOW   New York Int'l

DAYTON

Members:
      Shawn Sandridge—guitar, vocals, clarinet, talk box, synthesizer
      Chris Jones—vocals, percussion, clarinet
      Kevin Hurt—drums, percussion, vocals
      Craig E. Robinson—guitar, percussion, vocals (left group in 1983)
      Jennifer Matthews—vocals (left group in 1983)
      Rachel Beavers—vocals
      Justin Gresham—vocals (left group in 1983)
      Michael Dunlap—bass, vocals (left group in 1983)
      Evan Rogers—vocals (left group in 1983)
      Rahni Harris—vocals, keyboards, synthesizers—added in 1983
      Karen Harris Chappell—vocals
Hometown: Dayton, Ohio

After earning his bachelor's degree in music and science from Central State University, Shawn Sandridge taught school until teaming up with former Ohio Players lead guitarist, Junie Morrison. Following that stint, he joined Sun, and stayed for three years. With Chris Jones, Sandridge broke away from Sun and formed Magnum, later renamed Dayton. Dayton's history is marked by many personnel changes, particularly in 1983.

| July | 1982 | HOT FUN IN THE SUMMERTIME | Liberty |

DAZZ BAND

Members:
Bobby Harris—saxophone, vocals
Eric Fearman—guitar
Steve Cox—keyboards
Pierre DeMudd—trumpet, flugelhorn, vocals
Sennie "Skip" Martin III—trumpet, vocals
Michael Wiley—bass
Isaac Wiley, Jr.—drums
Kenny Pettus—percussion, vocals
Keith Harrison—vocals, keyboards—added in 1983
Hometown: Cleveland, Ohio

Years ago, Bobby Harris, leader of Dazz Band, was a member of a four-piece jazz combo called Bell Telephunk. When he wasn't playing with that combo, he was jamming with the band that played at the Kinsman Grill. Gradually the two bands merged to become Kinsman Dazz (*Dazz* for "danceable jazz") and released two albums. Three more musicians were added and the group's name changed to Dazz Band. In 1982, Dazz Band won a Grammy Award for "Let It Whip," which was cowritten by Harris and Leon Ndugu Chancler, now of the Crusaders.

April	1982	LET IT WHIP	Motown
February	1984	JOYSTICK	Motown
December	1984	LET IT ALL BLOW	Motown

DeBARGE

Members:
Eldra DeBarge—vocals, keyboards—born: June 4, 1961
Bunny DeBarge—vocals—born: March 10, 1955
Randy DeBarge—vocals, bass—born: August 6, 1958
Mark DeBarge—vocals, trumpet, saxophone—born: June 19, 1959
James DeBarge—vocals, keyboards—born: August 22, 1963—added in 1982
Hometown: Grand Rapids, Michigan

The members of DeBarge are only five of the ten DeBarge children, all of whom grew up harmonizing in their uncle's Pentecostal church choir, as well as on secular songs at home. Brothers Bobby and Tommy became members of a group called Switch, but promised not to forget their

DeBarge. *Left to right:* Mark, James, Eldra, Bunny, Randy.

siblings back home—and they didn't. They arranged an audition for the group that came to be known as DeBarge, and that audition led to a Motown Records contract. All of the members of the group write, but Eldra does most of the lead vocals. He has also become producer of the group's recordings, with assistance from Bobby DeBarge, who is not a member of the vocal group.

February	1983	1. I LIKE IT	Gordy
April	1983	2. ALL THIS LOVE	Gordy
October	1983	3. TIME WILL REVEAL	Gordy
March	1984	4. LOVE ME IN A SPECIAL WAY	Gordy
February	1985	5. RHYTHM OF THE NIGHT	Gordy

CHRIS De BURGH

Real Name: Christopher John Davidson
Born: October 15, 1950
Hometown: County Wexford, Ireland

Chris De Burgh adopted his surname De Burgh from his mother's family, whose ancesters reportedly date back to William the Conqueror. Chris was born the son of an officer in the British Foreign Service, so his childhood was spent in the exotic locales of his father's career, including Malta, Nigeria, and the Belgian Congo (now Zaire). He attended private school in the United Kingdom and in 1960, his family bought a dilapidated 12th century Norman castle in the south of Ireland, eventually transforming the structure into a resort hotel. Chris learned to play guitar there, often entertaining hotel guests. Once settled in Eire, Chris attended Trinity College in Dublin, the school immortalized in James Joyce's *Portrait of the Artist as a Young Man,* and graduated with degrees in English and French. By 1974, he secured a recording contract and toured the world, sometimes with a band, sometimes with just an acoustic guitar.

April	1983	DON'T PAY THE FERRYMAN	A & M
August	1983	SHIP TO SHORE	A & M
June	1984	HIGH ON EMOTION	A & M

DEELE

Members:
   Darnell "Dee" Bristol—vocals—born: June 29
   Carlos "Satin" Greene—vocals—born: October 31

Chris De Burgh

Stanley "Stick" Burke—guitar, keyboards, vocals—born: July 24
Kenny Edmonds—guitar, keyboards, vocals—born: April 10
Kevin "Kayo" Roberson—bass, vocals—born: September 30
Antonio "L. A." Marquis Reid—drums, percussion, vocals—born: June 7
Hometown: Cincinnati, Ohio

L. A., Kayo, Dee, and Satin have been playing together since high school.
Deele was formed in 1981, playing hometown clubs, colleges, and military
bases. The group's debut album, *Street Beat,* was released in late 1983
and contained the hit "Body Talk."

January   1984   BODY TALK   Solar

DEF LEPPARD

Members:

Joe Elliott—vocals—born: August 1, 1959
Steve "Steamin' " Clark—guitar—added in 1978—born: April 23, 1960
Phil Collen—guitar (replaced Pete Willis in 1982)—born: December 8, 1957
Rick Savage—bass—born: December 2, 1960
Rick Allen—drums—born: November 1, 1963
Hometown: Sheffield, England

Def Leppard. *Left to right:* Rick Savage, Phil Collen, Joe Elliot, Steve Clark, Rick Allen.

Pete Willis and Rick Savage (known to his friends as "Sav") played in youthful bands, and formed Atomic Mass after leaving school. The group was looking to replace its lead singer when Joe Elliott contacted Willis about buying one of his practice amps. Elliott fancied himself a drummer, but Willis and Sav convinced him he looked like a singer, and before long they had him singing a Thin Lizzy and a David Bowie song, as well as two original numbers. One day at college, Willis noticed that a classmate, Steve Clark, was reading a guitar manual. Later on, at a Judas Priest concert, they talked about guitars, and Pete invited Steve to a rehearsal. Steve was impressed, and accepted an invitation to join the band. Rick Allen then joined, and the group came to be known as Deaf Leopard, after a drawing Elliott had done of a feline beast with a hearing horn coming out of its ears. The spelling was later changed to Def Leppard. The group's first official live concert was in July 1978, at a school in Sheffield, where it earned $10. Meanwhile, most of Great Britain was absorbed in punk rock, and Def Leppard's brand of rock was unfashionable. Hard rock made a resurgence, however, and Def Leppard was there, ready to lead the way. Thanks to MTV, the group became more popular in the United States than back home. On New Year's eve, 1984, Rick Allen lost his left arm in a car crash in Sheffield, England.

March	1983	1. PHOTOGRAPH	Mercury
June	1983	2. ROCK OF AGES	Mercury
September	1983	3. FOOLIN'	Mercury
June	1984	4. BRINGIN' ON THE HEARTBREAK	Mercury

DELEGATION

Members:
    Ricky Bailey—vocals
    Bruce Dunbar—vocals
    Ray Patterson—vocals, guitar
Hometown: Birmingham, England

Ricky Bailey and Ray Patterson were born in Jamaica and came to Birmingham, England, with their families while still children. They went to school together in Birmingham, and played together in various bands for over a decade. Bruce Dunbar, originally from Texas, was in London appearing in a play, *The Little Willy Junior Resurrection Show*, when he answered the ad Ricky and Ray had placed in a local paper hoping to find a third vocalist. Dunbar was the very first to audition, and he impressed Bailey and Patterson so much that no further applicants were seen.

Delegation first appeared on the British pop scene in the summer of 1976. They released a few singles in the next year and a half, but "Oh, Honey," in 1979, was the vocal trio's only international hit.

| February | 1979 | OH, HONEY | Shadybrook |

TERI DESARIO

Hometown: Miami, Florida

Teri DeSario was first inspired to study music at age 10, when she heard the *West Side Story* soundtrack. After her high school years, DeSario performed in a Renaissance music group and then became a folk singer before joining the jazz group Abacus. She was discovered singing in a Miami club by producer Albhy Galuten, who recorded a demo tape with her and passed it on to his associate, Barry Gibb of the Bee Gees. Gibb liked what he heard and wrote her a hit, "Ain't Nothing Gonna Keep Me From You," which appeared on her debut LP. She later joined forces with K. C. of K. C. & the Sunshine Band.

July	1978	AIN'T NOTHIN' GONNA' KEEP ME FROM YOU	Casablanca
November	1979	YES, I'M READY (with K. C.)	Casablanca
June	1980	DANCIN' IN THE STREETS (with K. C.)	Casablanca

DEVO

Members:
   Mark Mothersbaugh—vocals, keyboards, guitar
   Jerry Casale—vocals, bass
   Bob Casale—guitar
   Bob Mothersbaugh—guitar
   Alan Myers—drums
Hometown: Akron, Ohio

According to the Devo tale, Jerry Casale met Mark Mothersbaugh in the art department at Kent State University. Jerry was reportedly into sporting ski masks and butcher aprons while playing his repertoire of one-chord original songs. Mark designed decals, wrote bizarre songs, and played electronic keyboards. When Jerry saw one of Mark's more obtuse decals, he tracked him down; they soon realized they were both devo. With Mark on keyboards, Jerry on bass, and both on vocals, they bullied their younger brothers, Bob and Bob, into playing guitars in the band. Alan Myers was recruited to play drums, and in a short time the group Devo (short for "de-evolution") moved to California. Little else is known about the band.

On the surface, Devo appears to be a band with a gimmick. Devo *is* that, but there is more. Although all the amazing rhetoric provided by the group is part of a master plan for creating a unique group identity, Devo does make sincere statements about the "de-evolution" of a world gone crazy. On the albums, on stage, and in the early trend-setting short movies (not videos), Devo is shown in odd uniforms playing quirky songs;

the group comments on the regressive nature of the human race, yet because of their colorful display, their statements on today's society become a form of black comedy.

August	1980	WHIP IT	Warner Bros.
September	1981	WORKING IN THE COAL MINE	Elektra
May	1983	THEME FROM DOCTOR DETROIT	Backstreet

Dennis De Young

DENNIS De YOUNG

Born: February 18, 1947
Hometown: Chicago, Illinois

In 1970, Dennis, along with Jim Young, John Curulewski, and Chuck and John Panozzo formed the group Styx. Two years later they had their first national hit, "Best Thing," and would go on to have fifteen more national hits including the number-one song, "Babe," in late 1979. In 1984, Dennis decided to try a solo project, and had a hit with "Desert Moon." See STYX, *Rock On: The Years of Change.*

September	1984	DESERT MOON	A & M
December	1984	DON'T WAIT FOR HEROES	A & M

JOEL DIAMOND

Joel Diamond is a record producer who has worked on a number of unrelated projects. By the time he made his first recording, a 1979 disco album, he had already produced records by Engelbert Humperdinck, Gloria Gaynor, Sister Sledge, Tommy James, Van McCoy, and Blood, Sweat & Tears' David Clayton-Thomas. Diamond is also credited with discovering Dr. Hook and the Addrisi Brothers. Later, he provided the theme music for the films *Raging Bull* and *Continental Divide.* In 1982, when medleys of classical composers' works were very popular, he recorded "Super-Strauss," a medley of waltz themes by Johann Strauss, the 19th century Austrian composer, performed by a full orchestra in traditional waltz time.

February   1981   THEME FROM RAGING BULL   Motown

DIESEL

Members:
      Rob Vunderink—guitar, vocals
      Mark Boon—guitar, vocals
      Frank Papendrecht—bass, vocals—replaced (1981) by Wijand Ott
      Pim Koopman—drums, keyboards, vocals
Hometown: The Netherlands

Mark Boon was born in Indonesia of Dutch and British parents, and moved to the Netherlands at the age of four. Years later, he emigrated to California and mastered the guitar in a series of garage bands before returning to his parents in Holland. Shortly after moving back, Boon met Rob Vunderink and they formed a musical relationship. With Pim Koopman, a noted producer in Holland, they formed Diesel, adding Frank Papendrecht to their ranks. The Dutch group's one and only American hit was a song about California.

September   1981   SAUSALITO SUMMERNIGHT   Regency

Dire Straits. *Left to right:* Terry Williams, Alan Clark, Mark Knopfler, Hal Lindes, John Illsley.

DIRE STRAITS

Members:
Mark Knopfler—vocals, guitar—born: August 12, 1949
David Knopfler—guitar (left group in 1980)—replaced by Hal Lindes
John Illsley—bass
Pick Withers—drums—replaced (1982) by Terry Williams
Alan Clark—guitar
Hometown: London, England

Mark Knopfler, a former newspaper journalist and English teacher, gave up his professions in the summer of 1977 when his brother David and David's roommate, John Illsley, formed a band. After Pick Withers joined, the quartet practiced intensely and played a few live dates in order to earn enough to pay for a weekend session in a recording studio. The result was a five-track demo tape, which was sent to a London rock writer/radio announcer, Charlie Gillett, who liked it enough to put the tape on the air. (They called themselves Dire Straits because of their financial situation at the time.) The group's debut single, "Sultans of Swing," established Dire Straits internationally. Mark Knopfler has since worked with Bob Dylan and Steely Dan.

February	1979	SULTANS OF SWING	Warner Bros.
July	1979	LADY WRITER	Warner Bros.
December	1980	SKATEAWAY	Warner Bros.

THOMAS DOLBY

Real Name: Thomas Morgan Dolby Robertson
Born: October 14, 1958
Hometown: Cairo, Egypt

Thomas Dolby spent his first 15 years travelling Europe with his British archeologist father, attending various boarding schools, teaching himself to play piano and guitar, singing in choirs, and running a film club. In the mid-seventies, when he was playing jazz piano in bars and restaurants throughout the United Kingdom, he developed an interest in home recording. From 1977 to 1980, while playing keyboards and engineering concerts with various British punk and new wave bands, he continued to explore home recording, working on other artists' music before recording his own work. In 1982, Dolby did his first concerts, one-man shows, in the United Kingdom. Dolby has appeared on or produced recordings by Foreigner, Joan Armatrading, Whodini, Adele Bertei, and Malcolm McLaren.

February	1983	SHE BLINDED ME WITH SCIENCE	Capitol
June	1983	EUROPA AND THE PIRATE TWINS	Capitol
February	1984	HYPERACTIVE	Capitol

JOE DOLCE

Born: 1947
Hometown: Painesville, Ohio

Joe Dolce was raised in a large Italian-American family that held traditional family gatherings and served meatballs and pasta on Sunday afternoons. Out of this experience and work in theater restaurants in Australia, Dolce concocted the Joe Dolce Music Theatre, consisting of the character Giuseppi, master of ceremonies, manager of several acts, and a singer in his own right. Dolce's Giuseppi had an international novelty hit, "Shaddap You Face," in 1981.

May	1981	SHADDAP YOU FACE	MCA

CHARLIE DORE

Hometown: London, England

Charlie Dore says her first band, Prairie Oyster, had almost as many members as gigs, going through seven drummers and about three of everything else (among the drummers who passed through was Pick Withers, who later joined Dire Straits). Even worse was the group's timing—Prairie Oyster was a country-rock group in late 1977, the height of Great Britain's punk rock upheaval. As Charlie's original tunes began to take shape, however, the band began getting steady club dates in London. By the time she was ready to record, Charlie was a solo act. Ultimately, her records were better received in the United States than in the United Kingdom.

February	1980	PILOT OF THE AIRWAVES	Island

DOUCETTE

Real Name: Jerry Doucette
Hometown: Montreal, Canada

Jerry Doucette's initiation into rock 'n' roll came at a party, when a band called the Reefers asked him to sit in on lead guitar for some Beatles' songs. Doucette was only 11 and didn't know what the name of the band meant, but he'd been playing guitar for five years, waiting for a moment like this. He stayed with the band for five years, hitting the club circuit at age 16. In 1972, an offer to play an album session took him to Vancouver. The sessions were never completed, but he stayed in British Columbia and joined the Seeds of Time, then the Rocket Norton Band. Afterwards Doucette went the solo route, forming a flexible band under the name Doucette. Jerry Doucette is married and has a son and three daughters.

April	1978	MAMA LET HIM PLAY	Mushroom

"D" TRAIN

Members:
    James Williams—vocals
    Hubert Eaves III—keyboards
Hometown: Brooklyn, New York

James Williams was nicknamed "D" Train at New York's Erasmus Hall High School, where he was starting defensive tackle on the 1979 division and city championship football team. Erasmus was also where Williams met Hubert Eaves, III. Together, they sorted out many musical ideas. One day, this duo wound up at Brooklyn's Sound Lab Studio, helping a mutual friend record a demo tape. Williams, who started singing in a church choir at the age of three and was an outstanding member of Erasmus's choral club, provided the vocals on his friend's project, while Eaves hit the bass and drums. Before long, Williams and Eaves became a recording and performing team.

January   1984   SOMETHING'S ON YOUR MIND   Prelude

GEORGE DUKE

Born: January 12, 1946
Hometown: San Rafael, California

George Duke traces his interest in jazz to the day his mother took him to a Duke Ellington concert. For weeks afterwards, George, only four years

George Duke

old, ran around the house telling his mom, "Get me a piano!" By age seven and a half George was taking lessons, and by high school he had worked with a rock band, a Latin group, and a jazz combo. At 16, he led his own trio at a club in San Francisco. After playing a variety of music with a number of local bands, Duke hooked up with noted jazz-rock fusion violinist Jean-Luc Ponty; Duke played on Ponty's album, and then toured rock clubs as his opening act. Duke has played in Frank Zappa's and Cannonball Adderly's bands, and has done team projects with both Billy Cobham and Stanley Clarke; Duke has also produced albums for A Taste Of Honey, Rufus, and Jeffrey Osborne.

January	1978	REACH FOR IT	Epic
May	1981	SWEET BABY (with Stanley Clarke)	Epic
February	1982	SHINE ON	Epic

DUKE JUPITER

Members:
    Marshall James Styller—keyboards, vocals
    Greg Walker—guitar, vocals
    David Corcoran—drums, percussion, vocals (replaced Earl Jetty in 1982)
    George Barajas—bass, vocals—replaced (1982) by Rick Ellis
Hometown: Rochester, New York

Duke Jupiter rose from the ashes of a local Rochester group called Joshua. The group has gone through several personnel changes and has recorded for several different record companies, but despite the ups and downs, Duke Jupiter plays about 250 dates per year. The band took its name from a sax player who hung out at a rehearsal but who never played with the band.

    Earl Jetty died as a result of delayed stress syndrome with possible Agent Orange complications incurred while serving in Viet Nam. George Barajas died after a long illness.

| March | 1982 | I'LL DRINK TO YOU | Coast to Coast |
| May | 1984 | LITTLE LADY | Motown |

ROBBIE DUPREE

Born: 1947
Hometown: Brooklyn, New York

As a youth, Robbie Dupree's big ambition was to be the best-dressed guy in Brooklyn. In the late fifties and early sixties, he sang a capella with neighborhood friends, later singing and playing guitar in a band that included Nile Rodgers, later of Chic. Now he says he doesn't care if he's the worst-dressed guy in Woodstock, where he moved and settled down during that upstate county's era in pop music. One thing led to another, and soon Robbie had a hit single, "Steal Away," which is reminiscent in its arrangement of the Doobie Brothers' "What A Fool Believes," and which earned him a Grammy nomination. Recently, Dupree converted his garage into a gym—he is a long-time boxing fan and admits to having a "fight jones" that predates his interest in music.

April	1980	STEAL AWAY	Elektra
July	1980	HOT ROD HEARTS	Elektra
May	1981	BROOKLYN GIRLS	Elektra

DURAN DURAN

Members:
    Simon Le Bon—vocals—born: October 27, 1958 (replaced Steve Duffy, Andy Wickett and Jeff Thomas in 1980)
    Andy Taylor—guitar—born: February 16, 1961 (replaced John Curtis in 1980)
    Nick Rhodes—keyboards—born: June 8, 1962
    John Taylor—bass—born: June 20, 1960
    Roger Taylor—drums—born: April 26, 1960
Hometown: Birmingham, England

Duran Duran. *Left to right:* Andy Taylor, Simon Le Bon, Nick Rhodes, John Taylor, Roger Taylor.

One day five young musicians walked into the Rum Runner nightclub in Birmingham, England, looking for work. Later that evening, they walked out with a management deal, their own independent record company, and the kind of support few bands get from club owners.

Duran Duran is named after a character in the film *Barbarella* and was formed in the spring of 1978 when Nick Rhodes, John Taylor, and since-departed clarinetist Simon Colley banded together with a rhythm box to play what John later described as "very much avant-garde English music." They met Roger Taylor (no relation) at a party, and decided he would be a suitable replacement for the machine. Soon, Colley left, and Andy Taylor (again, no relation), who responded to an ad for a "live wire guitarist," was asked to join. Simon Le Bon replaced a series of vocalists who didn't work out.

The Duran Duran we know today played its first gig at the Edinburgh Festival in Great Britain in July 1980, after which Le Bon quit school to pursue music full-time. Before long, the group was playing to screaming teenyboppers around the world. The United States was the last frontier, but when MTV began showing the band's colorful videos, American teenagers fell for the handsome British pop stars. The North Carolina State "Wolfpack" basketball team adopted "Hungry Like the Wolf" as its theme song.

In 1984 John and Andy Taylor, along with vocalist Robert Palmer and Chic's drummer Tony Thompson, recorded an album called *The Power Station* while on vacation from Duran Duran.

December	1982	1. HUNGRY LIKE THE WOLF	Harvest
April	1983	2. RIO	Capitol
June	1983	3. IS THERE SOMETHING I SHOULD KNOW	Capitol
November	1983	4. UNION OF THE SNAKE	Capitol
January	1984	5. NEW MOON ON MONDAY	Capitol
April	1984	★ 6. THE REFLEX	Capitol
November	1984	7. THE WILD BOYS	Capitol
February	1985	8. SAVE A PRAYER	Capitol

DYNASTY

Members:
Nidra Beard—vocals—born: August 12
Linda Carriere—vocals—born: August 4
Kevin Spencer—keyboards, vocals—born: June 30
Leon Sylvers III—bass, vocals—born: March 7, 1953—added in 1981
William Shelby—keyboards—born: September 30—added in 1981
Hometown: Los Angeles, California

Linda Carriere and Nidra Beard, a professional model, met at Maverick's Flat, a popular soul/pop nightclub in Los Angeles where the club owner was putting together a group called DeBlanc. For two years, DeBlanc toured Europe, Japan, Canada, and the United States, but broke up in 1975. Some of DeBlanc's original members, including Nidra and Linda, formed a new group called Starfire, which also toured the world for a year before disbanding.

While Linda was starring in a musical play, Nidra was filling in on live dates for the female members of the Sylvers who were minors. About the same time, Kevin Spencer auditioned as bass player for the Sylvers and got the job. Nidra developed a strong relationship with Leon Sylvers of the group. When Leon formed Dynasty in 1979, it was a vocal trio consisting of Nidra, Linda, and Kevin, and he was the producer. By 1981, he joined the group as a bass player and vocalist and brought along songwriter William Shelby.

September   1980   I'VE JUST BEGUN TO LOVE YOU   Solar

SHEENA EASTON

Born: April 27, 1959
Hometown: Belshill, Lanarkshire, Scotland

Sheena Easton was just finishing college and singing part-time in Glasgow clubs when she auditioned for an English BBC-TV show called *The Big Time*. The show's producers were looking for a young and talented hopeful to groom for a chance at stardom, and Sheena beat out over 200 other candidates. Week after week, viewers watched Sheena's progress; fortunately, she saved embarrassment by eventually landing a recording contract. She then had a series of hits in the United Kingdom. Sheena's pop tunes became international hits, and in short time she was singing before Her Majesty Queen Elizabeth and the Queen Mother at the Royal Variety Show. Not bad for a working class woman who started out as a drama student and speech therapist.

Sheena is a Grammy Award winner, and has been awarded gold records. She appeared in the opening sequence of a James Bond film singing "For Your Eyes Only." With Kenny Rogers she recorded Bob Seger's "We've Got Tonight," and Rogers was one of Sheena's guests

Sheena Easton

Dennis Edwards

when she hosted her first variety special for NBC-TV. In 1983, Home Box Office broadcast an hour-long concert special, and she also appeared on Bob Hope's 80th birthday NBC-TV special, on which she dueted with Kermit the Frog.

February	1981	★	1. MORNING TRAIN	EMI-America
May	1981		2. MODERN GIRL	EMI-America
July	1981		3. FOR YOUR EYES ONLY	Liberty
November	1981		4. YOU COULD HAVE BEEN WITH ME	EMI-America
April	1982		5. WHEN HE SHINES	EMI-America
September	1982		6. MACHINERY	EMI-America
October	1982		7. I WOULDN'T BEG FOR WATER	EMI-America
August	1983		8. TELEFONE (LONG DISTANCE LOVE AFFAIR)	EMI-America
December	1983		9. ALMOST OVER YOU	EMI-America
April	1984		10. DEVIL IN A FAST CAR	EMI-America
August	1984		11. STRUT	EMI-America
December	1984		12. SUGAR WALLS	EMI-America
March	1985		13. SWEAR	EMI-America

DENNIS EDWARDS

Born: February 3, 1943
Hometown: Birmingham, Alabama

Onetime member of the Temptations, Dennis Edwards went solo and had a hit in 1984.
See *THE TEMPTATIONS, Rock On: The Years of Change.*

May	1984	DON'T LOOK ANY FURTHER	Motown

WALTER EGAN

Born: July 12, 1948
Hometown: New York, New York

Elvis Presley's first appearance on "The Ed Sullivan Show" transformed eight-year-old Walter Egan into a rock 'n' roll fanatic. After years of watching every American Bandstand and listening to a transistor radio held to his ear, Egan joined his first group, The Malibooz, and tried to storm New York's Brill Building, where all the top rock 'n' roll songwriters worked. That plan didn't work, and Egan continued working with bands, moving around the country, until he signed a recording contract as a solo artist in 1976. His first two albums were produced by Lindsey Buckingham and Stevie Nicks of Fleetwood Mac.

June	1977	1. ONLY THE LUCKY	Columbia
May	1978	2. MAGNET AND STEEL	Columbia
October	1978	3. HOT SUMMER NIGHTS	Columbia
April	1983	4. FULL MOON FIRE	Backstreet

LARRY ELGART & HIS MANHATTAN SWING ORCHESTRA

Born: March 20, 1922
Hometown: New London, Connecticut

The "Elgart touch" reemerged on the charts thirty years after Larry formed an orchestra with his brother, Les.

Walter Egan

Larry Elgart

"Hooked on Swing" was the first song of its kind to have a full-length video which was played in clubs and on television.

| June | 1982 | HOOKED ON SWING | RCA |

JOE "BEAN" ESPOSITO

Hometown: Brooklyn, New York

A member of the group Brooklyn Dreams, Joe "Bean" Esposito had a lone chart entry in 1983 with a pretty ballad called "Lady, Lady, Lady," from the movie *Flashdance*.
See *BROOKLYN DREAMS*.

| October | 1983 | LADY, LADY, LADY | Casablanca |

EUCLID BEACH BAND

Members:
Richard Reising—vocals
Peter Hewlett—vocals
Hometown: Cleveland, Ohio

Although Richard Reising and Pete Hewlett both played in local Cleveland bands, including bands led by former members of the Raspberries, the two did not actually become friends until they ran into each other in England, where each was playing in recording sessions. In January 1978, Reising was working on a novelty song, "There's No Surf In Cleveland," and he called on Hewlett to sing the choruses. The song was released under the name the Euclid Beach Band. Taken from a defunct amusement park in Cleveland, the name was also meant to evoke the surf sound of the Beach Boys-inspired song. "There's No Surf In Cleveland" was a local hit and led to an album, which was produced by Raspberries founder Eric Carmen, and which had as one cut their 1979 hit, "I Need You."

March	1979	I NEED YOU	Cleveland International

EURYTHMICS

Members:
    Annie Lennox—vocals—born: December 25, 1954—Aberdeen, Scotland
    David Stewart—guitar—born: September 9, 1952—Sunderland, England

David Stewart first met Annie Lennox in 1977 when she was a waitress. He immediately persuaded her to quit her job and go full-time into music. They formed the Tourists with Pete Coombes and had a minor hit with a remake of a Dusty Springfield number, "I Only Want To Be With You." That band broke up in 1980. Lennox and Stewart planned to continue, but since they wanted to be free of the traditional rock format, they became a synthesizer-based duo. They figured they'd deliver a Euro-sound that was rhythmic, so they called themselves the Eurythmics.

The Eurythmics' androgynous look caught the public's eye. At one point Lennox was even mistaken for a male transvestite. The singer then went a step further, and on the 1984 Grammy Award telecast she performed wearing a suit, a dark Elvis-Presley-style wig, and fake sideburns.

May	1983	★ 1. SWEET DREAMS	RCA
September	1983	2. LOVE IS A STRANGER	RCA

Eurythmics. Annie Lennox and David Stewart.

Exile. *Left to right:* Sonny Lemaire, Marlon Hargis, J. P. Pennington, Steve Goetzman, Les Taylor.

January	1984	3. HERE COMES THE RAIN AGAIN	RCA
May	1984	4. WHO'S THAT GIRL	RCA
July	1984	5. RIGHT BY YOUR SIDE	RCA
November	1984	6. SEX CRIME (NINETEEN EIGHTY-FOUR)	RCA
May	1985	7. WOULD I LIE TO YOU?	RCA

EXILE

Members:
    Jimmy Stokley—vocals (left group in 1980)
    J. P. Pennington—guitar, vocals
    Buzz Cornelison—keyboards, vocals (left group in 1981)
    Marlon Hargis—keyboards, vocals—added in 1974
    Sonny Lemaire—bass, vocals
    Steven Goetzman—drums
    Les Taylor—guitar, vocals—added in 1980
    Mark Gray—keyboards, vocals—added in 1980 (left group in 1983)
Hometown: Berea, Kentucky

In 1965, a group of Kentucky boys calling themselves the Exiles were a local band in the strictest sense—they'd never even played Lexington, a mere 30 miles from home. One night, an agent for Dick Clark Productions heard them in a college pub, and got them a gig backing Bryan Hyland,

Tommy Roe, and others on four Dick Clark Caravan of Stars tours. Afterwards, the group returned to the Kentucky club circuit with professional experience and a good deal of advice from Dick Clark himself. While by the mid-seventies the renamed Exile was recording original tunes, its debut single, "Church St. Soul Rivival," was written and produced by Tommy James.

Controversy arrived in 1978 when a disc jockey refused to play Exile's first big hit, "Kiss You All Over," because of its overtly sexual theme. Elsewhere, a disc jockey at WBBM-FM determined that it takes the average person one hour and 48 minutes to "kiss you all over." Later, Exile toured South Africa successfully—a mixed blessing perhaps, in light of many Americans' feelings about that country's apartheid policies. The band has since changed its direction towards country music.

March	1977	1. TRY IT ON	Atco
July	1978	★ 2. KISS YOU ALL OVER	Warner/Curb
November	1978	3. YOU THRILL ME	Warner/Curb
April	1979	4. HOW COULD THIS GO WRONG	Warner/Curb

EYE TO EYE

Members:
    Deborah Berg—vocals
    Julian Marshall—keyboards
Hometown: London, England

Julian Marshall had a hit, "Dancing In The City," in early 1978, when he and a female singer named Kit Hain were in a group called Marshall Hain. Marshall Hain broke up later that year, and Julian headed back into the recording studio to record his own album, which has never been released.

One night, when Julian and his wife were visiting friends in San Diego, California, they went to see a performance by a dance troupe called Mostly Women Moving. As fate would have it, one of the dancers was Deborah Berg, who was born in Seattle, Washington, and raised in Lincoln, Nebraska, before relocating to San Francisco to pursue a career in dancing. That night, as the tour brought the Bay area troupe to San Diego, Berg sang improvisationally for half the show, attempting to create imagery for the dance. Julian was knocked out by what he heard. The two met backstage after the performance and exchanged addresses. Two months later, in January of 1980, Julian called Deborah from London, and offered to pay her way there to start working on Eye to Eye. With assistance from other musicians, the duo recorded the first Eye to Eye album in 1981.

| May | 1982 | NICE GIRLS | Warner Bros. |
| October | 1983 | LUCKY | Warner Bros. |

FABULOUS POODLES

Members:

Tony de Meur—vocals, guitar, harmonica—born: February 2, 1948

Richie C. Robertson—bass, vocals, guitar, keyboards, percussion—born: April 29, 1957

Bobby Valentino—violin, mandolin, vocals—born: June 22, 1954

Bryn B. Burrows—drums, percussion, vocals—born: June 30, 1954

Hometown: England

The name Fabulous Poodles was inspired by Frank Zappa, and like Zappa, the band members are rockers first, jokers second. Tony de Meur and Bobby Valentino started as a duo, before adding Richie C. Robertson and Bryn B. Burrows in 1974. Almost immediately, most of the quartet's original songs smacked of humor and satire. In concert, the group further enthused audiences by offering to play the very first record anyone in the audience ever bought. The British debut album, not released in America, was produced by John Entwistle of the Who.

| April | 1979 | MIRROR STAR | | Epic |

FACE TO FACE

Members:

Angelo Kimball—guitar—born: May 5, 1954

Stuart Kimball—guitar—born: December 1, 1956

John Ryder—bass—born: June 22, 1957

William Beard—drummer—born: June 18, 1954

Laurie Sargent—vocals—born: March 22, 1960

Hometown: Boston, Massachusetts

In 1981, five Boston college students met. Within three months they formed the group Face To Face, and made the semi-finals in Boston radio station WBCN's "Rock 'N' Roll Rumble" contest. In February 1982, Epic Records spotted Face To Face live, and signed the group. Face To Face appears in the film *Streets Of Fire*. It seems that Jimmy Iovine, producer of the group's debut record, was involved in the film and the group landed parts.

| June | 1984 | 10-9-8 | | Epic |

Face to Face. *Left to right:* (*top*) William Beard, Angelo, Stuart Kimball; (*bottom*) Laurie Sargent, John Ryder.

DONALD FAGEN

Born: January 10, 1948
Hometown: Passaic, New Jersey

Donald Fagen grew up in several parts of New Jersey before attending Bard College from 1965 to 1969 and graduating with a degree in English literature. There, he began collaborating with Walter Becker on the songs that would later become the basis of Steely Dan. While Steely Dan made many successful records, by the early eighties the two principals began pursuing separate projects. Fagen's first was a solo album, *The Nightfly.*

| October | 1982 | I.G.Y. (WHAT A BEAUTIFUL WORLD) | Warner Bros. |
| January | 1983 | NEW FRONTIER | Warner Bros. |

AGNETHA FALTSKOG

Born: April 5, 1950
Hometown: Jankoping, Sweden

As one fourth of ABBA, Agnetha Faltskog was an integral force behind one of the world's greatest pop institutions. Her high vocal range helped give the Swedish pop group hits around the world for 10 years. (See *ABBA, Rock On: The Years of Change.*)

Agnetha first started playing piano and writing melodies as a child and continued composing throughout her youth. After completing school, she had a brief job as a telephone operator, but she soon began singing with a dance band and recording. Her first hit was a self-penned song she recorded at age 18, "Jar Var Sa Kor" ("I Was So Much In Love"), which made it into Sweden's top 10. In 1971 she married Bjorn Ulvareus, and with Benny Andersson and Anni-Frid Lyngstad, they became ABBA. In 1982, Faltskog played a part in the movie *Raskenstam*, and a year later released her first English-language solo album, *Wrap Your Arms Around Me*. She has two children, Linda and Christian.

August   1983   CAN'T SHAKE LOOSE   Polydor

FARRAGHER BROS.

Members:
    Davey Farragher—bass, vocals
    Jimmy Farragher—guitar, vocals

Donald Fagen

Danny Farragher—keyboards, vocals
Tommy Farragher—keyboards, vocals
Marty Farragher—drums—added in 1978
Pammy Farragher—vocals—added in 1978
Hometown: California

Mrs. Farragher, a church choir singer, taught her boys early on how to sing and harmonize around the piano. A move toward entertainment began when Danny formed a band in grade school. When that band needed a bassist, Jimmy was added. Some initial recordings got early airplay, but in 1968, the group contracted to Dot Records and were named the Peppermint Trolley Company. They recorded a minor hit called "Baby You Come Rolling Across My Mind" and appeared once on a popular TV sitcom, *The Beverly Hillbillies*, before disbanding. Three years later Danny and Jimmy were again playing together, and before long were joined by Davey and Tommy for some sessions backing both Melissa Manchester and Kiss's drummer, Peter Criss. They started recording their own music as the Farragher Bros., later becoming simply the Farraghers.

February   1979   STAY THE NIGHT   Polydor

DON FELDER

Born: September 21, 1947
Hometown: Gainesville, Florida

Don Felder got his first guitar as an 11-year-old boy in Gainesville, a town with a small and tight music scene. (He says that he got the instrument in exchange for a "handful of cherry bombs," and that because it was in bad condition he "conned another kid out of his guitar.") Several years later Californian Bennie Leadon, who would later join the Eagles and who was a member of the Continentals (where he had replaced Stephen Stills, who in turn would join Buffalo Springfield and then Crosby, Stills & Nash), came to Florida with some hot bluegrass licks. However, Leadon had never played the electric guitar, so he and Felder traded lessons. Meanwhile, Felder also taught guitar to a youngster named Tom Petty, and helped with arrangements for Petty's band Mudcrutch. Felder later toured with David Blue and then with Graham Nash (of Crosby, Stills & Nash), but his biggest gig was when he joined the Eagles. His first work after the demise of the Eagles was two tracks for the film *Heavy Metal*. This was followed by "Never Surrender" for the film *Fast Times at Ridgemont High*, and a solo album, *Airborne*.

July   1981   HEAVY METAL   Full Moon/Asylum

SUZANNE FELLINI

Hometown: New York, New York

Suzanne brought loads of energy to her 1980 hit, "Love on the Phone," which she cowrote with keyboardist Jeff Waxman, Waxman, along with Sid McGinnis on guitar and Barry Lazarowitz on drums, made up her band.

March	1980	LOVE ON THE PHONE	Casablanca

FELONY

Members:
  Jeffrey Scott Spry—vocals
  Curly Joe Spry—guitars, vocals
  Danny Sands—keyboards
  Louis Ruiz—bass
  Arty Blea—drums
Hometown: Los Angeles, California

Brothers Jeffrey and Joe Spry founded Felony in the late seventies, and with a batch of original songs, established the group as a popular attraction on the Los Angeles club circuit. In April 1982, inspired by the new wave's do-it-yourself ethos, Felony recorded and produced its own single, "The Fanatic" b/w "Positively Negative." Both songs became hits on two Los Angeles radio stations, leading to a recording contract with a major record firm. After this contract was signed, "The Fanatic" went onto the national charts. Felony's debut album was released in January, 1983.

February	1983	THE FANATIC	Rock'N'Roll

JAY FERGUSON

Born: May 10, 1943
Hometown: San Fernando Valley, California

Jay Ferguson has been playing music since his high school days. While attending college at UCLA, Ferguson, together with Mark Andes, John Locke, Randy California, and Ed Cassidy, formed Spirit. Feeling that Spirit had become too progressive, Ferguson and Andes left the group and formed Jo Jo Gunne. In 1975, after a series of personnel changes and management shifts, Jo Jo Gunne disbanded. As a solo act, Jay Ferguson had his first hit single in 1977 with "Thunder Island."
See *SPIRIT* and *JO JO GUNNE, Rock On: The years of Change.*

December	1977	THUNDER ISLAND	Asylum
May	1979	SHAKEDOWN CRUISE	Asylum

MAYNARD FERGUSON

Born: May 4, 1928
Hometown: Verdun, Quebec

Maynard Ferguson has played jazz for decades, but in the late seventies, after moving to England, India, back to England, and finally back to North America, his music took a new turn, and Ferguson recorded disco tracks and TV and movie soundtracks in addition to his work in jazz. Each year, Ferguson gives about 30 lectures and performs about 150 concerts at universities and high schools, and in 1982, he took an active stand against federal and state cutbacks in music education. Ferguson also does about 100 other concerts each year, and teaches music clinics.

| April | 1977 | GONNA FLY NOW (THEME FROM *ROCKY*) | Columbia |
| August | 1979 | ROCKY II | Columbia |

RICHARD "DIMPLES" FIELDS

Hometown: San Francisco, California

Although at the time he fancied himself an aspiring young baseball star, Richard Fields accepted his friends' invitation to sing in their high school band. Inspired by the reaction he received, "Dimples" later opened a popular nightclub in the San Francisco Bay area, and as the club's headliner, gained a local following.

| April | 1982 | IF IT AIN'T ONE THING . . . IT'S ANOTHER | Boardwalk |

FIVE SPECIAL

Members:
    Bryan Banks—lead tenor vocals—born: March 22, 1958
    Mike Petillo—bass vocals—born: October 25, 1952
    Steve Harris—second tenor vocals—born: May 25, 1953
    Greg Finley—tenor, baritone vocals—born: April 18, 1952
    Steve Boyd—baritone vocals—born: October 3, 1960
Hometown: Detroit, Michigan

When Bryan Banks was still attending Cass Technical High School, neighbor Mike Petillo dropped by to trade vocal techniques, and the idea of starting a group was born. After rounding up three more vocalists, Bryan's brother, Ron Banks of the Dramatics, nudged them into a record contract. Although initially tagged a disco group, Five Special's five-part harmonies deserve broader characterization.

| July | 1979 | WHY LEAVE US ALONE | Elektra |

The Fixx. *Left to right:* Adam Woods, Cy Curnin, Rupert Greenall *(kneeling)*, Jamie West-Oram.

THE FIXX

Members:
    Cy Curnin—vocals—born: December 12, 1957
    Jamie West-Oram—guitar—born: February 19, 1954
    Adam Woods—drums, percussion—born: April 8, 1952
    Rupert Greenall—keyboards—born: March 30, 1950
    Charlie Barrett—bass (left group in 1983)
Hometown: London, England

The Fixx came together as the final line-up of a group called the Portraits. The band decided to change its name and approach when Jamie West-Oram joined after responding to an advertisement in a British music newspaper. His addition made such a difference to the group members— both musically and personally—that, filled with new enthusiasm, they decided to make a fresh start. Giving up their day jobs in 1979 to concentrate on writing and rehearsing, the Fixx released a single, "Lost Planes," and began to build a steady following on the London circuit.

October	1982	1. STAND OR FALL	MCA
May	1983	2. SAVED BY ZERO	MCA
August	1983	3. ONE THING LEADS TO ANOTHER	MCA
November	1983	4. THE SIGN OF FIRE	MCA
August	1984	5. ARE WE OURSELVES?	MCA
November	1984	6. SUNSHINE IN THE SHADE	MCA

FLASH AND THE PAN

Members:
> Harry Vanda (Harry Wandan)—guitar, vocals—born: March 22, 1947
> George Young—synthesizer, vocals—born: November 6, 1947
> Stevie Wright—vocals—added in 1982
> Les Karski—bass—added in 1980
> Ian Miller—drums—added in 1982

Hometown: Australia

Harry Vanda of Holland and George Young of Scotland had their first hits as members of the Australian-originated/British-based Easybeats in the 1960s. They later helped develop (among other acts) the hard-rocking Australian band AC/DC, which featured two of George's brothers. In 1978, with the idea of creating a rock poetry of the streets, they invented Flash and the Pan.

July	1979	HEY, ST. PETER	Epic

A FLOCK OF SEAGULLS

Members:
> Mike Score—guitar, vocals, keyboards—born: November 5, 1956
> Frank Maudsley—bass, vocals—born: November 10, 1959
> Paul Reynolds—lead guitar—born: August 4, 1962
> Ali Score—drums—born: August 8, 1955

Hometown: Liverpool, England

Before uniting as a band in 1979, A Flock of Seagulls were two hairdressers, an electrician, and an auto mechanic. The group took its name from the book *Jonathan Livingston Seagull*. They enjoyed moderate success in Great Britain, thanks to the song "Telecommunication," but seeking exposure outside their native land, A Flock of Seagulls took off for America. The Seagulls came to the States (where teens loved Mike Score's

A Flock of Seagulls. *Left to right:* Mike Score (*top*), Ali Score, Frank Maudsley, Paul Reynolds.

odd haircut as much as his music) intending to stay for three weeks; they remained seven months.

The quartet became known for its state-of-the-art techno-pop and its sci-fi-oriented lyrics. "I Ran," which is based on a photo Mike and Frank saw of a flying saucer chasing two people, became the group's biggest hit. Their most esteemed honor, however, was being the sole British band to win a Grammy Award in 1983.

July	1982	1. I RAN	Jive/Arista
November	1982	2. SPACE AGE LOVE SONG	Jive/Arista
May	1983	3. WISHING	Jive/Arista
August	1984	4. THE MORE YOU LIVE, THE MORE YOU LOVE	Jive/Arista

FLYING LIZARDS

Members:
    Deborah Lizard—vocals
    Julian Marshall—piano
    David Cunningham—other instruments
Hometown: England

While experimenting in a recording studio, record producer David Cunningham came up with an unusual interpretation of Eddie Cochran's "Summertime Blues." Along with Deborah Lizard and Julian Marshall, Cunningham recorded the song under the name Flying Lizards. The British public enjoyed the tune, and soon Cunningham's record company asked him to devise another low-budget/high-profit novelty reworking of a popular tune. It cost less than $14 to record "Money." Julian Marshall, whose studio Cunningham used, subsequently hooked up with another Deborah (Berg) to form Eye to Eye.

December   1979   MONEY   Virgin

ELLEN FOLEY

Hometown: St. Louis, Missouri

Ellen Foley has had a rich history of both music and acting since moving to New York in 1972. She first hooked up with Meat Loaf and Jim Steinman when all three were featured in the touring production of the National Lampoon Show in 1976. Her acting credits include NBC-TV's short-lived *3 Girls 3* in which she shared the lead with Debbie Allen and Mimi Kennedy in 1977, the soaps *Search For Tomorrow* and *One Life to Live*, the Broadway revival and film versions of *Hair*, and the film *Tootsie*, as well as off-Broadway work. Her singing career is highlighted by her duet with Meat Loaf on his "Paradise By The Dashboard Light" and a guest appearance on the Clash's "Hitsville, U. K." Her debut album was produced by Ian Hunter (formerly of Mott the Hoople) and Mick Ronson (formerly of David Bowie's Spiders from Mars and Bob Dylan's Rolling Thunder Revue), and her second album was produced by Mick Jones, then of the Clash (he was credited simply as My Boyfriend).

November   1979   WHAT'S A MATTER BABY   Cleveland International/
                                                               Epic

THE FOOLS

Members:
    Mike Girard—vocals
    Rich Bartlett—guitar, vocals
    Stacey Pedrick—guitar
    Doug Forman—bass, vocals
    Chris Pedrick—drums
Hometown: Boston, Massachusetts

Early in 1979, the Fools recorded a parody of Talking Heads' "Psycho Killer," called "Psycho Chicken," which got airplay around the country even though the homemade tape had not even been pressed into records. The Fools became a big draw on Boston's club circuit and won a record contract. Subsequent songs, however, were not novelty tunes, although the quintet included a degree of levity in their concerts and interviews.

| April | 1980 | IT'S A NIGHT FOR BEAUTIFUL GIRLS | EMI-America |
| March | 1981 | RUNNING SCARED | EMI-America |

STEVE FORBERT

Hometown: Meridian, Mississippi

When White's Auto Store in Meridian went out of business and Steve Forbert lost his job as a truck driver and warehouse man, he got on a train, and 25 hours later arrived in New York City. Back home, Forbert had played in local bands throughout his school years, but had more recently developed a one-man show, playing guitar and harmonica and singing his own tunes, and he believed that Greenwich Village was the place for him. Upon his arrival, he checked into a YMCA and began playing on street corners and in small clubs. He soon found an audience, a manager, and a record deal.

| December | 1979 | ROMEO'S TUNE | Nemperor |
| April | 1980 | SAY GOODBYE TO LITTLE JO | Nemperor |

FOTOMAKER

Members:
    Wally Bryson—guitar, vocals—born: July 10, 1949—Gastonia, North Carolina
    Lex Marchesi—guitar, vocals
    Frankie Vinci—keyboards, vocals
    Gene Cornish—bass, vocals—born: May 14, 1944—Ottawa, Canada
    Dino Danelli—drums—born: July 23, 1944—Jersey City, New Jersey
Hometown: New York, New York

After the exhaustive auditions that finally brought Lex Marchesi and Frank Vinci to their attention, former Rascals Gene Cornish and Dino Danelli thought to complete their new group with Wally Bryson, formerly of the Raspberries. Within six days, the new quintet began working on its first album. Fotomaker received only nominal public attention for its two albums, but the group did get to perform as the only rock band at the 10th Anniversary Special Olympics Benefit Night in Detroit's Cobo Hall in 1978.

| April | 1978 | WHERE HAVE YOU BEEN ALL MY LIFE | Atlantic |
| December | 1978 | MILES AWAY | Atlantic |

Fotomaker. *Left to right:* Dino Danelli, Wally Bryson, Frankie Vinci, Gene Cornish, Lex Marchesi.

FRANKE & THE KNOCKOUTS

Members:
    Franke Previte—vocals
    Billy Elworthy—guitar—replaced (1982) by Bobby Messano
    Blake Levinsohn—keyboards—replaced (1984) by Tommy Ayers
    Leigh Foxx—bass
    Claude LeHenaff—drums—replaced (1984) by Tico Torres
Hometown: New Brunswick, New Jersey

Franke Previte began singing a capella with friends in a train station hallway in his hometown of New Brunswick, New Jersey, grooving on the echo effect. He later recorded with the Oxford Watch Band and a heavy metal group called Bull Angus before forming Franke & The Knockouts in 1980.

March	1981	SWEETHEART	Millennium
July	1981	YOU'RE MY GIRL	Millennium
April	1982	WITHOUT YOU	Millennium

FRANKIE GOES TO HOLLYWOOD

Members:

Holly Johnson—vocals—born: February 19, 1960
Paul Rutherford—vocals—born: December 8, 1959
Brian ("Nasher") Nash —guitar—born: May 20, 1963
Peter (Ped) Gill—drums—born: May 8, 1964
Mark O'Toole—bass, drums—born: January 6, 1964

Hometown: Liverpool, England

Frankie Goes to Hollywood was named when its members found a vintage movie magazine with an article about Frank Sinatra's venture to California.

Frankie Goes to Hollywood. *Left to right:* Mark O'Toole, Paul Rutherford, Holly Johnson, Peter Gill, Brian Nash.

The flashy group gained instant notoriety when Holly Johnson and Paul Rutherford openly pronounced their homosexuality. The group's debut single, "Relax," was then banned by the BBC, but nevertheless went straight to number one, staying there for six weeks. A second single, "Two Tribes" entered the charts at number one, where it stayed for eight weeks, making it one of the five longest-running British hits of the past 20 years. While "Two Tribes" reigned at number one, "Relax" enjoyed a resurgence, going to number two. Only three other artists have occupied the number one and two positions on the U. K. singles chart simultaneously: the Beatles, Elvis Presley, and John Lennon.

While "Relax" was only a modest hit in the United States, the controversial video for "Two Tribes" was initially released to clubs only, where it caught the attention of rock fans. The song alludes to the world's superpowers' role in war, and the video, directed by the award-winning team of Kevin Godley and Lol Creme, featured actors resembling Ronald Reagan and Soviet leader Chernenko fighting dirty in a wrestling ring, intercut with archival footage of presidents Nixon and Kennedy. On British television, the video was restricted to after-midnight airings. A reedited version was made available to American television.

April	1984	1. RELAX	Island
October	1984	2. TWO TRIBES	Island
January	1985	3. RELAX (re-released)	Island
April	1985	4. WELCOME TO THE PLEASURE DOME	Island

ACE FREHLEY

Born: April 27, 1951
Hometown: Bronx, New York

Although a member of Kiss, Ace had a solo hit in 1978.
See *KISS, Rock On: The Years of Change*.

| October | 1978 | NEW YORK GROOVE | Casablanca |

GLENN FREY

Born: November 6, 1948
Hometown: Detroit, Michigan

Even as a child, Glenn Frey was ahead of the game; too smart for regular classes, he breezed through a special program for gifted students. After a brief stint in junior college, Frey gave up the classroom for rock and roll. He knocked around the Detroit bar scene, but quickly tired of the hometown bar and frat circuit and headed for southern California. There, he formed Longbranch Pennywhistle with J. D. Souther, and played rhythm guitar in Linda Ronstadt's band before forming the Eagles with two other Ronstadt musicians—Bernie Leadon and Don Henley—and with Randy Meisner. Some 50 million record sales later, the Eagles broke up, leaving all of its members to pursue solo careers. Frey's debut solo album, *No Fun Aloud,* was released in 1982.

June	1982	1. I FOUND SOMEBODY	Asylum
August	1982	2. THE ONE YOU LOVE	Asylum
December	1982	3. ALL THOSE LIES	Aslum
June	1984	4. SEXY GIRL	MCA
September	1984	5. THE ALLNIGHTER	MCA
December	1984	6. THE HEAT IS ON	MCA
April	1985	7. SMUGGLER'S BLUES	MCA

FRIDA

Real Name: Annifrid "Frida" Lyngstad
Born: November 15, 1945
Hometown: Stockholm, Sweden

Born in Norway and raised in Sweden, Annifrid Lyngstad was already a major television and recording star when she became one-fourth of Abba in the early 1970s. (See *ABBA, Rock On: The Years of Change.*) She had begun to sing professionally at age 13 and in 1967 had broken through to the masses via a Swedish television program called "Hyland's Corner."

Frida

Abba went on to become the biggest corporation in Sweden and the biggest-selling recording group in history. By the early eighties, however, members of the vocal quartet sought to establish their individual identities as well. In 1982, Frida released her debut solo album, *Something's Going On*, produced by Phil Collins. Shortly thereafter, she moved to England to be closer to the music industry and to live a bit more anonymously than she was able to in Sweden.

November   1982   I KNOW THERE'S SOMETHING GOING ON   Atlantic

RICHIE FURAY

Born: May 9, 1944
Hometown: Yellow Springs, Ohio

Richie Furay was in a folk-style vocal group called the Aw Go Go Singers when he met Stephen Stills. Less than a year later, Furay reencountered Stills and another friend from the Greenwich Village circuit, Neil Young, who had a bassist, Bruce Palmer, with him. With a drummer named Dewey Martin, they all formed Buffalo Springfield in April 1966. Two years and three albums later the group disbanded, but there were several country-rock offshoots. Furay formed Poco, and led the band for five years and six albums before leaving in 1973. A band called Souther-Hillman-Furay, with J. D. Souther and Chris Hillman, recorded two albums before each member resumed solo careers.

October   1979   I STILL HAVE DREAMS   Asylum

G

PETER GABRIEL

Born: May 13, 1950
Hometown: London, England

After nine years of fronting Genesis, Peter Gabriel quit the group in 1975. His hit single, "Solsbury Hill," was an acoustic-based examination of the artistic frustration that caused him to leave Genesis.
See *GENESIS, Rock On: The Years of Change.*

April	1977	1. SOLSBURY HILL	Atco
August	1980	2. GAMES WITHOUT FRONTIERS	Mercury
October	1982	3. SHOCK THE MONKEY	Geffen
August	1983	4. SOLSBURY HILL	Geffen

THE GAP BAND

Members:
    Charlie Wilson—vocals, keyboards—born: 1956—added in 1973
    Ronnie Wilson—keyboards, flugelhorn
    Robert Wilson—bass, guitar—added in 1975
Hometown: Tulsa, Oklahoma

The Gap Band's three Wilson Brothers are sons of a minister, and their first musical exposure came as members of a church choir. Ronnie Wilson founded the group in 1969, using an acronym for the three main arteries in Tulsa's black business community—Greenwood, Archer, and Pine Streets—as its name. Fellow Tulsa musician Leon Russell was so impressed with the Gap Band's music that he hired them as his backup band for a national concert tour in the mid-seventies. By 1978, the Gap Band became the three Wilson Brothers exclusively. Before long, the Gap Band was selling millions of records and climbing up the r&b sales charts to number one with "Shake" and "Oops (Upside Your Head)" before crossing over to the pop charts. Stevie Wonder liked them and asked them to contribute to his *Hotter Than July* album.

GAP BAND

February	1981	BURN RUBBER	Mercury
May	1981	YEARNING FOR YOUR LOVE	Mercury

THE GAP BAND

May	1982	EARLY IN THE MORNING	Total Experience
August	1982	YOU DROPPED A BOMB (ON ME)	Total Experience
March	1983	OUTSTANDING	Total Experience

GARY'S GANG

Members:
    Gary Turnier—drums—born: 1954
    Eric Matthew—guitar—born: 1954
    Bill Catlano—percussion—born: 1953
    Bob Forman—sax—born: 1955
    Al Lauricella—keyboard—born: 1960
    Rino Minetti—keyboard—born: 1959
    Jay Leon—trombone—born: 1956
Hometown: Richmond Hill, New York

Gary's Gang

Barry Gibb

Gary's Gang is basically a New York kind of band. It's America, it's good music, and it's happy.

Gary Turnier and Eric Matthew, who together write all of the group's material, were childhood friends from the Richmond Hill section of Queens, New York. Gary is the group drummer, and Eric handles the guitar and various other instruments. While Gary attended college, Eric built himself an eight-track studio in his family garage. He created work for himself by producing demo tapes and commercials. When a songwriter came to Eric's studio to do a demo the pair became friends and cowrote a number of songs which were recorded by established artists. Eric brought in Gary to do percussion work on songs he was coproducing and arranging for other artists.

Their first single, "Keep On Dancin'," was made on equipment purchased from a major record company that was selling its used recording equipment.

February   1979   KEEP ON DANCIN'   Columbia

BARRY GIBB

Born: September 1, 1946
Hometown: Manchester, England

A member of the Bee Gees, Barry Gibb has had several hits with Barbra Streisand.

Robin Gibb

See *THE BEE GEES, Rock On: The Years of Change.*

November	1980	GUILTY (with Barbra Streisand)	Columbia
January	1981	WHAT KIND OF FOOL (with Barbra Streisand)	Columbia
September	1984	SHINE SHINE	MCA

ROBIN GIBB

Born: December 22, 1949
Hometown: Manchester, England

Bee Gees member Robin Gibb had a few hits on his own.
See *THE BEE GEES, Rock On: The Years of Change.*

August	1978	OH DARLIN'	RSO
November	1980	HELP ME (with Marcy Levy)	RSO
June	1984	BOYS DO FALL IN LOVE	Mirage

TERRI GIBBS

Born: June 15, 1954
Hometown: Augusta, Georgia

Terri Gibbs was born blind, but her musical gifts transcended her handicap
almost from the beginning. At the age of three, she was playing piano for
her relatives, and she made her singing debut in gospel music before she
was even a teenager. By high school, Terri was winning talent contests,
singing in the school chorus, and appearing on stage locally. She recorded
her first demo at 18 and played in her first professional band, Sound
Dimension, two years later.

In 1975, Terri formed her own band and began her long-running gig

Terri Gibbs

at Augusta's Steak and Ale Restaurant. She paid her dues, singing 50 songs in three sets nearly every night for the next five years. All the while, she continually sent tapes of her original songs to Nashville, hoping to break into big-league country music.

The release of Terri's debut album, *Somebody's Knockin'*, immediately earned her nominations or awards by the Academy of Country Music, *Music City News, Record World* magazine, the Atlanta Songwriters Association, and the Country Music Association. She was also invited to play at the Grand Ole Opry. She's continued to win awards, including a Grammy.

Terri's father is a supervisor at Western Electric in Augusta, and the family lives comfortably on a sizeable piece of land near the suburb of Grovetown.

| January | 1981 | SOMEBODY'S KNOCKIN' | MCA |
| June | 1981 | RICH MAN | MCA |

NICK GILDER

Born: November 7, 1951
Hometown: London, England

When Nick Gilder came to Vancouver from London in 1971, he was a student at a technical college, not a singer. However, during a basement jam session he fell into a group that clicked. The group, called Sweeney Todd after a fictitious barber who liked to slash his customers' throats, got some attention and, before long, garnered a recording contract. Their records had little success outside of Vancouver until 1976, when "Roxy Roller" became a number-one smash in Canada. After a few false starts, Nick Gilder and his partner in Sweeney Todd, James McCulloch, began working on Gilder's solo album. Gilder's 1977 debut, *You Know Who You Are*, included a new version of "Roxy Roller," but it wasn't until "Hot Child In The City," from his second album, *City Nights*, that he broke ground in the United States.

June	1978	★ HOT CHILD IN THE CITY	Chrysalis
October	1978	HERE COMES THE NIGHT	Chrysalis
June	1979	YOU REALLY ROCK ME	Chrysalis

MICKEY GILLEY

Born: March 9, 1936
Hometown: Ferriday, Louisiana

Mickey Gilley had no plans for a career in music when he left Louisiana at age 17 for his first job in Houston, where he worked as a "grease monkey" in the construction business for 75 cents an hour. But his cousin Jerry Lee Lewis changed his mind for him when Lewis came to Houston for a concert after his first hit, "Crazy Arms." The two cousins had played piano together a lot as children, and Gilley was anxious to see Lewis's show. When he took Lewis to the airport afterwards and saw him pull out a wad of hundred-dollar bills, Gilley decided to quit the construction business and get into show biz.

Gilley began working in nightclubs around Houston, and financed his own first record. But local radio station programmers didn't give the record any airplay and, discouraged, Gilley moved to Memphis, then Nashville, New Orleans, Biloxi, and Mobile before settling in for nearly two years at a tiny lounge in Lake Charles, Louisiana. Disheartened, he finally gave up entertainment and went back to a construction job in Houston, performing at little clubs on the side for additional income. In 1959, he began making records again, but it took some 15 years for the public to notice.

In 1971, Mickey and his business partner Sherwood Cryer opened their own club, named "Gilley's," in Pasadena, Texas. The club was an instant success, and became the setting of the film *Urban Cowboy*. The soundtrack to the album of that name included Gilley's first major crossover hit, "Stand By Me." Gilley's success has led to performances at the Copacabana (the only country music show to have played there) in New York and the Aladdin in Las Vegas.

In 1978 Gilley opened a recording studio, also called "Gilley's," next to his club, and he bought a Cessna 210 aircraft, which he pilots. He has also ventured into western wear, a syndicated radio show called "Live At Gilley's," a magazine called *Gilley's*, and a rodeo arena he built next to his club in 1982.

June	1974	1. ROOM FULL OF ROSES	Playboy
June	1976	2. BRING IT ON HOME TO ME	Playboy
May	1980	3. STAND BY ME	Asylum
August	1980	4. TRUE LOVE WAYS	Epic
July	1981	5. YOU DON'T KNOW ME	Epic

DAVID GILMOUR

Born: March 6, 1947
Hometown: Cambridge, England

A member of Pink Floyd, David Gilmour had a chart entry in 1984 called "Blue Light."
See *PINK FLOYD, Rock On: The Years of Change.*

| April | 1984 | BLUE LIGHT | Columbia |

David Gilmour

LOUISE GOFFIN

Louise Goffin is the daughter of singer Carole King, who wrote many of the rock classics of the sixties. Louise's lone chart entry, "Remember (Walkin' in the Sand)," was originally done by the Shangri-Las.

August   1979   REMEMBER (WALKIN' IN THE SAND)   Asylum

THE GO-GO'S

Members:
   Belinda Carlisle—vocals—born: August 17, 1958
   Charlotte Caffey—guitar, keyboards, vocals—born: October 21, 1953
   Jane Wiedlin—guitar, vocals (left group in 1984)—replaced by Paula Jean
      Brown—bass—added in 1985
   Kathy Valentine—bass, now guitar—born: January 7, 1959—added in 1981
   Gina Schock—drums, percussion—born: August 31, 1957—added in 1979
Hometown: Los Angeles, California

The original members of the Go-Go's all lived in a rundown hotel in Hollywood when the group formed in May, 1978. They knew little about musicianship, but after a memorable debut performance at a basement punk club, the Masque, they decided they'd have to learn. After line-up changes, the revamped group did many shows in southern California, as well as a United Kingdom tour opening for Madness and the Specials. While in London, the Go-Go's recorded "We Got The Beat," which became popular at both British and American dance clubs. Before long, the group joined the ranks of pop pros, recording albums and touring the world, despite the music industry's early reluctance to believe an all-female pop group could hit.

Jane Wiedlin also hit the charts when she dueted on "Cool Places" with Russell Mael of Sparks. Several Go-Go's have written songs for other acts. The Go-Go's have a full-length home videocassette available called *Totally Go-Go's*. In 1985, the members of the group went their separate ways.

August	1981	1. OUR LIPS ARE SEALED	I.R.S.
January	1982	2. WE GOT THE BEAT	I.R.S.
July	1982	3. VACATION	I.R.S.
September	1982	4. GET UP AND GO	I.R.S.
March	1984	5. HEAD OVER HEELS	I.R.S.
June	1984	6. TURN TO YOU	I.R.S.
September	1984	7. YES OR NO	I.R.S

The Go-Go's. *Left to right:* *(top)* Charlotte Caffey, Belinda Carlisle; *(bottom)* Kathy Valentine, Jane Wiedlin, Gina Schock.

FRANNE GOLDE

Hometown: Chicago, Illinois

Franne Golde started in a group, Franny & Zooey with J. D., in 1971. Later, she went solo, playing the bathhouse circuit, and had her only hit, "Here I Go Again."

July   1979   HERE I GO AGAIN   Portrait

GOLDEN EARRING

Members:
George Kooymans—guitar, vocals
Barry Hay—vocals, guitar
Rinus Gerritsen—bass, keyboards
Cesar Zuiderwijk—drums (replaced Jaap Eggermont in 1969)
Eelco Gelling—guitar—added in 1976 (left group in 1978)
Robert Jan Stips—keyboards—added in 1975 (left group in 1976)
Hometown: Amsterdam, The Netherlands

Though Golden Earring was formed in the early sixties, it took several years for the band to establish a musical direction and a set line-up. Soon after it did so, however, the group did well in its native Holland, and by 1968 Golden Earring had broken all existing Dutch records for sales. That summer, the group set out to conquer America. Achieving only marginal success, they turned instead to Europe, where they gained popularity in Germany and England before a song called "Radar Love" in 1974 earned the group a following in the United States. Golden Earring rarely toured the States, and not all of their records were released internationally; it was not until "Twilight Zone" in 1982 that Golden Earring was reestablished around the world.

May	1974	1. RADAR LOVE	Track
October	1974	2. CANDY'S GOING BAD	Track
November	1982	3. TWILIGHT ZONE	21 Records
April	1983	4. THE DEVIL MADE ME DO IT	21 Records
March	1984	5. WHEN THE LADY SMILES	21 Records/Polygram

IAN GOMM

Born: March 17, 1947
Hometown: Ealing, England

At a young age, Ian Gomm landed a job as apprentice draftsman in the art department of the London offices of EMI Records. Only a few months into the job, Gomm went to the EMI boss and requested a recording contract. The label chiefs considered the request, but the possibility of sponsoring a band partly composed of musicians contracted to rival record companies didn't sit well, so Gomm had to literally return to the drawing board. Six years later, Gomm quit EMI and answered a musician's classified ad. In February, 1972, Gomm became a member of Brinsley Schwarz, which proved to be a pivotal band in London's pub-rock scene. Gomm appeared on five albums before the group split up. He then headed for Wales to engineer, produce, and write songs—one of his first projects was working with the Stranglers. Gomm only recorded his own work sporadically.

September	1979	HOLD ON	Stiff/Epic

ROBERT GORDON

Hometown: New York, New York

Former lead singer of the punk band Tuff Darts, Robert Gordon was paired with a country, rockabilly, and rock 'n' roll guitarist named Link Wray in 1977, and together they recorded the successful "Red Hot."

As a solo performer, Gordon had a hit in 1981 with "Someday, Someway."

October	1977	RED HOT (with Link Wray)	Private Stock
June	1981	SOMEDAY, SOMEWAY	RCA

LARRY GRAHAM

Born: August 14, 1946
Hometown: San Francisco, California

The Graham family moved from Beaumont, Texas, to Oakland, California, when Larry was two. At age five, Larry Graham was taking tap dance lessons; at age eight, he started on piano; and before he was in his teens, he'd learned to play guitar, harmonica, drums, and various keyboards, and had developed a three-and-a-half-octave vocal range. Larry's mother, Dell Graham, was a singer, and at age 15, Larry was accompanying her on guitar and organ in a San Francisco club, doing jazz standards such as "Time After Time," "The Shadow Of Your Smile," and others. One night, when the organ broke down and Larry went out to rent another, all he could get was a bass guitar: He's been playing bass ever since. In 1966, he met a local dj named Sylvester Stewart, and joined the group Stewart was forming, Sly and the Family Stone (Stewart became known as Sly Stone). Graham stayed in the group until 1972, all the while developing his unique thump-and-pluck technique of bass playing.

After Larry left Sly and the Family Stone he joined a band called Patryce Banks & Hot Chocolate. He restructured the group and in 1973 its name was changed to Graham Central Station (see *GRAHAM CENTRAL STATION, Rock On: The Years of Change*). After their self-titled debut album in December, the name became Larry Graham and Graham Central Station. In 1980 Graham left the group to pursue a solo career. Graham had two hits in his first year as a solo artist.

June	1980	ONE IN A MILLION	Warner Bros.
October	1980	WHEN WE GET MARRIED	Warner Bros.
September	1981	JUST BE MY LADY	Warner Bros.

EDDY GRANT

Born: March 5, 1948
Hometown: Palisance, British Guyana

While Patrick Grant was a professional trumpeter, playing calypso, salsa, and big-band jazz, his son Eddy wanted to be a doctor. When Eddy was 12, however, his family moved to England, and he discovered rock 'n' roll and soul music. Eddy made his first guitar (a replica of a Gibson Les Paul with Vox pickups) in his school's wood shop.

Eddy wound up forming the Equals, a quartet comprising two white and two black musicians. Though the group had a top 40 hit in the United States in 1968 with "Baby Come Back" and released two albums, they fared better abroad; in the United Kingdom, for instance, "Baby Come Back" hit number one, and was followed by two more hits, "Black-Skinned Blue-Eyed Boys" and "Viva Bobby Joe." Grant left the Equals at age 21 when he suffered a mild, stress-related heart attack.

Grant met with little success when he began producing his former group, the Equals, and a British reggae band, the Pioneers, so he took what he'd saved from his career earnings, bought a townhouse in North London, and installed a 24-track studio in the adjacent coach house. Coach House Studios, as it became known, was the first black-owned studio in Europe. In 1974, Grant formed his own record company, Ice Records, and later bought his own pressing plant. His first solo records

Eddy Grant

Lee Greenwood

under this new system did well in the Caribbean islands, Nigeria, and other parts of the Third World before hitting in England, Europe, the United States, Canada, Japan, Australia, and the U.S.S.R.

Grant now lives with his wife and four children on the 35-acre Bayley Plantation in St. Phillip, Barbados. His 48-track Blue Wave Studios is the only world-class black-owned recording facility in the Caribbean.

April	1983	ELECTRIC AVENUE	Portrait/Ice
August	1983	I DON'T WANNA DANCE	Portrait/Ice
May	1984	ROMANCING THE STONE	Portrait

LEE GREENWOOD

Born: October 27, 1942
Hometown: Los Angeles, California

Lee Greenwood was born in Los Angeles, raised in Sacramento, and spent some time in school in Anaheim, California. While studying music theory in school, he played in a Dixieland band at Disneyland. Later, he played saxophone in country singer Del Reeves's band, performed in a symphony orchestra in Sacramento, played in impromptu jazz or "kix" bands, and was also a member of a drum and bugle corps. He eventually formed the Lee Greenwood Affair, with which he toured the western states. While recording albums, he also wrote and arranged major Las Vegas stage productions.

Lee's big break came while singing at the Atrium Lounge in the Tropicana Hotel. It so happened that during one of his engagements there, a nationally televised show, "Country Top Twenty," was being taped there as well. After the tapings, many of the featured guests, such as Dottie West, T. G. Shepperd, and Mel Tillis, would drop by and see Greenwood perform his original songs. Soon, several of these artists requested tunes from him. By 1982, Greenwood was recording his compositions himself. Lee has moved to Nashville with his wife Melanie, who is a professional dancer and choreographer.

| May | 1983 | I.O.U. | MCA |
| October | 1983 | SOMEBODY'S GONNA LOVE YOU | MCA |

SAMMY HAGAR

Born: October 13, 1949
Hometown: Monterey, California

Sammy Hagar grew up in Fontana, a small steel town between San Bernardino and Los Angeles. His father was a boxer who, under the name Bobby Burns, won the bantamweight title in the mid-forties. Sammy himself was raised as an athlete, and he says this is where he got his sense of rhythm and timing. Sammy thought he'd be a boxer until he was about 16, when he heard Cream for the first time; he immediately set out to learn to play the guitar. A succession of garage bands led to the formation of Skinny, a group that became quite popular in San Bernardino clubs. In an attempt to widen the group's terrain, Skinny headed for San Francisco. There, the band was restructured and renamed Sammy Hagar & the Justice Brothers. However, when Sammy heard that Ronnie Montrose, a revered Bay area guitarist, had just left the Edgar Winter Group and needed a singer for a group he was forming, Sammy called him. They met, and soon they were writing songs together and forming a hard-rock band that would become known as Montrose.

Montrose recorded several albums and attained moderate success, but Sammy left two years later to pursue a solo career, ironically taking three Montrose members with him. After a few albums, he was voted "Bay Area Musician of the Year" by the readers of *BAM*, a regional music magazine, in its first annual poll in 1977. Sammy also recorded an album with Neal Schon (of Journey), Kenny Aaronson, and Michael Shrieve, under the group name Hagar-Schon-Aaronson-Shrieve.

Hagar's songs have been recorded by French pop star Johnny Halliday, and by Bette Midler, Rick Springfield, and others. Bette Midler sang one of Sammy's songs in her first film, *The Rose*, and Sammy himself cowrote and performed the title track for the animated film *Heavy Metal*.

December	1977	1. YOU MAKE ME CRAZY	Capitol
April	1979	2. THE DOCK OF THE BAY	Capitol
September	1979	3. PLAIN JANE	Capitol
January	1982	4. I'LL FALL IN LOVE AGAIN	Geffen
May	1982	5. PIECE OF MY HEART	Geffen
December	1982	6. YOUR LOVE IS DRIVING ME CRAZY	Geffen
March	1983	7. NEVER GIVE UP	Geffen
July	1984	8. TWO SIDES OF LOVE	Geffen
September	1984	9. I CAN'T DRIVE 55	Geffen

JIMMY HALL

A former member of Wet Willie, Jimmy Hall had several hits as a solo performer.
See *WET WILLIE, Rock On: The Years of Change.*

| September | 1980 | I'M HAPPY THAT LOVE HAS FOUND YOU | Epic |
| May | 1982 | FOOL FOR YOUR LOVE | Epic |

THE JOHN HALL BAND

Members:
John Hall—vocals, guitar—born: October 25, 1947
Bob Leinbach—vocals, keyboards
Eric Parker—drums
John Troy—vocals, bass

A former member of Orleans, John Hall had several hits with the John Hall Band.
See *ORLEANS, Rock On: The Years of Change.*

| December | 1981 | CRAZY | EMI-America |
| January | 1983 | LOVE ME AGAIN | EMI-America |

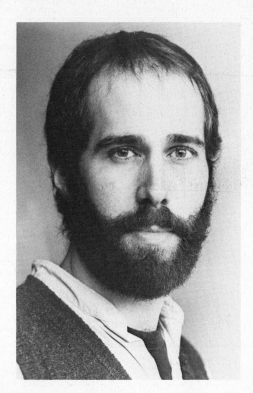

John Hall

HERBIE HANCOCK

Real Name: Herbert Jeffrey Hancock
Born: April 12, 1940
Hometown: Chicago, Illinois

Born and raised on Chicago's South Side, Herbie Hancock began studying the piano at the age of seven. At age 11, Herbie performed the Mozart D Major Piano Concerto with the Chicago Symphony Orchestra. At this time, Herbie also developed an interest in science and electronics. He later majored in electrical engineering, then music composition, at Grinnell College, where he received his Bachelor of Arts degree. The strong, danceable rhythms on Herbie's album *Future Shock* were produced by electronic devices and synthesizers combined with acoustic percussion and piano. His Grammy Award-winning track, "Rockit," became the largest selling 12-inch single in Columbia Records' history.

Herbie's many years of diverse musical experiences—his classical training, his solo ventures, and his explorations into electronic and computerized music—all contribute to his present sound.

| March | 1974 | CHAMELEON | Columbia |
| September | 1983 | ROCKIT | Columbia |

EMMYLOU HARRIS

Born: April 2, 1947
Hometown: Birmingham, Alabama

In 1967, Emmylou Harris began singing and playing acoustic guitar at East Coast colleges and folk clubs like Gerde's Folk City in New York's Greenwich Village. In 1970 she recorded her first album. The release of

Emmylou Harris

Debbie Harry

the album coincided with the birth of her first child, leading to the new mom's retirement from the music scene. A year later, however, she was back checking out the scene in New York and Nashville, and before the year was up, she was fronting a country/folk band in Washington, D. C. Emmylou was seen and heard by the Flying Burrito Brothers, and was invited to join the band; one week later, however, the group broke up. Chris Hillman, then a member of the band, introduced former member Gram Parsons to Harris. Harris sang in his band and on his albums until Parsons met an untimely death. Harris stayed in D. C., and by mid-1974 she had a record deal. "If I Could Only Win Your Love" was released as a single from her *Pieces Of The Sky* album in mid-1975 and became number one on the country charts. Many country hits and awards followed. Her reworking of the classic "Mister Sandman" was featured on the *Evangeline* album; the song also featured vocals by Dolly Parton and Linda Ronstadt.

August	1975	IF I COULD ONLY WIN YOUR LOVE	Reprise
March	1976	HERE, THERE AND EVERYWHERE	Reprise
February	1981	MISTER SANDMAN	Warner Bros.

DEBBIE HARRY

Born: July 1, 1945
Hometown: New York, New York

Deborah Harry, lead singer of Blondie, had a couple of solo hits in 1981. See *BLONDIE*.

| August | 1981 | BACKFIRED | Chrysalis |
| October | 1981 | THE JAM WAS MOVING | Chrysalis |

DAN HARTMAN

Born: December 8
Hometown: Harrisburg, Pennsylvania

After studying classical piano as a child, Dan Hartman began his professional career at age 13 in a group called the Legends. Years later, in 1971, he submitted a 13-song tape to Steve Paul, a well-known music industry leader who had operated an important sixties rock club called the Scene, and who managed Johnny Winter, Edgar Winter, Rick Derringer, and others. Paul liked Hartman's songs, and called him for an audition with Edgar Winter, who was assembling musicians for the Edgar Winter Group. They were immediately impressed with Hartman, who could play virtually every instrument, who wrote songs prolifically, and who fit in both musically and personally with everyone else in the organization.

Dan played bass, lead guitar, and keyboards, and wrote and sang on three Edgar Winter Group albums. When the group split up after a 60-city tour in 1975, Dan continued writing and producing while building a recording studio called the Schoolhouse in Westport, Connecticut. Although he engineered, produced, and mixed albums for both Johnny and Edgar Winter, and for Rick Derringer, Muddy Waters, Foghat, and .38 Special, he also came up with his own albums, which were more pop and dance-oriented than those of his hard-rock and blues cohorts.

The Three Degrees, Tavares, Rick Derringer, Johnny Winter, Montrose, and Sergio Mendes have all recorded Hartman's songs.

| October | 1978 | 1. INSTANT REPLAY | Blue Sky |
| February | 1979 | 2. THIS IS IT | Blue Sky |

Dan Hartman

April	1981	3. HEAVEN IN YOUR ARMS	Blue Sky
June	1981	4. IT HURTS TO BE IN LOVE	Blue Sky
May	1984	5. I CAN DREAM ABOUT YOU	MCA
October	1984	6. WE ARE THE YOUNG	MCA
February	1985	7. SECOND NATURE	MCA

JUSTIN HAYWARD

Born: October 14, 1946
Hometown: Swindon, Wiltshire, England

A member of the Moody Blues, Justin Hayward had himself a hit with "Forever Autumn" in 1978.
See *THE MOODY BLUES, Rock On: The Years of Change.*

| October | 1978 | FOREVER AUTUMN | Columbia |

LEON HAYWOOD

Hometown: Houston, Texas

The first instrument Leon Haywood recalls playing was a toy piano given to him by his mother one Christmas. For several years, receiving a new toy piano became a tradition until Leon convinced his mother to buy him a real one. By his early teens, Leon was already playing professionally in local clubs. In 1960, Leon began pursuing a recording contract, so he moved to Los Angeles and, again, played local clubs. Until 1963, he played in "Big" Jay McNeeley's orchestra. This led to a job playing piano for Sam Cooke. When Cooke died in December 1964, Leon decided to become a full-fledged singer/songwriter/musician/producer and solo artist. Several tunes got some attention, but his first chart success came in November, 1965, with an r&b song called "She's With Her Other Love." Leon continued to juggle a solo career with session work for other acts.

August	1967	1. IT'S GOT TO BE MELLOW	Decca
December	1967	2. MELLOW MOONLIGHT	Decca
March	1974	3. KEEP IT IN THE FAMILY	20th Century
February	1975	4. BELIEVE HALF OF WHAT YOU SEE	20th Century
		(AND NONE OF WHAT YOU HEAR)	
July	1975	5. COME AN' GET YOURSELF SOME	20th Century
September	1975	6. I WANT'A DO SOMETHING FREAKY TO YOU	20th Century
April	1980	7. DON'T PUSH IT, DON'T FORCE IT	20th Century

ROBERT HAZARD

Hometown: Philadelphia, Pennsylvania

The Philadelphia-based rocker Robert Hazard has developed a huge following in the City of Brotherly Love. His only national hit, "Escalator of Life," climbed the charts in 1983.

| March | 1983 | ESCALATOR OF LIFE | RCA |

Heaven 17. *Left to right:* Martyn Ware, Glenn Gregory, Ian Craig Marsh.

HEAVEN 17

Members:
    Glenn Gregory—vocals—born: May 16
    Martyn Ware—vocals—born: May 19
    Ian Craig Marsh—vocals—born: November 11
Hometown: London, England

In 1977, Ian, Martyn, and Philip Oakley were members of the Human League (see *HUMAN LEAGUE*), recording albums like *Reproduction* and *Travelogue*. In 1980, Ian and Martyn left the group, leaving Philip to form a new Human League. Ian and Martyn met former photographer Glenn Gregory and formed a trio called Heaven 17. (The name comes from a line in the film *A Clockwork Orange* when Alex walks into a record store looking for a certain song.)

Heaven 17 released an album in England and then recorded a video, "Penthouse and Pavement," that got them exposure on MTV in 1982. This led to a recording contract with Arista Records and a hit single in 1983.

March	1983	LET ME GO	Arista

DON HENLEY

Born: July 22, 1947
Hometown: Linden, Texas

Don Henley played in rock bands through high school, and then went on to college to please his well-meaning parents. Although he attended college for four years, he didn't graduate. In the early seventies, he decided to pursue his own dreams rather than his parents', and at the encouragement of Kenny Rogers, Henley took his band, Shiloh, to Los Angeles. Shiloh recorded an album that sold poorly, leaving Henley discouraged until Glenn Frey asked him to join Linda Ronstadt's band for $200 a week. Frey and Henley roomed together during a two-month tour with Ronstadt, and after working on the *Linda Rondstadt* LP, they formed the Eagles with fellow Ronstadt band member Bernie Leadon and ex-Poco member Randy Meisner. Henley wrote, sang, and played on many of the Eagles' biggest hits.

Don Henley first appeared as a solo artist in the summer of 1982 with a song called "Love Rules" on the soundtrack for the film *Fast Times At Ridgemont High*. A few weeks later, his debut solo album, *I Can't Stand Still*, was also released. The title song of this album was a hit.

August	1982	1. JOHNNY CAN'T READ	Asylum
October	1982	2. DIRTY LAUNDRY	Asylum
January	1983	3. I CAN'T STAND STILL	Asylum
November	1984	4. THE BOYS OF SUMMER	Geffen
February	1985	5. ALL SHE WANTS TO DO IS DANCE	Geffen

PATRICK HERNANDEZ

Born: 1949
Hometown: Paris, France

Born in Paris of a Spanish father, who played guitar in various bands, and an Austrian/Italian mother, who sang, Patrick Hernandez was introduced to music at an early age.

When he was sent to England to further his education in 1963, Patrick was caught up in the initial stirrings of Beatlemania and was inspired to pick up the guitar. Upon his return to France in 1966, he began working with a succession of rock groups, performing at many famous clubs and building his reputation.

After knocking around for more than a decade, Patrick, together with his collaborator Hervé Tholance, had a hit single with "Born To Be Alive." After the original rhythm and vocal tracks for the recording were done, Patrick and Hervé overdubbed new rhythm tracks, mingled the tracks, and remixed the record several times to produce a special sound. It became one of disco's biggest hits during the summer of 1979.

June   1979   BORN TO BE ALIVE   Columbia

BERTIE HIGGINS

Born: 1946
Hometown: Tarpon Springs, Florida

In 1962, Higgins worked as a drummer in a local combo. Two years later he was playing in a band called the Romans and had a recording contract with ABC-Paramount records, releasing several moderately popular local hits.

Patrick Hernandez

In 1968, Higgins, who is a direct descendant of the great German writer Goethe, finally got tired of touring and returned to the west coast of Florida to develop his writing and to learn to play the guitar.

Higgins' love for classic movies resulted in his 1981 major hit "Key Largo," named after the 1948 film starring Humphrey Bogart and Lauren Bacall. This film was a favorite of Higgins and his girlfriend, Beverly Seiberg. After the couple broke up, Higgins and his friend Sonny Limbo wrote the song "Key Largo" as a plea for Beverly to return to him, saying that they too had it all, just like Bogie and Bacall. The romantic ballad worked, for Seiberg heard it on the radio and returned to Higgins.

| November | 1981 | KEY LARGO | Kat Family |
| May | 1982 | JUST ANOTHER DAY IN PARADISE | Kat Family |

ROGER HODGSON

Born: May 21, 1950
Hometown: London, England

From 1975 until 1983, Roger sang and played keyboards for the highly successful group Supertramp. In 1984, he placed his first solo hit on the American charts.

| October | 1984 | HAD A DREAM (SLEEPING WITH THE ENEMY) | A & M |

JENNIFER HOLLIDAY

Born: October 19, 1960
Hometown: Houston, Texas

One of the stars from the Broadway production of *Dream Girls*, Jennifer first hit the charts in 1982 with a song from the show.

| July | 1982 | AND I'M TELLING YOU I'M NOT GOING | Geffen |
| October | 1983 | I AM LOVE | Geffen |

RUPERT HOLMES

Born: February 24, 1947
Hometown: Tenafly, New Jersey

Rupert Holmes spent most of his childhood in Nyack, New York, with occasional trips back to his mother's native Britain. Rupert, whose father played lead alto sax with many big bands in the forties, was introduced to music at a young age. His early skill on the clarinet eventually earned him a scholarship to the Manhattan School of Music. He quickly rejected the studies in classical music, however, switched to piano, and began hanging around recording studios.

In 1974, Holmes recorded his debut album, *Widescreen,* which critics applauded for its explorations of film themes. Barbra Streisand was impressed enough to ask him to produce her *Lazy Afternoon* album on which she sang some of Holmes's songs. The album became a gold record, and Streisand later recorded more of Holmes's tunes.

Holmes's songs have also been recorded by Barry Manilow, Dolly Parton, the Partridge Family, B. J. Thomas, Dionne Warwick, Mac Davis, Manhattan Transfer, Carol Douglas, and the Tymes. Holmes has produced albums for Sparks, Sailor, the Strawbs, and John Miles in addition to Streisand. Two of the seven songs written by Holmes that Streisand recorded were used in the film *A Star Is Born.*

September	1978	1. LET'S GET CRAZY TONIGHT	Private Stock
October	1979	★ 2. ESCAPE (THE PINA COLADA SONG)	Infinity
January	1980	3. HIM	MCA
May	1980	4. ANSWERING MACHINE	MCA
November	1980	5. MORNING MAN	MCA
April	1981	6. I DON'T NEED YOU	MCA

THE HONEYDRIPPERS

Members:
Robert Plant—vocals—born: August 20, 1947—Birmingham, England
Nile Rodgers—guitar—born: September 19, 1952—New York, New York
Jeff Beck—guitar—born: June 24, 1944—Surrey, England
Jimmy Page—guitar—born: January 9, 1945—Heston, Middlesex, England

Legendary rockers Robert Plant and Jimmy Page, formerly of Led Zeppelin, guitarist extraordinnaire Jeff Beck, and Nile Rodgers, famed producer of Chic and other musicians, pooled their talents to do an album of old rock 'n' roll songs. The album, *The Honeydrippers Volume One,* is a compilation of five songs written by performers like Ray Charles and Roy Brown and writers like Rudy Toombs and Doc Pomus. The production credit on the album is for Nugetre and the Fabulous Brill Brothers. Nugetre spelled backwards is Ertegun—as in Ahmet Ertegun, the chairman of Atlantic Records.

The debut single, "Sea Of Love," went as high as number two on the national charts when it was originally recorded by Phil Phillips during the summer of 1959.

Jimmy Page is busy today with his new band, the Firm; Nile Rodgers produced Madonna's new album; and Jeff Beck has been playing on new songs of Rod Stewart's, including "Infatuation."

October	1984	SEA OF LOVE	Es Paranza
January	1985	ROCKIN' AT MIDNIGHT	Es Paranza

HOTEL

Members:
    Marc Phillips—vocals, keyboards
    Tommy Colton—guitar
    George Creasman—bass—added in 1975
    Mike Reid—guitar—added in 1976
    Michael Cadenhead—drums—added in 1977
    Lee Bargeron—keyboards—added in 1978
Hometown: Birmingham, Alabama

While Hotel's music is described as commercial rock with classical overtones, the group has written a modern ballet, performed by the Birmingham Ballet Company, and a symphony, performed by the Atlanta Symphony Orchestra.

March	1978	1. YOU'LL LOVE AGAIN	Mercury
July	1979	2. YOU'VE GOT ANOTHER THING COMING	MCA
September	1979	3. HOLD ON TO THE NIGHT	MCA
July	1980	4. HALF MOON SILVER	MCA/Scotti Bros.

HUMAN LEAGUE

Members:
    Philip Oakey—vocals, synthesizers
    Adrian Wright—synthesizers
    Joanne Catherall—vocals—born: September 18, 1962—added in 1980
    Susanne Sulley—vocals—added in 1980
    Ian Burden—synthesizers—added in 1980
    Jo Callis—guitar, synthesizers—added in 1981
Hometown: Sheffield, England

Human League started in 1977, when computer operators Ian Craig Marsh and Martyn Ware teamed up with Philip Oakey. Although none was trained in music, they had a common desire to make pop music through electronics. The following year, the group released its first single in England, followed by an album, *Reproduction,* in 1979.

After a second album, *Travelogue,* in 1980, the group went through personnel changes. The regrouped Human League released its first album in America, *Dare,* and that album's first single, "Don't You Want Me," became an international smash. Another album, *Love and Dancing,* was released in the U.K. under the band's pseudonym, The League Unlimited Orchestra.

March	1982	★ 1. DON'T YOU WANT ME	A & M
May	1983	2. (KEEP FEELING) FASCINATION	A & M
October	1983	3. MIRROR MAN	A & M
June	1984	4. THE LEBANON	Virgin/A & M

Human League. *Left to right:* Joanne Catherall, Jo Callis, Adrian Wright, Philip Oakey, Susanne Sulley, Ian Burden.

IAN HUNTER

Born: June 3, 1946
Hometown: Shrewesbury, Shropshire, England

Leader of the group Mott the Hoople, Ian Hunter went solo in 1975 and had a chart entry in 1979.
See *MOTT THE HOOPLE, Rock On: The Years of Change.*

August   1979   JUST ANOTHER NIGHT   Chrysalis

I

ICICLE WORKS

Members:
    Ian McNabb—vocals, guitar
    Chris Layhe—bass guitar
    Chris Sharrock—drums
Hometown: Liverpool, England

An advertisement in a Liverpool newspaper in 1981 brought Icicle Works together. The group was named after a science fiction book. With the help of four opening slots on the Pretenders' United States tour, the group's career has taken off to the tune of a double debut on the charts: Both their single, "Whisper To A Scream (Birds Fly)," and their self-titled debut album were hits.

April   1984   WHISPER TO A SCREAM (BIRDS FLY)   Arista

Icicle Works. *Left to right:* Chris Layhe, Chris Sharrock, Ian McNabb.

BILLY IDOL

Real Name: William Broad
Born: November 30, 1955
Hometown: Surrey, England

Billy Idol was one of the original punk-rockers in London, along with the Clash, the Sex Pistols, and many others. In November 1976, with vocalist Gene October and bassist Tony James, he formed a band called Chelsea, which evolved into Generation X (the name derived from a book title). The group had five hit singles in England, but none in America. Eventually, Idol found the London punk scene to be stagnant, so in February 1981 he moved to New York City to launch a solo career. When "Dancing with Myself," which he originally recorded with his group (which had been renamed Billy Idol and Gen X), became a hit in American dance clubs, he rerecorded it for his mini-LP, *Don't Stop*. His first two solo albums, *Billy Idol* and *Rebel Yell*, both followed in 1983, and through hit songs, MTV rotation, and electrifying concerts, Billy Idol became a teen idol, despite or perhaps because of his rebellious look and attitude. Billy Idol turned down the lead role in *Lifeforce* due to tour commitments.

July   1982   1. HOT IN THE CITY   Chrysalis

May	1983	2. WHITE WEDDING	Chrysalis
January	1984	3. REBEL YELL	Chrysalis
May	1984	4. EYES WITHOUT A FACE	Chrysalis
August	1984	5. FLESH FOR FANTASY	Chrysalis
November	1984	6. CATCH MY FALL	Chrysalis

JULIO IGLESIAS

Born: September 23, 1943
Hometown: Madrid, Spain

At one time, it was estimated that one of Julio Iglesias's songs was played in some part of the world every 30 seconds. Iglesias has sold over 100 million albums in five languages, making him the best selling recording artist in history. Iglesias has given more than 2,100 live concerts and made over 790 television appearances in 69 countries. In 1984, he released *1100 Bel Air Place, California*, his first English-languge album, from which came two hits, both duets: "To All The Girls I've Loved Before," with country star Willie Nelson, and "All of You," with soul/pop songstress Diana Ross. These records finally made Iglesias a superstar in America.

March	1984	TO ALL THE GIRLS I'VE LOVED BEFORE (with Willie Nelson)	Columbia
July	1984	ALL OF YOU (with Diana Ross)	Columbia

JAMES INGRAM

Born: February 16
Hometown: Akron, Ohio

When James Ingram performed "Just Once" and "One Hundred Ways" on Quincy Jones's Grammy-winning album *The Dude,* he became the first artist in the history of pop music to win a Grammy (for best r&b male vocalist) without having released his own album. He also had a hit with "Baby, Come to Me," a duet with Patti Austin, which became the love theme for ABC-TV's popular daytime soap, *General Hospital.* Ingram also wrote "P.Y.T. (Pretty Young Thing)" which became a hit for Michael Jackson on his *Thriller* album.

In 1983, Ingram came into his own with a debut album, *It's Your Night.* Ironically, his two biggest hits from that album, "How Do You Keep the Music Playing" and "Yah Mo B There," were duets.

August	1981	1. JUST ONCE (with Quincy Jones)	A & M
December	1981	2. ONE HUNDRED WAYS (with Quincy Jones)	A & M
October	1982	★ 3. BABY, COME TO ME (with Patti Austin)	Qwest
May	1983	4. HOW DO YOU KEEP THE MUSIC PLAYING (with Patti Austin)	Qwest
December	1983	5. YAH MO B THERE (with Michael McDonald)	Qwest
April	1984	6. THERE'S NO EASY WAY	Qwest
September	1984	7. WHAT ABOUT ME (with Kenny Rogers and Kim Carnes)	RCA

INXS

Members:
Michael Hutchence—vocals—born: January 22
Tim Farriss—guitar—born: August 16
Kirk Pengilly—guitar, saxophone, vocals—born: July 4
Andrew Farriss—keyboard—born: March 27
Garry Gary Beers—bass, vocals—born: June 22
Jon Farriss—drums, vocals—born: August 10
Hometown: Sydney, Australia

INXS (pronounced "in excess") was formed in 1979 and the following year had a top 20 single in Australia, "Just Keep Walking," which gained the sextet a following. By the time INXS hit the United States with "The One Thing," the group had three gold albums and four hit singles back home. They incorporated a more American approach with their fourth album (second in the States) called *The Swing.* Their debut single from that album, "The Original Sin," was produced by Nile Rodgers of Chic and featured back-up vocals by Daryl Hall of Hall & Oates. That song caused some controversy when some people suggested it dealt with sex; the song was actually about racial injustice.

March	1983	1. THE ONE THING	Atco
July	1983	2. DON'T CHANGE	Atco
May	1984	3. ORIGINAL SIN	Atco
July	1984	4. I SEND A MESSAGE	Atco

DONNIE IRIS

Real Name: Don Ierace
Hometown: Beaver Falls, Pennsylvania

Singing has always been a part of Donnie Ierace's life, even at the age of five, when his mother used to accompany him at the piano. His talents brought him to the attention of Paul Whiteman, who invited the young boy to appear on his radio show. Donnie took first prize in the show's talent competition, winning a brand-new refrigerator.

Donnie played in several Pittsburgh-area bands during his adolescence, the most notable being the Jaggerz. (See *THE JAGGERZ, Rock On: The Years of Change.*) "The Rapper," written and sung by a then-renamed Donnie Iris, was a hit in 1970 for the Jaggerz and achieved gold status. Iris later joined Wild Cherry for a while before launching a solo career in 1980.

December	1980	1. AH! LEAH!	MCA/Carousel
October	1981	2. SWEET MERILEE	MCA/Carousel
December	1981	3. LOVE IS LIKE A ROCK	MCA

March	1982	4. MY GIRL	MCA
October	1982	5. TOUGH WORLD	MCA
July	1983	6. DO YOU COMPUTE	MCA
March	1985	7. INJURED IN THE GAME OF LOVE	HME

IRON HORSE

Randy Bachman, leader of Iron Horse, had several hits as the leader of BTO.

See *BACHMAN-TURNER OVERDRIVE (BTO), Rock On: The Years of Change.*

| March | 1979 | SWEET LUI LOUISE | Scotti Bros. |
| April | 1980 | WHAT'S YOUR HURRY DARLIN' | Scotti Bros. |

JANET JACKSON

Born: May 16, 1966
Hometown: Gary, Indiana

Janet began performing at age seven, appearing in Las Vegas with her famous brothers, the Jacksons, doing impressions of Mae West and Sonny & Cher.

At age ten, Janet was signed to play Penny Gordon on television's "Good Times."

December	1982	YOUNG LOVE	A & M
February	1983	COME GIVE YOUR LOVE TO ME	A & M

JOE JACKSON

Born: August 11, 1955
Hometown: Burton-on-Trent, England

Joe Jackson studied violin when he was 11, but writing songs interested the boy more than playing, so he persuaded his parents to buy a piano. He taught himself to play and began formal lessons at age 16. In 1974, Jackson graduated from the Royal Academy of Music and, with Mark Andrews, formed a band called Arms and Legs. That group dissolved, and Jackson saved enough money to record his own album, backed by a trio. *Look Sharp* was released in February 1979 and instantly garnered Jackson cult status in the United States.

After two more albums, Jackson moved to New York City, which he says was more stimulating musically and culturally than any other city. His next album was *Jumpin' Jive,* in which he featured his re-creations of classic jazz "jump" tunes of the forties. His next albums incorporated the Latin salsa sounds he picked up while living in downtown Manhattan.

Jackson was commissioned to do the soundtrack for a film called *Mike's Murder;* although the album was recorded and released, the film ultimately used little more than a minute of Jackson's music.

June	1979	1. IS SHE REALLY GOING OUT WITH HIM	A & M
August	1982	2. STEPPIN' OUT	A & M
January	1983	3. BREAKING US IN TWO	A & M
October	1983	4. MEMPHIS	A & M
April	1984	5. YOU CAN'T GET WHAT YOU WANT	A & M
July	1984	6. HAPPY ENDING	A & M

Joe Jackson

REBBIE JACKSON

Born: May 29, 1950
Hometown: Gary, Indiana

Rebbie, the oldest of the famous Jackson family, got her start in show business in 1974, when her famous brothers were playing the Celebrity Room of the MGM Grand Hotel in Las Vegas and she was asked to join the show. Rebbie travelled with her brothers until 1977, when she went to Hollywood to begin work on a solo career. After working with many artists and as a background singer on many dates, she decided to try a solo album. With her brothers Michael, Tito, and Randy, work began on her debut album for Columbia, called *Centipede*. The title cut, which was produced and written by Michael, became the song that launched her recording career in 1984.

October   1984   CENTIPEDE   Columbia

THE JAGS

Members:
    Nick Watkinson—vocals, guitar
    John Alder—guitar, vocals
    Steve Prudence—bass
    Alex Baird—drums

Formed in 1978, when they met during school, the Jags' only hit, "Back of my Hand," came from their debut LP.

June   1980   BACK OF MY HAND   Island

RICK JAMES

Born: February 1, 1952
Hometown: Buffalo, New York

Running AWOL from the United States Navy, Rick James headed for Toronto, where he met Neil Young. With other musicians, the two formed a band called the Mynah Birds which recorded a never-released album for Motown Records. James launched a successful solo career in 1978,

Rick James

and has been a high-profile superstar ever since. In addition to his own records, he helped launch Teena Marie's career by dueting with her, producing her early records and touring with her. He also formed the Mary Jane Girls, a female vocal quartet for which he wrote and produced an album that spawned three hits on urban contemporary-format radio stations. James also helped Bobby M., the Stone City Band, and Eddie Murphy, and sponsored a clothing line for a Hawaiian artist named Christopher Lee. On his own records he has collaborated with Teena Marie, the Temptations, Chaka Khan, Smokey Robinson, Grandmaster Flash, and even Billy Dee Williams.

Ever outspoken, James has gotten himself embroiled in controversy several times. He called MTV racist for not broadcasting videos of black artists; he accused Prince of stealing his Mary Jane Girls concept when Prince formed Vanity 6; and he openly smokes marijuana on stage, turning it into a scene when a roadie brings out a huge, fake joint.

July	1978	1. YOU AND I	Gordy
November	1978	2. MARY JANE	Gordy
April	1979	3. HIGH ON YOUR LOVE SUITE	Gordy
May	1979	4. BUSTIN' OUT	Gordy
May	1981	5. GIVE IT TO ME BABY	Gordy
August	1981	6. SUPER FREAK	Gordy
May	1982	7. STANDING ON THE TOP (with the Temptations)	Gordy
May	1982	8. DANCE WIT' ME	Gordy
July	1983	9. COLD BLOODED	Gordy
December	1983	10. EBONY EYES (and Smokey Robinson)	Gordy
July	1984	11. 17	Gordy
March	1985	12. CAN'T STOP	Gordy

AL JARREAU

Born: March 12, 1940
Hometown: Milwaukee, Wisconsin

Al Jarreau is the fifth of six children of a minister father and a mother who played piano in church. Al began singing in church before he was old enough to attend school, and later handled whatever part was assigned him in neighborhood street corner vocal groups. By high school, he was singing with local jazz bands.

Al earned degrees in psychology and at one time counseled for a living, but once he moved to northern California's Bay area, music began to claim his time and interest. Before long, he was working three nights a week in area clubs with George Duke's piano trio. In 1968, he quit his counseling job altogether and moved to Los Angeles hoping to be discovered. Jarreau lucked into nightclub engagements, which in turn led to performances on several nationally-televised variety shows. He spent the next few years moving around the country after promising gigs.

Jarreau's big break came in 1974, when he opened a show for Les McCann at the Troubadour in Hollywood. He was noticed and enjoyed

Al Jarreau

by several record company executives, and two weeks later he began recording his debut LP, *We Got By*. Quickly, jazz circles recognized Jarreau as a master vocalist, who sang and scatted. Jarreau won dozens of prestigious awards in short time.

Jarreau made his acting debut in the lead role of *The Nat King Cole Story*.

AL JARREAU

August	1981	1. WE'RE IN THIS LOVE TOGETHER	Warner Bros.
December	1981	2. BREAKIN' AWAY	Warner Bros.
April	1982	3. TEACH ME TONIGHT	Warner Bros.
October	1984	4. AFTER ALL	Warner Bros.

JARREAU

March	1983	MORNIN'	Warner Bros.
June	1983	BOOGIE DOWN	Warner Bros.
September	1983	TROUBLE IN PARADISE	Warner Bros.

GARLAND JEFFREYS

Hometown: Brooklyn, New York

Born and raised in Sheepshead Bay, Brooklyn, Jeffreys played back-up for many sixties performers.

Garland went solo in the seventies and finally made a mark with his 1981 revival of ? and the Mysterians' song, "96 Tears."

March	1981	96 TEARS	Epic

JOAN JETT AND THE BLACKHEARTS

Members:
  Joan Jett—vocals, guitar—born: September 22, 1960
  Ricky Byrd—guitar—born: October 20, 1958
  Gary Ryan—bass—born: July 3, 1964
  Lee Crystal—drums—born: February 3, 1958
Hometown: Los Angeles, California

Joan Jett's family moved 14 times during her youth, and she thinks this may be why she loves touring so much. The one constant in her childhood was a desire to play the guitar. As a grade-schooler in Rockville, Maryland, she was given a $20 Sears electric guitar and amp combination. By the age of 14, she had taught herself to play along with her record collection.

In 1972, Joan's family moved to Los Angeles, where she started hanging out in a club called Rodney's English Disco, which played nothing but early-seventies glitter rock. Joan started writing her first songs and met producer Kim Fowley. Together with Fowley and a drummer named Sandy West, a teenage all-female rock 'n' roll band called The Runaways was formed. The band cut three albums and toured for five years before splitting.

Joan Jett and The Blackhearts. *Left to right:* Gary Ryan, Lee Crystal, Joan Jett, Ricky Byrd.

Jett then recorded a solo album for a Dutch record label, Ariola. Since she couldn't get a record deal in America, she and her new producer, Kenny Laguna, used their personal savings to press records and set up their own system of independent distributors. After their own supply of records sold out, Joan was signed to Broadwalk Records. This first album led to the formation of Joan Jett and the Blackhearts.

Joan Jett and the Blackhearts seem to never stop touring, hitting every continent at least once a year. The group was the first American band to tour East Germany in the 37 years of the country's existence.

February	1982	★ 1. I LOVE ROCK 'N' ROLL	Broadwalk
May	1982	2. CRIMSON AND CLOVER	Boardwalk
July	1982	3. DO YOU WANNA TOUCH ME	Boardwalk
July	1983	4. FAKE FRIENDS	Blackheart/MCA
September	1983	5. EVERYDAY PEOPLE	Blackheart/MCA

TOM JOHNSTON

Hometown: Visalia, California

Founding member of the Doobie Brothers Tom Johnston left the group in 1977 and had a hit with "Savannah Nights" in the same year.
See *THE DOOBIE BROTHERS, Rock On: The Years of Change.*

| November | 1979 | SAVANNAH NIGHTS | Warner Bros. |

FRANCE JOLI

Born: 1963
Hometown: Montreal, Canada

As a youngster France took voice, acting, and dance lessons and listened to her two favorite performers, Barbra Streisand and Stevie Wonder. In 1979, after a few years of training, France's mother Michelle took her daughter to New York and made the rounds of the record companies. This resulted in a recording contract with Prelude Records and the hit single "Come To Me," which made the national top twenty.

In 1983, France signed with Epic Records and released the album *Attitude*.

September	1979	COME TO ME	Prelude

JON AND VANGELIS

Jon Anderson of Yes and Greek keyboard player Vangelis got together for several hits in the early eighties.
See *YES, Rock On: The Years of Change*, and *VANGELIS*

August	1980	I HEAR YOU NOW	Polydor
May	1982	I'LL FIND MY WAY HOME	Polydor

QUINCY JONES

Born: March 14, 1933
Hometown: Chicago, Illinois

By age 14, Quincy Jones was playing trumpet for Billie Holiday and developing composition and arrangement chops with his buddy Ray Charles. Jones and Charles formed a band, but by age 15, Q was ready to hit the road with Lionel Hampton, which he would have done were it not for the intervention of Mrs. Gladys Hampton, who threw him off the bus with an emphatic "Get that child out of here. . . . Let him finish school!"

Q ended up at the Berklee College of Music in Boston on a scholarship, taking ten courses a day and playing strip joints at night to pay for his lodging. His name got around, and he started going to New York on weekends to play on other people's sessions. Q subsequently moved to New York and joined the jazz club circuit. By the sixties, he'd worked arrangements and production for Sammy Davis, Jr., Frank Sinatra, Sarah Vaughan, Andy Williams, Johnny Mathis, Lesley Gore, and many other top names in jazz and pop, as well as creating the soundtracks for many films. In 1974, Jones almost died from neural aneurysms, but was saved with two operations.

Recently, Quincy wound up stealing the Grammy Awards in 1982 with his album *The Dude,* as producer of the *Thriller* album, he helped Michael Jackson dominate the Grammy presentation in 1984.

May	1970	1. KILLER JOE	A & M
March	1972	2. MONEY RUNNER	Reprise
October	1975	3. IS IT LOVE THAT WE'RE MISSIN' (featuring the Brothers Johnson)	A & M
March	1977	4. ROOTS (MEDLEY)	A & M
June	1978	5. STUFF LIKE THAT (with Ashford & Simpson and Chaka Khan)	A & M
April	1981	6. AI NO CORRIDA	A & M
August	1981	7. JUST ONCE (featuring James Ingram)	A & M
December	1981	8. ONE HUNDRED WAYS (featuring James Ingram)	A & M

RICKIE LEE JONES

Born: November 8, 1954
Hometown: Chicago, Illinois

Rickie Lee Jones was born into a show business family. Her grandparents were in vaudeville (he as a one-legged dancer, she as a member of a chorus line), and her father was a songwriter and musician.

Rickie Lee Jones

When she was about 23 years old, Rickie drifted to Los Angeles and started singing and playing piano in small bars in the Venice area, either solo or with a jazz trio. She had only performed five times as a soloist when she was discovered by a talent scout. A self-titled debut album was released in February 1979, and Jones became a sensation. Her albums since then have been sporadic.

April	1979	1. CHUCK E'S IN LOVE	Warner Bros.
July	1979	2. YOUNGBLOOD	Warner Bros.
October	1981	3. A LUCKY GUY	Warner Bros.
September	1984	4. THE REAL END	Warner Bros.

JOURNEY

Members:
 Steve Perry—vocals—born: January 22, 1949—added in 1978
 Neal Schon—guitar—born: February 27, 1954
 Gregg Rolie—keyboards—replaced (1981) by Jonathan Cain—guitar, keyboards—born: February 26, 1950
 Ross Valory—bass—born: February 2, 1949
 Steve Smith—drums—born: August 21, 1954—replaced Aynsley Dunbar in 1982
Hometown: San Francisco, California

In the mid-sixties, a teenage Herbie Herbert managed a band called Frumious Bandersnatch, which included Ross Valory. In 1968, Gregg Rolie, formerly with William Penn and His Pals, helped a then-unknown guitarist named Carlos Santana put together a group that would become the international supergroup, Santana. Bandersnatch broke up, and Herbert scored a position as production manager for Santana. Meanwhile, Valory played for various groups, including the Steve Miller Band.

In 1971, a 15-year-old guitar whiz named Neal Schon joined Santana after declining a similar offer from Eric Clapton. Santana split after its 1972 tour, and Herbert approached Schon with the idea of putting together a band with Valory and a rhythm guitarist named George Tickner. Rolie and drummer Prairie Prince also joined and Journey debuted in San Francisco on New Year's Eve in 1973. Prince left after two shows to join the Tubes, and he was replaced by Aynsley Dunbar, an Englishman who had played in John Mayall's band and led the short-lived Aynsley Dunbar Retalliation. Journey recorded a self-titled debut LP in 1974, after which Tickner left because he disliked touring.

In 1978, after three albums as a mostly instrumental, progressive rock band, the group decided to go for a mainstream sound by adding a vocalist. After several attempts, Herbert discovered Steve Perry via a demo tape. Perry joined the band, and the next album, *Infinity*, was the start of Journey's multi-platinum career. The group remained a supergroup

Journey. *Left to right:* Jonathan Cain, Steve Smith, Ross Valory, Neal Schon, Steve Perry.

even with additional personnel changes through the years. In 1983, a national Gallup poll described Journey as America's "most popular rock band." Journey also became the first group to have two video games modeled after its members' likenesses; one was a home cartridge game, the other an arcade game.

April	1978	1. WHEEL IN THE SKY	Columbia
July	1978	2. ANYTIME	Columbia
August	1978	3. LIGHTS	Columbia
April	1979	4. JUST THE SAME WAY	Columbia
July	1979	5. LOVIN', TOUCHIN', SQUEEZIN'	Columbia
January	1980	6. TOO LATE	Columbia
March	1980	7. ANY WAY YOU WANT IT	Columbia
May	1980	8. WALKS LIKE A LADY	Columbia
August	1980	9. GOOD MORNING GIRL/STAY AWHILE	Columbia
February	1981	10. THE PARTY'S OVER	Columbia
July	1981	11. WHO'S CRYING NOW	Columbia
October	1981	12. DON'T STOP BELIEVIN'	Columbia
January	1982	13. OPEN ARMS	Columbia
May	1982	14. STILL THEY RIDE	Columbia
February	1983	15. SEPARATE WAYS	Columbia
April	1983	16. FAITHFULLY	Columbia
July	1983	17. AFTER THE FALL	Columbia
September	1983	18. SEND HER MY LOVE	Columbia
January	1985	19. ONLY THE YOUNG	Columbia

JUDAS PRIEST

Members:
>Rob Halford—vocals—born: August 25, 1951
>Glenn Tipton—guitar—born: October 25, 1947
>K. K. Downing—guitar—born: October 27, 1951
>Ian Hill—bass—born: January 20, 1952
>Dave Holland—drums—born: April 5, 1948—replaced Les Binks in 1979

Hometown: Birmingham, England

In the early seventies, when K. K. Downing and Ian Hill started Judas Priest, they made a small living playing blues-flavored rock on the Midlands club circuit. In 1974, the group had a debut album, *Rocka Rolla,* made with a small British record company, which led to enough of a commotion to get the group on the bill of the annual heavy metal rock festival, the Reading Festival, in 1975. After one more album, *Sad Wings of Destiny,* on an independent record label in 1976, the group signed a worldwide recording contract and became a supergroup in Great Britain and Japan. In the United States, though heavy metal was not the hippest genre of music in the late seventies and early eighties, Judas Priest toured extensively, developing a growing audience that dismissed the trendiness of new wave for loud, abrasive rock and roll.

The members of Judas Priest wore leather and metal studs in abundance, giving heavy metal a visual image it previously lacked. Lead singer Rob Halford came on stage riding a Harley Davidson motorcycle, and during one song he cracked a whip over the heads of the audience to the

Judas Priest. *Left to right:* K. K. Downing, Rob Halford, Glenn Tipton.

beat of the music. In 1979 Dave Holland replaced Les Binks and Alan Moore. By the early eighties, Judas Priest was playing large arenas to sell-out audiences in the States. As the first group in the "new wave of British heavy metal," as the movement to metal music was called, Judas Priest became one of the most popular concert attractions around.

November   1982   YOU'VE GOT ANOTHER THING COMING   Columbia

JUMP 'N THE SADDLE BAND

Members:
    Peter Quinn—vocals, harmonica
    T. C. Furlong—guitar

Jump 'N The Saddle Band. *From the left:* (*top*) Tom Trinka, Rick Gorley, Vince Dee; (*bottom*) Barney Schwartz, Peter Quinn, T. C. Furlong.

Barney Schwartz—guitar
Tom "Shoes" Trinka—saxophone
Rick Gorley—bass
Vincent Dee—drums
Hometown: Chicago, Illinois

In 1973, Peter and T. C. joined a band called Rio Grande and played the Chicago suburbs performing country and rockabilly tunes. Four years later Barney and Anne Schwartz joined Peter and T. C. and they called themselves Jump 'N' the Saddle and began playing the bar and college circuit. A few years later Tom and Vince were added to the group, and in 1982 Rick joined, replacing Anne Schwartz who departed because she was pregnant.

During the spring of 1983, lead singer Peter Quinn was doing a little dance on stage, skipping backwards (something he got from watching the Three Stooges). Someone asked him what he was doing and he said "the Curly shuffle." Quinn then decided to write a song about this dance and one hour later it was done. They put the song into their live show and audiences went wild. Consequently, they recorded the song and eventually gave copies to local Chicago radio stations. The result was overwhelming approval, record sales, and a recording contract with Atlantic Records.

December   1983   THE CURLY SHUFFLE   Atlantic

K

KAJAGOOGOO

Members:
  Limahl (Chris Hamill)—vocals (left group in 1983)
  Steve Askew—guitar
  Stuart Croxford Neale—keyboards, synthesizer
  Nick Beggs—bass, vocals
  Jez Strode—drums, percussion
Hometown: Leighton Buzzard, England

In 1980, Nick Beggs, Steve Askew, Jez Strode, and Stuart Neale were playing experimental music as Art Nouveau, but called themselves the Handstands when booked into working-class clubs and cabaret stints. One day, Limahl (the name is an anagram of his real name) put a classified ad in a British rock paper saying that he was "22, a good looking, talented vocalist/songwriter with imagination and determination; I need four guys with the same qualifications." In addition to obscene phone calls, Limahl also heard from Beggs and company, who were considering incorporating a lead singer. The two parties exchanged tapes and liked what they heard. Limahl moved up to Leighton Buzzard. They sought a new name that meant nothing, and imagined a baby's first spoken sounds to be "ga-ga-goo-goo." From there, they adopted the name Kajagoogoo.

In 1982, Limahl met Nick Rhodes of Duran Duran in a London club, and before long, Rhodes helped Kajagoogoo get a recording contract. Limahl left the group after its 1983 debut album to pursue a solo career.

| April | 1983 | TOO SHY | EMI-America |
| August | 1983 | HANG ON NOW | EMI-America |

KAYAK

Members:
  Ton Scherpenzeel
  Pim Koopman—drums—replaced by Charles Louis Schouten in 1979
  Bert Veldkamp—bass—replaced by Theo De Jong in 1979
  John Slager—guitar
  Max Werner—mellotron, percussion
Hometown: The Netherlands

Founded in 1973 by Ton Scherpenzeel and Pim Koopman, Kayak has undergone numerous personnel changes. At the present time, their lineup is different from the one listed above that recorded their 1978 hit single.

Today the group consists of Ton Scherpenzeel, Charles Louis Schouten, Theo De Jong, John Slager, and Max Werner.

May	1978	I WANT YOU TO BE MINE	Janus

GREG KIHN BAND

Members:
    Greg Kihn—vocals, guitar
    Greg Douglas—guitar—replaced Dave Carpender and Robbie Dunbar in 1983
    Gary Phillips—keyboards, guitar, vocals—added in 1980
    Steven Wright—bass, vocals
    Larry Lynch—drum, percussion, vocals
Hometown: Berkeley, California

Greg Kihn started out in the small clubs of his native Baltimore. After a summer in Europe playing pass-the-hat engagements, he tried Los Angeles, then arrived in Berkeley in 1975, acoustic guitar in hand. He formed a band with Steve Wright, Larry Lynch, and Robbie Dunbar (who was soon replaced by Dave Carpender) and began holding down a series of Sunday night gigs at the seedy San Pablo Avenue music hall. In 1980 Gary Phillips was added to the band's roster. Year after year, the group remained a cult favorite until their sixth album, *Rockihnroll,* which featured "The Breakup Song (They Don't Write 'Em)," brought them national acclaim. In 1983, Greg Douglas replaced Dave Carpender.

GREG KIHN BAND

May	1981	1. THE BREAKUP SONG (THEY DON'T WRITE 'EM)	Beserkley
May	1982	2. HAPPY MAN	Beserkley
July	1982	3. EVERY LOVE SONG	Beserkley
January	1983	4. JEOPARDY	Beserkley
June	1984	5. LOVE NEVER FAILS	Beserkley

GREG KIHN

February	1985	LUCKY	Capitol

EVELYN "CHAMPAGNE" KING

Born: July 1, 1960
Hometown: Bronx, New York

The tale is that in 1976 Evelyn King was cleaning bathrooms in the Gamble & Huff studios while her mother was vacuuming nearby. Supposedly it was at Gamble & Huff that Evelyn was discovered by T. Life, a writer, producer, and artist at Philadelphia International Records. Life coached her and she recorded a single, "Shame," that became an instant disco hit upon its release in September 1977; it became a pop hit months later.

Evelyn "Champagne" King, just growing out of her teenage years, became a star among the world's teenagers. She continued to have hit

Evelyn "Champagne" King

records, made many TV appearances, and toured the world, playing countries most other acts skip over. Now King has grown into an independent woman; she owns her own home in New Jersey and is no longer accompanied by her parents on the road.

At one point, she was persuaded to drop her childhood nickname "Champagne" (it was actually "Bubbles," but was changed for the sake of show business) in order to present herself as a grown woman, but when the public failed to recognize Evelyn King as the same person with a track record of hits, she brought back the "Champagne."

EVELYN "CHAMPAGNE" KING

June	1978	1. SHAME	RCA
January	1979	2. I DON'T KNOW IF IT'S RIGHT	RCA
May	1979	3. MUSIC BOX	RCA
January	1984	4. ACTION	RCA

EVELYN KING

July	1981	I'M IN LOVE	RCA
August	1982	LOVE COME DOWN	RCA
January	1983	BETCHA SHE DON'T LOVE YOU	RCA

THE KINGBEES

Members:
Jamie James—vocals, guitar
Rex Roberts—drums

Michael Rummans—guitar
Hometown: Toronto, Canada

This Canadian trio had only one hit, "My Mistake," which surfaced in 1980.

The group's name came from a label on a set of drums leader Jamie James saw when he was nine years old.

June   1980   MY MISTAKE   RSO

THE KINGS

Members:
David Diamond—vocals, bass
Zero—guitar, vocals

The Kings. *Left to right:* David Diamond, Zero, Max Styles, Sonny Keyes.

Sonny Keyes—keyboards, vocals
Max Styles—drums
Hometown: Toronto, Canada

This rock 'n' roll quartet blasted their way onto the 1980 charts with their "beat rock" hit, "Switchin' to Glide," which proved to be their only hit.

August	1980	SWITCHIN' TO GLIDE	Elektra

THE KNACK

Members:
Doug Fieger—vocals, guitar—born: August 20
Berton Averre—guitar—born: December 13
Prescott Niles—bass—born: May 2
Bruce Gary—drums—born: April 7
Hometown: Los Angeles, California

The Knack formed in May 1978, and from its Hollywood homefront, moved into the southern California club circuit. By February of the following year, the Knack was Los Angeles' hottest new act. The band secured a record deal, then recorded and mixed their debut album, *Get The Knack*, in 11 days, with almost all the songs cut live in one take. Seven weeks after its release, the album hit the number one spot, selling over a million copies. (*Get The Knack* was certified gold 13 days after its release.) The group's debut single, "My Sharona," sold over one million units and became the fastest release-to-gold debut single by a rock band since the Beatles' "I Want To Hold Your Hand" 15 years earlier. (The Beatles comparisons continued: The Knack's outfits and stage sets often resembled those of the Fab Four.)

The Knack's popularity was quick and vast, but not long lasting. They never duplicated the impact of their initial success, and in 1982 the group broke up.

June	1979	★ 1. MY SHARONA	Capitol
September	1979	2. GOOD GIRLS DON'T	Capitol
February	1980	3. BABY TALKS DIRTY	Capitol
April	1980	4. CAN'T PUT A PRICE ON LOVE	Capitol
October	1981	5. PAY THE DEVIL	Capitol

FRED KNOBLOCK

Hometown: Jackson, Mississippi

Fred Knoblock (pronounced No-block) played for six years in a group called Let's Eat which got their name from the comics. He then went solo and reached the top 20 with "Why Not Me" in 1980.

Later in the same year Knoblock had a hit with Susan Anton on the duet, "Killin' Time."

| June | 1980 | WHY NOT ME | Scotti Bros. |
| November | 1980 | KILLIN' TIME (with Susan Anton) | Scotti Bros. |

THE KORGIS

Members:
James Warren
Andy Davis

James Warren and Andy Davis were in a British pop group called Stackridge before they split to form the Korgis in 1979.

Their only hit, "Everybody's Got To Learn Sometime," was recorded at a friend's house with a back-up group called the Short Wave Band.

| October | 1980 | EVERYBODY'S GOT TO LEARN SOMETIME | Asylum |

The Korgis

BILL LaBOUNTY

Hometown: Los Angeles, California

Bill LaBounty formed a group called Fat Chance while attending Boise College in Idaho during the early seventies. In 1978, he released his second solo LP, *This Love Won't Last Forever*, which included his only charted single record. This same tune proved to be highly successful for the Nashville singer Michael Johnson, who climbed into the top 20 with his version.

| May | 1978 | THIS NIGHT WON'T LAST FOREVER | Warner Bros. |

CHERYL LADD

Real Name: Cheryl Stoppelmoor
Born: July 2, 1951
Hometown: Huron, South Dakota

Cheryl Ladd played Kris Monroe in TV's *Charlie's Angels*. She had a hit with a song called "Think It Over" in 1978.

| July | 1978 | THINK IT OVER | Capitol |

GREG LAKE

Born: November 10, 1948
Hometown: Bournemouth, England

A member of King Crimson and Emerson, Lake & Palmer, Greg Lake had a chart entry with "Let Me Love You Once" in 1981.
See *EMERSON, LAKE & PALMER, Rock On: The Years of Change.*

December	1975	I BELIEVE IN FATHER CHRISTMAS	Atlantic
September	1977	C'EST LA VIE	Atlantic
November	1981	LET ME LOVE YOU ONCE	Chrysalis

ROBIN LANE & THE CHARTBUSTERS

Members:
    Robin Lane—vocals, guitar
    Leroy Radcliff—vocals, guitar
    Asa Brebner—vocals, guitar

Robin Lane & The Chartbusters

    Scott Baerenwald—vocals, bass
    Tim Jackson—drums
Hometown: Boston, Massachusetts

Led by California-born Robin Lane, the Chartbusters evolved out of
Boston in the late seventies and had one big hit in the summer of 1980,
"When Things Go Wrong."

July   1980   WHEN THINGS GO WRONG   Warner Bros.

LARSEN/FEITEN BAND

Members:
    Neil Larsen—keyboards—Siesta Key, Florida
    Buzzy Feiten—guitar—Centerport, Long Island, New York

Both together and separately, Neil Larsen and Buzzy Feiten have worked
as musicians with Bob Dylan, Bonnie Bramlett, the Rascals, George
Harrison, Dan Fogelberg, and Rickie Lee Jones.
    In 1980 they had a top 40 hit, "Who'll Be The Fool Tonite."

August   1980   WHO'LL BE THE FOOL TONITE   Warner Bros.

Larsen/Feiten Band.
Buzzy Feiten (*left*),
Neil Larsen.

NICOLETTE LARSON

Born: July 17, 1952
Hometown: Kansas City, Missouri

Nicolette Larson was born in Helena, Montana, but her dad's job caused the family to move around until they settled in Kansas City. Nicolette says that like most kids then, she took piano lessons and listened to the Beatles. In 1974, she moved to San Francisco and started working in music as a production secretary for the Golden State Country/Bluegrass Festival. A year later, she began singing in bars and clubs with David

Nicolette Larson

Nichtern and the Nocturnes, and then moved to Los Angeles, where she was a backup singer for Hoyt Axton. After leaving Axton, she sang in Commander Cody's band and began getting session work.

Before long, Nicolette became friendly with Emmylou Harris, Linda Ronstadt, and Neil Young, and sang on some of their recordings. This led to her own album, *Nicolette,* released in 1978, which featured her solo rendition of "Lotta Love," a popular Neil Young song the two had dueted on for his *Comes a Time* album.

Nicolette continues to appear on albums by other artists, including Ronstadt, Christopher Cross, the Doobie Brothers, and the Dirt Band. She appeared with the Doobie Brothers at the famous No Nukes benefit concert (and is in the subsequent film of the concert). Several of her tunes were featured in the film *Personals,* and she continues to record her own albums as well. Nicolette says her mother wanted to be a singer, so she feels a sense of accomplishment both for herself and for her mom.

November	1978	1. LOTTA LOVE	Warner Bros.
March	1979	2. RHUMBA GIRL	Warner Bros.
January	1980	3. LET ME GO, LOVE (with Michael McDonald)	Warner Bros.
August	1982	4. I ONLY WANT TO BE WITH YOU	Warner Bros.

STACY LATTISAW

Born: November 25, 1966
Hometown: Washington, D. C.

When Stacy Lattisaw was six years old, she began joining her mother in vocal duets around the kitchen sink. Her mother, Saundra Lattisaw, was no stranger to show business—in high school, she sang in a group that featured Marvin Gaye on piano.

At the age of 11, Stacy herself decided that she was "good enough to turn pro." Starting with local talent and fashion shows, she worked her way up to an appearance on a bill with Ramsey Lewis before 30,000 people in Fort Dupont Park. There she sang five songs and caused a sensation. A year later, she recorded her first LP, *Young And In Love,* and since then she's become the darling of Washington, D. C. Shortly after the release of her debut album in 1979, Stacy was feted by the Congressional Black Caucus at an evening reception on Capitol Hill. Later, she was invited to the White House, where she struck an immediate friendship with Amy Carter. In January 1981, Stacy joined Washington's Mayor Marion Barry, Stevie Wonder, and other prominent national figures at the head of the Martin Luther King Day march to the Washington Monument. Five months later, Stacy became the youngest person ever to be honored by the National Council for Negro Women, which presented her with the Mary McCleod Bethune Award. Mayor Barry also proclaimed a "Stacy Lattisaw Week," and Atlanta's Mayor Maynard Jackson named her an Honorary Citizen in 1981.

Stacy Lattisaw

Whenever she's in D. C. during football season, Stacy sings the national anthem at home games of the Washington Redskins.

Alongside her solo career, Stacy also records duets with her teenage playmate Johnny Gill.

August	1980	1. LET ME BE YOUR ANGEL	Cotillion
June	1981	2. LOVE ON A TWO WAY STREET	Cotillion
October	1982	3. ATTACK OF THE NAME GAME	Cotillion
August	1983	4. MIRACLES	Cotillion
March	1984	5. PERFECT COMBINATION (with Johnny Gill)	Cotillion

CYNDI LAUPER

Born: June 20, 1953
Hometown: Queens, New York

Cyndi Lauper says she was "almost born in a taxicab on the way to Boulevard Hospital in Queens." Her parents were divorced when she was five, and she was raised by her mother, who strongly encouraged individual creativity. Cyndi recalls her earliest performances as songs she sang for quarters to old ladies in her Ozone Park neighborhood. Cyndi also painted and wrote poetry as she grew up, but with a good memory for lyrics and melodies, singing became her passion. She took up guitar at age 12 and began writing songs with her sister, playing and writing in a folk style until her first rock 'n' roll band in college.

Lauper spent the mid-seventies paying her dues as a vocalist with various bands in and around New York. In 1977, she met John Turi, who played saxophone and keyboards, and left the cover-band circuit for good.

Over the next year, the two collaborated on original material and put together a band called Blue Angel, which quickly became a favorite on the New York club circuit. The group released one album in 1980 and broke up a year or so later. With the release of her debut solo album, *She's So Unusual,* in 1983, Lauper became an instant media star. Her soaring vocals, unusual hair and party dress, petite frame, and charming, dizzy personality even got her as far as television appearances on wrestling broadcasts and Johnny Carson's *Tonight* show. "Girls Just Want To Have Fun" and *She's So Unusual* each sold over a million units and "Time After Time" went to number one.

December	1983	1. GIRLS JUST WANT TO HAVE FUN	Portrait
April	1984	★ 2. TIME AFTER TIME	Portrait
July	1984	3. SHE BOP	Portrait
October	1984	4. ALL THROUGH THE NIGHT	Portrait
December	1984	5. MONEY CHANGES EVERYTHING	Portrait

ELOISE LAWS

Born: 1963
Hometown: Houston, Texas

Eloise Laws is a native of Houston, Texas, and attended Texas Southern University before going to New York to audition at the Improvisation, a showcase for new talent. Eloise worked the Playboy Club circuit, and

Cyndi Lauper

Ronnie Laws

after doing numerous talk shows, moved to Los Angeles. She is the sister of two well-known jazz artists, Hubert and Ronnie Laws.

January	1978	1,000 LAUGHS	ABC
March	1978	NUMBER ONE	ABC

RONNIE LAWS

Hometown: Houston, Texas

Ronnie Laws was born into a musical family that includes his brother Hubert, the world-renowned jazz and classical flautist; his sister Eloise, an actress-singer; and his mother Miolla, a gospel pianist.

Ronnie got his professional start leading the horn section behind Earth, Wind & Fire. In September 1981, he premiered on the charts with "Stay Awake."

September	1981	STAY AWAKE	Liberty

JOHNNY LEE

Hometown: Texas City, Texas

Johnny Lee says he was born in Texas City and raised on a dairy farm in Alta Loma in east Texas, listening to early rock 'n' roll while milking cows. In high school, he fronted Johnny Lee and the Road Runners. After winning several talent contests, including the state finals at a Future Farmers of America competition, the group became a hot item at teen hops. Meanwhile, Lee almost flunked science because he was busy composing songs like "My Little Angel."

Following high school, Lee spent four years in the United States Navy, which included a tour in Vietnam aboard a guided missile cruiser. After his discharge, he "bummed around California for a while," finally going back to Texas to play music again. One day, he met Mickey Gilley and said to him, "Mickey, do you remember me? I was on the Larry Kane TV show in Galveston with you." It was an outright lie. Johnny told him a few more lies before he asked if he could sit in with him. Gilley agreed, and the audience liked it. Lee sat in a few more times before Gilley offered him a job playing trumpet and singing backup. They became good friends and a successful team. Lee began recording his own singles in 1973, and had moderate success until he hit with "Lookin For Love" on the *Urban Cowboy* soundtrack. After some 10 years of playing Gilley's huge club in Pasadena, Texas, Lee opened up his own club down the road a piece. The club is called Johnny Lee's. Lee met actress Charlene Tilton on the set of *Urban Cowboy*. They married on Valentine's Day 1982 and had a daughter, Cherish.

| July | 1980 | LOOKIN' FOR LOVE | Asylum |
| October | 1981 | BET YOUR HEART ON ME | Full Moon/Asylum |

LARRY LEE

Born: 1947

Larry Lee gained his biggest fame as a member of the Ozark Mountain Daredevils, for whom he penned their biggest hit, "Jackie Blue."

He had a minor hit as a solo performer in 1982.

| June | 1982 | DON'T TALK | Columbia |

JULIAN LENNON

Real Name: John Charles Julian Lennon
Born: April 8, 1963
Hometown: Liverpool, England

John and Cynthia Lennon named their son Julian because that was the nearest they could get to Julia, John's mother's name. When Julian was a year old his family moved to London, exposing the young Lennon to "Beatlemania." In November 1968, John and Cynthia were divorced and Julian moved with his mother to Cheshire. A few years later, while at

Julian Lennon

Hoylake School, he became interested in the guitar and rock 'n' roll, playing a Les Paul model that his father gave him for Christmas in 1974.

After his father died in 1980, Julian became the center of a lot of attention in London, and he hid from people by getting lost in music, playing the piano and searching for his musical identity.

In 1983, Atlantic Records chairman Ahmet Ertegun was introduced to Julian and, recognizing his talent, signed him to his label. Julian, along with guitarist Justin Clayton and Jamaican-born Carlton Morales, went to the remote Manoir de Valotte, a French chateau, where he worked for several months on new songs. Shortly thereafter, Billy Joel's producer, Phil Ramone, was brought in as producer and they went to work recording the album "Valotte." The album was recorded in New York and at the Muscle Shoals Sound Studios in Alabama. The album's title song was released in late 1984, and a new career was launched.

October	1984	VALOTTE	Atlantic
January	1985	TOO LATE FOR GOODBYES	Atlantic
May	1985	SAY YOU'RE WRONG	Atlantic

LE ROUX

Members:

    Jeff Pollard—vocals, guitar
    Leon Medica—bass, vocals
    Rod Roddy—piano, organ, synthesizer, vocals
    David Peters—drums, percussion
    Bobby Campo—horns, flute, congas, percussion, vocals
    Tony Haseldon—guitar, vocals

This six-member band from the Bayou country in Louisiana, originally called Louisiana's Le Roux, provided four ear-catching hits on the charts between 1978 and 1983.

LOUSIANA'S LE ROUX

June	1978	NEW ORLEANS LADIES	Capitol

LE ROUX

February	1982	NOBODY SAID IT WAS EASY	RCA
May	1982	THE LAST SAFE PLACE ON EARTH	RCA
March	1983	CARRIE'S GONE	RCA

HUEY LEWIS AND THE NEWS

Members:

    Huey Lewis (Hugh Anthony Cregg III)—vocals—born: July 5, 1950
    Chris Hayes—guitar—born: November 24, 1957
    Johnny Colla—saxophone—born: July 2, 1952

Huey Lewis and the News

Sean Hopper—keyboards—born: March 31, 1953
Mario Cipollina—bass—born: November 10, 1954
Billy Gibson—drums—born: November 13, 1951
Hometown: San Francisco, California

The Huey Lewis and the News story pretty much picks up where the story of Clover, Huey's previous band, leaves off. Clover was a San Francisco-based bar band that released albums but remained relatively unknown. After the group broke up, Huey started a Monday night jam series at a Marin County club called Uncle Charlie's. When he was offered free time at a local recording studio called Different Fur, Huey went in with the Monday night jammers and cut a disco version of the theme from *Exodus*. Eventually, the group recorded enough songs for a demo tape, which led Huey to management and a recording contract. He then picked musicians out of his jam session regulars and formed Huey Lewis and the News.

February	1982	1. DO YOU BELIEVE IN LOVE	Chrysalis
May	1982	2. HOPE YOU LOVE ME LIKE YOU SAY YOU DO	Chrysalis
August	1982	3. WORKIN' FOR A LIVIN'	Chrysalis
September	1983	4. HEART AND SOUL	Chrysalis
January	1984	5. I WANT A NEW DRUG	Chrysalis
April	1984	6. THE HEART OF ROCK 'N' ROLL	Chrysalis
July	1984	7. IF THIS IS IT	Chrysalis
October	1984	8. WALKING ON A THIN LINE	Chrysalis

LIPPS, INC.

Members:
   Steven Greenberg—drums, keyboards, guitar
   Cynthia Johnson—vocals—replaced (1983) by Melanie Rosales and Margaret
   Cox
Hometown: Minneapolis/St. Paul, Minnesota

Lipps, Inc. is the concept of Steven Greenberg, who writes, arranges, produces and plays most of the instruments.

Steven was a professional rock 'n' roll drummer by age 15, and at age 20, wrote and produced his first record. Hoping to make it big in the music business, he went to Los Angeles, where his high hopes were deflated. He returned home to the Twin Cities area, and for the next six years, was half of a duo called Atlas and Greenberg. He became involved in several other music-industry projects before recording another tune, "Rock It," on which he played all the instruments except bass. He pressed 500 copies and promoted the song all over Minneapolis until it got considerable radio airplay.

In June of 1979, Greenberg began auditioning singers for his Lipps, Inc. project, and Cynthia Johnson won the audition. Cynthia had picked

Cynthia Johnson

up the saxophone at age eight, much to her mother's disapproval. Ten years later, she performed at her high school graduation, then went on to play sax and sing background vocals in local bands and church choral groups. One of these bands, Flyte Tyme, later came under the wing of Prince and became the Time.

Lipps, Inc.'s debut album, *Mouth To Mouth*, was released in 1980, and the first single, "Funkytown," hit number one. Greenberg's "Rock It" was rerecorded and released as the follow-up single, but Lipps, Inc. has yet to repeat the kind of success achieved with "Funkytown."

Cynthia left in 1982 to care for her newborn daughter.

| March | 1980 | ★ FUNKYTOWN | Casablanca |
| August | 1980 | ROCK IT | Casablanca |

LITTLE STEVEN & THE DISCIPLES OF SOUL

Born: November 22, 1950
Hometown: Asbury Park, New Jersey

Little Steven is Steve Van Zandt, formerly known as Miami Steve, an original member of the Asbury Park, New Jersey, collective that produced Bruce Springsteen & the E Street Band, Southside Johnny & the Asbury Jukes, Clarence Clemons & the Red Bank Rockers, and the comeback of Gary U. S. Bonds. Van Zandt wrote, produced, or played guitar for all those acts while gaining fame as Bruce Springsteen's guitarist. In 1982, while still a member of the E Street Band, Steve recorded an album called

Little Steven

Men Without Women with a band he called Little Steven & the Disciples of Soul, and by the time of his *Voice of America* album a year later, he had left Springsteen's band to go on strictly as a solo artist named Little Steven. A feature film was made from the concept of *Men Without Women*, featuring concert footage of Little Steven, but at presstime, the film is not yet scheduled for national release. In late 1984, he visited South Africa, researching material for a new album that will deal with the plight of the Blacks there.

December   1982   FOREVER   EMI-America

IAN LLOYD

Real Name: Ian Buonconciglio
Born: 1947
Hometown: Seattle, Washington

Lead singer of Stories, Ian Lloyd had a solo hit in 1979. In 1984 became the leader of the group Fast Forward.
See *STORIES, Rock On: The Years of Change.*

October   1979   SLIP AWAY   Scotti Bros.

LOVE AND KISSES

Members:
    Don Daniels—lead vocals
    Elaine Hill—lead vocals
    Dianne Brooks—vocal harmony
    Jean Graham—vocal harmony
Hometown: Los Angeles, California

Love and Kisses was signed by Casablanca Records shortly after they formed in 1977. They released two albums for the label: *Love and Kisses* and *How Much, How Much I Love You,* which were both moderately successful. However, it was the title cut from the hit movie *Thank God It's Friday* that landed the trio their only chart entry.

May	1978	THANK GOD IT'S FRIDAY	Casablanca

LOVERBOY

Members:
    Mike Reno—vocals—born: January 8, 1955
    Paul Dean—guitar, vocals—born: February 19, 1946
    Doug Johnson—keyboards—born: December 19, 1957
    Scott Smith—bass—born: February 13, 1955
    Matt Frenette—drums—born: March 7, 1954
Hometown: Vancouver, British Columbia

Loverboy. *Left to right:* Matt Frenette, Scott Smith, Mike Reno, Doug Johnson, Paul Dean.

Not long after Paul Dean set out to form his dream band, he was put in touch with Mike Reno (formerly of Moxy) and Doug Johnson. Paul had played with Matt Frenette in another band, and was able to recruit him also. Scott Smith joined while the group was recording its self-titled debut album.

Originally, the band was going to be called the Paul Dean Band, but Paul got zero reaction when he tried that name out on his girlfriend's 17-year-old brother. Paul leafed through glamour magazines in search of another name. From "covergirl" came "coverboy," which led to "Loverboy." That was 1978. By late 1980, the group's music was being played on rock radio stations across the United States and Canada. Within two years, their concert tours included headlining dates in major sports arenas. One coup was a performance on daytime TV's "Guiding Light" soap.

January	1981	1. TURN ME LOOSE	Columbia
June	1981	2. THE KID IS HOT TONITE	Columbia
November	1981	3. WORKING FOR THE WEEKEND	Columbia
April	1982	4. WHEN IT'S OVER	Columbia
June	1983	5. HOT GIRLS IN LOVE	Columbia
September	1983	6. QUEEN OF THE BROKEN HEARTS	Columbia

NICK LOWE

Born: March 25, 1949
Hometown: Suffolk, England

Nick Lowe's musical career started in 1965. He has worked with such influential British rockers as Brinsley Schwarz, Dave Edmunds & Rockpile,

Nick Lowe

Cheryl Lynn

Dr. Feelgood, the Damned, Elvis Costello, Graham Parker, the Rumour, and the Pretenders. Lowe can write well in almost any rock style.

Lowe's debut solo album, *Pure Pop For Now People*, was released in 1978. It was one of the highest-acclaimed albums of the year, as was his second album, *Labour Of Lust*, in 1979, on which his hit, "Cruel To Be Kind," appears.

July	1979	CRUEL TO BE KIND	Columbia

CARRIE LUCAS

Hometown: Los Angeles, California

Performing as a back-up singer with the Whispers and having recorded with D. J. Rogers, Carrie Lucas had her first solo hit in 1979 with "Dance With You." Her cool, sensuous voice is reminiscent of that of Sylvia or Donna Summer. Lucas was at one time a "Soul Train" act.

April	1977	I GOTTA KEEP DANCIN'	Soul Train
May	1979	DANCE WITH YOU	Solar

CHERYL LYNN

Born: 1956
Hometown: Culver City, California

Cheryl's career began with an appearance on Chuck Barris's "Gong Show," on which she finished in a tie with a female juggler. The next morning, record contract offers started coming her way. Lynn's first LP, *Got To Be Real,* has sold over 1.5 million copies.

December	1978	1. GOT TO BE REAL	Columbia
April	1979	2. STAR LOVE	Columbia
August	1981	3. SHAKE IT UP TONITE	Columbia
February	1984	4. ENCORE	Columbia

JEFF LYNNE

Born: December 30, 1947
Hometown: Birmingham, England

Jeff, the leader of the Electric Light Orchestra, decided to do a solo project in 1984, resulting in a hit single.
See *THE ELECTRIC LIGHT ORCHESTRA, Rock On: The Years of Change.*

| August | 1984 | VIDEO | Virgin/Epic |

M

Real Name: Robin Scott
Hometown: London, England

In the late sixties Robin began singing folk songs in local clubs in order to earn enough money to go to art school. By 1971, he realized he loved music more than painting, especially when he won £500 in a songwriting contest with the tune "Mr. Pop Star."

M

In 1975, Scott joined the famous French artist Johnny Halliday and got more involved with songwriting. A few years later he managed a band called Roogalator and then started up Do It Records, the label that would eventually discover Adam Ant.

In 1978, Robin moved back to Paris and began producing many artists. It was at this time, using the name M, that he recorded a big European hit called "Modern Man," followed by the number one national hit "Pop Muzik." Even though the song was an international hit, M never performed it live.

August   1979   ★ POP MUZIK   Sire

MADNESS

Members:
    Graham Suggs McPherson—vocals
    Carl Smyth—vocals, trumpet (replaced Chas Smash in 1982–3)

Madness

Mike Barson—keyboards
Mark Bedford—bass
Chris J. Foreman—guitar
Lee "Kix" Thompson—saxophone
Dan M. "Woody" Woodgate—drums
Hometown: London, England

Mike Barson, Chris Foreman, and Lee Thompson belonged to the same
Camden Town youth club in 1977, and with some friends, started a band
called the North London Invaders, playing cover versions of hit tunes.
Suggs joined the Invaders later, and his love for Jamaican "ska" music
changed the direction of the band. By September 1978, after several
personnel changes and local club dates, the group became Morris and the
Minors for a gig at the Music Machine.

Eventually, a friend of Mike Barson's older brother agreed to
produce a demo tape for the band. The tape was then sent off to the
Specials, another British-based, ska-oriented band that was likewise getting
much attention. The Specials had their own record label, 2-Tone, and,
impressed with the tape, offered to release a single by the group. Morris
and the Minors changed their name to Madness, named after a song by
an original ska performer, Prince Buster, and a debut single was released
in August 1979. Madness grew increasingly popular and secured its own
album deal elsewhere. In short time, they had 12 consecutive top 10
singles and several hit albums in Great Britain. Ironically, it wasn't until
the group dropped ska in favor of pop that Madness became popular in
America.

Madness's first feature film, *Take It Or Leave It*, documented the
group's career from 1976 to 1979, and featured the bandmembers starring
alongside professional actors. The film was never shown commercially in
the United States.

May	1983	OUR HOUSE	Geffen
August	1983	IT MUST BE LOVE	Geffen
March	1984	THE SUN AND THE RAIN	Geffen

MADONNA

Real Name: Madonna Louise Ciccone
Born: August 16, 1960
Hometown: Bay City, Michigan

Trained as a dancer from pre–high-school days, Madonna enrolled at the
University of Michigan to further her terpsichorean pursuits, studying
ballet, modern, and jazz dancing, and performing with the college's famed
dance company. In the late seventies, she moved to New York and

Madonna

performed for two years with both the Pearl Lange and Alvin Ailey dance troupes.

Madonna tried acting and moved to Paris to take singing lessons and become part of disco artist Patrick Hernandez's touring entourage. She grew frustrated, however, and moved back to New York, where she taught herself to play guitar, keyboards, and drums. She joined a series of club circuit bands, but again grew restless. Finally, she set out to record her original pop/soul songs. A number of her songs became instant dance club hits, eventually crossing over to pop radio.

October	1983	1. HOLIDAY	Sire
March	1984	2. BORDERLINE	Sire
August	1984	3. LUCKY STAR	Sire
November	1984	★ 4. LIKE A VIRGIN	Sire
February	1985	5. MATERIAL GIRL	Sire
March	1985	★ 6. CRAZY FOR YOU	Geffen
May	1985	7. ANGEL	Sire

BARBARA MANDRELL

Born: December 25, 1948
Hometown: Oceanside, California

Thanks to her talented mother, Barbara Ann Mandrell learned to play the accordion even before she learned how to read. Barbara was still a youngster when her father, who sang and played guitar, bought a music store in Oceanside, California, and moved the family there. At age 11,

Barbara made her television debut as a regular on a live local show called "Town Hall Party," and at age 12, she appeared on ABC's "Five Star Jubilee." By the time Barbara reached her teens, she had learned to play steel guitar, saxophone, banjo, and bass guitar. Her father eventually formed a family musical group, the Mandrells, with Barbara, her mother Mary, himself, and two young men on guitar and drums.

In 1967, Barbara married that drummer, Ken Dudney, and temporarily gave up her musical aspirations to become a serviceman's wife. Ken was overseas in the Navy when Barbara and her family moved to Nashville. She went to see the Grand Ole Opry with her dad, and was immediately reinspired to work as an entertainer herself. With Irby as her manager, she began performing in Nashville and landed a recording contract. She has since won dozens of music industry awards. After many television appearances, she became the host of her own successful series, "Barbara Mandrell and the Mandrell Sisters," on NBC-TV.

Barbara lives in Gallatin, Tennessee, with Ken and their two children, Matthew (born May 8, 1970) and Jamie (born February 23, 1976). They also maintain a condominium in Aspen, Colorado, and a lakeside retreat in Dedeville, Alabama. She has business interests in real estate, cattle, and Barbara Mandrell One-Hour Photo Centers. On September 11, 1984, Barbara was involved in a near fatal car accident, which she feels has changed her life dramatically.

March	1978	WOMAN TO WOMAN	ABC/Dot
March	1979	IF LOVING YOU IS WRONG	ABC
October	1979	FOOLED BY A FEELING	MCA

Barbara Mandrell

CHUCK MANGIONE

Real Name: Charles Frank Mangione
Born: November 29, 1940
Hometown: Rochester, New York

Chuck Mangione took piano lessons for two years before turning to trumpet at age 10. He grew up with jazz musicians coming by the house to dine and play. Throughout high school, Chuck continued to study trumpet, flugelhorn, and music theory at the Preparatory Department of the Eastman School of Music. With his brother, pianist Gap Mangione, Chuck formed a quintet called the Jazz Brothers in 1958; the group stayed together for six years and recorded three albums. In 1962, Chuck recorded his first solo album, *Recuerdo*, for Jazzland Records.

In 1965, Chuck moved to New York City, where he played with many established and up-and-coming jazz musicians. Intermittently, Mangione taught music at schools in Rochester. Chuck's first big event was in 1969, when he personally hired fifty musicians and presented a concert called "Kaleidoscope" in order to hear some music he had written for an orchestra. On the basis of this concert, Chuck was invited to be a guest conductor of the Rochester Philharmonic Orchestra in a concert of Mangione music; the concert, called "Friends And Love," sold out the Eastman Theater and was videotaped by the local PBS television station for national broadcast. The soundtrack of that concert led to a major recording contract and his first Grammy Award nomination. Since then, Mangione has won many prestigious awards for musical excellence and has been featured on many television shows. His subsequent albums have sometimes featured orchestras and sometimes featured only a small group of musicians.

Chuck composed and performed the theme song ("The Cannonball Run Theme") for the Burt Reynolds movie *Cannonball Run*.

July	1971	1. HILL WHERE THE LORD HIDES	Mercury
July	1975	2. CHASE THE CLOUDS AWAY	A & M
June	1977	3. LAND OF MAKE BELIEVE	Mercury
February	1978	4. FEELS SO GOOD	A & M
January	1980	5. GIVE IT ALL YOU GOT	A & M

TEENA MARIE

Real Name: Mary Christine Brockert
Born: 1957
Hometown: Venice, California

Teena, born in Santa Monica and raised in nearby Venice, grew up listening to all kinds of music, from the Beatles and the Rolling Stones to Sarah Vaughan and Marvin Gaye. By the time she was 13 she formed her first group, with her brother, and began doing the L. A. club circuit performing soul music. After a few years of performing she enrolled in college, but still kept singing. It was during her freshman year that she met a producer from Motown records who eventually signed her to the label.

In 1979, Teena debuted her first album for Motown, called *Wild and Peaceful*. This resulted in the r&b hit "I'm A Sucker For Your Love." After that album, Rick James suggested she begin producing her own albums, which she has done since that time.

Teena Marie

In 1983, Teena signed with Epic Records and released her first album for them, called *Robbery*.

November	1980	1. I NEED YOUR LOVIN'	Gordy
July	1981	2. SQUARE BIZ	Gordy
December	1984	3. LOVER GIRL	Epic
May	1985	4. JAMMIN'	Epic

MOON MARTIN

Originally from the American Southwest, Moon Martin became a phenomenon in Europe before he ever had hits in the United States.

In 1979, he made two chart appearances with "Rolene" and "No Chance."

August	1979	ROLENE	Capitol
November	1979	NO CHANCE	Capitol

STEVE MARTIN

Born: August 1946
Hometown: Orange County, California

In addition to being one of the hottest comedians in the business today, Steve Martin has made guest appearances on "The Tonight Show"; has hosted "The Tonight Show" and "Saturday Night Live" on numerous occasions; and has appeared in motion pictures. In 1969 Martin won an Emmy for his work as one of ten writers on "The Smothers Brothers Comedy Hour." Two years later he performed in concert as the opening

Steve Martin

Mass Production. *Left to right:* Gregory McCoy, Ricard Williams, Kevin Douglas, Joe Redding, Lecoy Bryant, Tyrone Williams, Agnes Kelly, Larry Marshall, Otis Drumgole, Sam Williams.

act for the Nitty Gritty Dirt Band. It came as no surprise to many when Martin became a recording artist.

Today Martin is very involved in making films, like *The Jerk, Pennies from Heaven,* and *All of Me.*

December	1977	GRANDMOTHER'S SONG	Warner Bros.
May	1978	KING TUT	Warner Bros.
November	1979	CRUEL SHOES	Warner Bros.

CAROLYNE MAS

Born: 1956
Hometown: Bronxville, New York

Carolyne took opera lessons at age 11 and was accepted at Julliard at age 18, but opted to attend a folk music festival in Pennsylvania instead.

She had a minor hit in 1979 called "Stillsane."

September	1979	STILLSANE	Mercury

MASS PRODUCTION

Members:
Tyrone Williams—keyboards
Ricardo Williams—vocals, drums
Lecoy Bryant—guitar

Agnes "Tiny" Kelly—vocals
Larry Marshall—vocals
Emmanuel Redding—percussion
Kevin Douglass—bass
Gregary McCoy—sax—died: September 24, 1984
James Drumgole—brass
Joe Redding
Sam Williams
Hometown: Norfolk, Virginia

This army of r&b/funk players came together at Norfolk State College in Virginia.

Mass Production had a mild hit, "Welcome to Our World," in 1977, and their biggest hit, "Firecracker," in the summer of 1979.

| February | 1977 | WELCOME TO OUR WORLD | Cotillion |
| August | 1979 | FIRECRACKER | Cotillion |

IAN MATTHEWS

Real Name: Ian McDonald
Born: 1946
Hometown: Lincolnshire, England

Ian Matthews's first professional band, in 1966, was called the Pyramid. From there, he went on to found three bands of note, leaving each of these groups just as they were about to break into Britain's pop big-time.

Ian Matthews

In 1967 he founded Fairport Convention, recorded two albums and departed during sessions for the third; in 1969 he founded Matthews Southern Comfort, and in 1971 he founded Plainsong, after which he became a solo artist. Matthews moved to Los Angeles in 1973, then moved to Seattle in August 1977.

February	1972	DA DOO RON RON	Vertigo
November	1978	SHAKE IT	Mushroom
April	1979	GIVE ME AN INCH	Mushroom

MAZE

Members:
  Frankie Beverly—vocals, piano
  Roame Lowry—congas, vocals
  McKinley Williams—percussion, vocals
  Robin Duhe—bass
  Sam Porter—organ, synthesizers
  Ron Smith—guitar
  Billy (Shoes) Johnson—drums
  Phillip Woo—piano, synthesizers
Hometown: San Francisco, California

Maze is led by Frankie Beverly, who wrote, arranged, and produced all of the group's hits.

This eight-man funk-pop band surfaced in San Francisco after migrating from Philadelphia, where Frankie and the original members had started a band in 1971 known as Raw Soul.

May	1977	1. WHILE I'M ALONE	Capitol
June	1979	2. FEEL THAT YOU'RE FEELIN'	Capitol
June	1983	3. LOVE IS THE KEY	Capitol
March	1985	4. BACK IN STRIDE	Capitol

MAC McANALLY

Real Name: Lyman Corbitt McAnally Jr.
Born: 1957
Hometown: Belmont, Mississippi

Mac McAnally's songs are based on true events and real people from his quiet upbringing. Trombone and piano were Mac's major instruments until he switched to guitar at the age of 15. At age 17 he began playing clubs in local country bands. After leaving Belmont, Mississippi, where he was raised, Mac wound up in Muscle Shoals, Alabama, where he was sought after as an acoustic session guitarist. Mac's big break came when he was discovered by producers Terry Woodford and Clayton Ivey, who handled his first album.

| July | 1977 | IT'S A CRAZY WORLD | Ariola American |
| March | 1983 | MINIMUM LOVE | Geffen |

DELBERT McCLINTON

Born: November 4, 1940

Delbert McClinton was the leader of a group called the Ron-Dels. His claim to fame was that he played harmonica on Bruce Channel's "Hey! Baby" in 1962. (See *Bruce CHANNEL, Rock On: The Solid Gold Years.*)

| December | 1980 | GIVING IT UP FOR YOUR LOVE | Capitol |
| March | 1981 | SHOTGUN RIDER | Capitol/Mss |

MICHAEL McDONALD

One-time lead voice of the Doobie Brothers, Michael McDonald had several hits on his own.
See *THE DOOBIE BROTHERS, Rock On: The Years of Change.*

August	1982	I KEEP FORGETTIN'	Warner Bros.
November	1982	I GOTTA TRY	Warner Bros.
December	1983	YAH MO B THERE (with James Ingram)	Qwest

RONNIE McDOWELL

When Elvis died on August 16, 1977, Ronnie McDowell recorded a tribute song called "The King Is Gone," sounding very much like the king of rock and roll. The song became a big success in the fall of 1977. Several months later McDowell had a hit with "I Love You, I Love You, I Love You."

| September | 1977 | THE KING IS GONE | Scorpion |
| March | 1978 | I LOVE YOU, I LOVE YOU, I LOVE YOU | Scorpion |

McFADDEN & WHITEHEAD

Gene McFadden and John Whitehead were background singers who sang on Arthur Conley's hit "Sweet Soul Music" in 1967. McFadden & Whitehead had their lone chart entry in 1979.

| April | 1979 | AIN'T NO STOPPING US NOW | P.I.R. |

BOB McGILPIN

Hometown: Omaha, Nebraska

Bob McGilpin was born in Fort Dix, New Jersey, and grew up in a military environment.

McGilpin got his first guitar by age 10, wrote songs during his teen years, and had his only hit to date, "When You Feel Love," in 1978.

| September | 1978 | WHEN YOU FEEL LOVE | Butterfly |

McFadden & Whitehead. Gene McFadden (*left*), John Whitehead.

McGUFFEY LANE

Members:
  Terry Efaw—guitar
  Stephen Reis—vocals, bass
  Bob McNelley—vocals, guitar
  Stephen "Tebes" Douglass—keyboards, harmonica, vocals
  John Schwab—vocals, guitar
  Dave Rangeler—drums

McGuffey Lane played for ten years before they finally had their first hit, "Long Time Lovin' You," in 1981.

The group's name was taken from Stephen Reis's address; McGuffey Lane was the name of the street he lived on in Athens, Ohio.

January	1981	LONG TIME LOVIN' YOU	Atco
February	1982	START IT ALL OVER	Atco

McGuffey Lane. *Left to right:* John Schwab, Dave Rangeler, Bob McNelley, Terry Efaw, Stephen Reis.

McGUINN, CLARKE & HILLMAN

Members:
  James Joseph "Roger" McGuinn III—guitar, vocals—born: July 13, 1942—Chicago, Illinois
  Eugene Clarke—guitar—born: November 17, 1944—Tipton, Missouri
  Christopher Hillman—bass—born: December 4, 1942—Los Angeles, California

Roger McGuinn, Gene Clarke, and Chris Hillman are all former members of the Byrds. They combined their talents and had one hit song in 1979. See *THE BYRDS, Rock On: The Years of Change.*

| March | 1979 | DON'T YOU WRITE HER OFF | Capitol |

BOB & DOUG McKENZIE

Rick Moranis and Dave Thomas of SCTV were so popular among fans that they signed a record contract and had a big hit in 1982, using the names Bob and Doug McKenzie.

| January | 1982 | TAKE OFF | Mercury |

McGuinn, Clark & Hillman. *Left to right:* Chris Hillman, Roger McGuinn, Gene Clark.

Bob & Doug McKenzie

KRISTY & JIMMY McNICHOL

Kristy—born: September 9, 1963
Hometown: Los Angeles, California

Kristy, who played Buddy Lawrence on TV's "Family," and her brother Jimmy, got together and had a hit in 1978 with the song "He's So Fine," which was originally done by the Chiffons in 1963.

July	1978	HE'S SO FINE	RCA

CHRISTINE McVIE

Born: July 12, 1943

A member of Fleetwood Mac, Christine McVie had several solo hits in 1984.
See *FLEETWOOD MAC, Rock On: The Years of Change.*

January	1984	GOT A HOLD ON ME	Warner Bros.
May	1984	LOVE WILL SHOW US HOW	Warner Bros.

RANDY MEISNER

Born: March 8, 1946
Hometown: Scottsbluff, Nebraska

The grandson of a Russian classical violinist, Randy Meisner was an easy convert to music. He learned to play guitar, then switched to bass and

JOHN COUGAR MELLENCAMP 211

joined his first band, the Dynamics. In the mid-sixties, Randy left Nebraska and joined a band in Denver; this band moved to Los Angeles, where it shared management with Buffalo Springfield and Sonny & Cher. When Buffalo Springfield split up, Jim Messina and Richie Furay formed Poco and persuaded Meisner to join. Meisner became disenchanted, however, and left Poco to help form Rick Nelson's Stone Canyon Band, which was basically the group Meisner had come with to L. A. He stayed for two albums and a tour of Europe before hooking up with Glenn Frey, Don Henley, and Bernie Leadon, backing up Linda Ronstadt. In 1972, the quartet became the nucleus of the Eagles.

The Eagles became one of America's most popular home-grown bands. Meisner cowrote and sang lead on the hit "Take It To The Limit," but left the group in 1977, after the *Hotel California* album, to pursue a solo career. He was first heard as a solo artist the following year on the soundtrack of the film *FM;* ironically, the song "Bad Man," was written for Randy by Eagle Glenn Frey and good friend J. D. Souther. A self-titled debut album was released in June 1978; his third album, released in 1982, was also self-titled.

October	1980	DEEP INSIDE MY HEART	Epic
January	1981	HEARTS ON FIRE	Epic
July	1982	NEVER BEEN IN LOVE	Epic

JOHN COUGAR MELLENCAMP

Real Name: John Mellencamp
Born: October 7, 1951
Hometown: Seymour, Indiana

John Mellencamp came to New York City in 1975 with two cassettes of songs and a whole lot of nerve. Before long, he had a high-powered manager who renamed him John Cougar and released his unfinished demos as an album. Disillusioned, he parted company with the manager and returned home to Bloomington, Indiana, where he rehearsed new songs with his band, the Bone, and recorded another solo album. The hits started snowballing, but John took a break in 1983 to produce a Mitch Ryder album, *Never Kick a Sleeping Dog,* under the name Little Bastard.

Cougar made news in 1983 when he suffered a head wound requiring six stitches while performing for 51,000 people at a Who concert at the Sun Devil Stadium in Tempe, Arizona. A beer bottle thrown from the crowd hit him on the side of the head and knocked him unconscious. He was carried offstage, where his head was bandaged; he rested 20 minutes, then resumed his set, singing "Hurt So Good" as he came back onstage.

John Cougar Mellencamp

Cougar is also recognized for giving a free concert to 20,000 high school students who sandbagged for eight days in March 1983, saving Fort Wayne, Indiana, from its worst flood crisis ever. Meanwhile, at another midwest concert, he found the sound system inadequate, told the audience to demand its admission fee refunded and stormed offstage in mid-concert. Cougar also cancelled his 1983 US Festival booking when the promoters insisted on all rights to videos made of that performance.

JOHN COUGAR

October	1979	1. I NEED A LOVER	Riva
February	1980	2. SMALL PARADISE	Riva
September	1980	3. THIS TIME	Riva
January	1981	4. AIN'T EVEN DONE WITH THE NIGHT	Riva
April	1982	5. HURTS SO GOOD	Riva
July	1982	★ 6. JACK AND DIANE	Riva/Mercury
November	1982	7. HAND TO HOLD ON TO	Riva

JOHN COUGAR MELLENCAMP

October	1983	CRUMBLIN' DOWN	Riva
December	1983	PINK HOUSES	Riva
March	1984	THE AUTHORITY SONG	Riva

MEN AT WORK

Members:

    Colin Hay—vocals, guitar
    Ron Strykert—guitar, vocals
    Greg Ham—saxophone, flute, harp, keyboards, vocals
    John Rees—bass, vocals

Jerry Speiser—drums, vocals
Hometown: Melbourne, Australia

For most of 1980, Men At Work was a low-profile group that nevertheless drew full houses at the Cricketers Arms Hotel pub in the Melbourne suburb of Richmond. Men At Work quickly became Australia's highest-paid unrecorded band. Then Peter McIan appeared. McIan had emigrated from Los Angeles to Australia in order to produce another artist; once he was on the streets of Melbourne, he was amazed by the number of small clubs featuring live music as well as by the musical calibre of those bands. McIan discovered Men At Work and produced a single, "Who Can It Be Now?" which was certified gold in Australia. A second single, "Down Under," did even better, hitting the number one spot. A year later, both singles and a debut album, *Business As Usual,* were released around the world. The album was certified quadruple-platinum back home, and did equally impressively here in the States; *Business As Usual* became the first album in five years to produce two number-one hits, and the album itself stayed at number one for 15 weeks, selling more than 4 million copies. The group has retained its popularity with the release of subsequent records.

July	1982	★ 1. WHO CAN IT BE NOW?	Columbia
November	1982	★ 2. DOWN UNDER	Columbia
April	1983	3. OVERKILL	Columbia
July	1983	4. IT'S A MISTAKE	Columbia
September	1983	5. DR. HECKYLL & MR. JIVE	Columbia

Men at Work. *Left to right:* Greg Ham, John Rees, Colin Hay, Ron Strykert, Jerry Speiser.

MIDNIGHT STAR

Members:
Reginald Calloway—trumpet, flute, percussion, keyboards, vocals—born: January 23, 1955
Vincent Calloway—trombone, trumpet, flute—born: January 5, 1957
Jeffrey Cooper—guitar—born: July 2, 1956
Kenneth Gant—bass, vocals—born: December 28, 1956
Melvin Gentry—vocals, guitar, drums, bass, percussion—born: March 18, 1957
Belinda Lipscomb—vocals—born: April 19, 1957
William Simmons—saxophone, keyboards, percussion—born: March 2, 1953
Boas "Bo" Watson—vocals, clarinet, synthesizers—born: April 19, 1957
Hometown: Louisville, Kentucky

Midnight Star was formed in September 1976 on the campus of the University of Kentucky. The group members solidified their bond by living together in the home of Reggie and Vincent Calloway's grandparents in Louisville. Eventually, they moved to Cincinnati, this time to the home of Reggie and Vincent's parents, and began to work the clubs. In 1979, the group signed a record deal. In 1983, Midnight Star received its first platinum album for *No Parking On The Dance Floor*, which spawned three hit singles.

Reggie Calloway produced and helped launch the career of another Cincinnati-based combo, the Deele, in 1983. Brothers Reggie and Vincent also produced a song for funk star William "Bootsy" Collins, also from Cincinnati.

August	1983	1. FREAK-A-ZOID	Solar
November	1983	2. WET MY WHISTLE	Solar
March	1984	3. NO PARKING (ON THE DANCE FLOOR)	Solar
December	1984	4. OPERATOR	Solar
March	1985	5. SCIENTIFIC LOVE	Solar

FRANKIE MILLER

Hometown: Glasgow, Scotland

Frankie Miller's career began when he hooked up with Jimmy Dewar. In 1971 they formed the group Jude, with Robin Trower (who had left Procul Harum) and Clive Bunker (who had left Jethro Tull), but the group disbanded before the release of their debut LP. Miller then became immersed in the British pub-rock scene, during which time he released four albums.

He had a chart entry in 1982 with "To Dream The Dream."

| June | 1977 | FULL HOUSE | Chrysalis |
| June | 1982 | TO DREAM THE DREAM | Capitol |

STEPHANIE MILLS

Born: 1956
Hometown: Brooklyn, New York

At age 11, Stephanie Mills won a talent contest at New York's Apollo Theater, and received a week's engagement there opening for the Isley Brothers. Shortly thereafter, she, Irena Cara, and several other children wound up on Broadway in the cast of *Maggie Flynn* with Shirley Jones and the late Jack Cassidy.

Stephanie's first major break, however, came at age 15, when she was cast in the lead role of *The Wiz*, Broadway's all-black version of *The Wizard of Oz*. Stephanie played the role of Dorothy for the show's entire five-year run. She then turned to records, and cut her first album, *For The First Time*, in 1975. The album was a collection of Burt Bacharach/Hal David songs, and did not sell well. Four years later, *Whatcha' Gonna Do With My Lovin'* became her first gold album. Before long, Stephanie was on a winning streak and received many prestigious awards from the music industry.

There were disappointments as well. The role of Dorothy in the movie version of *The Wiz* was given to Diana Ross. Her marriage to Jeffrey Daniel of Shalamar on June 13, 1980, ended shortly thereafter. Nevertheless, Mills found new happiness in religion—she became a born-again Christian. Stephanie has appeared on the NBC-TV soap "Search For Tomorrow," and performed at the White House for Presidents Reagan and Carter.

In 1983 and 1984, Stephanie resumed her role of Dorothy with a touring company of *The Wiz*. The show received bad reviews when it returned to Broadway, however, and closed quickly.

Stephanie lives in Los Angeles.

July	1979	1. WHATCHA' GONNA DO WITH MY LOVIN'	20th Century
June	1980	2. SWEET SENSATION	20th Century
August	1980	3. NEVER KNEW LOVE LIKE THIS BEFORE	20th Century
May	1981	4. TWO HEARTS (with Teddy Pendergrass)	20th Century
October	1984	5. THE MEDICINE SONG	Casablanca

RONNIE MILSAP

Born: January 16, 1946
Hometown: Robbinsville, North Carolina

Blind since birth, Ronnie Milsap was enrolled in the state school for the blind, where by the age of 12 he became a multi-instrumentalist. By 1977, Ronnie had established himself as a top country-music performer and won three of the Country Music Association's biggest awards.

Ronnie Milsap

September	1974	1. PLEASE DON'T TELL ME HOW THE STORY ENDS	RCA
June	1977	2. IT WAS ALMOST LIKE A SONG	RCA
January	1978	3. WHAT A DIFFERENCE YOU'VE MADE IN MY LIFE	RCA
July	1978	4. ONLY ONE LOVE IN MY LIFE	RCA
October	1979	5. GET IT UP	RCA
November	1980	6. SMOKEY MOUNTAIN RAIN	RCA
June	1981	7. NO GETTIN' OVER ME	RCA
October	1981	8. I WOULDN'T HAVE MISSED IT FOR THE WORLD	RCA
May	1982	9. ANY DAY NOW	RCA
August	1982	10. HE GOT YOU	RCA
March	1983	11. STRANGER IN MY HOUSE	RCA
August	1983	12. DON'T YOU KNOW HOW MUCH I LOVE YOU	RCA
August	1984	13. SHE LOVES MY CAR	RCA

MINK DeVILLE

Members:
　　Willy Deville—vocals, guitar—born: August 25, 1950
　　Rick Bordia—guitar—born: October 29, 1951
　　Ken Margolis—organ, piano—born: July 28, 1954
　　Louis Cortelezzi—saxophone—born: May 5, 1952
　　Bob Curiano—bass—born: September 27, 1952
　　Boris Kinberg—percussion—born: April 27, 1951
　　Shawn Murray—drums—born: January 28, 1954
Hometown: New York, New York

Willy Deville spent a great deal of time in New York before heading to
London and San Francisco in the early seventies. By the mid-seventies,

Willy was back in New York, playing in punk rock clubs with a band he called Mink DeVille, even though the group was hardly of the punk rock genre—their music was inspired by rhythm & blues. In 1976, Mink DeVille appeared on an anthology album called *Live at CBGB's,* and this led the way to the group's own recording deal. The debut album, *Cabretta* in 1977, established Mink DeVille in the United States and Great Britain as a solid cult attraction.

The group's lineup changed substantially after 1981. In that year, Bordia replaced Louie X. Erlanger, Margolis replaced Bobby Leonards, Cortelezzi replaced Steve Douglas and Jackie Kelso, and Curiano replaced Ruben Siguenza.

February   1984   EACH WORD'S A BEAT OF MY HEART   Atlantic

MISSING PERSONS

Members:
      Dale Bozzio—vocals—born: March 2, 1955
      Warren Cuccurullo—guitar, vocals—born: December 8, 1956
      Chuck Wild—keyboards—left the group in 1984
      Patrick O'Hearn—bass, synthesizer—born: September 6, 1954
      Terry Bozzio—drums, keyboards, vocals—born: December 27, 1950
Hometown: Los Angeles, California

Willy DeVille

Missing Persons. *Left to right:* *(top)* Terry Bozzio, Dale Bozzio *(center)* Warren Cuccurullo; *(bottom)* Patrick O'Hearn, Chuck Wild.

Dale Bozzio, her husband Terry, and Warren Cuccurullo all worked in Frank Zappa's bands at one time or another, and in 1980 decided to form their own group. With the addition of studio veteran Chuck Wild and a fellow Zappa alumnus, Patrick O'Hearn, Missing Persons was born. When more than 10,000 copies of a homemade mini-LP quickly sold in L. A., Capitol Records signed the group, in March 1982, and re-released the mini-album. It sold more than 250,000 units, an unprecedented number for an EP by a new band. By the time the group's debut LP, *Spring Session M*, was released in October, Missing Persons already had a strong following. Dale Bozzio, who was a Playboy bunny in 1976, also became something of a rock 'n' roll sex kitten in her stunning and unusual costumes.

July	1982	1. WORDS	Capitol
October	1982	2. DESTINATION UNKNOWN	Capitol
January	1983	3. WINDOWS	Capitol
March	1983	4. WALKING IN L.A.	Capitol
March	1984	5. GIVE	Capitol

MOLLY HATCHET

Members:

Jimmy Farrar—vocals (replaced Danny Joe Brown in 1980)—born: August 24, 1951—replaced (1982) by Brown

Duane Roland—guitar—born: December 3, 1952
Dave Hlubek—guitar—born: August 28, 1951
Steve Holland—guitar—replaced in 1984 by John Galvin—keyboards—
    born: May 21, 1955
Banner Thomas—bass—replaced (1982) by Riff West—born: April 13, 1950
Bruce Crump—drums—replaced in 1982 by B. B. Borden—replaced by
    Crump in 1984—born: July 17, 1957
Hometown: Jacksonville, Florida

The name Molly Hatchet comes from 17th century Salem, where a woman
known as Hatchet Molly reportedly decapitated her lovers. Coming in at
the tail end of the burst of southern rock bands to go national, Molly
Hatchet proved to be the hardest rocking of them all. Pat Armstrong, a
manager who helped guide Lynyrd Skynyrd and .38 Special, drilled Molly
Hatchet through the obligatory southern roadhouse/club/bar circuit until
the sextet was ready to hit the big time. The group signed a record deal
at the end of 1977, and their self-titled debut album the following year
was awarded platinum status. The follow-up album, *Flirtin' With Disaster*,
sold even better—over 1.5 million copies. This heavy touring band played
as many as 275 shows a year.

In early 1980, Danny Joe Brown left the band, and Jimmy Farrar
joined for two albums, while Brown tried leading his own band. In mid-
1982, Molly Hatchet's popularity began to fade, and Brown, who had not

Molly Hatchet. *Left to right:* Danny Joe Brown, Duane Roland, John Galvin, Bruce Crump,
Riff West, Dave Hlubek.

been able to make inroads on his own, rejoined Molly Hatchet, replacing Jimmy Farrar.

January	1980	1. FLIRTIN' WITH DISASTER	Epic
March	1981	2. THE RAMBLER	Epic
February	1982	3. POWER PLAY	Epic
October	1984	4. SATISFIED MAN	Epic

EDDIE MONEY

Real Name: Eddie Mahoney
Born: March 2, 1949
Hometown: Brooklyn, New York

Because Eddie Mahoney comes from a family where the men traditionally become police officers, he dutifully enrolled at the New York Police Academy. But although he studied law enforcement by day, he lived a rock 'n' roll lifestyle and rehearsed with bands by night. Ultimately, the

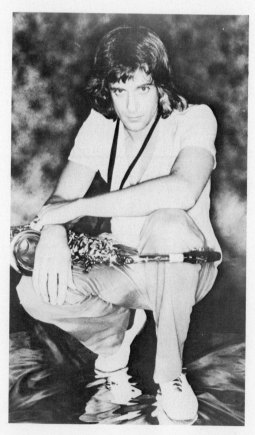

Eddie Money

rock 'n' roll lifestyle took over, and Eddie packed his Bob Dylan albums and a surf board and headed for California.

Renamed Eddie Money, he led a locally popular band called the Rockets while in Berkeley, and portrayed a 90-year-old former rock star in Richard Bailey's one-man play, *Back Tracks*, in San Francisco in 1977. One day, while trying to sneak into a west coast rock club, he was caught by the club's manager. That manager, Bill Graham, ultimately went on to manage Eddie Money's career.

In 1980, a post-tour accident left Money with nerve damage in one leg, but after an 18-month hiatus he picked up where he left off.

February	1978	1. BABY HOLD ON	Columbia
June	1978	2. TWO TICKETS TO PARADISE	Columbia
November	1978	3. YOU'VE REALLY GOT A HOLD ON ME	Columbia
January	1979	4. MAYBE I'M A FOOL	Columbia
May	1979	5. CAN'T KEEP A GOOD MAN DOWN	Columbia
August	1979	6. GET A MOVE ON	Columbia
September	1980	7. RUNNING BACK	Columbia
October	1980	8. LET'S BE LOVERS AGAIN (with Valerie Carter)	Columbia
July	1982	9. THINK I'M IN LOVE	Columbia
October	1982	10. SHAKIN'	Columbia
November	1983	11. BIG CRASH	Columbia
February	1984	12. CLUB MICHELLE	Columbia

MELBA MOORE

Hometown: New York, New York

After graduation from Columbia University's Teachers College in New York in the sixties, Melba taught music in a public school for about a year. However, she knew her first love was performing so she began singing in piano bars, which led to studio work as a background singer at recording sessions. In 1969, she was doing some background singing for the album of *Hair*. All the vocalists were invited to audition for the show, which she did, landing a part in the "tribal love rock musical." Before leaving the show after a year and a half, Moore took over the female lead of Sheila, which got her a lot of publicity. From *Hair* she moved on to the role of Luttibelle in the musical *Purlie*, in which she costarred with Cleavon Little. This role won her a Tony, the New York Drama Critics Award, and the Drama Desk Award. Her performance in the show, especially singing the song "I Got Love," made the music industry take notice of her talents.

This recognition resulted in a recording contract with Buddah Records and her first national pop hit in 1976.

April	1976	THIS IS IT	Buddah
January	1979	YOU STEPPED INTO MY LIFE	Epic

THE MOTELS

Members:
Martha Davis—vocals, guitar—born: January 19, 1951
Tim McGovern—guitar, vocals—(replaced Jeff Jourard in 1979)—replaced in 1981 by Guy Perry—born: March 20, 1951
Martin Life Jourard—keyboards, saxophone, vocals—born: August 25, 1954
Michael Goodroe—bass—born: February 8, 1950
Scott Thurston—keyboards, horns, guitar—joined in 1981—born: January 10, 1952
Brian Glascock—drums—born: July 17, 1948
Hometown: Berkeley, California

The Motels began in July 1978 when Martha Davis and Jeff Jourard hastily assembled a band to play Hollywood's Whisky Au Go Go. That makeshift group included Martin Life Jourard and the classically-trained guitarist-turned-bassist Michael Goodroe. The group relocated to Los Angeles, and after rejecting 85 drummers, they took on Brian Glascock, who'd played in a British band called Toe Fat. The Motels resurfaced on January 2, 1979, and began working the L. A. club circuit. (During this year Jeff Jourard left the group and was replaced by Tim McGovern.) Word about the group's music traveled fast, and six weeks later the record companies were bidding against one another to sign the Motels. One Friday night, the group played a gig at Madame Wong's; they signed a record deal the day after, and were in a recording studio by Monday. A self-titled debut album was released in September 1979.

The Motels. *Left to right:* Marty Jourard, Scott Thurston, Brian Clascock, Martha Davis, Michael Goodroe, Guy Perry.

Tim McGovern has since left the Motels to lead Burning Sensations.

April	1982	1. ONLY THE LONELY	Capitol
September	1982	2. TAKE THE L	Capitol
November	1982	3. FOREVER MINE	Capitol
September	1983	4. SUDDENLY LAST SUMMER	Capitol
December	1983	5. REMEMBER THE NIGHT	Capitol

MÖTLEY CRÜE

Members:
    Vince Neil (Vince Neil Wharton)—vocals—born: February 8, 1961
    Mick Mars—guitar, vocals—born: April 4, 1955
    Nikki Sixx—bass—born: December 11, 1958
    Tommy Lee—drums, vocals—born: October 3, 1962
Hometown: Los Angeles, California

Nikki Sixx left a band called London about the same time Tommy Lee left Suite 19. They started talking about music, and answered Mick Mars's classified ad in a local publication; the ad read "loud, rude, aggressive guitarist available." Mars then spotted Vince Neil singing with a band called Rock Candy; they met and found that not only was their hair similar, but so were their musical tastes. Mötley Crüe was finally born in February 1981.

Mötley Crüe set out to conquer the Los Angeles rock club circuit, which at the time was patronized by short-haired new wavers wearing skinny ties. In time, the band developed a following and worked steadily. In June 1981, the Crüe had a thousand copies of a single, "Stick To Your

Mötley Crüe. *Left to right: (top)* Vince Neil; *(bottom)* Tommy Lee, Nikki Sixx, Mick Mars.

Guns" b/w "The Toast of the Town," distributed, mostly for promotional purposes. A few months later, the group recorded an album, *Too Fast For Love*, and released it independently; the entire original pressing of 20,000 copies sold out in a few months. The album was remixed and rereleased later that year when the group went on to a major record firm. By the time a second album, *Shout At The Devil*, was released in 1983, Mötley Crüe had become one of America's biggest heavy-metal attractions.

On December 8, 1984, Vince Neil and Hanoi Rocks drummer Nicholas Dingley were involved in an auto crash in Redondo Beach, California, a crash that claimed Dingley's life.

| February | 1984 | LOOKS THAT KILL | Elektra |
| June | 1984 | TOO YOUNG TO FALL IN LOVE | Elektra |

MR. MISTER

Members:
  Richard Page—vocals, bass—born: May 16, 1953
  Steve George—keyboards—born: May 20, 1955

Mr. Mister. *Left to right:* Steve Farris, Richard Page, Steve George, Pat Mastelotto.

M + M. Martha Johnson and Mark Gane.

Steve Farris—guitar—born: May 1, 1957
Pat Mastelotto—drummer—born: September 10, 1955
Hometown: Los Angeles, California

Before forming Mr. Mister in mid-1983, Page and George had left their hometown of Phoenix, Arizona, for Los Angeles and worked as studio musicians for artists ranging from Molly Hatchet to James Ingram. They also wrote songs for Donna Summer and Al Jarreau and even made a Budweiser commercial. When Men At Work's producer Peter McIan offered to produce Mr. Mister, RCA quickly made a deal and signed them. From this came their first album, *I Wear the Face,* which included "Hunters Of The Night."

While Mr. Mister is clean-cut in appearance, they specialize in a fairly rugged brand of rock 'n' roll with haunting undertones.

March   1984   HUNTERS OF THE NIGHT   RCA

M + M

Members:
    Martha Johnson—born: December 18, 1950
    Mark Gane—born: December 17, 1953
Hometown: Toronto, Canada

In 1975, Martha was working a conventional day job while working at night at various Toronto clubs with her group Martha and the Muffins. It was at this time that she met Mark, a recent art college graduate who was painting and doing some songwriting, and persuaded him to join her group. The group gained a large local following, and in 1979 they recorded an album in England called *Metro Music*, which yielded the European hit single "Echo Beach." This song would gain them worldwide popularity and become the "single of the year" in Canada.

After several other albums, including *Trance And Dance* and *This Is The Ice Age*, the group disbanded, leaving Martha and Mark to continue as a duo under the name M+M.

In early 1984, they released the album *Mystery Walk*, from which came their first charted United States single, "Black Stations/White Stations."

June	1984	BLACK STATIONS/WHITE STATIONS	RCA

MTUME

Members:
    Mtume—vocals, keyboards
    Raymond Johnson—bass
    Phillip Fields—keyboards
    Tawatha Agee—vocals
Hometown: Philadelphia, Pennsylvania

Growing up in Philadelphia, Mtume's goal was to be an Olympic swimming champion. In fact, in high school he received acclaim as the first black to

Mtume. Mtume and Tawatha Agee.

be public high school champion two years in a row and the first black high school All-American. For this he received a scholarship and went to Pasadena College in California. However, while at college Mtume became more interested in music than swimming, especially South African music. It was at this time that he mastered the difficult African drum.

In 1970, he moved to Newark, New Jersey, and a year later, while performing at New York's Village Gate, he met Miles Davis. In 1972, Mtume joined Davis's group as a percussionist and stayed with him for several years, developing his craft. After this he joined Roberta Flack's band and met guitarist Reggie Lucas. The two of them collaborated on a dozen gold and platinum albums, including Flack's 1978 platinum album *Blue Light In the Basement*.

In 1981, Mtume launched his self-titled group. His album, *Kiss This World Goodbye* was followed by the albums *Search Of The Rainbow Seekers* and the gold *Juicy Fruit*.

| June | 1983 | JUICY FRUIT | Epic |
| September | 1984 | YOU, ME AND HE | Epic |

THE MUPPETS

Jim Henson's character Kermit the Frog had a hit in 1979. The song was featured in the Muppet movie.

| September | 1979 | RAINBOW CONNECTION | Atlantic |

MUSICAL YOUTH

Members:
     Dennis Seaton—vocals—Born: 1966
     Kelvin Grant—guitar—Born: 1971
     Michael Grant—keyboards—Born: 1969
     Patrick Waite—bass—Born: 1968
     Junior Waite—drums—Born: 1967
Hometown: Birmingham, England

In 1980, Kelvin, Michael, Patrick, Junior, and the latter pair's dad, Freddie, a prominent reggae singer in Jamaica, began performing in their hometown with Freddie as the lead singer. John Peel, whose London radio show, "Radio One," would play demos of unknown groups, began playing some of the group's songs. Charlie Ayre, the director of A&R for MCA records in London, heard the group on his car radio and liked them so much that he went to one of their concerts. Although he liked them very much, he felt that the father should not sing with the group, but that they should have someone close to their own age instead. It was then that Dennis joined the group as the new lead voice.

Musical Youth. *Left to right:* Junior Waite, Dennis Seaton, Patrick Waite, Kelvin Grant, Michael Grant.

After months of rehearsals they recorded a song they had in their repertoire called "Pass the Dutchie," the "Dutchie" being a type of cooking pot. In 1982, the song became an international smash.

December	1982	PASS THE DUTCHIE	MCA
January	1984	SHE'S TROUBLE	MCA

N

NAKED EYES

Members:
  Pete Byrne—vocals—born: June 9, 1954
  Rob Fisher—keyboards—born: November 5, 1956
Hometown: Bath, England

When Rob Fisher first entered the University of Bath, he probably had no idea that his course of study, electronics, would lead to a career in music. At the university he met Pete Byrne, who'd sung for several local bands, and the two discovered their shared affinity for music. Fisher and Byrne wrote prolifically and recorded several demos, and they secured a publishing deal in the summer of 1980. Although Naked Eyes' self-titled debut album features Fisher playing eight electronic keyboards as well as a grand piano, the synthesizer-based music also necessitated several session musicians. The duo's first single was a synthesizer/vocal-based reworking of Burt Bacharach's "Always Something There To Remind Me."

March	1983	1. ALWAYS SOMETHING THERE TO REMIND ME	EMI-America
July	1983	2. PROMISES, PROMISES	EMI-America
October	1983	3. WHEN THE LIGHTS GO OUT	EMI-America
August	1984	4. (WHAT) IN THE NAME OF LOVE	EMI-America

Naked Eyes. Pete Byrne (*left*), Rob Fisher.

DAVID NAUGHTON

Hometown: Cheshire, Connecticut

David Naughton, star of TV's "Makin It" and a Dr. Pepper TV commercial, had a hit with a song from the motion picture *Meatballs*. The record made the nation's top ten.

March   1979   MAKIN' IT   RSO

WILLIE NELSON

Born: April 30, 1933
Hometown: Abbott, Texas

It is said that Willie Nelson comes by his talents naturally; his grandparents, who raised him in the latter years of the Depression, earned mail-order music degrees. Willie's musical career began at age 10, when one night he played rhythm guitar with a bohemian polka band. In the fifties, after a hitch in the Air Force, Willie supported his first wife and daughter by peddling vacuum cleaners, encyclopedias, and Bibles before starting as a disc jockey at a San Antonio radio station. Still singing nights and weekends in honky tonks, he worked at radio stations in other cities in Texas and even in Oregon. Willie began writing songs, and one night Hank Cochran heard him at Tootsie's Orchid Lounge in Nashville and signed him to a publishing firm then partly owned by Ray Price. When Price told Willie he needed a bassist, Willie told him he could do it, and

Willie Nelson

learned how to play overnight. Eventually, Willie began recording his own albums for a variety of record companies; many of the more obscure records are now collectors' items.

By the mid-seventies, Willie Nelson was a country music superstar. He's been awarded countless plaques, trophies and tributes. His songs have been recorded by Frank Sinatra, Bing Crosby, Stevie Wonder, Aretha Franklin, Lawrence Welk, Elvis Presley, Harry James, and dozens of other artists. Thousands of fans turn out at his concerts, including his "picnic" concerts around Independence Day, and equally famous athletes and entertainers routinely make guest appearances on stage. Willie has starred in the films *The Electric Horseman, Honeysuckle Rose,* and *Barbarosa.* He has dueted with Leon Russell, Ray Price, Merle Haggard, Waylon Jennings, and Julio Iglesias (with whom he had a hit). Perhaps Willie is the only person who can get away with visiting the President of the United States (Jimmy Carter in particular) at the White House dressed in his customary faded blue jeans, T-shirt, and sneakers.

August	1975	1. BLUE EYES CRYING IN THE RAIN	Columbia
January	1976	2. REMEMBER ME	Columbia
May	1978	3. GEORGIA ON MY MIND	Columbia
February	1980	4. MY HEROS HAVE ALWAYS BEEN COWBOYS	Columbia
September	1980	5. ON THE ROAD AGAIN	Columbia
March	1982	6. ALWAYS ON MY MIND	Columbia
August	1982	7. LET IT BE ME	Columbia
March	1984	8. TO ALL THE GIRLS I'VE LOVED BEFORE (with Julio Iglesias)	Columbia

NENA

Members:
   Nena Kerner—vocals
   Carlo Karges—guitar
   Uwe Fahrenkrog-Petersen—keyboards
   Jurgen Demel—bass
   Rolf Brendel—drums
Hometown: Berlin, West Germany

Nena is the name of both a person and a band. Nena Kerner and Rolf Brendel both played in a power pop group in Hagen called Stripes before moving to Berlin in 1980 in search of better musical opportunities. They banded with Uwe Fahrenkrog-Petersen, who had previously performed with Stripes on the group's final tour, and two rock veterans, Jurgen Demel and Carlo Karges, to become Nena.

After several months' rehearsal, Nena (the group) went into a recording studio and came out with what became the group's first number-one hit in Germany, "Just A Dream." This was followed by another number-one hit, "99 Luftballons," and a platinum-certified (West German) number-one album. When a disc jockey on KROQ-FM in Los Angeles began

Nena

playing an imported copy of "99 Luftballons" in heavy rotation, two versions of the song, one in German and one in English, were released in the United States. "99 Luftballons" became an international hit.

December　1983　99 LUFTBALLONS　　　　　　　　　　　Epic

NEW EDITION

Members:
　　Ralph Tresvant—vocals—born: May 16, 1968
　　Ronald DeVoe—vocals—born: November 17, 1967
　　Michael Bivins—vocals—born: August 10, 1968
　　Bobby Brown—vocals—born: February 5, 1969
　　Ricky Bell—vocals—born: September 18, 1967
Hometown: Boston, Massachusetts

Maurice Starr discovered New Edition at a talent show and signed the teenage vocal quintet to Streetwise Records, with himself as the producer. With a vocal sound and melodies that closely matched the Jackson 5, but backed with electronic music, these boys became immediate heartthrobs. Right after the release of the debut LP, *Candy Girl,* the group sought a release from both Streetwise and Starr. The record company and producer claimed they owned the name of the group, and Starr suggested that "New Edition" was a concept and he could find five other teenage boys to work under the name. A United States District Court in Boston ruled that another group using the name would be defrauding the public, and disavowed the group's contracts by virtue of infancy—the boys were minors and the contracts were never approved by any court. As a result, the group kept its name, enlisted the aid of Ray Parker, Jr., as producer, and signed with MCA Records in 1984.

May	1983	1. CANDY GIRL	Streetwise
October	1983	2. IS THIS THE END	Streetwise
September	1984	3. COOL IT NOW	MCA
December	1984	4. MR. TELEPHONE MAN	MCA
March	1985	5. LOST IN LOVE	MCA

New Edition. *Left to right:* Ronald DeVoe, Ralph Tresvant, Ricky Bell, Bobby Brown, Michael Bivens.

JUICE NEWTON

Real Name: Judy Cohen
Born: February 18, 1952
Hometown: Virginia Beach, Virginia

Juice Newton performed traditional folk music in acoustic duos and trios during her high school years. She moved to Los Gatos, California, in the late sixties to attend college. With guitarist Otha Young and bassist Tom Kealey, she formed Juice Newton and Silver Spur in 1972. The group moved to Los Angeles, where they occasionally added a drummer, and by 1975 concentrated almost entirely on original material. Frustrated by the public's assumption that Silver Spur was a country music band—Newton always maintained she was rock or country-rock—the group

Juice Newton

broke up in 1978. (Newton had also developed minor voice problems, and dissolving the band gave her time to rest her voice.) Newton soon went solo, still accompanied by Young. She has more recently chosen to describe her music as "country/pop."

Newton has received numerous music industry awards, and was named National Chairperson for the Kidney Foundation in 1983. Also, the Southern California Collegiate Panhellenic listed Newton among the country's 10 most influential women in 1983.

April	1978	1. IT'S A HEARTACHE	Capitol
February	1981	2. ANGEL OF THE MORNING	Capitol
May	1981	3. QUEEN OF HEARTS	Capitol
October	1981	4. THE SWEETEST THING	Capitol
May	1982	5. LOVE'S BEEN A LITTLE BIT HARD ON ME	Capitol
August	1982	6. BREAK IT TO ME GENTLY	Capitol
November	1982	7. HEART OF THE NIGHT	Capitol
August	1983	8. TELL HER NO	Capitol
November	1983	9. DIRTY LOOKS	Capitol
June	1984	10. A LITTLE LOVE	RCA
August	1984	11. CAN'T WAIT ALL NIGHT	RCA

STEVIE NICKS

Born: May 26, 1948
Hometown: Phoenix, Arizona

Stevie Nicks received a classical guitar as a gift on her 16th birthday. Singing and songwriting came quickly and naturally to Nicks, who became lead vocalist with a Bay area band called Fritz (Nicks had been raised in California), in which she met guitarist Lindsey Buckingham. She and Buckingham subsequently moved to Los Angeles, where they recorded an album, *Buckingham Nicks*, in 1973. The record brought them to the attention of Mick Fleetwood, at whose invitation they joined Fleetwood Mac two years later. Fleetwood Mac quickly became a supergroup. As each member of the group pursued individual goals between band commitments, Nicks prepared for her solo recordings, the first of which, *Bella Donna*, was released in 1981. In 1982, Home Box Office aired a special one-hour program called "Stevie Nicks In Concert," taped in December 1981 at the Wilshire Fox Theater in Los Angeles.

July	1981	1. STOP DRAGGIN' MY HEART AROUND (with Tom Petty & The Heartbreakers)	Modern
October	1981	2. LEATHER AND LACE (with Don Henley)	Modern
February	1982	3. EDGE OF SEVENTEEN	Modern
May	1982	4. AFTER THE GLITTER FADES	Modern
June	1983	5. STAND BACK	Modern
September	1983	6. IF ANYONE FALLS	Modern
December	1983	7. NIGHTBIRD	Modern

NIELSEN/PEARSON

Members:
  Reed Nielsen—vocals, drums
  Mark Pearson—vocals, piano, guitar
Hometown: Sacramento, California

Reed Nielsen and Mark Pearson both learned to play musical instruments before their teen years. The duo's talents were discovered while taking music classes north of Sacramento. Initially, they were signed to a contract at Epic Records, but two years later they joined Capitol, where they have enjoyed two hit records: "If You Should Sail" and "The Sun Ain't Gonna Shine Anymore."

September	1980	IF YOU SHOULD SAIL	Capitol
August	1981	THE SUN AIN'T GONNA SHINE ANYMORE	Capitol

NIGHT RANGER

Members:
  Brad Gillis—guitar, vocals—born: June 15, 1957
  Jeff Watson—guitar—born: November 4, 1956
  Alan "Fitz" Fitzgerald—keyboards, vocals—born: July 16, 1949
  Jack Blades—bass, vocals—born: April 24, 1954
  Kelly Keagy—drums, vocals—born: September 15, 1952
Hometown: San Francisco, California

Night Ranger can be traced back to Rubicon, a seven-piece funk-rock group of the late seventies that recorded two albums. Jack Blades and Brad Gillis were in that group, and Kelly Keagy had joined on for the group's last tour in 1979. This trio went on to form a short-lived rock 'n' roll band called Stereo. One day, Alan Fitzgerald, who'd played bass for Ronnie Montrose and keyboards for Sammy Hagar, called Blades, his former roommate, to tell him he had access to recording equipment and was he interested in forming a band. Jack said yes. He brought Brad and Kelly along, and the four recorded eight songs in just a few weeks. In short time, Fitz persuaded local hot-shot guitarist Jeff Watson to fill out Night Ranger. The group's debut album, *Dawn Patrol*, was released in December 1982, after Brad did a brief tour as Ozzy Osbourne's guitarist. Night Ranger opened a national tour for Sammy Hagar and was on its way to success when Boardwalk Records suddenly folded in June 1983. Momentum picked up again, however, with the release of the *Midnight Madness* album in October of that year.

January	1983	1. DON'T TELL ME YOU LOVE ME	Boardwalk
April	1983	2. SING ME AWAY	Boardwalk

Night Ranger. *Left to right:* Kelly Keagy, Jack Blades, Alan Fitzgerald, Brad Gillis (*in front*), Jeff Watson.

December	1983	3. (YOU CAN STILL) ROCK 'N' ROLL IN AMERICA	Camel/MCA
March	1984	4. SISTER CHRISTIAN	Camel/MCA
July	1984	5. WHEN YOU CLOSE YOUR EYES	Camel/MCA

ALDO NOVA

Hometown: Montreal, Canada

After high school Aldo got a job in a recording studio, where he learned to become a producer and recording engineer. At the same time he also learned to play the guitar and keyboards. In 1979, Aldo began his first musical project in which he wrote the songs, sang them, played guitar,

Aldo Nova

and engineered the sessions. When his demo came to the attention of Sandy Pearlman, the manager of Blue Öyster Cult, Pearlman signed Nova to a managerial contract and then got him signed to Portrait Records. This led to his debut album, *Aldo Nova*.

March	1982	FANTASY	Portrait
July	1982	FOOLIN' YOURSELF	Portrait

Gary Numan

GARY NUMAN

Born: March 8, 1958
Hometown: London, England

In 1977, Gary formed a group called Tubeway Army that became very popular throughout Great Britain. During the next few years, while they recorded such albums as *Tubeway Army* and *Replicas,* the group went through several personnel changes.

It was during this time, 1979, that the Tubeway Army simply became known as Gary Numan. During that same year the album *The Pleasure Principle* was released, yielding the hit single and video "Cars" in 1980.

Because of the special effects the video became a hit on MTV and the single became a top-ten national hit in America.

By 1981, Numan was spending a lot of time flying around the world just for the sake of adventure; consequently, he was not spending much time on his recording career. The result of this was that people began to forget about him. After tax problems in 1982, Numan made an attempt to get back into singing once again.

February   1980   CARS   Atco

OAK

Members:

Rick Pinette—vocals, guitar, piano
Daniel Caron—drums, percussion
Scott Weatherspoon—vocals, guitar
David Stone—vocals, keyboards
John Foster—vocals, bass

Rick Pinette actually started Oak when he was in grammar school in his native New Hampshire. Although the members changed over the years, they've always performed as Oak.

After playing classic rock 'n' roll tunes in Maine beachtowns for years, they finally scored on the charts with a summertime hit, "This Is Love."

July	1979	THIS IS LOVE	Mercury
May	1980	KING OF THE HILL	Mercury
December	1980	SET THE NIGHT ON FIRE	Mercury

THE OAK RIDGE BOYS

Members:

Duane Allen—vocals, guitar—born: April 29, 1943—Taylortown, Texas
Joe Bonsall—tenor—born: May 18, 1948—Philadelphia, Pennsylvania
William Lee Golden—baritone—born: January 12, 1939—Brewton, Alabama
Richard Sterban—bass vocals—born: April 24, 1943—Camden, New Jersey
Hometown: Hendersonville, Tennessee

The Oak Ridge Boys, known for their four-part harmonies, have been accepted by both country and pop music fans. An international success, the group has done command performances before royalty in Sweden, Monaco, and Great Britain, as well as entertaining President and Mrs. Jimmy Carter at Ford's Theatre in Washington, D. C. The Oaks are also active in a national campaign for the prevention of child abuse; they produce an annual benefit concert with top name performers, with proceeds donated to provide educational material and rehabilitation for abused children and their families. The Oak Ridge Boys were also the official spokespersons for the Boy Scouts of America. The group has done commercial endorsements for IT&T, Dr. Pepper, and the Boy Scouts of America. The only controversy ever linked with this clean-cut group was

The Oak Ridge Boys. *Left to right:* Joe Bansall, Duane Allen, William Lee Golden, Richard Sterban.

the song "Easy," which they released in 1978. Although the song was essentially a touching and optimistic love song, it touched on the theme of illegitimacy, and so was banned on all radio and television in South Africa and encountered difficulty getting airplay in England.

May	1981	1. ELVIRA	MCA
January	1982	2. BOBBIE SUE	MCA
June	1982	3. SO FINE	MCA
March	1983	4. AMERICAN MADE	MCA

BILLY OCEAN

Born: January 21, 1950
Hometown: London, England

While growing up in his native Trinidad, Billy got interested in music by playing a ukelele his mother bought him. At the age of eight, his family moved to London, where, as a teenager, he got a job working as a cutter in ladies' tailoring. Billy was very involved in the clothing industry until he bought his first piano. He then would tailor by day and play music with bands like Shades of Midnight and Dry Ice at night. When this schedule became too hectic Billy gave up tailoring for the full-time pursuit of music. He got work as a session singer, whereupon he met Ben Findon, who became Billy's writing partner; this led to the two of them signing

Billy Ocean

with GTO Records and in 1976 writing a top-ten English hit, "Love Really Hurts Without You," and later that same year, the hit "LOD (Love On Delivery)."

A few years later Billy Ocean came to America where he collaborated with Ken Gold and started writing for artists like LaToya Jackson, Lenny Williams, and the Nolans. In 1982, he was voted "Top New Male Artist" by *Cash Box* magazine for his r&b hit "Nights (Feel Like Getting Down)."

In 1984, Billy signed with Jive Records and released his debut album, *Suddenly*, from which came the smash hit single he cowrote with Keith Diamond called "Caribbean Queen (No More Love On The Run)."

August	1984	★ CARIBBEAN QUEEN (NO MORE LOVE ON THE RUN)	Jive/Arista
December	1984	LOVER BOY	Jive/Arista
March	1985	SUDDENLY	Jive/Arista

NIGEL OLSSON

Nigel Olsson, Elton John's drummer from 1971 to 1976, had several solo hits in the seventies.

March	1975	ONLY ONE WOMAN	Rocket
December	1978	DANCIN' SHOES	Bang
April	1979	LITTLE BIT OF SOAP	Bang

JEFFREY OSBORNE

Born: March 9, 1948
Hometown: Providence, Rhode Island

Nigel Olsson

As the son of a trumpet player, Jeffrey Osborne became more interested in mastering an instrument than his voice, and so learned to play drums. In 1971, he joined L.T.D., and before long, his fellow band members learned he could sing and pushed him up front. Osborne sang all the group's hits, but began to think about starting a solo career. In 1979, he decided to leave, but in the interest of the band he stayed on for another tour and another album. He officially left in 1981, after the group's *Shine*

Jeffrey Osborne

On album. Osborne launched his solo career in fine form; his self-titled debut LP in 1982 produced three hits and his 1983 followup, *Stay With Me Tonight*, produced three more.

June	1982	1. I REALLY DON'T NEED NO LIGHT	A & M
September	1982	2. ON THE WINGS OF LOVE	A & M
March	1983	3. EENIE MEENIE	A & M
July	1983	4. DON'T YOU GET SO MAD	A & M
October	1983	5. STAY WITH ME TONIGHT	A & M
February	1984	6. WE'RE GOING ALL THE WAY	A & M
August	1984	7. THE LAST TIME I MADE LOVE (with Joyce Kennedy)	A & M
October	1984	8. DON'T STOP	A & M
January	1985	9. THE BORDERLINES	A & M

OUTLAWS

Members:
  Hughie Thomasson—guitar, vocals
  Freddie Salem—guitar, vocals
  Rick Cua—bass
  David Dix—drums
Hometown: Tampa, Florida

This band formed in the mid-seventies and became a big local favorite. Ronnie Van Zant, the leader of Lynyrd Skynyrd, saw Outlaw perform and liked them so much that he took them on the road as his opening act. In 1975, Van Zant approached Clive Davis, president of Arista Records, about signing the group. He did, and their first album, *Outlaws*, went gold. From that album came their first chart single, "There Goes Another Love Song," launching the group's southern rock sound.

Today Hughie Thomasson is the only original Outlaw in the line-up.

September	1975	1. THERE GOES ANOTHER LOVE SONG	Arista
July	1976	2. BREAKER-BREAKER	Arista
July	1977	3. HURRY SUNDOWN	Arista
December	1980	4. (GHOST) RIDERS IN THE SKY	Arista

PAGES

Members:
    Richard Page—vocals
    Steve George—vocals, piano, synthesizer
Hometown: Phoenix, Arizona

Richard and Steve have been singing harmoniously since they met as youngsters in the Phoenix Boys Choir. They formed Pages in 1977, when they blended their jazz-influenced harmonies with synthesizers. Their big break came when they became the back-up group for Andy Gibb, prompting Epic Records to sign them. In 1979 they had their only chart accomplishment, "I Do Believe in You."

December	1979	I DO BELIEVE IN YOU	Epic

ROBERT PALMER

Born: January 19, 1949
Hometown: Batley, Yorkshire, England

Robert Palmer began his musical career in the Mandrakes with a few fellow art students. It was in this band that the 19-year-old singer was spotted by Alan Bown, who recruited him for his own band. Palmer stayed with the well-known bandleader for a year and a half, until guitarist Pete Gage persuaded him to help start a new jazz-rock ensemble called Dada, which was ultimately trimmed down to become Vinegar Joe. This group, which featured vocals by Palmer and Elkie Brooks, became a popular pub band in England, but Palmer quit in February 1974, after 18 months, to launch his own career. He recorded demo tapes and landed a record deal, releasing his debut *Sneakin' Sally Through The Alley* LP a year later. While he has continued to record his own albums, Palmer has also produced albums for Moon Martin and Peter Baumann.

December	1976	1. MAN SMART, WOMAN SMARTER	Island
March	1978	2. EVERY KINDA PEOPLE	Island
July	1979	3. BAD CASE OF LOVING YOU	Island
December	1979	4. CAN WE STILL BE FRIENDS	Island
June	1983	5. YOU ARE IN MY SYSTEM	Island

GRAHAM PARKER

Hometown: London, England

During the mid-seventies Parker, who worked as a gas station attendant, went to a small recording studio and met Dave Robinson, the manager of the popular group Brinsley Schwarz. Parker presented Robinson with a tape of a few songs he had written. Robinson arranged for a recording session and then took one of the songs to Charlie Gillet to play on his local radio show. This airing resulted in a contract with Phonogram Records and the album *Howlin' Wind*.

In 1977, the EP "The Pink Parker" was released, from which came the single "Hold Back The Night," released on Mercury Records in the United States during the spring.

Even though Parker is a very exciting visual performer, this talent has not been translated into large record sales.

| April | 1977 | HOLD BACK THE NIGHT | Mercury |
| September | 1983 | LIFE GETS BETTER | Arista |

THE ALAN PARSONS PROJECT

Members:
    Alan Parsons—synthesizer
    Eric Woolfson—vocals
Hometown: London, England

Alan Parsons' record-making career began during the sessions for the Beatles' *Abbey Road* album, for which he served as assistant engineer.

The Alan Parsons Project. Eric Woolfson (*left*), Alan Parsons.

After the break-up of the Beatles, Parsons went on to engineer McCartney & Wings' *Wildlife* and *Red Rose Speedway* albums. Parsons also worked on five Hollies albums, Pink Floyd's *Dark Side Of The Moon* LP, and Al Stewart's *Year Of The Cat* LP as well as records by John Miles, Ambrosia, Pilot, Steve Harley & Cockney Rebel, and others.

Parsons started producing his own albums as the Alan Parsons Project with Eric Woolfson in 1974. A debut LP, *Tales Of Mystery And Imagination*, was released in the spring of 1976; the album was a musical interpretation of Edgar Allan Poe's classic stories. The albums that followed often delved into science fiction or mystical concepts.

Guest artists contribute lead vocals on much of the Project's music. These vocalists have included Colin Blunstone, John Miles, Lesley Duncan, and the English Chorale.

July	1976	1. DOCTOR TARR AND PROFESSOR FETHER	20th Century
October	1976	2. THE RAVEN	20th Century
August	1977	3. I WOULDN'T WANT TO BE LIKE YOU	Arista
January	1978	4. DON'T LET IT SHOW	Arista
September	1978	5. WHAT GOES UP	Arista
September	1979	6. DAMNED IF I DO	Arista
December	1980	7. GAMES PEOPLE PLAY	Arista
April	1981	8. TIME	Arista
October	1981	9. SNAKE EYES	Arista
July	1982	10. EYE IN THE SKY	Arista
November	1982	11. PSYCHOBABBLE	Arista
November	1983	12. YOU DON'T BELIEVE	Arista
March	1984	13. DON'T ANSWER ME	Arista
May	1984	14. PRIME TIME	Arista
February	1985	15. LET'S TALK ABOUT ME	Arista
May	1985	16. DAYS ARE NUMBERS (THE TRAVELLER)	Arista

LESLIE PEARL

Hometown: Bucks County, Pennsylvania

Before Leslie ever had a hit record, she wrote, sang, and produced jingles for New York Telephone, Gillette, Clairol, Pepsi, and Ford, to name just a few. Pearl has also written songs for Johnny Mathis, Mary MacGregor and Crystal Gayle.

In 1982, she had her only hit on her own to date. "If The Love Fits, Wear It" reached the top 40.

May	1982	IF THE LOVE FITS, WEAR IT	RCA

DAN PEEK

Born: 1950
Hometown: Florida

Onetime member of the group America, Dan Peek had a solo hit in 1979. See *AMERICA, Rock On: The Years of Change*.

September	1979	ALL THINGS ARE POSSIBLE	Lamb & Lion

TEDDY PENDERGRASS

Born: March 26, 1950
Hometown: Philadelphia, Pennsylvania

Teddy Pendergrass was reared in a very religious home, and was ordained as a minister by the age of 10. As a child, Teddy accompanied his mother to her job at Skioles, a Philadelphia club popular in the early sixties for performances by Frank Sinatra, Connie Francis, Bobby Rydell, and others. Taking advantage of the equipment on hand, Teddy soon taught himself how to read music and play drums. In his adolescence, Teddy joined a variety of local bands. One band, the Cadillacs, backed Harold Melvin & the Blue Notes. Within a year, lead vocalist John Atkins exited that group, and Teddy moved up from behind the drums. Harold Melvin & the Blue Notes began enjoying a string of hits. (See *HAROLD MELVIN & THE BLUE NOTES, Rock On: The Years of Change.*) In 1976, however, Pendergrass left the group to launch a solo career. In short time, he was nicknamed Teddy Bear and became a sex symbol; some of his concerts were billed as "For Women Only." Phone hookups called "Teddy Lines" were set up, and "Teddy" jeans and chocolate lollipops called "Teddy Pops" were introduced. Pendergrass was also set to star in *The Otis Redding Story,* but the film was never made. Pendergrass did make a cameo appearance in concert in the film *Soup For One.*

In March 1982, Pendergrass was in an automobile accident that left him partially paralyzed. Pendergrass returned to recording in 1984 with the *Love Language* album, which was produced by Luther Vandross and Michael Masser.

May	1977	1. I DON'T LOVE YOU ANYMORE	Philadelphia International
July	1978	2. CLOSE THE DOOR	Philadelphia International
July	1979	3. TURN OFF THE LIGHTS	P.I.R.
August	1980	4. CAN'T WE TRY	P.I.R.
November	1980	5. LOVE T. K. O.	P.I.R.
January	1982	6. YOU'RE MY LATEST, MY GREATEST INSPIRATION	P.I.R.
June	1984	7. HOLD ME (with Whitney Houston)	Asylum

STEVE PERRY

Born: January 22, 1949
Hometown: Hanford, California

When Steve Perry was singing with Alien Project, around 1977, the group was close to signing a record contract. While driving home one night, however, the band's bass player was killed in an auto accident, and rather than find a replacement, the group members agreed to split up.

Shortly thereafter, Perry was called by Herbie Herbert, manager of Journey, who had heard Alien Project's demo tape. Perry was persuaded to join the San Francisco-based band, which was looking for a lead singer who could propel them beyond cult status. Perry's vocals and songs

Steve Perry

helped make Journey a supergroup; the band was voted the Most Popular Rock Band in the National Gallup Poll in 1983. (See *JOURNEY.*)

Between Journey commitments, the band members explored outside interests. Steve Perry released his debut solo album, *Street Talk,* in 1984, and the record was an instant success. His hit single "Oh, Sherrie," was inspired by his girlfriend, Sherrie Swafford.

August	1982	1. DON'T FIGHT IT (with Kenny Loggins)	Columbia
April	1984	2. OH, SHERRIE	Columbia
June	1984	3. SHE'S MINE	Columbia
September	1984	4. STRUNG OUT	Columbia
November	1984	5. FOOLISH HEART	Columbia

BERNADETTE PETERS

Real Name: Bernadette Lazzara
Born: February 28, 1948
Hometown: Ozone Park, Queens, New York

Bernadette, who took her father's first name Peter and called herself Bernadette Peters, appeared in several movies. She scored big in 1980 with a Carla Thomas hit from 1961, "Gee Whiz."

March	1980	GEE WHIZ	MCA
August	1981	DEDICATED TO THE ONE I LOVE	MCA

TOM PETTY & THE HEARTBREAKERS

Members:

> Tom Petty—vocals, guitar—born: October 20, 1953
> Mike Campbell—guitar—born: February 1, 1954
> Benmont Tench—keyboards, vocals—born: September 7, 1954
> Howie Epstein—bass, vocals
> Stan Lynch—drums, vocals—born: May 21, 1955

Hometown: Gainesville, Florida

Although all the Heartbreakers are from one area of Florida, they moved to Los Angeles independently. There, their common roots drew them together and they formed a band. The group's self-titled debut album was released in 1976, just as a new punk-rock scene was attracting public attention. Initially, Tom Petty & the Heartbreakers were thought to be part of that scene, simply because they were a new act, but the group quickly showed themselves to be past any limiting labels.

TOM PETTY & THE HEARTBREAKERS

November	1977	1. BREAKDOWN	Shelter/ABC
June	1978	2. I NEED TO KNOW	Shelter/ABC
September	1978	3. LISTEN TO HER HEART	Shelter/ABC
November	1979	4. DON'T DO ME LIKE THAT	Backstreet
January	1980	5. REFUGEE	Backstreet
April	1980	6. HERE COMES MY GIRL	Backstreet
May	1981	7. THE WAITING	Backstreet
July	1981	8. STOP DRAGGIN' MY HEART AROUND (with Stevie Nicks)	Modern
August	1981	9. A WOMAN IN LOVE	Backstreet
November	1982	10. YOU GOT LUCKY	Backstreet
February	1983	11. CHANGE OF HEART	Backstreet

TOM PETTY

March	1985	DON'T COME AROUND HERE NO MORE	MCA

MIKE PINERA

Mike Pinera, a member of Iron Butterfly, had a solo hit in 1980. See *IRON BUTTERFLY, Rock On: The Years of Change.*

January	1980	GOODNIGHT MY LOVE	Spector

ROBERT PLANT

Born: August 20, 1948
Hometown: Bromwich, Staffordshire, England

Robert Plant might have become an accountant had he not been entranced by the blues. By the mid-sixties, Plant was a fixture in the Birmingham music scene, singing in a string of bands, including the Band of Joy, which featured drummer John Bonham. Plant then cut a few singles under his own name, backed by the Band of Joy.

In 1968, guitarist Jimmy Page, upon the recommendation of pop singer Terry Reid, recruited Plant, as well as Bonham and bassist John Paul Jones, to form a new band. Page's former band, the Yardbirds, had

Robert Plant

just broken up, so the new group called themselves the New Yardbirds. They soon changed their name to Led Zeppelin. After nine multi-million selling albums, Led Zeppelin ended in 1980 with the death of John Bonham, but the group's popularity never decreased. (See *LED ZEPPELIN, Rock On: The Years of Change.*)

Plant was the first to actively pursue a solo career, with his *Pictures at Eleven* LP in 1982. While his post-Zep music was mellower, the legend of Led Zeppelin among hard-rock bands assured Plant an immediate following. Today, he is involved with his new group, *THE HONEY-DRIPPERS.*

September	1982	1. BURNING DOWN ONE SIDE	Swan Song
November	1982	2. PLEDGE PIN	Swan Song
August	1983	3. BIG LOG	Swan Song
November	1983	4. IN THE MOOD	Esparanza

PLASTIC BERTRAND

Real Name: Plastoc Bertrand
Born: 1960

Plastic first came to the attention of French and Belgian audiences through combined new wave and disco play in late 1977. In early 1978, he became the third new wave act signed by Sire Records (following the Ramones, with "Sheena Is A Punk Rocker," and the Talking Heads, with "Psycho Killer").

His first release for the label was "Ça Plane Pour Moi," which translates to "It Flies For Me." This was a good-feeling rock tune with Beach Boys-style harmonies.

April	1978	ÇA PLANE POUR MOI		Sire

POCKETS

Members:
    Larry Jacobs—vocals, percussion—born: 1951
    Jacob Sheffer—guitar, percussion—born: 1953—replaced (1979) by Allan Thomas
    Albert McKinney—keyboards, vocals
    Charles Williams—trumpet, flugel horn, vocals, percussion—born: 1955
    Irving Madison—saxophone, vocals, percussion—born: 1958
    Kevin Barnes—trombone, vocals, percussion—born: 1960
    Gary Grainger—bass, vocals—born: 1954
    George Gray—drums, vocals, percussion—born: 1953
Hometown: Baltimore, Maryland

All the members of Pockets grew up together in Baltimore, each playing in different local bands, exchanging places with one another, forming new bands out of old bands and growing up in the music world. Al McKinney, Pockets' keyboardist and leader, had been playing with Luther Ingram when he decided it was time to form a new group. He recruited friends and neighbors, and the band, named Pockets by Ingram, was born. A mutual friend sent a tape of the group's original music to Verdine White of Earth, Wind & Fire, who was so interested in the music that he made arrangements for Pockets to come to Los Angeles to stage a showcase performance before industry executives. Verdine White and Earth, Wind & Fire wound up giving Pockets many of the group's earliest breaks in the music business.

January	1978	COME GO WITH ME		Columbia

POINT BLANK

Members:
    Bubba Keith—vocals
    Rusty Burns—guitar, vocals
    Kim Davis—guitar, vocals
    Michael Hamilton—keyboards
    "Wild" Bill Randolph—bass, vocals
    Peter "Buzzy" Gruen—drums, percussion, vocals
Hometown: Texas

Point Blank was hardly born before the group earned an encore as the opening act for the Marshall Tucker Band and J. J. Cale in New Orleans.

The group was soon recording albums and opening concerts for many top-name hard-rock and heavy-metal acts. Although Point Blank did more road work than most bands, they remained essentially a group with a cult following. "Wild" Bill Randolph joined in 1978 to replace Phillip Petty. In 1980 Bubba Keith replaced John O'Daniel and Michael Hamilton replaced Steve Hardin and Karl Berke.

June	1981	NICOLE	MCA

BONNIE POINTER

Born: July 11, 1951
Hometown: East Oakland, California

Bonnie Pointer was an original member of the Pointer Sisters, but left in 1978 to pursue a solo career. She released several albums, but after three initial hits, has had no more chart songs.

November	1978	FREE ME FROM MY FREEDOM	Motown
June	1979	HEAVEN MUST HAVE SENT YOU	Motown
December	1979	I CAN'T HELP MYSELF	Motown

THE POLICE

Members:
    Sting (Gordon Sumner)—vocals, bass—born: October 2, 1951
    Andy Summers—guitar—born: December 31, 1942
    Stewart Copeland—drums—born: July 16, 1952
Hometown: London, England

Bonnie Pointer

The Police. *Left to right:* Stewart Copeland, Andy Summers, Sting.

Stewart Copeland organized the Police in January of 1977 with Henri Padovani on guitar and Sting, whom he'd discovered playing in a Newcastle jazz combo called Last Exit, on bass. Copeland persuaded Sting to leave his daytime teaching job and come to London. The trio then put out a first single, "Fall Out" b/w "Nothing Achieved," themselves. Andy Summers joined later as a fourth band member, but then Padovani left them as a trio once again.

The members of Police worked on various projects both separately and as a group (Copeland had a dual career as a mythical artist named Klark Kent), but the three committed themselves to the Police's success when their single "Roxanne" got a lot of attention in England upon its release in April 1978. The song also generated attention on American radio waves, leading to the immediate success of the group's debut album, *Outlandos d'Amour,* in early 1979. The Police quickly became an international supergroup, garnering multiple hits and awards. One of the group's biggest coups, however, was a 1983 tour of SRO stadium concerts, highlighted by Shea Stadium in New York. Sting has also gotten good notices for his acting roles in films *Quadrophenia, Brimstone & Treacle* and *Dune.*

February	1979	1. ROXANNE	A & M
November	1979	2. MESSAGE IN A BOTTLE	A & M
October	1980	3. DE DO DO DO, DE DA DA DA	A & M

February	1981	4. DON'T STAND SO CLOSE TO ME	A & M
September	1981	5. EVERY LITTLE THING SHE DOES IS MAGIC	A & M
January	1982	6. SPIRITS IN THE MATERIAL WORLD	A & M
April	1982	7. SECRET JOURNEY	A & M
June	1983	★ 8. EVERY BREATH YOU TAKE	A & M
August	1983	9. KING OF PAIN	A & M
November	1983	10. SYNCHRONICITY II	A & M
January	1984	11. WRAPPED AROUND YOUR FINGER	A & M

GARY PORTNOY

Born: 1956
Hometown: Valley Stream, New York

Gary Portnoy says that no one in his family was particularly musically inclined, but that there was a piano in the house, so at age nine he started fooling with it. Unlike most recording artists, Portnoy has had little performance experience (outside of playing keyboards in a local band called Kark when he was a senior in high school). Years later, he made several attempts to hook up with a record producer or publishing company, but little of consequence happened until he signed with the Entertainment Company, which successfully farmed Portnoy's songs to Dolly Parton, Glen Campbell, Cheryl Ladd, Samantha Sang, and others. Portnoy's own self-titled debut album was released in 1980.

| April | 1983 | HERE EVERYBODY KNOWS YOUR NAME | Applause |

POUSETTE-DART BAND

Members:
    Jon Pousette-Dart—guitar, vocals
    John Troy—bass, vocals
    John Curtis—guitar, vocals
    Michael Dowe—drums, percussion, vocals
Hometown: Boston, Massachusetts

Pousette-Dart began as a duo in 1970 when Jon met John Troy while attending college in Stockton, California. The two separated for a few years, then reunited in 1973 to form the full band. The group emerged nationally in the late seventies with a charted album, and in 1979 had a charted single, "For Love."

| September | 1979 | FOR LOVE | Capitol |

PRETENDERS

Members:
    Chrissie Hynde—vocals—born: September 7, 1951—Akron, Ohio
    James Honeyman-Scott—guitar, vocals, keyboards—died: June 16, 1982—
        replaced (1982) by Robbie MacIntosh—born: October 25, 1957

Pretenders—1980. *Left to right:* James Honeyman-Scott, Martin Chambers, Chrissie Hynde, Pete Farndon.

Pete Farndon—bass—born: 1953—died: April 14, 1983—replaced (1982)
   by Malcolm Foster—born: January 13, 1956
Martin Chambers—drums—born: September 4, 1951
Hometown: Hereford, England

Chrissie Hynde, an American, had shuffled back and forth among the
United States, England, and France, singing in a number of bands and at
a few recording sessions, before hooking up with James Honeyman-Scott,
Pete Farndon, and Martin Chambers, all friends from Hereford who had
played together in various combinations. The group recorded a cover
version of the Kinks' "Stop Your Sobbing" in January 1979 with Nick
Lowe producing. The single did well in the United Kingdom, and was

Pretenders—1983. *Left to right:* Martin Chambers, Rob MacIntosh, Chrissie Hynde, Malcolm Foster.

followed that same year with two other successful non-cover singles, "Kid" and "Brass In Pocket." Their self-titled debut album, released in January 1980, immediately established the group as a hit band. In 1982, James Honeyman-Scott died, and Pete Farndon left the group; Farndon subsequently died also. The two musicians were replaced by Robbie MacIntosh and Malcolm Foster, respectively.

February	1980	1. BRASS IN POCKET	Sire
June	1980	2. STOP YOUR SOBBING	Sire
December	1982	3. BACK ON THE CHAIN GANG	Sire
December	1983	4. MIDDLE OF THE ROAD	Sire
March	1984	5. SHOW ME	Sire
June	1984	6. THIN LINE BETWEEN LOVE AND HATE	Sire

PRINCE

Real Name: Prince Rogers Nelson
Born: June 7, 1958
Hometown: Minneapolis, Minnesota

After playing briefly in local bands, Prince became widely known when at the age of 19 he signed a lucrative deal with Warner Brothers Records, which allowed the virtually unknown musician to compose, arrange, play all the instruments on, and produce his debut album, *For You.* In short time, Prince became known not only for his precedent-setting deal with the major record firm, but for his skimpy stage outfits (neckerchief, bikini briefs, and legwarmers) and his taboo subject matter (oral sex, incest). By the early eighties, Prince had lent his hand to a group called the Time, and helped form an all-female vocal trio called Vanity 6 (now Apollonia 6), pulling together an empire of daring, creative musicians. Although Prince himself kept something of a low profile (he turns down *all* requests for interviews, photo sessions, television appearances, etc.), his *1999* album, released in late 1982, made him a superstar by the end of 1983. Prince then conceived and starred in a film he called *Purple Rain,* filmed in Minneapolis in late 1983 and released in the summer of 1984. All members of his "empire" were featured in starring roles in *Purple Rain.* The act became known as Prince and the Revolution in 1984.

PRINCE

November	1978	1. SOFT AND WET	Warner Bros.
November	1979	2. I WANNA BE YOUR LOVER	Warner Bros.
October	1981	3. CONTROVERSY	Warner Bros.
October	1982	4. 1999	Warner Bros.
February	1983	5. LITTLE RED CORVETTE	Warner Bros.
June	1983	6. 1999	Warner Bros.
September	1983	7. DELIRIOUS	Warner Bros.
December	1983	8. LET'S PRETEND WE'RE MARRIED/IRRESISTABLE BITCH	Warner Bros.

PRINCE AND THE REVOLUTION

June	1984	★ 1. WHEN DOVES CRY	Warner Bros.
August	1984	★ 2. LET'S GO CRAZY	Warner Bros.
October	1984	3. PURPLE RAIN	Warner Bros.
December	1984	4. I WOULD DIE 4 U	Warner Bros.
February	1985	5. TAKE ME WITH U (with Appolonia)	Warner Bros.

PRISM

Members:
 Ron Tabak—vocals
 Lindsey Mitchell—guitar
 Tom Lavin—guitar

Ab Bryant—bass
John Hall—keyboards
Rodney Higgs—drums
Henry Small—vocals—added in 1981
Hometown: Toronto, Canada

Prism, a Canadian-bred band with platinum-record status, was preparing to try to win over more American rock fans when a number of personnel changes left the group's future in doubt. Bruce Allen, who was managing Loverboy and other Canadian rock acts as well as Prism, turned to Loverboy's Paul Dean for a solution. Dean recommended vocalist Henry Small, who had fronted his previous band, Scrubbaloe Caine. They located Small in southern California, where he was trying to put together a band after coming off a Burton Cummings tour as guest vocalist. Allen persuaded the New York native to go to Vancouver and join Prism. Together, the new Prism recorded the *Small Change* album, which was released in January 1982. The group broke up, however, so Small began touring and recording subsequent albums (with other musicians) as Prism.

October	1977	1. SPACESHIP SUPERSTAR	Ariola
January	1978	2. TAKE ME TO THE KAPTAIN	Ariola
July	1978	3. FLYIN'	Ariola
January	1982	4. DON'T LET HIM KNOW	Capitol
April	1982	5. TURN ON YOUR RADAR	Capitol

THE PRODUCERS

Members:
    Van Temple—guitar, vocals
    Wayne Famous—keyboards, vocals
    Kyle Henderson—bass, vocals
    Bryan Holmes—drums, vocals
Hometown: Atlanta, Georgia

The members of the Producers learned to play their instruments in an assortment of original and cover bands in and around Atlanta's club circuit. On New Year's Eve 1979, Kyle Henderson caught Van Temple, Wayne Famous, and Bryan Holmes playing at Uncle Tom's Tavern, and in a few minutes the quartet became the Producers. The group spent the next few months rehearsing and writing new material before returning to the club circuit, mixing original sets with cover jobs to keep the money flowing. In August, the band's manager worked out a showcase gig in New York, which landed the Producers a producer and then a record deal.

| June | 1981 | WHAT SHE DOES TO ME | Portrait |

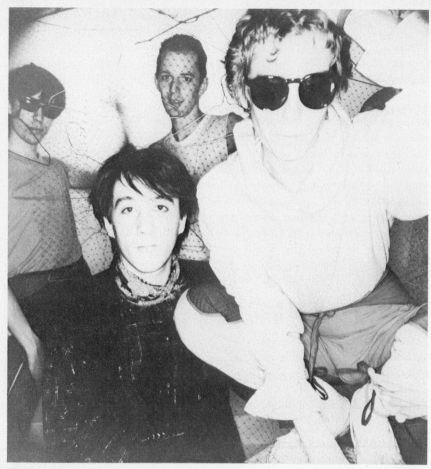

The Psychedelic Furs. *Left to right:* Tim Butler, John Ashton, Vince Ely, Richard Butler.

THE PSYCHEDELIC FURS

Members:
 Richard Butler—vocals
 John Ashton—guitar
 Tim Butler—bass
 Phil Calvert—drums, percussion—replaced (1984) by Keith Forsey
Hometown: London, England

In 1977, when punk rock ruled England, Richard and Tim Butler, guitarist Roger "Dog" Morris, and saxophonist Duncan Kilburn were formulating an idea for a new band. As they developed their sound, the group went through the requisite personnel changes. John Ashton was added as a second guitarist in November 1978, and Vince Ely became the drummer in the spring of 1979. Thanks to a successful single in late 1979, the Psychedelic Furs' self-titled debut album was an instant best seller when it was released in March 1980. Success in America came more slowly, and by the time "Love My Way" from the *Forever Now* album charted, the Furs were a quartet. Vince Ely had played on the first three albums, but left in 1982. He was replaced by Phil Calvert, who was replaced in turn by producer Keith Forsey.

| March | 1983 | LOVE MY WAY | Columbia |
| May | 1984 | THE GHOST IN YOU | Columbia |

PURE PRAIRIE LEAGUE

Members:
Vince Gill—vocals, guitar, fiddle, banjo—added in 1980
Jeff Wilson—guitar, vocals—added in 1980
Michael Connor—keyboards
Michael Reilly—bass, vocals
Billy Hinds—drums
Hometown: Cincinnati, Ohio

None of Pure Prairie League's original members were in the line-up that had hits. Originally conceived as a trio, the first current member to join was Billy Hinds in 1971, who arrived in time to join singer/guitarist Craig Fuller, pedal steel guitarist John Call, and rhythm guitarist George Powell for the group's second album, *Bustin' Out*. Michael Reilly and Michael Connor had played on the sessions for that album, and in July 1972 officially joined Pure Prairie League. When RCA Records dropped Pure Prairie League from its roster, the group continued to tour. In April 1975, when RCA re-signed PPL and released *Two Lane Highway*, the lineup included Powell, Hinds, Connor, Reilly, Call, and temporary lead guitarist Larry Goshorn. John Call exited the group in 1977 and was replaced by Larry's brother, Timmy Goshorn, on lead guitar and vocals. Both Goshorn brothers left in late 1978, and Patrick Bolin and Vince Gill beat over fifty guitar players for the jobs. Bolin was replaced by Jeff Wilson in January 1980. There's no telling who will be in PPL by the time you read this, but last we heard, Vince Gill left to go solo.

March	1975	1. AMIE	RCA
June	1975	2. TWO LANE HIGHWAY	RCA
May	1980	3. LET ME LOVE YOU TONIGHT	Casablanca
August	1980	4. I'M ALMOST READY	Casablanca
December	1980	5. I CAN'T STOP THE FEELIN'	Casablanca
April	1981	6. STILL RIGHT HERE IN MY HEART	Casablanca
July	1981	7. YOU'RE MINE TONIGHT	Casablanca

QUARTERFLASH

Members:
  Rindy Ross—vocals, saxophone—born: June 26, 1951
  Marv Ross—guitar, vocals—born: January 30, 1951
  Jack Charles—guitar, vocals (left in 1984)
  Rick DiGiallonardo—keyboards (left in 1984)
  Rich Gooch—bass—born: November 2, 1948
  Brian David Willis—drums—born: June 14, 1958
Hometown: Portland, Oregon

Marv and Rindy Ross have been musical partners since their high school days, and gained considerable reputation in a group called Seafood Mama, which had a local hit in 1980 with "Harden My Heart." Eventually, the husband and wife team joined forces with another Portland club band, Pilot, and became Quarterflash, the name taken from an Australian folk saying: "a quarter part flash and three parts foolish." They recorded "Harden My Heart" along with other songs for an album, and this time

Quarterflash. *Left to right:* Rick DiGiallonardo, Jack Charles, Rich Gooch, Rindy Ross, Marv Ross, Brian David Willis.

the song became a hit across the nation. The group had several hits, including the theme song for the movie *Night Shift*.

October	1981	1. HARDEN MY HEART	Geffen
February	1982	2. FIND ANOTHER FOOL	Geffen
May	1982	3. RIGHT KIND OF LOVE	Geffen
August	1982	4. NIGHTSHIFT	Geffen
June	1983	5. TAKE ME TO HEART	Warner Bros.
October	1983	6. TAKE ANOTHER PICTURE	Geffen

SUZI QUATRO

Born: June 3, 1950
Hometown: Detroit, Michigan

Although Suzi Quatro first appeared onstage at the age of eight, playing bongo drums for her father's jazz trio, she waited until she was 15 to form her own band, Suzie Soul and the Pleasure Seekers (later called Cradle), with her three sisters.

When Quatro left Detroit and headed for England in 1971, she said she wouldn't return until she'd proven herself in rock 'n' roll. Dressed in black leather outfits, she became part of the short-lived glitter rock fad and enjoyed enough hits in the United Kingdom to become a rather big name in the mid-seventies.

Suzi's first success in America was several appearances as Leather Tuscadero in ABC-TV's "Happy Days" series. Suzi lives in England with her husband/guitarist/collaborator, Len Tuckey.

September	1974	1. ALL SHOOK UP	Bell
February	1976	2. CAN THE CAN	Big Tree
January	1979	3. STUMBLIN' IN (with Chris Norman)	RSO
May	1979	4. IF YOU CAN'T GIVE ME LOVE	RSO
September	1979	5. I'VE NEVER BEEN IN LOVE	RSO
November	1979	6. SHE'S IN LOVE WITH YOU	RSO
January	1981	7. LIPSTICK	Dreamland

QUIET RIOT

Members:
    Kevin DuBrow—vocals—born: October 29
    Carlos Cavazo—guitar, vocals—born: July 8
    Rudy Sarzo—bass, vocals—born: November 18—left group in 1985
    Frankie Banali—drums, vocals—born: November 14
Hometown: Los Angeles, California

Quiet Riot has had two incarnations. The original Quiet Riot was formed in 1975 by Kevin DuBrow and the late Randy Rhoads, best known as lead guitarist with Ozzy Osbourne. Although the group had a strong local following, American record companies weren't interested. Japanese com-

Quiet Riot. *Left to right:* Frankie Banali, Kevin DuBrow, Carlos Cavazo.

panies were, however, and *Quiet Riot* (1977) and *Quiet Riot II* (1978),
were released in the Far East. The group soon split up, when Rhoads and
Rudy Sarzo, who was in the original Quiet Riot's final line-up, joined
Ozzy Osbourne's band while DuBrow led another hard-rock band, DuBrow,
through L. A. clubs. DuBrow finally landed a record deal and not only
received permission from Rhoads and Sarzo to use the name Quiet Riot,
but also confirmation that they would guest on one tune, "Thunderbird."
Rhoads died in a plane crash shortly before the session was to take place,
however. Sarzo went in to do the one song, but liked it so much that he
joined the new band.

Quiet Riot's American debut album, *Metal Health*, was released in
early 1983 and sold over 4 million copies.

September	1983	CUM ON FEEL THE NOIZE	Pasha
January	1984	BANG YOUR HEAD (METAL HEALTH)	Pasha
July	1984	MAMA, WEER ALL CRAZEE NOW	Pasha

R

EDDIE RABBITT

Born: November 27, 1944
Hometown: East Orange, New Jersey

Eddie Rabbitt was raised in East Orange, New Jersey, by an Irish father who played the fiddle and accordion, but he learned his first guitar chords at age 12 from his scoutmaster. In 1964, Rabbitt filled in for a piano player in a Paterson, New Jersey bar, then parlayed that gig into many more in country bars around New York and New Jersey. After three years, Rabbitt grew restless and moved to Nashville. He began by writing songs that were then recorded by other artists, including Elvis Presley's "Kentucky Rain," and then in 1975, started recording some himself.

In late 1978, the *Chicago Tribune* polled insiders of the Nashville music industry as to which artist would become the next country-pop superstar. Almost unanimously, the music moguls named Eddie Rabbitt, and the prediction shortly became reality. Rabbitt's hits came quickly, turning him into a major crossover sensation and sex symbol.

Rabbitt sang the title song for the 1978 film *Every Which Way But Loose* and hosted his own hour-long TV special for NBC in 1979. In 1982, he volunteered his time and services to the National Mental Health Association and appeared in a public service announcement for TV broadcast.

Eddie Rabbit

July	1976	1. ROCKY MOUNTAIN MUSIC	Elektra
June	1977	2. I CAN'T HELP MYSELF	Elektra
June	1978	3. YOU DON'T LOVE ME ANYMORE	Elektra
January	1979	4. EVERY WHICH WAY BUT LOOSE	Elektra
June	1979	5. SUSPICIONS	Elektra
May	1980	6. GONE TOO FAR	Elektra
June	1980	7. DRIVIN' MY LIFE AWAY	Elektra
November	1980	★ 8. I LOVE A RAINY NIGHT	Elektra
July	1981	9. STEP BY STEP	Elektra
November	1981	10. SOMEONE COULD LOSE A HEART TONIGHT	Elektra
April	1982	11. I DON'T KNOW WHERE TO START	Elektra
October	1982	12. YOU AND I (with Crystal Gayle)	Elektra
April	1983	13. YOU CAN'T RUN FROM LOVE	Warner Bros.
September	1983	14. YOU PUT THE BEAT IN MY HEART	Warner Bros.

RAES

Members:
Robbie Rae—vocals
Cherrill Rae—vocals
Hometown: Cardiff, Wales

Robbie Rae was born in Resolven, Wales, where he gained early musical training in Welsh choirs as a boy soprano, a tradition handed down from his father. Through his teenage years, Robbie sang and toured with his brother. By the early seventies, Robbie was hosting a variety show on Welsh television, and one week his guest happened to be the future Mrs. Rae. Cherrill was born in Carlisle, near the Scottish-English border. As a child, she moved to Canada with her parents, where she became fascinated with soul music. She later led a variety of rock and soul groups playing bars throughout Canada, but eventually headed to Cardiff, Wales, to attend the College of Music there. Three days after their first meeting, Robbie and Cherrill were engaged. Each pursued a solo career, and because of their individual successes, the Raes found it impossible to perform in Great Britain as a duo. They consequently moved to Canada in 1974.

December	1978	A LITTLE LOVIN' (KEEPS THE DOCTOR AWAY)	A & M

GERRY RAFFERTY

Hometown: Scotland

Gerry Rafferty began his musical career in 1968 when he and Brian Connoly formed the Humblebums. Three years later, Rafferty recorded his first solo album *Can I Have My Money Back?* Then, along with Joe Egan, a childhood friend who had worked on the album with him, Rafferty formed Stealer's Wheel. Their debut album in 1973 included a hit, "Stuck In The Middle With You," but the group broke up two years later.

April	1978	1. BAKER STREET	United Artists
August	1978	2. RIGHT DOWN THE LINE	United Artists

December	1978	3. HOME AND DRY	United Artists
June	1979	4. DAYS GONE DOWN	United Artists
August	1979	5. GET IT RIGHT NEXT TIME	United Artists
July	1980	6. THE ROYAL MILE	United Artists

RAINBOW

Members:

Joe Lynn Turner—vocals (replaced Ronnie James Dio and Graham Bonnett in 1980)

Ritchie Blackmore—guitar—born: April 14, 1945

David Rosenthal—keyboards (replaced Mickey Lee Soule, Tony Carey, David Stone & Don Airey in 1982)

Roger Glover—bass (replaced Craig Gruber, Jimmy Bain, Mark Clarke, and Bob Daisley)

Chuck Burgi—drums (replaced Gary Driscoll, Cozy Powell, and Bob Rondinelli)

Originally called Blackmore's Rainbow, this group was formed in 1975 after Ritchie Blackmore left Deep Purple. Rainbow goes through rapid personnel changes; at presstime, the group has yet to record even two consecutive albums with the same line-up. "Street of Dreams" was recorded by the line-up listed above. In 1984 Ritchie Blackmore joined a re-formed Deep Purple, and Joe Lynn Turner recorded his debut solo album.

November	1979	SINCE YOU'VE BEEN GONE	Polydor
April	1982	STONE COLD	Mercury
November	1983	STREET OF DREAMS	Mercury

RAMONES

Members:

Joey Ramone (Jeffrey Hyman)—vocals—born: May 19, 1951

Johnny Ramone (John Cummings)—guitar—born: October 8, 1948

Dee Dee Ramone (Douglas Colvin)—bass—born: September 18, 1951

Tommy Ramone (Tommy Erdelyi)—drums—replaced (1977) by Marky Ramone (Marc Bell)—Marky replaced (1983) by Richie Ramone (Richie Beau)—born: August 11, 1957

Hometown: Queens, New York

When the Ramones formed in 1974 and began playing at CBGB's and elsewhere on the New York City club circuit, there was no other group like it, and to this day, they remain a unique quartet. The Ramones' brand of rock 'n' roll is pop music with silly lyrics backed by a fast and thunderous wall of power chords. The group starred in and supplied much of the music for the 1979 film *Rock 'N' Roll High School*, and was featured in an underground film short, *Punking Out*. They were one of the first new wave acts signed to a major label.

Ramones. *Left to right:* Johnny, Richie, Joey, Dee Dee.

All four members, though unrelated, have taken on Ramone as their last name.

July	1977	SHEENA IS A PUNK ROCKER	Sire
January	1978	ROCKAWAY BEACH	Sire
April	1978	DO YOU WANNA DANCE	Warner Bros.

BILLY RANKIN

Born: April 25, 1959
Hometown: Glasgow, Scotland

Billy Rankin served his apprenticeship in various local bands. At 17, he was invited to play guitar in a band called Zal; although reportedly received enthusiastically by the press and the public, the group split when the leader, Zal Cleminson, took his leave. Rankin went on to other groups, but his major break came when he was asked to join Nazareth. Within days of accepting, he was on his way to the United States for a tour that was recorded and filmed for a live album and video. He left Nazareth before they had their first hit single in 1975. Billy's solo career started with the *Growin' Up Too Soon* album in January 1984.

March	1984	BABY COME BACK	A & M

Ratt. *Left to right:* Warren DeMartini, Bobby Blotzer, Stephen Pearcy, Robbin Crosby, Juan Croucier.

RATT

Members:
Stephen Pearcy—vocals—born: July 3, 1959
Robbin Crosby—guitar, vocals—born: August 4, 1960
Warren DeMartini—guitar, vocals—born: April 10, 1963
Juan Croucier—bass, vocals—born: August 22, 1959
Bobby Blotzer—drums—born: October 22, 1958
Hometown: Los Angeles, California

In 1982, Ratt began appearing before capacity crowds in Los Angeles clubs, including the Troubador, the Roxy, the Starwood, and the Whisky, where they eventually became the house band. It was while appearing at the Whisky that the group was seen by Marshall Berle, nephew of comedian Milton Berle, who became their manager and financed their first recording session. An album was recorded and released on the local Time Coast label, with several cuts finding their way to local major radio stations like KMET and KLOS. This exposure led to large album sales and interest by major labels. Ratt was signed to Atlantic and recorded the album *Out Of The Cellar*, which produced the single "Round and Round" and the video of the same name in which Milton Berle made a guest appearance.

| June | 1984 | ROUND AND ROUND | Atlantic |
| October | 1984 | WANTED MAN | Atlantic |

GENYA RAVAN

Real Name: Goldie Zelkowitz
Born: 1940
Hometown: New York, New York

Goldie Zelkowitz was raised in a tenement on New York's Lower East Side, where she joined an all-girl street gang, the Furies. One evening in Brooklyn's Lollipop Lounge, she jumped on stage with the house band on a dare. The group was the Escorts, led by Richard Perry, and Goldie became their lead singer. Four years later, she formed an all-girl group called Goldie and the Gingerbreads. Eric Burdon heard them in a rock club and was so intrigued that his group, the Animals, produced the first single for Goldie and the Gingerbreads. The group toured for three years with all the British Invasion groups.

In 1968, Goldie took the name Genya Ravan and became the lead singer of a nine-person jazz-rock group called Ten Wheel Drive, which lasted for three years and three albums. Becoming Goldie again, she released a solo album before readopting the name Genya. Ravan released more solo albums, produced local New York rock artists like the Dead Boys, the Shirts, and even Ronnie Spector, and formed a short-lived independent record company. These days, Ravan is teaching record production.

August   1978   BACK IN MY ARMS AGAIN   20th Century

RAYDIO

Members:
 Ray Parker, Jr.—guitar, vocals—born: May 1, 1954
 Charles Fearing—guitar—born: September 16, 1956
 Arnell Carmichael—keyboards—born: October 29, 1952
 Darren Carmichael—vocals
 Larry Tolbert—drums—born: July 21, 1950
Hometown: Detroit, Michigan

The evolution of Ray Parker, Jr. and Raydio began with four musicians who grew up together in the Dexter/Davison section of Detroit, home territory for Diana Ross, the Temptations, George Clinton, and other music luminaries. Larry Tolbert lived next door to Ray and taught Ray his basics. Brothers Arnell and Darren Carmichael also lived nearby. Arnell played in a back-up group with Ray when they were in their early teens, and even played in a band with Ray's brother. Ray completed the Raydio line-up in Los Angeles when he met Barry White's former guitarist, Charles Fearing.

Ray's own musical odyssey began on the clarinet. At age nine, a solo on that instrument won him first prize in a talent show. Soon afterwards,

Ray Parker, Jr.

he was accepted into the All-City Band, and also played in a trio with drummer Ollie E. Brown and trumpeter Nathan Watts. At age 12, Ray switched to electric guitar and wound up playing back-up for many of the big-name artists who came to play the 20 Grant, the biggest club in town. The back-up band, which also included Michael Henderson, Ollie Brown, and Hamilton Bohamon, wound up playing behind Stevie Wonder, Gladys Knight, the Temptations, and others. This led to Ray's becoming a local session musician, eventually touring as Stevie Wonder's guitarist on a 1972 tour opening for the Rolling Stones. Once in Los Angeles, he became known not only as a session musician, but as a songwriter; Rufus had a big hit with lead vocalist Chaka Khan belting out Parker's "You Got The Love," and Herbie Hancock's interpretation of Ray's "Keep On Doin' It" was nominated for a Grammy Award. Ray knew it was time to move to the forefront, and formed Raydio.

The versatile Parker composed, played, sang, arranged, engineered, and produced Raydio's self-titled debut album in 1977. The album and its debut single, "Jack & Jill," both went gold. By the third album the group was renamed Ray Parker, Jr. and Raydio. After four albums, all of which went gold, Parker officially disbanded Raydio. More than ever, the man who plays guitar, piano, synthesizer, bass, and drums was becoming a one-man operation.

Parker has produced records for Deniece Williams, Cheryl Lynn, Brick, Diana Ross, and New Edition. Aside from the aforementioned Herbie Hancock and Rufus, Diana Ross, Barry White, Helen Reddy, LaBelle, Bobby Womack, and Seals & Crofts have also recorded Parker's tunes. Well established now as a solo artist, songwriter, and producer, Parker may produce a group led by Arnell Carmichael; the group will be called Raydio.

RAYDIO

January	1978	JACK & JILL	Arista
April	1979	YOU CAN'T CHANGE THAT	Arista

RAY PARKER, JR. & RAYDIO

April	1980	TWO PLACES AT THE SAME TIME	Arista
March	1981	A WOMAN NEEDS LOVE	Arista
July	1981	THAT OLD SONG	Arista

RAY PARKER, JR.

March	1982	1. THE OTHER WOMAN	Arista
July	1982	2. LET ME GO	Arista
December	1982	3. BAD BOY	Arista
November	1983	4. I STILL CAN'T GET OVER LOVING YOU	Arista
June	1984	★ 5. GHOSTBUSTERS	Arista
November	1984	6. JAMIE	Arista

RAY, GOODMAN & BROWN

Members:
Harry Ray—tenor & falsetto vocals—born: December 15, 1946
Al Goodman—bass vocals—born: March 31, 1947
Billy Brown—falsetto vocals—born: June 30, 1946
Hometown: Hackensack, New Jersey

When the Moments left All Platinum Records in 1977, they left their name behind them, since the firm owned the copyrights. Harry Ray, Al Goodman, and Billy Brown carried on as Ray, Goodman & Brown. When Harry Ray left in 1982 to pursue a solo career, Goodman and Brown found a replacement and continued to use the name Ray, Goodman & Brown for club dates. Ray's solo career started and ended with a little-noticed solo album. He rejoined Ray, Goodman & Brown in 1983, replacing his own replacement.

January	1980	SPECIAL LADY	Polydor
May	1980	INSIDE OF YOU	Polydor
August	1980	MY PRAYER	Polydor

CHRIS REA

Born: 1951
Hometown: Middlesborough, England

Chris Rea hadn't thought much about a career in music until hooking up with a band called the Beautiful Losers. After five years on the club and concert circuit, Rea signed a publishing deal and recording contract. He quickly scored an international hit, "Fool (If You Think It's Over)," from his 1978 debut album, *Whatever Happened To Benny Santini?* and earned a Grammy nomination as best new artist. Also that year, Rea was commissioned to write the music for the film *Black Joy*, which reportedly did well in the United Kingdom.

July	1978	1. FOOL (IF YOU THINK IT'S OVER)	Magnet
November	1978	2. WHATEVER HAPPENED TO BENNY SANTINI?	Allied
April	1979	3. DIAMONDS	United Arists
April	1982	4. LOVING YOU	Columbia

REAL LIFE

Members:
    David Sterry—guitar, vocals
    Richard Zatorski—keyboards, violin, vocals
    Allan Johnson—bass, synthesizer, vocals
    Danny Simcic—drums, percussion
Hometown: Melbourne, Australia

David Sterry had played with various bands and taught guitar part-time when he replied to Richard Zatorski's advertisement for a cowriter in

Real Life. *Left to right:* (*top*) Richard Zatorski, David Sterry; (*bottom*) Allan Johnson, Danny Simcic.

1980. The two became a team, joined by Allan Johnson later that year. In 1982, Danny Simcic beat out 64 other drummers in an audition for the drummer's seat. Real Life became a hard-working band, at one time doing 110 shows in 132 days. A debut album, *Heartland*, was released in late 1983.

November	1983	SEND ME AN ANGEL	MCA/Curb
March	1984	CATCH ME I'M FALLING	MCA/Curb

THE RECORDS

Members:
  Huw Gower—guitar, vocals—replaced (1979) by Jude Cole—Cole replaced
    (1981) by Dave Whelan (Whelan left group in 1982)
  John Wicks—guitar, vocals
  Phil Brown—bass, vocals
  Will Birch—drums, vocals
  Chris Gent—vocals, saxophone—added in 1981
Hometown: England

When the Kursaal Flyers disbanded in Great Britain in 1977, Will Birch, the group's drummer and songwriter, and John Wicks, singer and rhythm guitarist for the last three months of its existence, formed a songwriting partnership. For the next two months, the duo divided its time between staring at the walls and writing songs. By February 1978, Phil Brown was recruited and after listening to over 200 guitarists, Birch spotted Huw Gower playing guitar in a band called the Ratbites from Hell, and persuaded him to join the Records.

The Records played in local pubs and clubs throughout Britain, and were soon invited to back Rachel Sweet on an American tour; they were subsequently asked to be the opening act as well.

September	1979	STARRY EYES	Virgin

LEON REDBONE

Leon Redbone won't tell *anyone* how old he is or where he's from originally. The earliest we can trace him is early 1970, by which time he was gaining fame playing small clubs in and around the Toronto area, as far west as Ann Arbor, Michigan, and as far east as Buffalo, New York. Redbone often performs with little more than an acoustic guitar and harmonica, singing the blues, ragtime, and other American folk music dating from as far back as the late 1800s. He moves with an odd gait and wears a Groucho Marx moustache, glasses, and antique three-piece suits. His face remains expressionless and he sings with a rumbling timbre,

Leon Redbone

hardly moving his lips. While he appears to be a novelty act, Redbone's repertoire is a course in music history.

April   1981   SEDUCED   Emerald City

THE REDDINGS

Members:
    Dexter Redding—vocals, bass—born: 1960
    Mark Lockett—vocals, keyboards, drums—born: 1957
    Otis Redding III—guitar
Hometown: Macon, Georgia

The Reddings is made up of two sons of the late soul singer, Otis Redding, Dexter and Otis III, and their cousin Mark Lockett. Dexter has been playing guitar since age four and bass since age 13, Otis has played guitar since he was 12, and Mark has been playing both keyboards and drums, also, since he was 12; all are self-taught. The three musicians played in various local bands until they called themselves the Reddings in 1979. Shortly thereafter, the trio scored a record contract and began opening concert dates for Teddy Pendergrass, Stephanie Mills, Chaka Khan, the Time, Maze, and Rick James.

| November | 1980 | REMOTE CONTROL | Believe In A Dream |
| June | 1982 | THE DOCK OF THE BAY | Believe In A Dream |

RED RIDER

Members:
  Tom Cochrane—vocals, guitar—born: May 14, 1953
  Ken Greer—guitar—born: July 25, 1954
  Jeff Jones—bass, vocals—born: September 20, 1953
  Peter Boynton—keyboards, vocals—replaced (1982) by Steve Sexton—replaced (1984) by John Webster—born: December 18, 1957
  Rob Baker—drums, percussion—born: May 24, 1951
Hometown: Toronto, Canada

Red Rider was formed in Toronto in 1976 by Peter Boynton, Ken Greer, and Rob Baker, and gigged as a trio before Tom Cochrane joined in November 1977. Cochrane had already recorded several singles and an album, *Hang On To Your Resistance*, under his own name, and had written the soundtrack to the film, *My Pleasure Is My Business*. Jeff Jones had already filled out Red Rider when the debut album, *Don't Fight It*, was released in 1980. Red Rider has toured with the Kinks and the Beach Boys.

| April | 1980 | WHITE HOT | Capitol |
| June | 1984 | YOUNG THING, WILD DREAMS (ROCK ME) | Capitol |

RED ROCKERS

Members:
  John Griffith—vocals, guitar, keyboards—born: April 3, 1962
  James Singletary—guitar—replaced (1983) by Shawn Paddock—born: July 7, 1962
  Darren Hill—bass—born: December 4, 1961
  Jim Reilly—drums—born: May 9, 1960
Hometown: Algiers, Louisiana

Even as the Ratfinks in 1980, the original Red Rockers' line-up didn't look or sound like any other band in town. Their amps were decorated with hammer and sickle drawings and their songs had titles like "Guns of Revolution," "Dead Heroes," and "White Law." After the band changed its name and won a battle of the bands contest, the four members decided there wasn't much else they could do in the New Orleans area, so they

Red Rockers. *Left to right:* Jim Reilly, Darren Hill, John Griffith, Shawn Paddock.

moved to California—except for the drummer, who turned back after a show in Austin, Texas. The remaining three members arrived in California on New Year's Day 1981 with no drummer, no place to stay, and no gigs lined up. Independently-pressed singles of "Guns of Revolution" were played on more adventurous California radio stations, providing Red Rockers with a following and gigs at all of the Bay area's better clubs. After Jeff Greenberg, who left in 1981, and Patrick Jones, who left in 1982, the drummer is Jim Reilly.

June   1983   CHINA   Columbia

RE-FLEX

Members:
> Baxter—vocals, guitar
> Paul Fishman—keyboards, computer, vocals
> Nigel Ross-Scott—bass, vocals
> Roland Vaughan Kerridge—drums, computers, vocals
Hometown: London, England

Baxter and Paul Fishman spent a great deal of time developing their musical ideas and experimenting with different personnel until, by the beginning of 1982, a band was solidified for a series of live dates. For nine months, Re-Flex toured the United Kingdom, performing in clubs and universities. In October, the band underwent changes in both line-up and approach when Nigel Ross-Scott was recommended to the band by a mutual friend, Thomas Dolby. At the same time, the band turned to computers for sounds. In the spring of 1983, Re-Flex found management and before the end of the year, they released a debut album, *The Politics of Dancing*.

| November | 1983 | THE POLITICS OF DANCING | Capitol |
| May | 1984 | HURT | Capitol |

R.E.M.

Members:
    Michael Stipe—vocals
    Pete Buck—guitar
    Mike Mills—bass, vocals
    Bill Berry—drums, vocals
Hometown: Athens, Georgia

When R.E.M. was formed in April 1980, the original intention was to play one party at an abandoned church Pete Buck and Michael Stipe were

R.E.M. *Left to right:* Michael Stipe, Mike Mills, Bill Berry, Peter Buck.

living in at the time. That party led to others, and before long the four musicians had a solid following and were opening for bands in Atlanta's largest clubs. They selected the name R.E.M. in a random skim through a dictionary; R.E.M. is an abbreviation for *rapid eye movement*, a natural phenomenon during a deep sleep. In July 1981, R.E.M. released "Radio Free Europe" as an independent single, and got substantial press. The single was rereleased two years later by a larger record firm and became a national hit.

| July | 1983 | RADIO FREE EUROPE | I.R.S. |
| June | 1984 | SOUTH CENTRAL RAIN (I'M SORRY) | I.R.S. |

MIKE RENO AND ANN WILSON

Mike Reno—born: January 8, 1955
Ann Wilson—born: June 19, 1950
Hometown: Vancouver, British Columbia

Mike Reno of Loverboy and Ann Wilson of Heart combined their talents for a big hit in the spring of 1984.
See *LOVERBOY*; see *HEART, Rock On, The Years of Change*.

| May | 1984 | ALMOST PARADISE . . . LOVE | Columbia |

REO SPEEDWAGON

Members:
    Kevin Cronin—vocals, guitar, piano—born: October 6, 1951
    Gary Richrath—guitar—born: October 18, 1949
    Neal Doughty—keyboards, synthesizers—born: July 29, 1946
    Bruce Hall—bass, vocals—born: May 3, 1953 (replaced Gregg Philbin in 1977)
    Alan Gratzer—drums—born: November 9, 1948
Hometown: Champaign, Illinois

The original REO Speedwagon began in 1968 as a bar band from the University of Illinois at Champaign-Urbana; in 1971, after a self-titled debut album, vocalist Terry Luttrell left the band to join another midwestern group. Desperate for a new lead singer, Gary Richrath called what he believed was a musician's referral service in Chicago, unaware that it was a fictitious setup Kevin Cronin had devised only two days earlier because he was looking for a gig. Richrath told him REO was looking for a really good singer who could play some rhythm guitar, and Cronin replied that he knew just the person—himself! Cronin and Richrath met, and less than two weeks later they were in Memphis, recording REO's second album. Cronin left in 1973 to pursue a solo career, but rejoined in 1975 at the band's invitation, replacing Mike Murphy, his own replacement.

REO Speedwagon. *Left to right:* Alan Gratzer, Bruce Hall, Kevin Cronin, Gary Richrath, Neal Doughty.

The band had a hardcore following in the midwest, but relocated to Los Angeles in 1976. Soon afterwards, their albums began reaching gold and platinum status. REO hit a peak in 1981 when the *Hi Infidelity* album spawned four hit singles and sold over six million LPs, making it the second biggest seller in the history of CBS Records at the time.

The band took its name from the first brand of high-speed fire trucks, designed by Ransom Eli Olds in 1911.

May	1977	1. RIDIN' THE STORM OUT	Epic
May	1978	2. ROLL WITH THE CHANGES	Epic
July	1978	3. TIME FOR ME TO FLY	Epic
May	1980	4. TIME FOR ME TO FLY (rereleased)	Epic
November	1980	★ 5. KEEP ON LOVING YOU	Epic
March	1981	6. TAKE IT ON THE RUN	Epic
June	1981	7. DON'T LET HIM GO	Epic
August	1981	8. IN YOUR LETTER	Epic
June	1982	9. KEEP THE FIRE BURNIN'	Epic
August	1982	10. SWEET TIME	Epic
October	1984	11. I DO WANNA KNOW	Epic
January	1985	★ 12. CAN'T FIGHT THIS FEELING	Epic
March	1985	13. ONE LONELY NIGHT	Epic

BURT REYNOLDS

Born: February 11, 1936
Hometown: Waycross Georgia

Movie superstar Burt Reynolds turned vocalist in 1980 with a song from the film *Smokey & the Bandit II.*

| October | 1980 | LET'S DO SOMETHING CHEAP AND SUPERFICIAL | MCA |

TURLEY RICHARDS

Born: June, 1941
Hometown: Charleston, West Virginia

Turley Richards's music career has been a string of promising starts that through unpredictable events were foiled, leaving him back at the starting point. His first group met with only minimal success in his southern environs, perhaps because it was interracial. Then, at age 17, he began making local TV appearances but an unfortunate experience with his first manager and recording contract led to his decision to get out of the business. In 1964 he came to New York, and a new manager and record company persuaded him to make another record; when the records were pressed, the first 5000 copies had no grooves! In 1970 and 1971, he

Turley Richards

released two more albums, this time for Warner Brothers, but the records did not sell, despite touring and TV shows. That, combined with a failing marriage and the fact that he had been going blind since 1969, precipitated a decision to quit once again. Richards headed for Louisville, Kentucky, where he played three-week engagements at a club and hosted his own weekly variety show on local television. He became involved in a small production company that eventually folded. Richards met and married Patty Kirchner, and once he became the father of a boy, Adam, in the summer of 1978, he decided to try recording again. With the backing of some friends who were financing a demo-production company, he cut ten songs. On a trip to Los Angeles, he connected with Fleetwood Mac's Mick Fleetwood, who liked the tape. With Fleetwood's help, Richards secured management and another record deal. The subsequent album, *Therfu*, was moderately successful.

April	1970	LOVE MINUS ZERO—NO LIMIT	Warner Bros.
June	1970	I HEARD THE VOICE OF JESUS	Warner Bros.
January	1980	YOU MIGHT NEED SOMEBODY	Atlantic

LIONEL RICHIE

Born: June 20, 1949
Hometown: Tuskegee, Alabama

After 15 years and many hits with the Commodores, Lionel Richie, who'd written and sung all of the group's latter-day hits, tried a few side

Lionel Richie

projects. First, a duet with Diana Ross for the theme song to the film *Endless Love* was a number-one hit, and then the songs he wrote and produced for Kenny Rogers were also hits. While still a member of the Commodores, Richie recorded a solo album which was a smash and produced three hit singles. Shortly thereafter, Richie left the Commodores to fully pursue a solo career.

July	1981	★ 1. ENDLESS LOVE (with Diana Ross)	Motown
October	1982	★ 2. TRULY	Motown
January	1983	3. YOU ARE	Motown
April	1983	4. MY LOVE	Motown
September	1983	★ 5. ALL NIGHT LONG (ALL NIGHT)	Motown
November	1983	6. RUNNING WITH THE NIGHT	Motown
February	1984	★ 7. HELLO	Motown
June	1984	8. STUCK ON YOU	Motown
October	1984	9. PENNY LOVER	Motown

THE RINGS

Members:
   Mark Sutton—guitar, keyboards, vocals—born: 1954
   Mike Baker—guitar, keyboards, vocals—born: 1955
   Bob Gifford—bass, vocals—born: 1952
   Matt Thurber—drums, vocals—born: 1959
Hometown: Boston, Massachusetts

Mark Sutton and Mike Baker met at college in 1975. Although they jammed a lot together, they never managed to work out anything professionally at the time. A couple of years later, Sutton, Baker, Gifford, and a drummer connected and began rehearsing top-40 hits in the basement of an artists' collective in Jamaica Plain outside Boston. They hoped to make money on the cover-band circuit, but after auditioning some 30 singers, found no one suitable. Without a good singer, they could not crack the circuit, so the four musicians began working on original material. The Rings went public in the summer of 1977 by playing a Boston rock club, shortly after which Matt Thurber replaced the original drummer. Three years later, the Rings had a recording contract.

| March | 1981 | LET ME GO | MCA |

LEE RITENOUR

Born: January 11, 1952
Hometown: Los Angeles, California

Lee Ritenour, sometimes known as "Captain Fingers," started playing guitar at the age of six, and began formal music lessons at age 10. Later he took lessons from well-known jazz guitarist Joe Pass, and at the age of 21 he taught others at University of Southern California. In 1974, Ritenour was hired by Sergio Mendes, who immediately took him on a Brazilian tour. Once back in Los Angeles, he began working sessions for Barbra Streisand, Steely Dan, John Denver, Carly Simon, Herbie Hancock, Johnny Mathis, Melissa Manchester, Kenny Loggins, Natalie Cole, Flora Purim, and the Brothers Johnson. Later, he began performing live with other musicians and recording his own albums, but continued contributing to other artists' recordings as well. He's played on the soundtracks of several films, including *Saturday Night Fever, The Champ* and *An Officer and a Gentleman.* In 1980, Ritenour married Gail Davis and they moved to Malibu. He still teaches master classes and conducts seminars at USC and the Guitar Institute of Technology, and he holds guitar clinics between dates when on tour in Japan.

| April | 1981 | IS IT YOU | Elektra |
| December | 1982 | CROSS MY HEART | Elektra |

ROCKIE ROBBINS

Hometown: Minneapolis, Minnesota

Rockie Robbins had had little formal training or experience when in the mid-seventies, he abandoned a secure position with Munsingwear to front a series of bands. When disco dried up local gigs for performing groups, Rockie and his wife decided they should take a drastic step—they took out a second mortgage on their house to finance a demo tape for Rockie. The self-produced tape was finished and mailed to the record companies. The Robbinses waited. Although the chances were slim, Rockie did get a recording contract in 1978. After three albums and the promise of becoming a teen idol, Rockie disappeared from the music world in 1981; some say he found religion and quit show business. Reportedly even his record company and management couldn't locate him. Sources also indicate that he will return shortly with a new album.

| July | 1980 | YOU AND ME | A & M |

ROCKETS

Members:
> David Gilbert—vocals—added in 1976
> Jim McCarty—guitar, vocals
> Dennis Robbins—guitar, vocals (left group in 1981)
> Donnie Backus—piano, vocals—added in 1978
> David Hood—bass—replaced (1979) by Dan Keylon—Keylon replaced (1980)
> by Bobby Neil Haralson
> John "The Bee" Badanjek—drums, percussion, vocals

Hometown: Detroit, Michigan

Jim McCarty and John Badanjek spent their early teens jamming together in Badanjek's attic. Both were playing drums then, but McCarty began fooling around with a guitar. By 1963 they were joined with other local musicians, and Billy Lee and the Rivieras were playing soul-infused rock 'n' roll on Detroit's club circuit. The band had national hits once its name was changed to Mitch Ryder and the Detroit Wheels. In 1966, Ryder decided to go on his own; Badanjek, still a teenager, went with Ryder as his drummer, then moved on to play for Edgar Winter, Alice Cooper, and Dr. John, while McCarty, also a teenager, joined the Siegel-Schwall Blues Band and then the Buddy Miles Express. Both continued to play in big rock attractions until late 1972, when they gave it all up to form the Rockets. The group's debut LP, *Love Transfusion*, was released in 1977.

April	1979	CAN'T SLEEP	RSO
July	1979	OH WELL	RSO
February	1980	DESIRE	RSO

ROCKPILE

Members:
  Dave Edmunds—vocals, guitar, piano, organ—born: April 15, 1944—Cardiff, Wales
  Nick Lowe—vocals, bass
  Billy Bremner—guitar, vocals
  Terry Williams—drums
Hometown: London, England

Rockpile. *Left to right:* Terry Williams, Nick Lowe, Dave Edmunds, Billy Bremner.

Dave Edmunds, Nick Lowe and Billy Bremner (formerly of The Rutles) were enjoying substantial success as solo artists when they joined with Williams to form Rockpile in spring 1977, performing their combined repertoires. For three years, Rockpile toured to promote Lowe and Edmunds' solo albums. In concert, each of the 3 original members took turns singing his songs through the performance, and each played on the other's albums. Edmunds's contractual agreements prohibited him from recording as Rockpile, but when that contract expired in 1980, the first— and only—Rockpile album was finally released. Ironically, after five tours as Rockpile, the group split up only shortly after the release of the *Seconds of Pleasure* LP.

November   1980   TEACHER TEACHER   Columbia

ROCKWELL

Real Name: Kennedy Gordy
Born: March 15, 1964
Hometown: Detroit, Michigan

Although his identity was kept hidden at first, the secret circulated quickly. Rockwell is Kennedy (after President John F. Kennedy) Gordy,

Rockwell

son of Motown Records founder Berry Gordy, Jr., who hoped that by adopting a pseudonym, he might be able to "make it" without cashing in on his father's name. (While playing with a high school band named Essence he had been nicknamed *Rock*. He later changed this to *Rockwell* because he would rock well.)

Michael Jackson sang the chorus of Rockwell's single "Somebody's Watching Me," which was released at the peak of Jackson's career. The novelty song, which featured clever lyrics about acute paranoia, as well as a put-on British/ghoulish accent by Rockwell, was a big hit. A novelty follow-up "Obscene Phone Caller," which again featured Rockwell's vocal parody, but did not feature Jackson, was also a hit, but not as big as his first.

| January | 1984 | SOMEBODY'S WATCHING ME | Motown |
| May | 1984 | OBSCENE PHONE CALLER | Motown |

RODWAY

Hometown: Kent, England

Steve Rodway credits the Buggles' 1979 hit, the all-electronic and vocal "Video Killed the Radio Star," as a musical turning point for him. He was so taken with the ideas and production of the song that shortly after hearing it, he tracked down the Buggles' Trevor Horn, hoping to interest Horn in producing a record for him by presenting him with a homemade demo tape. Horn liked what he heard, and soon Steve was programming synthesizers for the Buggles. Shortly thereafter, Horn offered him a deal on his label, Perfect Records, and began plans to record Steve in partnership with his brother-in-law and producer of Foreigner's first album, John Sinclair. Midway through the sessions, Sinclair was called off to Los Angeles. After holding on for some months, Rodway decided that rather than sit around and wait until the recording resumed, he would leave the U. K. for New York and start all over again. His debut album, *Horizontal Hold*, was released in 1982.

| December | 1982 | DON'T STOP TRYING | Millennium |

ROGER

Hometown: Hamilton, Ohio

Roger, as Roger Troutman likes to be called, juggles a solo career with his obligations to Zapp, a group he fronts that also features his three brothers and other musicians. After the release of the second Roger album, *The Many Facets of Roger*, in 1981, his solo career was put on hold, since his third album, *The Saga Continues*, is the object of a lawsuit, and its release has been delayed.

| November | 1981 | I HEARD IT THROUGH THE GRAPEVINE | Warner Bros. |

THE ROMANTICS

Members:
>Coz Canler—guitar, vocals
>Wally Palmer—guitar, harmonica, vocals
>Mike Skill—bass, guitar, vocals
>Jimmy Marinos—drums, percussion, vocals

Hometown: Detroit, Michigan

The Romantics had a simple start. They formed in early 1977 and began playing clubs. After a while the group grew popular enough to tour the country's rock clubs, and eventually won a record deal in May 1979. The original group was comprised of Wally Palmer and Mike Skill on guitars, Rich Cole on bass, and Jimmy Marinos on drums. In 1981, Cuban-born Coz Canler replaced Mike Skill on lead guitar. In late 1982, Cole left the band and was replaced by Skill, who now played bass, since that's what the vacancy was. In 1984 this lineup became one of the first rock and roll groups to appear on the syndicated TV series *Soul Train*.

February	1980	WHAT I LIKE ABOUT YOU	Nemperor
October	1983	TALKING IN YOUR SLEEP	Nemperor
February	1984	ONE IN A MILLION	Nemperor

ROMEO VOID

Members:
>Debora Iyall—vocals—born: April 29, 1954
>Ben Bossi—saxophone—born: September 7, 1953
>Frank Zincavage—bass—born: September 30, 1952

Romeo Void. *Left to right:* Frank Zincavage, Aaron Smith, Debora Iyall, Peter Woods, Ben Bossi.

Peter Woods—guitar—born: December 26, 1954
Aaron Smith—drums—born: September 3, 1950
Hometown: San Francisco, California

Debora and Frank met in 1978, while attending San Francisco's Art Institute, and talked about forming a band. They recruited guitarist Peter Woods and another friend to play drums, and by 1979 were performing in the area as Romeo Void, a name chosen by Debora. A year later Ben Bossi joined the band and they recorded their first album, called *It's A Condition,* for 415 Records. This album enabled them to become an opening act for other groups as they travelled across the U. S. building a following.

In 1982, Ric Ocasek of the Cars produced a four-song EP called "Never Say Never," the title cut of which became a dance classic.

Next came the album *Benefactor* and then *Instincts,* which produced their first chart single, "A Girl In Trouble."

September   1984   A GIRL IN TROUBLE (IS A TEMPORARY THING)   Columbia

ROSSINGTON COLLINS BAND

Members:
    Dale Krantz—vocals
    Barry Harwood—guitar, vocals
    Gary Rossington—guitar
    Allen Collins—guitar
    Billy Powell—keyboards
    Leon Wilkeson—bass
    Derek Hess—drums
Hometown: Jacksonville, Florida

In 1977 a tragic plane crash took the lives of Lynyrd Skynyrd's lead vocalist Ronnie Van Zant, guitarist Steven Gaines, and his sister, backing vocalist Cassie Gaines. After a few years of thinking and reorganizing, most of the remaining band, Gary Rossington, Allen Collins, Billy Powell, and Leon Wilkeson, recruited new musicians and formed Rossington Collins Band. Krantz and Rossington eventually married, reportedly, and then left the band after two albums. Collins later carried on with the Allen Collins Band, but the public has not heard from the Rossingtons.

July   1980   DON'T MISUNDERSTAND ME   MCA

ROUGH TRADE

Members:
    Carol Pope—vocals—born: August 6, 1949
    Kevan Staples—guitar, keyboards, synthesizer
    David McMorrow—synthesizers, vocals

Terry Wilkins—bass, vocals
Bucky Berger—drums, vocals
Hometown: Toronto, Canada

Carol Pope was born in Manchester, England, but moved to Canada with her family when she was five, ultimately settling in Toronto in 1959. At 17, she worked as a commercial artist and began hanging out with rock musicians and one road manager in particular, Kevan Staples. Staples began teaching himself to play both keyboards and guitar, and Pope began writing songs. Their first band was called O, and later became the X-rated Bullwhip Brothers. Rough Trade similarly seeks to outrage audiences— Carol sometimes performs in complete bondage suit or begins concerts by informing the crowd what boring towns they live in. In 1976, Rough Trade reportedly became the first rock group anywhere to make a direct-to-disc recording. The nucleus of Rough Trade remains Pope and Staples.

December   1982   ALL TOUCH   Boardwalk

DEMIS ROUSSOS

Hometown: Greece

In 1968, while en route to London, Demis was rerouted to Paris. Two months later, the public heard "Rain and Tears," now a multi-million seller. Blending western pop with folk and religious influences from a childhood spent by the shores of the Mediterranean, he has sold millions of records and performed over a thousand concerts in 35 countries.

June   1978   THAT ONCE IN A LIFETIME   Mercury

THE ROVERS

Members:
Will Millar—vocals, guitar, mandolin, banjo, drums, whistle
George Millar—vocals, guitar
Joe Millar—bass, harmonica, accordion, vocals
Jimmy Ferguson—vocals
Wilcil McDowell—accordion, keyboards, synthesizer
Hometown: Alberta, Canada

All originally from Ireland and all residents of Canada since their teens, the Rovers came together as a group (originally called the Irish Rovers) in 1964 under the leadership of Will Millar, who brought together his brother George, cousin Joe and two boyhood friends, Jimmy Ferguson and Wilcil McDowell. As their reputation grew in Canada, interest sparked in the United States and resulted in a 22-week engagement at San Francisco's Purple Onion, beginning New Year's Eve 1965. The Rovers had a CBS-TV series which lasted for six seasons, as well as many TV "super specials." They are a headline attraction around the world.

THE IRISH ROVERS

March	1968	THE UNICORN	Decca
June	1968	WHISKEY ON A SUNDAY	Decca
September	1968	THE BIPLANE EVER MORE	Decca

THE ROVERS

| February | 1981 | WASN'T THAT A PARTY | Cleveland International |

KEVIN ROWLAND & DEXYS MIDNIGHT RUNNERS

Members:
  Kevin Rowland—vocals
  Helen O'Hara—violin
  Billy Adams—banjo, guitar
  Micky Billingham—accordian, piano, organ
  Giorgio Kilkenny—bass
  Seb Shelton—drums
  Brian Maurice—saxophone
  Paul Speare—flute, whistle, saxophone
  Big Jimmy Patterson—trombone
Hometown: Birmingham, England

Kevin Rowland originally wanted to be a priest, but took up the guitar
and formed the original Dexy's Midnight Runners in 1978. (The name of
the group was a reference to the stimulant Dexedrine.) The group's music
was soulful, their look was that of a street gang, and their records were
great successes in England. In 1981, the group revamped and redirected

Kevin Rowland & Dexys Midnight Runners. Kevin Rowland (*second from right*).

themselves to become more self-disciplined. Members jogged to rehearsals, wore track suits and boxing boots, and banned alcoholic beverages from all their concerts. By 1983, the members described themselves as Celtic Soul Brothers and dressed as farmers and hippies, with overalls, sandals, and bandanas. All this time, the renamed Kevin Rowland & Dexys Midnight Runners saw their music leaning more towards folk elements, while maintaining a rock approach. An album called *"Too-Rye-Ay"* with this new communal-living look and sound produced a number-one song, "Come On Eileen." On the video, Eileen was played by Rowland's wife, Helen O'Hara.

January	1983	★ COME ON EILEEN	Mercury
May	1983	THE CELTIC SOUL BROTHERS	Mercury

ROXY MUSIC

Members:
  Bryan Ferry—vocals—born: September 26, 1945
  Phil Manzanera—guitar—born: January 31, 1951
  Andy Mackay—horns—born: July 23, 1946
  Gary Tibbs—bass—born: January 25, 1958 (replaced John Wetton, John Gustafson, and Graham Simpson in 1979)
  Paul Thompson—drums—born: May 13, 1951
  Dave Skinner—keyboards (replaced Eddie Jobson in 1979)
Hometown: London, England

While in his late teens and early 20s, Bryan Ferry studied fine art at the University of Newcastle by day and played American soul music in local bands by night. He then taught painting in London for a year before

Roxy Music. *Left to right:* Phil Manzanera, Paul Thompson, Dave Skinner, Bryan Ferry, Gary Tibbs, Andy Mackay.

deciding that music offered a more potent and far-reaching form of artistic expression. In spring 1975 he formed Roxy Music, and by Christmas the group was performing in and around London. Through the years, the band's line-up has changed regularly, and has at times been augmented by additional musicians and vocalists, but the core—Bryan Ferry, Phil Manzanera, and Andy Mackay—remains intact. Former members John Wetton, Eddie Jobson, and Brian Eno went on to work with major bands, and Ferry, Manzanera, and Mackay have all recorded solo albums.

December	1975	LOVE IS THE DRUG	Atco
April	1979	DANCE AWAY	Atco
August	1980	OVER YOU	Atco

THE ROYAL PHILHARMONIC ORCHESTRA

Conductor Louis Clark and the Royal Philharmonic Orchestra not only performed a pop medley of classical themes to a dance beat, but a year later also recorded an album of songs originally done by the hard-rock group Queen. The orchestra has also played many movie scores.

| October | 1981 | HOOKED ON CLASSICS | RCA |

RUBICON

Members:
    Max Haskett—vocals, trumpet
    Dennis Marcellino—vocals, saxophone, flute
    Gerald Martini—horns
    Bradley Gillis—guitar
    Jim Pugh—keyboards
    Jack Blades—bass
    Greg Eckler—drums, vocals
Hometown: San Francisco, California

After helping to put together Sly & the Family Stone in the San Francisco Bay area in 1966 and then spending 10 years arranging its horn parts, Jerry Martini put those acquired skills to work when he organized Rubicon. The group was short-lived, but Brad Gillis and Jack Blades went on to form the very successful Night Ranger years later.

| February | 1978 | I'M GONNA TAKE CARE OF EVERYTHING | 20th Century |

RUSH

Members:
    Alex Lifeson—guitar—born: August 27, 1953
    Geddy Lee—bass, vocals—born: July 29, 1953
    Neil Peart—drums—born: September 12, 1952
Hometown: Toronto, Canada

Rush. *Left to right:* Alex Lifeson, Neil Peart, Geddy Lee.

Rush had another drummer, Jon Rutsy, and worked one-nighters on the club circuit, when the group decided it was time to record an album in early 1973. The initial tracks for the album were laid down in one eight-hour stretch, with overdubbing and remixing completed a few months later. Rather than shop around for a record deal, the band and its managers set up Moon Records and released the LP independently in early 1974. The trio's management later went to the American Talent International booking agency, which signed Rush on the spot and sent a copy of the LP to Mercury Records. Just 24 hours later, Rush was signed to Mercury, and the LP was rereleased in August.

Six days before a four-month tour of the States with Aerosmith and Kiss, Neil Peart replaced Rutsy. Despite continual criticism from the press, Rush's popularity gradually grew to the point where the trio was headlining all of America's biggest concert arenas.

January	1977	1. FLY BY NIGHT/IN THE MOOD	Mercury
November	1977	2. CLOSER TO THE HEART	Mercury
February	1980	3. THE SPIRIT OF RADIO	Mercury
March	1981	4. LIMELIGHT	Mercury
June	1981	5. TOM SAWYER	Mercury
December	1981	6. CLOSER TO THE HEART	Mercury
September	1982	7. NEW WORLD MAN	Mercury

PATRICE RUSHEN

Born: September 30, 1954
Hometown: Los Angeles, California

A genuine child prodigy, Patrice Rushen began studying music at age three, when she was enrolled in a special music preparatory program under the auspices of the University of Southern California. By the age of six she was giving piano recitals. Rushen studied successively with three piano teachers, first playing on an old upright, then on a Yamaha baby grand she acquired at age 11. A year later, she picked up the flute and quickly got first chair in the student orchestra. In time, she learned to improvise.

When Patrice went professional, she was much in demand. She worked sessions for many jazz and soul acts, as well as playing for commercials and movie scores. She also began recording her own jazz-oriented albums, continuing her studies in U. S. C. right through to the late seventies. Recently, her music has taken a more pop direction, but Patrice is still her own guiding light; she composes, plays, and sings her own songs, and arranges and produces her albums.

January	1980	HAVEN'T YOU HEARD	Elektra
May	1982	FORGET ME NOTS	Elektra
June	1984	FEEL SO REAL (WON'T LET GO)	Elektra

BRENDA RUSSELL

Hometown: Brooklyn, New York

Brenda Russell was backstage at a club in Toronto when a man asked her if she sang. She'd been working with bands, and answered yes. Without hearing her sing a single note, the man hired her on the spot for a female group he managed called the Tiaras. Brenda later moved to New York where she landed a role in a road-show production of *Hair* that brought her right back to Toronto. There she married Brian Russell, and with him cohosted a Canadian TV series called *"Music Machine."* She had three Canadian hits and even did a weekly gospel radio show that required a brand new hymn every seven days.

In 1973, Brian and Brenda came to Los Angeles, where they got TV and session work as well as a record contract. When the duo divorced, Brenda continued recording and writing. Her songs have been recorded by Jermaine Jackson, Earth, Wind & Fire, Roberta Flack, Joe Cocker, Patrice Rushen, Anne Murray, Tata Vega, Cheryl Ladd, and Rufus. She has also performed or recorded with Elton John, Barbra Streisand, Bette Midler, Neil Sedaka, Robert Palmer, Donna Summer, and many others.

| August | 1979 | SO GOOD, SO RIGHT | Horizon |

SAD CAFÉ

Members:
>   Paul Young—vocals, percussion
>   Ashley Mulford—guitar, vocals
>   Ian Wilson—guitar, vocals, percussion
>   Vic Emerson—piano, synthesizer
>   Dave Irving—drums, vocals, percussion
>   John Stimpson—bass, vocals
>   Lenni Zaksen—saxophone, vocals

Hometown: Manchester, England

Sad Café was formed in 1976, when members of two bands, Byro and Mandala, merged. (The group took its name from Carson McCullers's book, *The Ballad Of The Sad Café.*) Although their 1977 debut album, *Fanx Ta-Ra,* was not released in America, Sad Café came to the States the following year to promote its second album, *Misplaced Ideals,* and toured as opening act to both Santana and Toto. Dave Irving joined in 1978, replacing Tony Creswell.

| January | 1979 | RUN HOME GIRL | A & M |
| August | 1981 | LA DI DA | Swan Song |

SAGA

Members:
>   Michael Sadler—vocals, keyboards, bass
>   Ian Crichton—guitar
>   Jim (Daryl) Gilmour—keyboards, vocals (replaced Peter Rochon in 1980)
>   Jim Crichton—bass, keyboards
>   Steve Negus—drums, percussion

Hometown: Toronto, Canada

Jim Crichton, Michael Sadler, and Steve Negus began Saga in 1976 after leaving the popular Canadian band Flood. With the addition of Jim's younger brother Ian and Peter Rochon, Saga began exploring progressive keyboard- and synthesizer-oriented rock. The group's self-titled 1978 debut album did not do well commercially and, discouraged by the thought that a second album might not be properly promoted, Saga accepted its contract back. Saga's music began to do well in Europe, particularly in Germany, where the group gained even greater popularity when they toured there; after a while, even fellow Canadians believed

Sad Café. *Left to right:* Ian Wilson, Paul Young, Vic Emerson, John Stimpson, Ashley Mulford, Lenni Zaksen, Dave Irving.

Saga was from Germany. More albums were successfully released in Europe before *Worlds Apart* was released internationally in 1982 and turned the rest of the world on to Saga's music. Saga toured the United States, opening for Jethro Tull, Pat Benatar, Billy Squier, and Quiet Riot.

December	1982	ON THE LOOSE	Portrait
April	1983	WIND HIM UP	Portrait
November	1983	THE FLYER	Portrait

CAROLE BAYER SAGER

Born: March 8, 1947

A two-time Academy Award nominee, Carole Bayer Sager wrote the lyrics to popular songs used in the soundtracks of many films: *The Spy Who Loved Me, Ice Castles, Chapter Two, "10", All That Jazz, Starting Over, It's My Turn, Coast To Coast, Middle Aged Crazy, It Seems Like Old Times,* and *The Devil and Max Devlin.* Since her first hit as a teenager, when she wrote "Groovy Kind of Love" for the Mindbenders, she has collaborated on dozens of standards with top songwriters, including Peter Allen, David Foster, Marvin Hamlisch, Melissa Manchester, Michael Masser, Michael McDonald, and Bruce Roberts. Her songs have been hits for the Doobie Brothers, Aretha Franklin, Michael Jackson, Bette Midler, Dolly Parton, Leo Sayer, Carly Simon, Frank Sinatra, and others. Sager also cowrote the score for Broadway's *They're Playing Our Song* with Marvin Hamlisch. Her one album as a performer, *Sometimes Late At Night*, was a concept album cowritten with Burt Bacharach.

| October | 1977 | YOU'RE MOVING OUT TODAY | Elektra |
| May | 1981 | STRONGER THAN BEFORE | Boardwalk |

SAINT TROPEZ

Members:
Phyllis Rhodes—vocals
Teresa Burton—vocals
Kathy Deckard—vocals

Although Rhodes, Burton, and Deckard gave interviews, toured discos, and lipsynched on TV shows, none are included among the many credits on the *Belle DuJour* album, from which came the hit "One More Minute." The disco tracks were actually a studio project by multi-instrumentalist W. Michael Lewis and percussionist Laurin Rinder, both of whom played on and produced the album.

| April | 1979 | ONE MORE MINUTE | Butterfly |

SANTA ESMERALDA

Real Name: Jimmy Goings
Born: 1955
Hometown: South Dakota

Santa Esmeralda was a studio project that featured Jimmy Goings on vocals. Tailored for the dance floor, the Santa Esmeralda records were lengthy disco records that borrowed elements from samba, salsa, and cha-cha. The best-known Santa Esmeralda tunes were disco reworkings of two songs originally recorded by the Animals, "Don't Let Me Be Misunderstood" and "House of the Rising Sun."

| November | 1977 | DON'T LET ME BE MISUNDERSTOOD | Casablanca |
| April | 1978 | HOUSE OF THE RISING SUN | Casablanca |

SCANDAL

Members:
Patty Smyth—vocals—born: June 26, 1957
Zack Smith—guitars—born: January 29
Hometown: New York, New York

Scandal. Zack Smith and Patty Smyth.

Patty Smyth's mother was involved in club management in New York's Greenwich Village; years later Patty worked the city's clubs herself, but in another capacity—as the leader of her band. Meanwhile, Zack Smith of Westport, Connecticut, was playing the same circuit with a band called Scandal. Smith felt his band needed a female vocalist, and after a month of auditioning over 80 female singers, a mutual friend suggested that Zack meet Patty. It took him so long to reach her that their first conversation was an argument. They finally joined forces and recorded a five-song EP in 1982 (the biggest selling mini-LP in Columbia Records' history) and toured with John Cougar, the Kinks, and Hall & Oates. Although they used some of Zack's old band members, the core of Scandal was Patty and Zack.

Following the release of their first full-length album, *Warrior*, in 1984, Zack left to concentrate on producing and song writing. Patty gathered a lineup of new musicians and the new Scandal toured extensively with John Waite.

November	1982	1. GOODBYE TO YOU	Columbia
April	1983	2. LOVE'S GOT A LINE ON YOU	Columbia

June	1984	3. THE WARRIOR (featuring Patty Smyth)	Columbia
October	1984	4. HANDS TIED (featuring Patty Smyth)	Columbia
January	1985	5. BEAT OF A HEART (featuring Patty Smyth)	Columbia

JOEY SCARBURY

Born: June 7, 1955
Hometown: Ontario, California

At age five, Joey (*not* Joseph) Scarbury did an Elvis Presley imitation for show-and-tell in his kindergarten class. By age nine, when his family moved to Thousand Oaks, Joey was winning talent contests. Four years later, the father of singer/songwriter Jimmy Webb came into the furniture store where Joey's mother worked, and in short time, Joey recorded his first single, "She Never Smiles Anymore," written and produced by Jimmy Webb. Nothing more really happened until later, when Joey began singing back-up vocals for producer Mike Post. After a three-year stint as backing vocalist for Loretta Lynn, Joey auditioned to sing "Believe It Or Not" at the invitation of Post, who had composed the song for the ABC-TV series *The Greatest American Hero.* Joey won the part, and the song went on to be a hit. Scarbury also plays second base for his Thousand Oaks softball league, and shares his home with his wife D'On (pronounced Dee-on) and a West Highland terrier named Maggie.

May	1981	THEME FROM "THE GREATEST AMERICAN HERO"	Elektra
		(BELIEVE IT OR NOT)	
October	1981	WHEN SHE DANCES	Elektra

PETER SCHILLING

Born: January 28, 1956
Hometown: Stuttgart, Germany

At the age of 20, Peter Schilling began playing and singing his songs on the German folk club circuit. A year later, he took a job in the merchandising division of WEA Records, where he learned the mechanics of the music business. Upon his discharge from the army in 1978, Schilling signed with an international song publisher, Peer-Southern Music, and by the beginning of 1982, he had organized a performing band for his songs and signed a recording contract. His first single, "Major Tom (Coming Home)," became an international hit in both German and English.

| September | 1983 | MAJOR TOM (COMING HOME) | Elektra |

TIMOTHY B. SCHMIT

Born: October 30, 1947
Hometown: Oakland, California

Onetime member of Poco and the Eagles, Tim Schmit had a lone chart
entry in 1982 with the song "So Much In Love," which was featured in
the movie *Fast Times At Ridgemont High*.

October	1982	SO MUCH IN LOVE	Full Moon/Asylum

JOHN SCHNEIDER

Born: 1955
Hometown: Mt. Kisco, New York

John Schneider began his show business career in New York at a very
young age. By the time he was in high school in Atlanta, Georgia, he was
already an accomplished actor, singer, and musician. Schneider's first
national starring role was in *A Few Good Men,* a documentary made for
the United States Marine Corps. Thereafter, he appeared in *Smokey and
the Bandit,* and, in January 1979, as Bo Duke in CBS-TV's "The Dukes
of Hazzard" series. In 1977, while still relatively unknown, he recorded
a children's Christmas album, *Small One,* which has since become a
collector's item. In addition to being a television star and recording artist,
Schneider is interested in racing cars and competes in celebrity jeep races
and the like.

May	1981	1. IT'S NOW OR NEVER	Scotti Bros.
September	1981	2. STILL	Scotti Bros.
May	1982	3. DREAMIN'	Scotti Bros.
August	1982	4. IN THE DRIVERS SEAT	Scotti Bros.

EDDIE SCHWARTZ

Hometown: Toronto, Canada

In 1977, after a brief stint in a band called Charity Brown, Eddie Schwartz
became a staff songwriter for ATV Music. In 1979, he signed an international recording deal with Infinity Records, but just as he completed his
debut album, the firm went out of business. It appeared that Schwartz's
record would never be heard, but by mid-1980, another record company
agreed to distribute the album, titled *Schwartz,* throughout Canada. By
early 1981, Schwartz negotiated yet another record deal and saw his *No
Refuge* album released internationally.

Schwartz's songs have been recorded by Greg Lake, Eddie Money,
Rachel Sweet, Mickey Thomas, Long John Baldry, and others. He also
won a prestigious Juno Award in Canada as 1980 Composer of the Year
for Pat Benatar's hit, "Hit Me With Your Best Shot."

December	1981	ALL OUR TOMORROWS	Atco
March	1982	OVER THE LINE	Atco

Eddie Schwartz

SCORPIONS

Members:
    Klaus Meine—vocals—born: May 25
    Matthias Jabs—guitar—born: October 25
    Rudolf Schenker—guitar—born: August 31
    Francis Buchholz—bass—born: February 19
    Herman Rarebell—drums—born: November 18
Hometown: Hanover, West Germany

Klaus and Rudolf first formed Scorpions in their native Germany in 1971, and debuted that year with their first album, *Lonesome Crow*. Over the next few years, they did a lot of touring as an opening act with other heavy-metal performers like Ted Nugent, UFO, and Rainbow. Other albums, such as *Fly to the Rainbow* (1974), *In Trance* (1975), *Virgin Killer* (1976), *Taken by Fire* (1977), and *Tokyo Tapes* (1978) established them as one of the premier heavy-metal bands of the seventies. In fact, top bands like Van Halen and Iron Maiden are said to have been influenced a lot by this German band.

It was during the seventies that the band went through various personnel changes, with Buchholz joining in 1974, Jabs in 1979, and Rarebell in 1977.

It wasn't until 1982 that the group started placing hit singles on the American charts, becoming one of the hottest acts in this country.

June	1982	NO ONE LIKE YOU	Mercury
March	1984	ROCK YOU LIKE A HURRICANE	Mercury
July	1984	STILL LOVING YOU	Mercury

SEA LEVEL

Members:

  Jimmy Nalls—guitar, vocals
  Chuck Leavell—keyboards, vocals
  Lamar Williams—bass, vocals (left in 1980)
  Jai "Jaimoe" Johanny Johanson—drums, percussion (left group in late 1970s)
  Randall Bramblett—keyboards, saxophone, vocals—added in 1977
  Davis Causey—guitar—added in 1977
  George Weaver—drums—added in 1977—replaced (1978) by Joe English
    (left group in 1980)
Hometown: Macon, Georgia

During their tenure in the Allman Brothers Band, Chuck Leavell, Lamar Williams, and Jaimoe Johanson could often be found jamming backstage before a concert or during afternoon soundchecks. And when the ABB wasn't touring, the three would get together to play. By the summer of 1976, the ABB broke up, and Sea Level (the name is a play on Chuck's first initial plus his last name) was able to rise from the ashes. Chuck called Jimmy Nall, with whom he'd played in Alex Taylor's Friends & Neighbors band, and after jamming, the four previously-skeptical musicians committed themselves to Sea Level. One of the group's earliest gigs was at President Carter's inaugural.

By their second album, *Cats On The Coast*, Sea Level had expanded to seven members. Johanson eventually left the group to rejoin a re-formed Allman Brothers Band. In late 1982 Chuck Leavell joined the group Betts, Hall, Leavell & Trucks.

| February | 1978 | THAT'S YOUR SECRET | Capricorn |

MICHAEL SEMBELLO

Hometown: Philadelphia, Pennsylvania

At the age of 17, Michael Sembello became Stevie Wonder's guitarist, touring with him for eight years and performing on every Wonder album from 1973 to 1979. After relocating to Los Angeles in the mid-seventies, Sembello quickly became a much-sought-after composer and session artist. He wrote, sang, and/or played guitar on sessions for albums by Donna Summer, Jeffrey Osborne, Cheryl Lynn, Diana Ross, Chaka Khan, The Jacksons, Seals & Crofts, Art Garfunkel, Sergio Mendes, and many more.

Michael Sembello

He only came into his own when he worked on the *Flashdance* soundtrack, and his song, "Maniac," became the movie's second biggest hit.

| June | 1983 | ★ MANIAC | Casablanca |
| September | 1983 | AUTOMATIC MAN | Warner Bros. |

707

Members:
    Kevin Russell—guitar, vocals—born: 1955
    Duke McFadden—keyboards, vocals—born: 1955 (left group in 1981)
    Phil Bryant—bass, vocals—born: 1957
    Jim McClarty—drums, percussion—born: 1956
Hometown: Los Angeles, California

Kevin Russell played in a popular local band with his brothers, and one night, during a jam, was joined by Jim McClarty, who'd played in several jazz and rock bands. Although Phil Bryant, who'd played in local bands since the age of 10 (and who, coincidentally, admired Russell's work from afar), had become friends with McClarty when he was 16, they had never played together.

Bryant moved to Los Angeles in 1978, and Russell and McClarty soon followed suit, although they each moved independently of the others. When the three happened into each other's lives in L. A., they figured they were meant to be together, and formed a group, adding Duke McFadden to their ranks. Named 707, the group first appeared in April 1979 and met instant success at L. A.'s premier rock clubs. A self-titled debut album was released in March 1980, launching 707's professional career.

| October | 1980 | I COULD BE GOOD FOR YOU | Casablanca |
| July | 1982 | MEGA FORCE | Boardwalk |

SHALAMAR

Members:
    Gary Mumford—vocals—born: 1952—replaced (1979) by Howard Hewett—
        vocals—born: October 1
    Jody Watley—vocals—born: January 30,1959 (left group in 1983)
    Jeffrey Daniel—dancing—born: August 24, 1956 (left group in 1983)
    Micki Free—guitar, vocals—added in 1983
    Delisa Davis—vocals, keyboards—added in 1984
Hometown: Los Angeles, California

Shalamar started as an anonymous studio group and later became a trio consisting of a dancing duo, Jody Watley and Jeffrey Daniel, recruited from the syndicated TV show "Soul Train," and a lead singer, Gary Mumford, who was soon replaced by Howard Hewett. At about the time the group's pivotal album, *The Look,* was released in the summer of 1983, Watley and Daniel quit Shalamar to pursue individual interests. Guitarist Micki Free, who'd earlier been managed by Diana Ross, was recruited to join Howard Hewett, and a nationwide talent contest was held to select a third member. Delisa Davis, a graduate of Tennessee State University, won the contest and completed the Shalamar line-up in early 1984. Shalamar's songs for the *D.C. Cab* and *Footloose* soundtracks were recorded during this period of flux. "Deadline USA" from *D.C. Cab* featured Howard Hewett alone, while "Dancing in the Sheets" from *Footloose* featured Hewett and Free; Davis had not yet joined the group at the time of the recording.

March	1977	1. UPTOWN FESTIVAL	Soul Train
January	1979	2. TAKE THAT TO THE BANK	Solar
December	1979	3. THE SECOND TIME AROUND	Solar
December	1980	4. FULL OF FIRE	Solar
April	1981	5. MAKE THAT MOVE	Solar
April	1982	6. A NIGHT TO REMEMBER	Solar
June	1983	7. DEAD GIVEAWAY	Solar
March	1984	8. DANCING IN THE SHEETS	Columbia
November	1984	9. AMNESIA	Solar

SHANNON

Hometown: Washington, D. C.

While majoring in accounting and minoring in music at York University, Shannon Green's professors encouraged her to pursue her singing potential. She worked a number of day jobs before recording "Let The Music Play"

Sheila

in 1983. The success of the hot 12-inch dance track, released by a small independent record company, led to a rerelease of the record by a larger firm as well as to Shannon's own record contract.

November	1983	LET THE MUSIC PLAY	Mirage
March	1984	GIVE ME TONIGHT	Mirage/Emergency
April	1985	DO YOU WANNA GET AWAY	Mirage

SHEILA AND B. DEVOTION

Hometown: Paris, France

The daughter of a Parisian street market vendor, Sheila's first record in the seventies endowed her with celebrity status; her second single, "School Is Over," astounded the French record industry by selling an amazing 1.5 million copies in that country alone. Her sole American success came with "Little Darlin'," a song written and originally recorded by the New York–based group called Spider. Sheila has since moved to Los Angeles.

| December | 1981 | LITTLE DARLIN' | Carrere |

SHEILA E.

Real Name: Sheila Escovedo
Born: December 12, 1959
Hometown: San Francisco, California

As the daughter of Bay area percussionist Pete Escovedo, Sheila was introduced to the congas at the age of five, playing with the Escovedo Brothers. At age 15, she toured South America with her father and the group Azteca. She has worked in the past with George Duke, Prince,

Herbie Hancock, Lionel Richie, Marvin Gaye, Jeffrey Osborne, and several other recording artists.

Stepping out of the background and into the spotlight, Sheila E. had her first chart entry with "The Glamorous Life."

| June | 1984 | THE GLAMOROUS LIFE | Warner Bros. |
| October | 1984 | THE BELLE OF ST. MARK | Warner Bros. |

T. G. SHEPPARD

Real Name: Bill Browser
Born: July 20, 1944
Hometown: Jackson, Tennessee

T. G. Sheppard's mother, a piano teacher, reserved Sundays for musical get-togethers. By the time T. G. reached his mid-teens, he had outgrown the local music scene in his hometown, so he joined the Travis Womack Band in Memphis as a singer and guitarist before quitting the road for a more secure job as a promotion man in the music business.

One day, a song written by an unknown songwriter, Bobby David, came to T. G.'s attention. T. G. pitched the song to eight record companies, and all eight turned it down. He left the tape of the song sitting on the corner of his desk for months trying to decide what to do with it; apparently, he was the only one who believed the song could be a hit. Finally, T. G. recorded the song himself, and "Devil In The Bottle" became a country & western hit for him. For a while, T. G. kept his day

T. G. Sheppard

job while more of his songs became hits; he became a full-time entertainer when he found himself booked on television variety shows. T. G. and his wife Diane were close friends of the late Elvis Presley, whom T. G. had met in 1961 when he came out of the armed services. T. G. Sheppard is a pseudonym, short for The Good Shepherd.

January	1975	1. DEVIL IN THE BOTTLE	Melodyland
May	1975	2. TRYIN' TO BEAT THE MORNING HOME	Melodyland
July	1976	3. SOLITARY MAN	Hitsville
March	1981	4. I LOVE 'EM EVERY ONE	Warner/Curb
January	1982	5. ONLY ONE YOU	Warner/Curb
April	1982	6. FINALLY	Warner Bros.
February	1984	7. MAKE MY DAY (with Clint Eastwood)	Warner/Curb

SHERBS

Members:
  Daryl Braithwaite—vocals
  Harvey James—guitar—replaced (1981) by Tony Leigh
  Garth Porter—keyboards
  Tony Mitchell—bass
  Alan Sandow—drums
Hometown: Australia

Sherbs

Sherbs (later the Sherbs) is a reorganized version of Sherbet. Formed in 1969, Sherbet went on to become the biggest-selling music group in Australian history. A dozen Sherbet albums were released in the seventies, each achieving gold or platinum status. But in 1979, Sherbet withdrew from the public eye to adopt a new musical direction, shifting from their previous pop approach to a more aggressive rock 'n' roll emphasis. When they reemerged, the line-up of Sherbs was the same as it had been in Sherbet since 1976. One change occurred in 1981, when Tony Leigh replaced Harvey James, although James was credited for "additional guitar" on the Sherbs' second album, *Defying Gravity*.

SHERBET
August   1976   HOWZAT   MCA

SHERBS
March   1981   I HAVE THE SKILL   Atco

SHERIFF

Members:
    Freddy Curci—vocals
    Arnold David Lanni—keyboards, guitar, vocals
    Steve DeMarchi—guitar, vocals
    Wolf D. Hassel—bass, vocals
    Rob Elliott—drums
Hometown: Canada

Most people in the music business had never heard of Sheriff until the group signed a recording contract and released a self-titled debut album in August 1982, three years after forming. According to the band's chief songwriter, Arnold Lanni, Sheriff devised a deliberate three-year plan to play outside of the major cities in order to be able to present a defined sound, refined repertoire, and a solid performing unit down the road. After the release of the album, Sheriff toured the United States opening for the Kinks.

May   1983   WHEN I'M WITH YOU   Capitol

SHOES

Members:
    Jeff Murphy—guitar, vocals, percussion, synthesizer
    Gary Klebe—guitar, vocals, percussion, harmonica
    John Murphy—bass, vocals, guitar, percussion, synthesizer
    Skip Meyer—drums, backing vocals—added in 1976
Hometown: Zion, Illinois

Although brothers Jeff and John Murphy and friend Gary Klebe did some live shows at one time, unlike most new bands, Shoes was basically born in the studio, not on stage. Their debut album, *Black Vinyl Shoes*, was recorded in Jeff's living room on a Teac four-track machine, and before long Shoes gained a reputation and a national following, without ever leaving their hometown of Zion. The record became an underground sensation, and Shoes received fan letters from 30 states and seven countries.

November   1979   TOO LATE   Elektra

SHOOTING STAR

Members:
>   Van McLain—vocals, guitar—born: May 3, 1955
>   Gary West—vocals, keyboards, guitars—born: June 27, 1953
>   Charles Waltz—violin, vocals—born: January 27, 1958
>   Bill Guffey—keyboards (left group in 1981)
>   Ron Verlin—bass—replaced (1984) by Norm Dahlor—born: April 29, 1956
>   Steve Thomas—drums—born: May 10, 1953

Hometown: Kansas City, Missouri

At age 10, Van McLain joined a local band whose other members averaged 17 years old. His friend Gary West spent nine years in a group called Chessman Square, a popular midwest band, until in the mid-seventies he moved to New York and joined and recorded an album with the Beckies. McLain met Ron Verlin, meanwhile, together worked with a fifties-style show band billed as "The Shooting Stars featuring the Galaxies." West soon left the Beckies and began collaborating with McLain and Verlin on the Shooting Stars. The three joined up with Waltz, Guffey and Thomas, and in 1978, the newly-named hard-rock band Shooting Star traveled to New York twice to showcase before record companies. The group was signed, and a self-titled debut album was released in January 1980.

| April | 1980 | YOU GOT WHAT I NEED | Virgin/Atlantic |
| March | 1982 | HOLLYWOOD | Virgin/Epic |

GLENN SHORROCK

Born: June 30, 1944
Hometown: Sydney, Australia

Born in Great Britain but raised in the migrant town of Elizabeth, near Adelaide in southern Australia, Glenn Shorrock was already leading a popular band, the Twilights, in 1964. That group recorded 13 singles and two albums before splitting up in 1969, after which Shorrock formed another Australian favorite, Axiom, which had three big hits before they too split up. After a two-album stint with Esperanto, Shorrock caught up with the remnants of Mississippi, a soft-rock group from Adelaide; he, along with Graham Goble, Beeb Birtles, and Derek Pellicci, formed Little River Band in 1975. (See *LITTLE RIVER BAND, Rock On: The Years of Change*.) Although Shorrock's seven years with this internationally successful group were creatively and financially rewarding, the members had differences, prompting Shorrock to quit in 1982 in favor of a solo career. His debut solo album was *Villain of the Peace*.

September   1983   DON'T GIRLS GET LONELY   Capitol

THE SILENCERS

Members:
    Frank Czuri—vocals
    Warren King—guitar
    Dennis Takos—keyboards
    Michael Pella—bass
    Ronnie Foster—drums
Hometown: Pittsburgh, Pennsylvania

Frank Czuri and Ronnie Foster hark back to the Igniters, a blue-eyed soul band that released two singles in the mid-sixties. Foster later recorded an album with Sweet Lightning and three albums with Roy Buchanan, while Czuri recorded three albums with Warren King in Diamond Reo. When Diamond Reo split up in 1979, King, Czuri, and Foster formed the Silencers, adding Takos and Pella to their ranks. The group's debut LP, *Rock 'N' Roll Enforcers*, was released in 1980 and their second album, *Romanic*, in 1981.

July   1980   SHIVER AND SHAKE   Precision

SILVER CONDOR

Members:
    Joe Cerisano—vocals
    Earl Slick—guitar—replaced (1983) by Steve Plunkett and Nick Brown
    John Corey—keyboards—replaced (1983) by Steve Goldstein
    Jay Davis—bass—replaced (1983) by Kenny Aaronson
    Claude Pepper—drums—replaced (1983) by Craig Krampf

Tired of nonstop session work, in late 1979 Earl Slick decided to form a band. Via recommendations, Slick met Joe Cerisano, and within a week they'd cowritten two songs. As soon as the final line-up was set, the quintet made a live garage tape using only one microphone. The tape led to management, which led to a professional demo tape and then to a recording contract. A self-titled debut album was released in April 1981, but true to the nature of session musicians, the group's line-up changed radically by the time it released a follow-up album, *Trouble At Home*, two years later. Slick and Cerisano were the only members to stay in the group. The new line-up, now a sextet, also comprised session musicians; they too dispersed shortly after recording the album.

July   1981   YOU COULD TAKE MY HEART AWAY   Columbia

GENE SIMMONS

Born: August 25, 1949
Hometown: Queens, New York

A member of Kiss, Gene Simmons had a chart entry in 1978 with his song "Radioactive."

December	1978	RADIOACTIVE	Casablanca

PATRICK SIMMONS

Born: January 23, 1950
Hometown: Aberdeen, Washington

By the time he was seven years old and his family moved to San Jose, California, Patrick Simmons was already a devotee of rock 'n' roll. A year later, he picked up a guitar and by the time of the California music explosion in the mid-sixties, he was playing anywhere he could. In 1970 Simmons met Tom Johnston and John Hartman, who along with Greg Murphy invited him to turn their hard-rocking trio into a quartet. Simmons hesitated at first because he was working steadily, but eventually he did join; within a year, this nucleus turned into the Doobie Brothers.

Although a majority of the Doobie's hits were written by Tom Johnston and later Michael McDonald, it was Simmons's "Black Water" in 1974 that gave the group its first gold single. Simmons was the only original member remaining in the Doobie Brothers when the group split in 1982.

Simmons now lives on his farm in the Santa Cruz Mountains, where he raises, tends, cultivates, cares for, feeds, and otherwise shares space with llamas, lizards, goats, burros, rabbits, chickens, ducks, finches, parrots, macaws, dogs, and cats, as well as his lemon, apple, apricot, avocado, and peach trees and raspberry, strawberry, and blueberry vines. Simmons juggles that rural existence with a solo recording career.

March	1983	SO WRONG	Elektra
June	1983	DON'T MAKE ME DO IT	Elektra

SINGLE BULLET THEORY

Members:
    Michael Maurice Garrett—vocals, guitar, saxophone
    Gary Alan Holmes—guitar, vocals
    Barry C. Fitzgerald—keyboards, vocals
    Mick Muller—bass, vocals
    Dennis Madigan—drums
Hometown: Richmond, Virginia

In 1978 Dennis Madigan and Michael Maurice Garrett decided to name their rock group Single Bullet Theory. Although the name is based on the

Warren Commission's report on the John F. Kennedy assassination, it has less to do with the late president than with that particular era and its legacy, according to Dennis Madigan. An independently-recorded and -released four-song EP sold out and eventually led to a major record-company deal.

March   1983   KEEP IT TIGHT   Nemperor

SISTER SLEDGE

Members:
     Debbie Sledge—vocals—born: July 9, 1954
     Joni Sledge—vocals—born: September 13, 1956
     Kim Sledge—vocals—born: August 21, 1957
     Kathy Sledge—vocals—born: January 6, 1959
Hometown: Philadelphia, Pennsylvania

Sister Sledge. *Left to right:* Debbie, Kathy, Joni, Kim.

Viola Williams, a former opera singer, did her best to encourage her four grandchildren to sing, and so at an early age, the Sledge sisters began singing at Second Macedonia Church in Philadelphia, quickly graduating to occasional back-up vocals for Gamble & Huff sessions at Sigma Sound Studios. After securing their own record contract in 1973, the vocal quartet appeared on television around the world and performed at Muhammed Ali's championship festivities in Zaire.

Sister Sledge's signature hit is "We Are Family" which was written, arranged, and produced by Chic's Nile Rodgers and Bernard Edwards. The song became the anthem for the world champion Pittsburgh Pirates baseball team in 1979 and was later adapted for a Pepsi-Free ad campaign.

February	1979	1. HE'S THE GREATEST DANCER	Cotillion
April	1979	2. WE ARE FAMILY	Cotillion
January	1980	3. GOT TO LOVE SOMEBODY	Cotillion
March	1981	4. ALL AMERICAN GIRLS	Cotillion
May	1981	5. NEXT TIME YOU'LL KNOW	Cotillion
January	1982	6. MY GUY	Cotillion

SKY

Members:
> John Williams—guitar—born: 1941
> Kevin Peek—guitar—born: December 21, 1946
> Francis Monkman—keyboards—born: June 9, 1949
> Herbie Flowers—bass
> Tristan Fly—drums, percussion—born: 1946

Sky is a collaboration among five of contemporary music's most gifted practitioners, devoted to exploring a fusion of rock, jazz, and classical music. Each member takes time off from his solo career to write, rehearse, and record for Sky. Though the quintet has done few concerts, one notable performance was the first rock concert ever held at Westminster Abbey, commemorating the 20th anniversary of Amnesty International; all profits from the show, which was videotaped for future broadcast, went to the Nobel Peace Prize-winning human rights organization. The group has yet to enjoy in America the kind of attention and acclaim it receives in Great Britain.

January	1981	TOCATTA	Arista

SKYY

Members:
> Denise Dunning Crawford—vocals
> Bonny Dunning—vocals
> Delores Dunning—vocals
> Solomon Roberts, Jr.—vocals, guitar, drums

Anibal "Butch" Sierra—guitar
Wayne Wilentz—keyboards (replaced Larry Greenburg in 1981)
Gerald Lebon—bass
Tommy McConnell—drums
Hometown: Brooklyn, New York

Skyy and fellow Brooklyners Brass Construction started out in the basement of Solomon Roberts's parents' house, where all the musicians they knew would gather and jam. Skyy's self-titled debut album was released in 1979. Even the success of "Call Me" in 1982 changed nothing—the group still rehearses in the basement they affectionately call "Hole in the Ground Studios."

| January | 1982 | CALL ME | Salsoul |

SLADE

Members:
    Noddy Holder—vocals, guitar—born: June 15, 1950
    Dave Hill—guitar—born: April 4, 1952
    Jim Lea—bass, violin—born: June 14, 1952
    Don Powell—drums—born: September 10, 1950
Hometown: England

Slade initially rose to stardom in Great Britain in 1972 during the days when glitter rock propelled the careers of T. Rex, Gary Glitter, Suzi Quatro, and other pop acts. Although this era was short-lived, it influenced an entire generation of rock acts, most notably Kiss.

While many rock fans assumed that Slade split up after glitter rock died, the group actually continued to play sporadically at festivals and other rock events. Interest in the group was regenerated when a number of artists covered Slade's British hits, particularly Quiet Riot's "Cum On Feel the Noize." But Slade's 1984 comeback album, *Keep Your Hands Off My Power Supply*, was not marked by the group's original, distinctive sound.

September	1972	1. TAKE ME BAK 'OME	Polydor
November	1972	2. MAMA WEER ALL CRAZEE NOW	Polydor
March	1973	3. GUDBUY T JANE	Polydor
May	1973	4. CUM ON FEEL THE NOIZE	Polydor
April	1984	5. RUN, RUNAWAY	CBS Associated
July	1984	6. MY, OH MY	CBS Associated

SLAVE

Members:
    Steve Arrington—vocals, drums, percussion—added in 1979 (left group in 1982)
    Danny Webster—guitar, vocals, percussion
    Kevin Johnson—guitar (replaced Marc Hicks in 1981, left group in 1982)

Slave. *Left to right:* Floyd Miller, Larry Houston, Ronny Cochran, Aubrey Rivers, Mark Adams, Kenny Anderson, Danny Webster, Marvin Wheatly.

Sam Carter—keyboards, percussion, vocals (replaced Ray Turner and Carter Bradley in 1981)—replaced (1982) by Marvin Wheatley

Delburt C. Taylor—keyboards, flugel horn, trumpet, vocals (replaced Stevie Washington in 1981)

Charles C. Carter—keyboards, flute, saxophone, vocals (replaced Tom Lockett and Orion Wilhoite in 1980, left group in 1982)

Floyd Miller—trombones, trumpet, percussion, vocals

Mark L. Adams—rap, bass, synthesizer

Roger Parker—drums, percussion (replaced Tim Dozier in 1981)—replaced (1982) by Ronny Cochran

Larry Houston

Aubrey Rivers

Kenny Anderson

Hometown: Dayton, Ohio

A band called Black Satin Soul, which included "Tiny" Tim Dozier, Marc "Drac" Hicks, and Steve Washington, joined with Thomas Lockett, Mark Adams, and Floyd Miller to form a band. After the group's first rehearsal, in November 1976, Danny Webster, Carter Bradley, and Orion Wilhoite joined. Ray Turner joined the following year.

One day, Floyd came to rehearsal wearing a T-shirt with the word *slave* on it. The word captured the imagination of the others, who thought it described the dedication they felt to their music. Later, when the group adopted a cosmic image, a written statement explained that "all of humanity is a slave to the universe," and that Slave would relate this message—through hard-core funk. Slave's self-titled debut LP was released in February 1977. The group moved to the New York area in April 1978 and through the years changed personnel with dizzying speed before moving back to Ohio sometime later as a very different group.

Steve Arrington has gone on to a successful solo career. Steve Washington is producing Aurra, which features three former Slave back-up vocalists, Curt Jones, Starleana Young, and Jennifer Ivory.

June	1977	SLIDE	Cotillion
January	1981	WATCHING YOU	Cotillion
October	1981	SNAP SHOT	Cotillion

GRACE SLICK

Born: October 30, 1943
Hometown: Chicago, Illinois

As Jefferson Airplane and Jefferson Starship evolved through the years, Grace Slick became less of a spotlighted frontperson than she was originally. The first album released under her own name, *Manhole*, in 1973, was not really a solo album: it featured most of Jefferson Starship, only the group didn't have a name yet. Grace quit Jefferson Starship in 1978, and her first real solo album was the 1980 *Dreams*, which produced her hit single "Seasons." Grace rejoined Starship in 1981. She simultaneously continues a solo career.
See *JEFFERSON STARSHIP, Rock On: The Years of Change.*

April	1980	SEASONS	RCA

FRANKIE SMITH

After several years of touring as a performer, Frankie Smith was hired by Philadelphia International Records in 1977 as a songwriter. Shortly after his first song, "Hard Not To Like You," was recorded by Archie Bell & the Drells, Frankie was given the opportunity to produce as well as write for P. I. R.'s roster of artists. In 1980, Frankie signed with WMOT Records as a writer and producer as well as a recording artist. His one hit for the label was a novelty record that capitalized on the increased interest in double-dutch jump rope competitions. "Double Dutch Bus" was originally released in August of 1980, but was picked up by radio only after months of word-of-mouth. Most of Smith's vocal parts were sung in a Wolfman Jack-type growl and many of the lyrics were word plays in pig Latin. The success of the single placed him on a brief tour opening for Rick James.

May	1981	DOUBLE DUTCH BUS	WMOT

PATTI SMITH

Born: December 31, 1946
Hometown: Chicago, Illinois

Patti Smith was a latter-day beat poet when on February 10, 1971, well-known rock journalist Lenny Kaye plugged in an electric guitar behind her at a reading in a New York City church. In 1974, Smith and Kaye recorded their first single, "Hey Joe" b/w "Piss Factory," and one by one, expanded their musical accompaniment until a whole band was formed. Patti was then not only one of the hippest poets in New York literary circles, but she became the princess of the then-burgeoning punk rock scene. In 1977, Smith fell off a stage in Florida and had to put her neck in traction, causing a temporary halt to her career, but she resumed in 1978. After her 1979 album, *Wave*, however, she fell in love with Fred "Sonic" Smith, formerly of the MC5, moved to Michigan, married, and disappeared from the music scene.

| April | 1978 | BECAUSE THE NIGHT | Arista |
| August | 1979 | FREDERICK | Arista |

REX SMITH

Hometown: Jacksonville, Florida

As a child, Smith moved around a lot with his family, finally settling in Atlanta, Georgia, where young Rex played in bands and appeared in amateur theater productions. In 1975, he moved to New York, planning to give up rock 'n' roll and attend acting school. Ironically, he quickly met a big-time rock manager, who negotiated Rex a lucrative record deal. After two hard-rocking albums by a band called Rex, he launched a career as Rex Smith, individual. In 1979 he landed the male lead in a teen drama TV-movie called *Sooner or Later,* in which he played a 17-year-old rock singer with a crush on a 13-year-old fan he believes is 15. This role and storyline instantly turned Smith into a teen idol, and "You Take My Breath Away," a song from the *Sooner Or Later* soundtrack, became his first hit single.

Smith went on to play the male lead in *Grease* on Broadway and then in an east coast road show. He sang the theme for and appeared in the film *Headin' For Broadway,* which was released only in the midwest and parts of Canada. The high point of his acting career was costarring with Linda Ronstadt and Kevin Kline in both the Broadway and film versions of Gilbert & Sullivan's *The Pirates of Penzance* in 1980. All the while, Smith continued recording albums and making occasional television appearances.

In 1981, in the middle of *Pirates'* Broadway run, Smith led an ad-hoc band called Crime and Punishment for a special benefit concert for the Santa Fe Festival Theater. Crime featured *Star Trek–The Movie's* Steven Collins on bass, *Pirates'* costar Kevin Kline on piano, *Dog Day Afternoon's* Chris Sarandon on drums, and *Animal House's* Peter Riegert on percussion; the Punishment back-up vocalists were Susan Sarandon, Brooke Adams, Carol Kane, and Jill Eikenberry!

Rex Smith

| April | 1979 | YOU TAKE MY BREATH AWAY | Columbia |
| June | 1981 | EVERLASTING LOVE (with Rachel Sweet) | Columbia |

SNAIL

Members:
>   Bob O'Neill—vocals, guitar
>   Ken Kraft—vocals, guitar
>   Jack Register—bass
>   Jim Norris—drums

Hometown: Santa Cruz, California

Snail started out as an excuse for the leaders of two different bands to get together and jam. That was circa 1968, and both Bob O'Neill and Ken Kraft were just out of high school. In ten years of playing together, Snail went from copying British rock bands to country-rock and acoustic sets. Back in the duo's country-rock days, a close friendship was started with another country-rock band, Fly By Night. When that group disbanded in 1977, drummer Jimmy Norris joined Snail. With Jack "Cash" Register on bass, the quartet finally put out a long-awaited album, *Snail*, in 1978.

| September | 1978 | THE JOKER | Cream |

SNEAKER

Members:
>   Mitch Crane—vocals, guitar
>   Michael Carey Schneider—vocals, keyboards
>   Tim Torrance—guitar
>   Jim King—keyboards, synthesizer, vibes
>   Michael Cottage—bass, vocals
>   Mike Hughes—drums, vocals

Hometown: Los Angeles, California

The genesis of Sneaker was in 1973, when Michael Cottage moved west from New Orleans to play in a club band. In time, he met Mitch Crane of Blackhawk County, Iowa, and they formed a new band, Sneaker, named after the Steely Dan song, "Bad Sneakers." The duo recruited Michael Carey Schneider of southern California when his band broke up. Mike Hughes of Houston joined in 1978, and Jim King of Los Angeles and Tim Torrance of Seattle, shortly thereafter. Sneaker's self-titled debut album was produced by Jeff "Skunk" Baxter, formerly of the Doobie Brothers and Steely Dan.

| October | 1981 | MORE THAN JUST THE TWO OF US | Handshake |
| February | 1982 | DON'T LET ME IN | Handshake |

Sniff 'N' The Tears. *Left to right: (top row)* Mick Dyche, Nick South, Loz Netto; *(middle row, second from left)* Paul Roberts, Keith Miller.

SNIFF 'N' THE TEARS

Members:
 Paul Roberts—vocals, guitar
 Loz Netto—guitar—replaced (1980) by Les Davidson

Mick Dyche—guitar—replaced (1980) by Les Davidson
Alan Fealdman—keyboards—replaced (1979) by Keith Miller—Miller replaced (1980) by Mick Taylor
Chris Birkin—bass—replaced (1979) by Nick South
Luigi Salvoni—drums, percussion—replaced (1980) by Jamie Lane
Hometown: London, England

Sniff 'N' the Tears is the brainchild of Paul Roberts, who not only leads the band and writes all their material, but illustrates their album covers with his original paintings. Roberts began by leading bands through the London club circuit in the early seventies. He then moved to France, where he played occasional dates as a solo artist and developed his skill in painting. In 1976, he found himself in a London studio recording a selection of his songs with a pickup band. On the strength of "Driver's Seat," the band, which named themselves Sniff 'N' the Tears, toured America as opening act for both Kenny Loggins and Kansas.

July   1979   DRIVER'S SEAT   Atlantic

SNUFF

Members:
James "Jimbo" Gray Bowling—guitar, vocals
Robbie House—guitar, vocals
Chuck Larson—guitar, vocals
Cecil Hooker—violin
C. Scott Trabue—bass
Michael A. Johnson—drums, vocals
Hometown: Virginia Beach, Virginia

In 1971, Bowling and two other musicians formed a trio for a local club gig. As of the night of the engagement, they still hadn't named the group. Shortly before going onstage, a waitress at the club suggested the name Snuff, and that's what went up on the marquee.

Snuff played cover tunes at all the local clubs until the trio split up. Trabue and Johnson joined with Bowling in 1973 to form a new Snuff. They were joined by Hooker and House a year later and by Larson in 1979. By 1980, the group had begun performing out-of-state. They played original tunes, and financed the recording of an album.

August   1983   BAD, BAD BILLY   Warner Bros.

GINO SOCCIO

Born: September 1955
Hometown: Montreal, Canada

Gino Soccio's early training in classical piano gave way to a passion for rock 'n' roll, at which time he switched to guitar. He formed a band while still in high school and played the hits of the day at parties and dances. Later, while studying philosophy at the University of Montreal, Soccio simultaneously trained extensively in music at the famous Vincent D'Indy Conservatory. He returned to keyboards and supported himself as a studio musician on commercial jingles and demo tapes for other aspiring artists. In 1974, he recorded his own demo of jazz-rock material; when the record industry paid no attention, he switched to disco. Soccio's first effort was the French language "Sauve Qui Peut," which was successful in Quebec. He then recorded an album alone, playing over 20 instruments, under the fictitious name Kebekelektrik before releasing English-language disco records under his own name. Soccio also produced a disco album for Gothan Flasher, was production consultant for an album by Ruby Winters and put together the fictitious group Witch Queen for an album. He also wrote the score for *Babe*, a film starring Buddy Hackett that was never released.

April   1979   DANCER   RFC

SOFT CELL

Members:
    Marc Almond—vocals, percussion—born: 1957
    David Ball—synthesizers, percussion—born: 1959
Hometown: Leeds, England

Soft Cell. Marc Almond (*left*), David Ball.

Marc Almond from Southport and David Ball from Salford and Blackpool, England, met at Leeds Polytechnic, where they both graduated with degrees in Fine Arts. They were friends for a year before forming Soft Cell in October 1979.

The two-man Soft Cell made its performance debut at a Christmas party and released an independent four-song EP in the summer of 1980. While the duo has enjoyed considerable success in Great Britain, its only hit single in the United States was "Tainted Love," a cover of a song originally recorded by American soul singer Gloria Jones in the late sixties. Marc Almond also released an album, *Untitles*, under the name Marc and the Mambas.

"Tainted Love" set a record for the most consecutive weeks on the charts: 43.

January	1982	TAINTED LOVE	Sire

THE S. O. S. BAND

Members:
  Mary Davis—vocals, keyboards
  Abdul Raoof—vocals, trumpet, flugel horn, percussion—added in 1981
  Billy R. Ellis—saxophone, flute, keyboards, vocals
  Willie "Sonny" Killebrew—saxophone, flute, vocals
  Bruno Speight—guitar, vocals
  Jason "T. C." Bryant—keyboards, vocals, synthesizer
  John Alexander Simpson III—bass, keyboards, vocals
  Jerome "J. T." Thomas—drums, percussion (replaced James Earl Jones III in 1981)
Hometown: Atlanta, Georgia

The S. O. S. Band established itself with its debut single, "Take Your Time (Do It Right)," which sold over two million copies in 1980. Although the group toured nationally with the Isley Brothers and the Commodores, their first two albums did not sell as well. The S. O. S. Band made a comeback in 1983 with songs from their *On The Rise* LP that were produced by the red-hot team of Terry Lewis and Jimmy "Jam" Harris, formerly of the Time.

May	1980	1. TAKE YOUR TIME (DO IT RIGHT)	Tabu
August	1983	2. JUST BE GOOD TO ME	Tabu
November	1983	3. TELL ME IF YOU STILL CARE	Tabu
August	1984	4. JUST THE WAY YOU LIKE IT	Tabu

J. D. SOUTHER

Real Name: John David Souther
Hometown: Detroit, Michigan

John David Souther was raised in Amarillo, Texas, but it wasn't until he moved to Los Angeles that he was recognized by the music industry as a prolific singer/songwriter. His first album, *John David Souther*, was released in 1972, after which he joined with ex-Flying Burrito Brother Chris Hillman and ex-Poco/ex-Buffalo Springfield member Richie Furay to form a collective called the Souther-Hillman-Furay Band. (See *SOUTHER-HILLMAN-FURAY BAND, Rock On: The Years of Change.*) After the demise of the short-lived supergroup following two albums, Souther recorded albums sporadically. All this time, however, he also collaborated occasionally with a network of southern California musicians.

| September | 1979 | YOU'RE ONLY LONELY | Columbia |
| March | 1981 | HER TOWN TOO (with James Taylor) | Columbia |

SOUTHSIDE JOHNNY & THE ASBURY JUKES

Members:
   "Southside" Johnny Lyon—vocals, harmonica—born: December 4, 1948
   William Rush—guitars, vocals (replaced "Miami" Steve Van Zandt in 1976)

Southside Johnny

Joel Gramolini—guitar, vocals—added in 1979
Richard "La Bamba" Rosenberg—trombone
Stan Harrison—saxophone, flute (replaced Carlo Novi in 1978)
Ed Manion—saxophone—replaced by Joseph Stann in 1979
Walter "Rick" Gazda—trumpet
Bob Muckin—trumpet, fluegelhorn (replaced Tony Palligrosi in 1978)—
    replaced (1980) by Mike Spengler
Kevin Kavanaugh—keyboards, vocals
Allan Berger—bass—replaced (1980) by Gene Boccia
Steve Becker—drums, vocals, percussion (replaced Kenny Pentifallo in 1978)
Hometown: Asbury Park, New Jersey

In the late sixties and early seventies, Asbury Park in the wee hours was the meeting place for both local musicians who'd just finished gigs in the area and out-of-work musicians. Clubs in that seaside town were receptive to early morning jams. "Southside" Johnny Lyon recalls that bands came and went, since few musicians seriously sought anything permanent. In October 1974, however, Johnny joined a local outfit called the Blackberry Booze Band and took it over, ultimately changing personnel so drastically that the guy who originally formed the band left. "Miami" Steve Van Zandt joined on guitar and became coleader of the band, renamed Southside Johnny & the Asbury Jukes, until Bruce Springsteen drafted him for his E Street Band. Van Zandt remained involved with the Jukes, however, and produced the group's demo tape. The group's debut album, *I Don't Want To Go Home,* was released in April 1976, and although the Jukes have yet to achieve national stardom, they are a main attraction in the northeast. Southside Johnny & the Asbury Jukes appeared as an up-and-coming band in the film *Between The Lines.*

September   1979   I'M SO ANXIOUS   Mercury

SPACE

Space is the creative vehicle of Didier "Ecama" Marovani, who composes with keyboard player Roland Romanelli. They teamed up with French producer Jean Philippe Iliesco and English session vocalist Madeline Bell to record several dance tracks under the name Space. The songs did well in France, and were played in American discos.

April   1979   MY LOVE IS MUSIC   Casablanca

SPANDAU BALLET

Members:
    Tony Hadley—vocals
    Gary Kemp—guitar, vocals
    Steve Norman—saxophone, percussion
    Martin Kemp—bass
    John Keeble—drums, percussion
Hometown: London, England

Spandau Ballet. *Left to right:* Gary Kemp, John Keeble, Tony Hadley, Steve Norman, Martin Kemp.

Spandau Ballet emerged from an underground scene centered around a handful of fashionable dance clubs in late 1979. The scene was caught up in what was called a "new romantic" fashion, which its adherents promised would be the "next big thing," but which, like all fads, died a quick death. As a result, the flamboyantly dressed Spandau Ballet went from maintaining a high profile in England to relative obscurity in 1982. A year later, Spandau Ballet returned to the music scene with another look, one which is timeless but perhaps ironic for rock 'n' roll—dark suits, white shirts, dark ties, shoes, and socks.

August	1983	1. TRUE	Chrysalis
November	1983	2. GOLD	Chrysalis
March	1984	3. COMMUNICATION	Chrysalis
July	1984	4. ONLY WHEN YOU LEAVE	Chrysalis

SPARKS

Members:
> Russell Mael (Dwight Russel Day)—vocals—born: October 5, 1953
> Ron Mael (J. Ronald Day)—keyboards—born: August 12, 1948

Hometown: Culver City, California

Sparks. Ron Mael (*left*), Russell Mael.

Although they have used many backing musicians through the years, the two Mael brothers are the nucleus of Sparks. The duo began recording in 1970 as Halfnelson, with Harley Feinstein (drums) and two other brothers, Earl (bass) and Jim (guitar) Mankey. When they were persuaded to change the name of the group in 1971, their debut album was repackaged and released under the name Sparks. America was virtually unaware of Sparks' existence until the Mael brothers headed for the United Kingdom. The British rock journals made a big deal of Sparks, igniting some interest back in America, and making the group quite big throughout Europe. Nevertheless, through the years, Sparks has remained more of a cult favorite than a main attraction in the States. "Cool Places" was a vocal duet between Sparks' Russell Mael and Jane Wiedlin of the Go-Go's.

| May | 1982 | I PREDICT | Atlantic |
| April | 1983 | COOL PLACES (with Jane Wiedlin) | Atlantic |

SPELLBOUND

Members:
   Barry Flast—vocals, keyboards, guitar
   Bill Burgess—guitar, vocals
   David Lenchner—keyboards, synthesizer, vocals

Ralph Carter—bass, vocals
Joey Kluchar—drums (replaced Jim Preston)
Hometown: California

Hours after he left a band called Kingfish, Barry Flast formed a new group called Spellbound. David Lenchner was from Flast's old neighborhood in New York City and had played extensively over the years. Ralph Carter had played with Flast on the west coast in Flast's earlier band, Trouble. Bill Burgess had toured with Van Morrison and Bill Quateman, and original drummer Jim Preston had just found himself jobless as the Sons of Champlin split up. The Bay area–based Spellbound had no major hits after their first album.

| July | 1978 | RUMOUR AT THE HONKY TONK | EMI-America |

SPIDER

Members:
    Amanda Blue—vocals
    Keith Lentin—guitar, vocals
    Holly Knight—keyboards, vocals
    Jimmy Lowell—bass, vocals
    Anton Fig—drums, vocals
Hometown: New York, New York

Amanda Blue, Keith Lentin, and Anton Fig, all natives of South Africa, were involved in Hammak, a short-lived band that played Capetown clubs until Anton went off to the New England Conservatory of Music in Boston, Keith to Boston's Berklee College of Music, and Amanda to London. By the mid-seventies, all three had relocated to New York. With two Americans, Holly Knight and Jimmy Lowell, they formed Siren, playing the New York rock clubs, and later changed their name to Spider. The band recorded two albums, and a revamped line-up became Shanghai, which continued to play New York clubs.

April	1980	NEW ROMANCE (IT'S A MYSTERY)	Dreamland
August	1980	EVERYTHING IS ALRIGHT	Dreamland
May	1981	IT DIDN'T TAKE LONG	Dreamland

SPLIT ENZ

Members:
    Tim Finn—vocals
    Neil Finn—guitar, vocals (replaced Phill Judd in mid-1970s)
    Eddie Rayner—keyboards
    Nigel Griggs—bass
    Malcolm Green—bass (left group in 1981)
    Noel Crombie—percussion (moved to drums when Green left)
Hometown: Auckland, New Zealand

When Split Enz started up in October 1972, the group prepared a gimmick—outrageous black-and-white stage costumes and even more outrageous geometrically shaped hairstyles. But success eluded the band after three albums, and by the end of 1978, not only had founding member Phil Judd, saxophone player Robert Gillie, and the original rhythm section left, but the group also found itself without a record contract. Within a year, Split Enz was reformed and a record deal was secured. The ensuing album, *True Colours,* was an international success, and the Australian government chose to include a videocassette of the album in a time capsule. The group's following in the States has remained moderate at best, however.

August   1980   I GOT YOU   A & M

THE SPORTS

Members:
  Stephen Cummings—vocals
  Andrew Pendlebury—guitars, vocals
  Martin Armiger—guitars, vocals—added in 1978
  James Niven—keyboards, vocals
  Robert Glover—bass
  Paul Hitchins—drums
Hometown: Melbourne, Australia

The Sports was formed in 1977, the brainchild of Steve Cummings, an art school student and avid record collector. The group worked the Melbourne pub-hotel-university circuit. They had one hit in America, then disappeared.

October   1979   WHO LISTENS TO THE RADIO   Arista

SPYRO GYRA

Members:
  Jay Beckenstein—saxophone—born: May 14, 1951
  Jeremy Wall—keyboards (left group in 1977)
  Jim Kurzdorfer—bass—replaced (1981) by David Wofford—Wofford replaced
    (1983) by Kim Stone—born: April 18, 1954
  Geraldo Velez—congas, timbales—born: August 15, 1947
  Chet Catallo—guitar—replaced (1984) by Julio Fernandez—born: August
    29, 1954
  Eli Konikoff—drums—replaced (1983) by Richie Morales—born: December
    8, 1952
  Tom Schuman—piano, oberheim, keyboards—born: January 31, 1958
  Dave Samuels—vibraphone, marimba—born: October 9, 1948
Hometown: Buffalo, New York

Spyro Gyra. *Top row:* Dave Samuels, Geraldo Velez, Tom Schuman. *Middle:* Jay Beckenstein. *Bottom row:* Julio Fernandez, Kim Stone, Richie Morales.

Jay Beckenstein had been playing saxophone with the federally funded Buffalo Jazz Ensemble when, with Jeremy Wall, Jim Kurzdorfer, and Tom Schuman, he graduated to the bars of Buffalo, where they led an open-house jam session on Tuesday and Thursday nights. Thus began Spyro Gyra. The group eventually recorded its own album and put it out in

1977, hoping to break even. A small record firm called Amherst, in upstate New York, bought and repackaged the album. Amherst then negotiated with Infinity Records, a larger company, and a second album, *Morning Dance*, was recorded by a somewhat larger Spyro Gyra line-up. When Infinity Records disintegrated, all the label's contracts reverted to the parent company, MCA Records. So, ironically, though all the major record companies passed on Spyro Gyra when they sent out their initial homemade tape, the group eventually wound up on a major label, though by unpredictable circumstances. By 1981, Beckenstein's partner and cofounder in Spyro Gyra, Kurzdorfer, chose to pursue his own projects while continuing to write, arrange, and assist in the production of the group's recording, and so he is no longer a musician for the band.

June	1978	1. SHAKER SONG	Amherst
June	1979	2. MORNING DANCE	Infinity
April	1980	3. CATCHING THE SUN	MCA
February	1981	4. CAFE AMORE	MCA

SPYS

Members:
    Al Greenwood—keyboards
    Ed Gagliardi—bass

Al Greenwood and Ed Gagliardi, two former members of Foreigner, combined their talents for their lone hit in 1982 under the group name Spys.

| August | 1982 | DON'T RUN MY LIFE | EMI-America |

SQUEEZE

Members:
    Chris Difford—guitar, vocals—born: November 4, 1954
    Glenn Tilbrook—guitar, vocals—born: August 31, 1957
    Paul Carrack—keyboards, vocals (replaced Jools Holland in 1976)—replaced (1980) by Don Snow
    John Bentley—bass, vocals (replaced Harry Kakoulli in 1980)
    Gilson Lavis—drums (replaced Paul Gunn in 1976)
Hometown: London, England

Back in 1974, two aspiring young musicians, guitarist Glenn Tilbrook and lyricist Chris Difford, teamed up with their old buddy, pianist Jools Holland, and formed the nucleus of U. K. Squeeze. Another friend, Harry Kakoulli, was persuaded to switch from guitar to bass and join them, and Paul Gunn joined to play drums. With an electric repertoire, the group began playing clubs in 1975 and in due time, changed personnel and shortened their name. Although Squeeze had attracted a large following by the time of its farewell concert tour in 1982, their single American hit was the only Squeeze tune sung by Paul Carrack, who was in the group only briefly. Jools Holland went on to form his own band, the Millionaires, and Paul Carrack launched a solo career; Squeeze finally split when Chris Difford and Glenn Tilbrook decided to work as a duo rather than with a group.

August	1981	TEMPTED	A & M

BILLY SQUIER

Born: May 12, 1950
Hometown: Wellesley, Massachusetts

An only child, Billy Squier became a great fan of the early Beatles and Rolling Stones, but "got hooked on guitar" one day while listening to Eric Clapton on a John Mayall's Bluesbreakers album. After a brief stint at Boston University, Squier moved to New York to be at the center of the music business. His early bands went nowhere, but he jammed with Jimi Hendrix and Johnny Winter, among others. In 1973, he joined the Sidewinders, who had already released one album and were club favorites in Boston. In 1976, he formed and led a promising band called Piper; after two albums, however, Squier succumbed to the paradox of being both the leader of the group and just "one of the boys" in a band. Frustrated, he signed a solo deal with Capitol Records in 1979. Aside from several successful Billy Squier LPs, the singer/songwriter also wrote, performed, and produced the title track to the film *Fast Times At Ridgemont High*, and worked with producer Giorgio Moroder on the score for the film *Metropolis*.

May	1981	1. THE STROKE	Capitol
September	1981	2. IN THE DARK	Capitol
November	1981	3. MY KINDA LOVER	Capitol
August	1982	4. EMOTIONS IN MOTION	Capitol
October	1982	5. EVERYBODY WANTS YOU	Capitol
February	1983	6. SHE'S A RUNNER	Capitol
July	1984	7. ROCK ME TONITE	Capitol
October	1984	8. ALL NIGHT LONG	Capitol
December	1984	9. EYE ON YOU	Capitol

FRANK STALLONE

Hometown: Philadelphia, Pennsylvania

Frank Stallone began songwriting at age 14. After high school, he moved to New York, where he shared a small apartment with his brother Sylvester, who was then pursuing an acting career. Within a few years and after numerous odd jobs, Frank began performing in New Jersey clubs with his band, Valentine. The group disbanded after one unsuccessful album, and Frank started a solo career. He is seen singing a capella in the first *Rocky* film and playing in Cynthia Rhodes's band in *Stayin' Alive*.

September	1980	CASE OF YOU	Scotti Bros.
July	1983	FAR FROM OVER	RSO
May	1984	DARLIN'	Polydor

MICHAEL STANLEY BAND

Members:
  Michael Stanley—vocals, guitar, percussion—born: March 25, 1948
  Kevin Raleigh—vocals, keyboards, synthesizer, percussion—added in 1978—born: February 27, 1952
  Gary Markasky—guitar (replaced in 1984 by Dan Powers—born: November 20, 1956)
  Bob Pelander—keyboards, vocals, guitar, synthesizer—added in 1975—March 25, 1951
  Rick Bell—saxophone (left group in 1984)
  Michael Gismondi—bass, saxophone—born: July 5, 1955—replaced Daniel Pecchio in 1979
  Tommy Dobeck—drums—born: October 28, 1952
Hometown: Cleveland, Ohio

Michael Stanley Band. *Left to right:* Rick Bell, Bob Pelander, Dan Powers, Michael Stanley, Michael Gismondi, Kevin Raleigh, Tommy Dobeck.

Everywhere the MSB goes, the leader of the group gets the same question: Why is the group so super-popular in Ohio and only lukewarm everywhere else? There's really no answer for this, but while the group was headlining multiple nights at the biggest arenas in the midwest, they were also trekking east for small club dates in New York.

Michael Stanley put out two solo albums in the folk mode, then took a nine-to-five job. Before being transferred in 1974 to another city, he played in a jam session for TV's "Don Kirshner's Rock Concert" with fellow Clevelander Joe Walsh, and with Joe Vitale, David Sanborn, and Paul Harris. After the jam Stanley set out to assemble a band. He found guitarist-composer-vocalist Jonah Koslen, and together they wrote and performed songs. Also in 1974 he found Bell, Gismondi, and Dobeck. Bob Pelander joined the group the following year, and Kevin Raleigh came in 1978. Jonah has since left the group to form his own band, Breathless.

November	1980	1. HE CAN'T LOVE YOU	EMI-America
March	1981	2. LOVER	EMI-America
August	1981	3. FALLING IN LOVE AGAIN	EMI-America
September	1982	4. WHEN I'M HOLDING YOU TIGHT	EMI-America
December	1982	5. TAKE THE TIME	EMI-America
October	1983	6. MY TOWN	EMI-America
December	1983	7. SOMEONE LIKE YOU	EMI-America

PAUL STANLEY

Born: January 20, 1952
Hometown: New York, New York

A member of Kiss, Paul Stanley had a hit in 1978 with "Hold Me, Touch Me."

November	1978	HOLD ME, TOUCH ME	Casablanca

STARGARD

Members:
  Rochelle Runnells—vocals
  Debra Anderson—vocals (left group in 1981)
  Janice Williams—vocals
Hometown: Los Angeles, California

Rochelle Runnells and Debra Anderson had sung in many bands together in Los Angeles when Rochelle was selected from over 100 candidates to back up Anthony Newley's dinner-club act. Newley's agent left the choice of a second girl to her, so Rochelle immediately recruited her ex-singing partner, Debra. After a while, Debra left to pursue a solo career, and was replaced by Janice Williams. During a break in the tour, Rochelle and Janice returned to L. A., where they did a background vocal session for

Candi Staton's "Young Hearts Run Free," when they received a phone call from producer Norman Whitfield saying he wanted to form a female vocal group. Rochelle and Janice called Debra, and Stargard was formed. The group's first hit was the theme from the Richard Pryor film, *Which Way Is Up?* Later the trio appeared in the film *Sgt. Pepper's Lonely Hearts Club Band* as the Diamonds. Rochelle also had a hand in the soundtrack to *Cheech & Chong's Next Movie.* Meanwhile, Stargard Corp., a business formed by Stargard, is a thriving real estate concern. Debra Anderson left the band in 1981.

| January | 1978 | WHICH WAY IS UP | MCA |
| March | 1978 | DISCO RUFUS | MCA |

STARS ON 45

The concept of stringing together a lengthy medley of pop tunes from the sixties and early seventies to a steady dance rhythm was conceived by Dutch producer Jaap Eggermont, onetime drummer for the group Golden Earring, who used session vocalists and musicians and then invented the group name—Stars on 45. The idea was then imitated in nearly every field of music, including classical and big band swing. Various producers also used the format to tribute individual performers, such as Frankie Valli & the Four Seasons, but no medley record of that nature was as big as the original Stars on 45 single.

April	1981	★ 1. MEDLEY: INTRO VENUS/SUGAR SUGAR/NO REPLY/I'LL BE BACK/DRIVE MY CAR/DO YOU WANT TO KNOW A SECRET/WE CAN WORK IT OUT/I SHOULD HAVE KNOWN BETTER/NOWHERE MAN/YOU'RE GOING TO LOSE THAT GIRL/STARS ON 45	Radio Records
July	1981	2. MEDLEY II	Radio Records
September	1981	3. MORE STARS ON 45	Radio Records
March	1982	4. STARS ON 45 III (A TRIBUTE TO STEVIE WONDER)	Radio Records

STEEL BREEZE

Members:
    Ric Jacobs—vocals
    Ken Goorabian—guitar
    Waylin Carpenter—guitar
    Rod Toner—keyboards
    Vinnie Pantleoni—bass
    Barry Lowenthal—drums
Hometown: Sacramento, California

After years of bashing out rock 'n' roll in California night clubs and on demo tapes, the members of Steel Breeze took a bold step—they amassed a minor fortune of $120,000 and recorded a full album. They figured a record company might take a chance with a finished product, and they were right. The group's first hit, "You Don't Want Me Anymore," was adapted for a Budweiser beer commercial in early 1983.

| August | 1982 | YOU DON'T WANT ME ANYMORE | RCA |
| January | 1983 | DREAMIN' IS EASY | RCA |

JIM STEINMAN

Hometown: New York, New York

Jim Steinman spent much of his early life in Claremont, California, near Los Angeles, but moved back to his hometown of New York City before entering high school. His interest in writing for theater was nurtured while attending Amherst College in Massachusetts.

Steinman first met Meat Loaf when he auditioned Meat for a part in his show, *More Than You Deserve*. Meat got the part, and they became a team. After a short tour for both with *The National Lampoon Show*, Steinman and Loaf spent two years putting together Meat Loaf's dramatic *Bat Out of Hell* album. As the duo and a band toured to promote the record, *Bat Out of Hell* went on to sell eight million copies worldwide, taking the tour from dates opening for Cheap Trick to closing as headliners at the 20,000-seat Nassau Coliseum on Long Island, New York, in a span of about one year.

The duo began working on a follow-up album, but a series of delays led Steinman to record the *Bad For Good* album himself.

| May | 1981 | ROCK 'N' ROLL DREAMS COME THROUGH | Epic/Cleveland International |

VAN STEPHENSON

Hometown: Nashville, Tennessee

At age 10, Van Stephenson was relocated from Ohio to Nashville, Tennessee, where instead of getting turned on to country & western music, he discovered the Beatles, grew his hair, and bought a guitar. Throughout his high school years, Stephenson played in garage bands and jammed informally. After graduation, he began playing clubs in Tennessee, Florida, and Oklahoma. His rapidly maturing songwriting skills came to the attention of the House of Gold publishing house, where he was subsequently hired as a songwriter. By 1980, Stephenson was becoming a recording artist. His debut album, *China Girl*, was put out by a small record label, Handshake, and got some attention via the song "You've Got A Good Love Coming." Three years later, his second album, *Righteous Anger*, produced another hit, "Modern Day Delilah."

September	1981	YOU'VE GOT A GOOD LOVE COMING	Handshake
April	1984	MODERN DAY DELILAH	MCA
August	1984	WHAT THE BIG GIRLS DO	MCA

Van Stephenson

SHAKIN' STEVENS

Real Name: Mike Barratt
Born: March 4, 1948
Hometown: Cardiff, South Wales

Shakin' Stevens (as his schoolmates nicknamed him) was around 10 years old when he discovered rockabilly music. At age 15, at a time when American bands were trying to sound like British bands, Shakey (as his friends and fans call him) left school and formed a band called the Sunsets to play this American hybrid of country music and rock 'n' roll.

Stevens did not get a lot of attention at first, but after starring in the musical *Elvis* in London's West End, and with Lulu in a 36-week syndicated TV show called "Let's Rock," Stevens became a major star throughout Europe. In February 1982, the viewers of BBC television and the readers of the London Daily Mirror voted Stevens "Male Vocalist of the Year." After placing top-ten hits in 15 European countries, Stevens hoped in 1980 to begin reaching the American market.

April   1984   I CRY JUST A LITTLE BIT   Epic

AMII STEWART

Born: 1956

Born in America, Amii Stewart groomed her talents in England, Italy, and Germany. In 1978, while codirecting, choreographing, and starring in the

London production of *Bubbling Brown Sugar*, she met producers/song-writers Barry Leng and Simon May; together they gave Amii a British single, "You Really Touched My Heart." Later on, her debut American single, a disco reworking of Eddie Floyd's "Knock On Wood," was a big hit. Stewart has also worked on the films *King Kong, The Greatest,* and *The Return Of The Pink Panther*.

January	1979	★ KNOCK ON WOOD	Ariola
June	1979	LIGHT MY FIRE	Ariola
August	1980	MY GUY/MY GIRL (with Johnny Bristol)	Handshake

JOHN STEWART

Born: September 5, 1939
Hometown: San Diego, California

The son of a racehorse trainer, John Stewart learned the guitar as a teenager and formed a band called John Stewart & the Furies, cutting one single, "Rocking Anna," for Vita Records. While at Mt. San Antonio Junior College in Pomona, California, Stewart grew interested in folk music and played local dates with a trio. He attended a Kingston Trio concert in 1959 and played the folk group a couple of his songs. The Trio recorded two of his songs, "Molly Dee" and "Green Grasses," while Stewart banded with his choir teacher from Pomona and another guy to become a similar group, the Cumberland Three. After three albums with that group, Stewart was called in 1959 to replace Dave Guard in the Kingston Trio, then the largest-selling group in the world. Stewart stayed with the Kingston Trio until 1966, then left because he was bored. He went off to write "Daydream Believer" for the Monkees (later recorded by Anne Murray) and other hit tunes for other artists. After an album with his wife, Buffy Ford, John Stewart launched a solo career with 1969's *California Bloodlines* LP. His first pop hits, "Gold" and "Midnight Wind," featured assistance from Lindsey Buckingham and Stevie Nicks of Fleetwood Mac.

September	1969	1. ARMSTRONG	Capitol
May	1979	2. GOLD	RSO
August	1979	3. MIDNIGHT WIND	RSO
December	1979	4. LOST HER IN THE SUN	RSO

STILLWATER

Members:
    Jimmy Hall—vocals
    Bobby Golden—guitar
    Michael Causey—guitar
    Bob Spearman—keyboards
    Rob Walker—guitar

Allison Scarborough—bass
Sebie Lacey—drums
Hometown: Warner Robins, Georgia

During the late sixties, the various members of Stillwater played in
different bands around the Robins Air Force Base in Warner Robins,
Georgia. Around 1970, Bobby Golden, Michael Causey, Bob Spearman,
Jimmy Hall, and Sebie Lacey joined the local group Coldwater Army. In
the fall of 1972 they asked Allison and Rob to join with them to form
Stillwater.

This southern rock ensemble got their big break in 1975, when asked
to play at the annual Capricorn Records barbeque. This engagement led
to a contract with the label and an eventual hit single.

| January | 1978 | MINDBENDER | Capricorn |

STRAY CATS

Members:
    Brian Setzer—guitar, vocals—born: April 10, 1960
    Lee Rocker (Leon Drucker)—bass—born: August 3, 1961
    Slim Jim Phantom MacDonnell—percussion—born: March 21, 1961
Hometown: Massapequa Park, New York

After Brian Setzer left a successful local group called Bloodless Pharoahs,
he started playing rock 'n' roll at Long Island bars with just his acoustic
guitar as his accompaniment. Once he teamed up with Lee Rocker and
Slim Jim Phantom, they moved to England, where they hoped their
rockabilly revival would be accepted. They were right; the Stray Cats
became very popular throughout Europe, recording two albums before
returning to the United States, where selected tracks from those two
albums were packaged as the *Built For Speed* LP.

In 1984, the group and its record company were sued by the holders
of the late Eddie Cochran's publishing rights, who claimed that when the
Stray Cats changed 85 of the 191 words in a reworking of the song
"Jeanie Jeanie Jeanie," the original intent of the song was changed to
emphasize sex and "booze." The judge sided with the complainant, adding
that the members of the Stray Cats should have checked with the
copyright holders before releasing the revised version of the song.

On March 21, 1984, Slim Jim married actress Britt Ekland. In late
1984, the group disbanded.

September	1982	1. ROCK THIS TOWN	EMI-America
December	1982	2. STRAY CAT STRUT	EMI-America
August	1983	3. (SHE'S) SEXY + 17	EMI-America
October	1983	4. I WON'T STAND IN YOUR WAY	EMI-America
January	1984	5. LOOK AT THAT CADILLAC	EMI-America

STREEK

Members:
> Billy DeMartines—keyboards, vocals
> Ron Abrams—guitar, vocals
> Daniel J. Ricciardelli—saxophone, vocals
> Randy Oviedo—bass, vocals
> Guivanni Bartoletto—drums, vocals

Hometown: Los Angeles, California

In 1979, childhood friends Billy DeMartines and Ron Abrams decided they wanted to front a rock band—separately. Both kept to their ambition until someone convinced the California guitarist and the Florida-born pianist that they should team up and build a band around themselves. After they found Daniel Ricciardelli, the three tried any means necessary, including promises of $500 a week, to convince Randy Oviedo and Guivanni Bartoletto to quit their top-40 copy band for Streek. The group

Streek

never hit the club circuit, however; they rehearsed and rehearsed and rehearsed, and eventually talent scouts came by to listen. The group released one album, *Streek*, in 1981.

October   1981   ONE MORE NIGHT   Columbia/Badland

STREETS

Members:
   Steve Walsh—vocals, keyboards—born: 1950
   Mike Slamer—guitar

Streets. *Left to right:* Billy Greer, Tim Gehrt, Mike Slamer, Steve Walsh.

Billy Greer—bass, vocals
Tim Gehrt—drums, percussion
Hometown: Atlanta, Georgia

After leaving the group Kansas in 1981, Steve Walsh formed Streets, which was designed to be a democratic band rather than a back-up band for him. His first recruit was Tim Gehrt, who'd played on Walsh's solo album in 1979, *Schemer-Dreamer*. Next was Mike Slamer, whom Walsh didn't actually meet until the first day of rehearsal. Two weeks later, the trio went into a studio to record a demo tape. Shortly thereafter, Walsh lured Billy Greer away from a band called QB1, and Streets was born. The group then made its performance debut before 10,000 people at the annual Volunteer Jam in Nashville in January 1983. A debut album, *1st*, was released later that year.

| December | 1983 | IF LOVE SHOULD GO | Atlantic |

JOE SUN

Hometown: Rochester, Minnesota

After a stint in the armed forces and at Brown Institute in Minneapolis, where he studied radio broadcasting, Joe Sun worked as an air personality at WKIZ in Key West, Florida, and at country station WMAD in Madison, Wisconsin. In Madison, he moonlighted in a band called the Branded Men, until he left the radio station. Sun moved to Chicago, then Nashville, where he worked as a promotion man for a then-fledgling father-and-daughter team, the Kendalls. This led to his own recordings, which started with a single called "Old Flames (Can't Hold A Candle To You)."

| May | 1980 | SHOTGUN RIDER | Ovation |

SUPERTRAMP

Members:
    Rick Davies—vocals, keyboards—born: July 22, 1944
    Roger Hodgson—vocals, keyboards, guitar (left group in 1983)—born: March 21, 1950
    John Anthony Helliwell—keyboards—added in 1974
    Dougie Thomson—bass—added in 1974
    Bob C. Benberg—drums—added in 1974
Hometown: London, England

Rick Davies recruited Roger Hodgson, along with Richard Palmer and Bob Millar, to form Supertramp (a name taken from a book titled *The Autobiography Of A Supertramp*) in 1970. The group revamped in the early seventies and the line-up for Supertramp's third album, *Crime Of*

The Century, in 1974 proved the most rewarding. Shortly afterward, the quintet relocated to southern California. Roger Hodgson left in 1983 to pursue a solo career.

April	1975	1. BLOODY WELL RIGHT	A & M
June	1977	2. GIVE A LITTLE BIT	A & M
March	1979	3. THE LOGICAL SONG	A & M
July	1979	4. GOODBYE STRANGER	A & M
October	1979	5. TAKE THE LONG WAY HOME	A & M
September	1980	6. DREAMER	A & M
December	1980	7. BREAKFAST IN AMERICA	A & M
October	1982	8. IT'S RAINING AGAIN	A & M
January	1983	9. MY KIND OF LADY	A & M

SURVIVOR

Members:
> David Bickler—vocals, keyboards, synthesizer—replaced (1984) by Jimmie Jamison
> Frankie Sullivan—guitar, vocals
> Jim Peterik—piano, guitar
> Stephan Ellis—bass (replaced Dennis Keith Johnson in 1981)
> Marc Droubay—drums (replaced R. Gary Smith in 1981)

Hometown: Chicago, Illinois

In 1970, Jim Peterik was in a band called Ides of March, whose hit song, "Vehicle," he wrote. (See *IDES OF MARCH, Rock On: The Years of Change.*) In 1973, the group disbanded and Peterik pursued a solo career, releasing an album called *Don't Fight The Feeling* in 1976. He also cowrote several songs for 38 Special and the theme song for the film *Heavy Metal.*

Peterik met David Bickler while both were recording advertising jingles. He met Frankie Sullivan when Sullivan was in a band called Mariah. In 1978, the three formed Survivor. With the addition of a rhythm section they became a quintet and released a self-titled debut album in 1979. The group's major break was the theme song to the film *Rocky III,* "Eye Of The Tiger," which was written by Peterik and Sullivan after discussing the music for the soundtrack with the film's director and star, Sylvester Stallone.

February	1980		1. SOMEWHERE IN AMERICA	Scotti Bros.
October	1981		2. POOR MAN'S SON	Scotti Bros.
February	1982		3. SUMMER NIGHTS	Scotti Bros.
June	1982	★	4. EYE OF THE TIGER	Scotti Bros.
September	1982		5. AMERICAN HEARTBEAT	Scotti Bros.
January	1983		6. THE ONE THAT REALLY MATTERS	Scotti Bros.
October	1983		7. CAUGHT IN THE GAME	Scotti Bros.
June	1984		8. THE MOMENT OF TRUTH	Casablanca
September	1984		9. I CAN'T HOLD BACK	Scotti Bros.
January	1985		10. HIGH ON YOU	Scotti Bros.
May	1985		11. THE SEARCH IS OVER	Scotti Bros.

RACHEL SWEET

Born: 1963
Hometown: Akron, Ohio

Rachel Sweet's show business career began when she was five years old, when her grandfather, who worked on the staff of Akron's *Beacon Journal*, urged her to enter the talent contest at the newspaper's annual picnic, which she won. Within a year, she'd appeared four times on a local "amateur hour" television program, *The Gene Carroll Show*, and went as far as the quarter-finals. By the time she was seven years old, she'd sung and danced her way through summer-stock productions of *The Sound Of Music, Fiddler On The Roof,* and *Music Man,* and was soon commuting back and forth to New York, where she cut numerous commercials. By age 11, Sweet had already toured with both Mickey Rooney and Bill Cosby. Later, she auditioned for Linda Blair's role in *The Exorcist,* but unbeknownst to her parents, she turned down the part on account of "all that bad language." Although she'd been discovered many times throughout her childhood, her debut LP, *Fool Around,* was not released until late 1978. In 1982, Sweet starred in the 3D film *Rock 'n Roll Hotel* with Dick Shawn, and also served as the movie's musical director; the film was never released theatrically.

| June | 1981 | EVERLASTING LOVE (with Rex Smith) | Columbia |
| February | 1983 | VOO DOO | Columbia |

Rachel Sweet

SWITCH

Members:
> Gregory Williams—keyboards, bass
> Jody Sims—drums, percussion, vocals
> Philip Ingram—(left group in 1982)
> Eddie Fluellen—keyboards, trombone, vocals
> Tommy DeBarge—(left group in 1982)
> Bobby DeBarge—(left group in 1982)
> Renard Gallo—percussion, vocals—added in early 1980s
> Gonzales Ozen—percussion, vocals—added in early 1980s

Hometown: Mansfield, Michigan

In December 1976, Gregory Williams formed Switch and promised the members that they'd cut a demo tape and get a record deal. After the demo was recorded, he and Jody Sims went to Los Angeles. As fate would have it, they met Jermaine and Hazel Jackson in an elevator in the Motown Records building, and handed them a copy of the demo tape. Jermaine later listened to the tape and liked it enough to take Switch under his wing. Jermaine and Hazel managed Switch for a time and got the group signed to Gordy Records. There, Switch earned one platinum and two gold records.

The name Switch signifies how, in the group's early days, all the members would constantly switch instruments with one another, from piano, to drums, to bass, to guitar, etc.

October	1978	THERE'LL NEVER BE	Gordy
July	1979	BEST BEAT IN TOWN	Gordy
November	1979	I CALL YOUR NAME	Gordy

SYLVESTER

Real Name: Sylvester James
Hometown: Los Angeles, California

Sylvester James says he comes from a middle-class black family in Los Angeles, and that in 1967 he moved to San Francisco, where he felt free. After appearing as Sylvester & the Hot Band both independently and as part of a campy, colorful, drag-queen theatrical group called the Cockettes, Sylvester went on to become a disco darling in the late seventies.

March 11, 1979, was declared Sylvester Day by San Francisco Mayor Dianne Feinstein, and Sylvester was presented with the keys to the city at his Opera House concert that evening. He appeared in the film *The Rose* as a female impersonator doing a Diana Ross act. On April 14, 1980, he was falsely arrested for passing a bad check in New York City; someone else had impersonated *him*, and charges were dropped when the complainant admitted that the person who wrote the bad check was not Sylvester.

Sylvia

August	1978	DANCE, DISCO HEAT	Fantasy
January	1979	YOU MAKE ME FEEL MIGHTY REAL	Fantasy
April	1979	I WHO HAVE NOTHING	Fantasy

SYLVIA

Real Name: Sylvia Kirby Allen
Hometown: Kokomo, Indiana

Sylvia had her lone chart entry, "Nobody," in 1982 on RCA records. The song made the nation's top 20.

August	1982	NOBODY	RCA

THE SYSTEM

Members:
    Mic Murphy—guitar, vocals
    David Frank—synthesizers
Hometown: New York, New York

The System's story begins with Mic Murphy, who was born in Raleigh, North Carolina, but grew up in New York City. At age 14, Murphy was already playing original material with a band he called Mic & the Soul Shakers. Over the years, Murphy continued playing in local bands, mostly

The System. David Frank (*left*), Mic Murphy.

hard-rock groups, also working as roadie, sound man, road manager, production person, and background vocalist.

David Frank was born in Dayton, Ohio, but raised from age eight in the Boston suburb of Weston, Massachusetts. By ninth grade, he supplemented his training in classical piano with a series of mostly rock 'n' roll bands which, like Murphy's band, were also primarily playing original work. In 1980, he moved to New York and began playing in area bands. One day, Mic Murphy spotted David Frank in the backing band for a vocalist, and was struck by Frank's ability. In May 1982, the two began working together. The System's debut LP, *Sweat*, was released in February, 1983.

March   1983   YOU ARE MY SYSTEM   Mirage

T

TACO

Real Name: Taco Ockerse
Born: 1955
Hometown: Hamburg, Germany

Taco was born to Dutch parents in Jakarta, Indonesia, and spent his early years travelling the world with his globe-trotting family. They eventually settled in Germany, where Taco studied dance and theater. By 1975, he had appeared in a number of musical comedies and by 1979 he was touring Germany as Chino in *West Side Story*.

In 1980, Taco created his own band called Taco's Bizz and appeared in Hamburg's trendy nightclubs. Since his show of nostalgic songs was so popular, he decided to do an album of such material: *After Eight* featured remakes of such classics as "Cheek to Cheek," "Singin' in the Rain" and the Irving Berlin tune "Puttin' on the Ritz." The latter song was released

Taco

as a single and became an international hit. It made Taco a very big success in the U. S. during the summer of 1983.

June   1983   PUTTIN' ON THE RITZ   RCA

TALKING HEADS

Members:
   David Byrne—guitar, vocals—born: May 14, 1952
   Jerry Harrison—keyboards, guitar, vocals—born: February 21, 1949
   Martina Weymouth—bass—born: November 22, 1950
   Chris Frantz—drums—born: May 8, 1951
Hometown: New York, New York

David Byrne, Chris Frantz, and Tina Weymouth met at the Rhode Island School of Design, where David and Chris formed a group called the Artistics. Following Chris's graduation in 1974, David and Chris moved to New York and, bored and disenchanted with the contemporary art scene, decided to continue making music. They invited Tina to join as a singer, but she decided to play bass instead.

The trio moved into a loft in lower Manhattan in January 1975 and together worked on music. Taking its name from TV terminology for close-up face shots in news programs and talk shows, Talking Heads debuted in June at CBGB's, a New York club that served as a clearing house for up-and-coming musicians. The group played there often, many times as opening act to bigger groups before becoming headliner in their own right. In early 1977, they recruited Jerry Harrison, who'd previously played in Jonathan Richman's Modern Lovers. A few months later, Weymouth and Frantz were wed.

By 1980, Talking Heads began using more musicians and leaning

Talking Heads. *Left to right:* Chris Frantz, Jerry Harrison, Martina Weymouth, David Byrne.

towards more percussive sound. Weymouth and Frantz also recorded music as Tom Tom Club between Talking Heads commitments, and David Byrne composed music called *The Catherine Wheel* for the Twyla Tharp dance company's Broadway production. In 1984 the group starred in a hit movie, *Stop Making Sense.*

February	1978	1. PSYCHO KILLER	Sire
November	1978	2. TAKE ME TO THE RIVER	Sire
November	1979	3. LIFE DURING WARTIME	Sire
July	1983	4. BURNING DOWN THE HOUSE	Sire
November	1983	5. THIS MUST BE THE PLACE	Sire

MARC TANNER BAND

Members:
      Marc Tanner—vocals, guitar, piano
      Michael Stevens—guitar
      Ron Edwards—bass
      Joe Romersa—drums
      Linda Stevens—back-up vocals
Hometown: Los Angeles, California

As an exchange student in high school, Marc Tanner studied in London, England, and Rome, Italy. While in London, he grew to love English rock. Upon his return from Europe, he moved out of the family home, determined to take a chance on music. He worked day jobs and played clubs as well as on other people's demo sessions, and he visited record companies whenever he could. He landed a record deal in 1978 and released *No Escape.* Soon after, Tanner formed a band and played to audiences for the first time.

March	1979	ELENA	Elektra

THE TARNEY SPENCER BAND

Members:
      Alan Tarney—guitar, bass, keyboards, vocals
      Trevor Spencer—drums
Hometown: Australia

Alan Tarney and Trevor Spencer first met in Australia in the late sixties. They moved to England and worked with bands that came to nothing, so after a while they opted to sell their original songs and do studio work. They played, produced, or wrote for Cliff Richard, Olivia Newton-John, Bonnie Tyler, the New Seekers, and the Drifters. By 1976, Tarney and Spencer decided to start developing their own careers again. The duo's first album, in 1978, was called *Three's A Crowd.*

July	1978	IT'S REALLY YOU	A & M
May	1979	NO TIME TO LOSE	A & M
September	1981	NO TIME TO LOSE	A & M

B. E. TAYLOR GROUP

Members:
 B. E. Taylor—vocals
 Rick Witkowski—guitars, vocals
 Dave "Nat" Kerr—keyboards, vocals
 Joe Macre—bass, vocals
 Joe D'Amico—drums, vocals
Hometown: Pittsburgh, Pennsylvania

Taylor has been playing with bar bands since as far back as 1964. He formed a duo with fellow Pittsburgh recording artist Donnie Iris just after Donnie's group, the Jaggerz, split up. They played as a duo for a year and a half, until Iris joined Wild Cherry. Taylor then teamed up with Rick Witkowski, Joe Macre, and Joe D'Amico, all formerly of Crack the Sky, to form the B. E. Taylor Group. Nat Kerr, a former member of Sojourn, joined the band later. Incidentally, the group's one hit, "Vitamin L," is the only song recorded on the group's albums that was not sung by Taylor; the song was sung by Joe D'Amico.

| January | 1984 | VITAMIN L | MCA/Sweet City |

LIVINGSTON TAYLOR

Born: November 21, 1950
Hometown: Boston, Massachusetts

Livingston Taylor came from a musical family. After the success of brother James Taylor, siblings Livingston, Alex, and Kate all released albums, but of James's three family members, only Livingston kept recording. Born in Boston and raised in North Carolina, Liv resettled in a semi-rural Boston suburb in Massachusetts. He lives with his wife Maggie.

February	1971	1. CAROLINA DAY	Capricorn
February	1972	2. GET OUT OF BED	Capricorn
October	1978	3. I WILL BE IN LOVE WITH YOU	Epic
March	1979	4. I'LL COME RUNNING	Epic
July	1980	5. FIRST TIME LOVE	Epic

BRAM TCHAIKOVSKY

Members:
 Bram Tchaikovsky (Peter Bramall)—vocals, guitar, bass—born: 1951
 Micky Broadbent—bass, guitar, keyboards, vocals
 Keith Boyce—drums—replaced (1980) by Keith Line
 Dennis Forbes—guitar, vocals, bass, keyboards—added in 1979
Hometown: Lincolnshire, England

After leaving the Motors in 1978, Bram Tchaikovsky made it clear that his new group would be named after himself. This unique moniker continued to puzzle the public, especially when the British press reported that Bram Tchaikovsky broke up so that Bram Tchaikovsky could pursue a solo career. In any case, Bram Tchaikovsky (neither the group nor the individual) has not been heard from since the *Funland* album in 1981.

| July | 1979 | GIRL OF MY DREAMS | Polydor/Radar |

T-CONNECTION

Members:
 Theophilus "T" Coakley—vocals, keyboards, guitar
 Dave Mackey—guitar, vocals
 Kirkwood Coakley—bass, drums, vocals
 Anthony Flowers—percussion, vocals
 Steve Colebrook—vocals—added in 1984
Hometown: The Bahamas

T Coakley began his music career in 1965, playing maracas in a calypso quartet in the Bahamas. In 1973, he formed his own band in Nassau with his brother Kirk, Dave Mackey, and Anthony Flowers, and the group became the most popular band in the Islands. In 1976, during the disco era, T-Connection's rhythmic music was accepted in the United States.

| March | 1977 | DO WHAT YOU WANNA DO | Dash |
| March | 1979 | AT MIDNIGHT | Dash |

TEARS FOR FEARS

Members:
 Curt Smith—vocals, bass, keyboards
 Roland Orzabal—vocals, guitar, keyboards, rhythm programming
Hometown: Bath, England

Curt Smith and Roland Orzabal have known each other since age 13, when they met in school. Six years later, they formed their first band called Graduate, later changing the name to History of Headaches and then Tears for Fears. The duo has been assisted by drummer Manny Elias, keyboard programmer Ian Stanley, and others.

| August | 1983 | CHANGE | Mercury |
| March | 1985 | ★ EVERYBODY WANTS TO RULE THE WORLD | Mercury |

THIRD WORLD

Members:
 William "Bunny Rugs" Clarke—vocals, guitar (replaced Milton Hamilton in 1976)

Stephen H. "Cat" Coore—guitar, bass, vocals—born: 1960
K. Michael "Ibo" Cooper—keyboards, vocals, guitar—born: 1956
Richard "Bassheart" Daley—bass—born: 1955
William John Lee "Root" Stewart—drums—born: February 15, 1953 (replaced
    Cornell Marshall in mid-1970s)
Irvin "Carrot" Jarrett—percussion—born: 1951
Hometown: Kingston, Jamaica

Third World was conceived in July 1973 by Ibo and Cat, who called on those musician friends they knew were dissatisfied with what they claim was a prevailing lack of imagination in Jamaican music. Together, the members of Third World sought to utilize influences from Africa and North and Central America, and ultimately became well-known in many parts of the world for this approach.

February   1979   NOW THAT WE FOUND LOVE   Island

38 SPECIAL

Members:
Donnie Van Zant—vocals—born: June 11, 1952
Don Barnes—vocals, guitar—born: December 3, 1952
Jeff Carlisi—guitar—born: July 15, 1952
Larry Junstrom—bass (replaced Ken Lyons in 1977)—born: June 22, 1949
Steve Brookins—drums—born: June 2, 1951
Jack Grondin—drums—born: October 3, 1951
Hometown: Jacksonville, Florida

38 Special. *Left to right:* Jack Grondin, Larry Junstrom, Steve Brookins, Jeff Carlisi, Donnie Van Zant, Don Barnes.

On Donnie Van Zant's 16th birthday, his parents gave him a 1938 Buick Special, which he quickly converted into an equipment van for his band, Standard Production. The following year, Van Zant lured Jeff Carlisi away from a band called Doomsday Refreshment Committee, and together with Ken Lyons, formed Sweet Rooster, which would also include Steve Brookins. Carlisi quickly left to attend architecture classes at Georgia Tech and was replaced by Don Barnes. Sweet Rooster died, but Van Zant and Barnes continued working together in various bands throughout the early seventies, while Van Zant worked as a railroad brakeman and Barnes delivered chickens in Van Zant's converted Buick. Lyons became an expert house painter and Steve Brookins drove a semi.

In the summer of 1975, Van Zant, Barnes, Carlisi, Lyons, Brookins, and Jack Grondin formed 38 Special and played the club circuit for a year and a half while Donnie's brother Ronnie was getting a taste of stardom in Lynyrd Skynyrd. In 1977, 38 Special released its self-titled debut LP. Most of the group's biggest hits were cowritten with Jim Peterik of the group Survivor, and were sung by Don Barnes.

On April 26, 1981, 38 Special did a benefit concert in Richmond, Virginia, for the March of Dimes; the concert was free to "WalkAmerica" walkers who raised money for the March's fight against birth defects. In 1982, Donnie was arrested for drinking in public when he toasted the audience after a concert in Tulsa. The group averages 200 concerts each year.

February	1980	1. ROCKIN' INTO THE NIGHT	A & M
February	1981	2. HOLD ON LOOSELY	A & M
June	1981	3. FANTASY GIRL	A & M
May	1982	4. CAUGHT UP IN YOU	A & M
August	1982	5. YOU KEEP RUNNIN' AWAY	A & M
November	1983	6. IF I'D BEEN THE ONE	A & M
February	1984	7. BACK WHERE YOU BELONG	A & M
September	1984	8. TEACHER, TEACHER	Capitol

CHRIS THOMPSON

A member of Manfred Mann's Band from 1976 to 1979, Chris Thompson had two hits after he left the group. He played with a group called Night between his two hit singles.

| August | 1979 | IF YOU REMEMBER ME | Planet |
| November | 1983 | ALL THE RIGHT MOVES (with Jennifer Warnes) | Casablanca |

ROBBIN THOMPSON BAND

Members:
Robbin Thompson—vocals, guitar—born: 1949
Velpo Robertson—guitar, vocals
Eric Heiberg—keyboards, vocals

Michael Lanning—bass, vocals
Bob "Rico the Fox" Antonelli—drums, vocals
Hometown: Richmond, Virginia

In the early seventies, Robbin Thompson played in a band called Steel Mill with Bruce Springsteen, after which he won the American Song Festival twice. A solo album in 1976 was not a success, but Thompson received considerable attention after forming the Robbin Thompson Band in 1978. Nine months later, this ensemble recorded a debut LP, entitled *(two "b's" please)*.

October   1980   BRITE EYES   Ovation

THOMPSON TWINS

Members:
Tom Bailey—vocals, synthesizer, drum programs, keyboards, percussion—
    born: January 18, 1956
Alannah Currie—xylophone, percussion, vocals—born: September 28, 1957
Joe Leeway—conga, synthesizer, vocals
Hometown: Chesterfield, England

Thompson Twins. *Left to right:* Alannah Currie, Tom Bailey, Joe Leeway.

There are no Thompsons and there are no twins. The members of the original Thompson Twins band adapted this group's name from two characters in a famous comic called "Horsay's Adventures of Tin Tin."

Back in 1977, Tom Bailey and two friends, Pete Dodd and John Roog, formed the Thompson Twins. The group expanded beyond its hometown of Chesterfield and developed a following in Sheffield and other northern cities before moving to London. The band evolved into a shifting line-up, which often included members of its audiences. The group became popular in England, where their first headlining tour benefited the No Nukes movement. By 1983, the Thompson Twins was a nucleus of three with additional musicians; only Tom Bailey remains from the original line-up.

January	1983	1. LIES	Arista
April	1983	2. LOVE ON YOUR SIDE	Arista
February	1984	3. HOLD ME NOW	Arista
May	1984	4. DOCTOR! DOCTOR!	Arista
August	1984	5. YOU TAKE ME UP	Arista
November	1984	6. INTO THE GAP	Arista

ALI THOMSON

Born: 1959
Hometown: Glasgow, Scotland

Ali Thomson was singing by the age of five and fronting bands by his early teens. In his mid-teens, he moved to London, England, and worked at Mountain Records while continuing to play in bands. Eventually, he decided to join his brother, Supertramp's Dougie Thomson, in California. There, he began thinking about pursuing a solo career instead of always joining bands. Once back in England, he worked for a publishing company. Ali's first success as a writer was Gary Wright's "Dream Weaver." *Take A Little Rhythm*, Ali's debut LP, was released in March 1980.

| June | 1980 | TAKE A LITTLE RHYTHM | A & M |
| September | 1980 | LIVE EVERY MINUTE | A & M |

BILLY THORPE

Real Name: William Richard Thorpe
Hometown: Manchester, England

Born in England, young William Richard Thorpe emigrated to Australia with his parents. At age 10, he began his professional career by performing on Australian television. Six years later, he formed a rock band, Billy Thorpe & the Aztecs. The group scored 15 number-one albums and 12 number-one singles. Selected as a semifinalist in the first annual American

International Song Festival in 1975, Thorpe visited the United States and became enamored with the high quality of recording and staging technology here, and after 20 successful albums in Australia, he sought to try his luck elsewhere by moving to Los Angeles in 1976. Since then, his American albums have encompassed a continuing sci-fi saga.

July	1979	CHILDREN OF THE SUN	Capricorn

TIERRA

Members:
  Steve Salas—vocals, trombone, timbales
  Rudy Salas—guitar, vocals
  Bobby Navarrete—reeds, vocals
  Joey Guerra—keyboards, vocals
  Steve Falomir—bass
  Phil Madayag—drums
  Andre Baeza—congas, percussion
Hometown: East Los Angeles, California

Tierra (Spanish for *earth*) is led by brothers Rudy and Steve Salas, who have been making music since they were eleven and nine, respectively, performing at family reunions and high school dances. They played in several bands, including El Chicano, before forming Tierra in 1972. The group's reworking of the Intruders' "Together" was a local hit with a small record company before Tierra signed with a national firm and rereleased the single.

November	1980	TOGETHER	Boardwalk
March	1981	MEMORIES	Boardwalk
October	1981	LA LA MEANS I LOVE YOU	Boardwalk

TIGGI CLAY

Members:
  Fizzy Qwick—vocals
  Romeo "Breath" McCall—keyboards
  William "Billy" Peaches—bass
Hometown: Oakland, California

Tiggi Clay is the name of a perhaps mythical bully that Breath McCall supposedly had it out with after school one day. Tiggi Clay is now the name of a new wave trio as well. The group traces its origins to 1979, when Billy Peaches was playing behind Lenny Williams. McCall was a security guard at the venue, and after Peaches and McCall exchanged musical ideas, they exchanged phone numbers and began frequenting a club called Ivy's. There they met Fizzy Qwick, and the three began writing songs together. A debut LP, *Flashes*, was released in 1984.

February   1984   FLASHES   Morocco

THE TIME

Members:
> Morris Day—vocals—born: 1959
> Jesse Johnson—guitar, vocals
> Jimmy "Jam" Harris—keyboards, vocals—replaced (1984) by Paul Peterson
> Monte Moir—keyboards, vocals (left group in 1982)—replaced (1984) by Mark Cardenas
> Terry Lewis—bass, vocals (left group in 1982)—replaced (1984) by Jerry Hubbard
> Jellybean Johnson—drums, percussion
> Jerome Benton—percussion

Hometown: Minneapolis, Minnesota

The Time's lead singer, Morris Day, played drums in a band called Grand Central along with Prince and Prince's then-roommate and later bassist, Andre Cymone. Once Prince became a big star, he took Morris under his wing and formed a group around him, circa 1980.

About the same time, a group called Flyte Tyme was playing around the Minneapolis area; that group consisted of Jimmy "Jam" Harris, Monte Moir, Terry Lewis, and Jellybean Johnson. Morris recruited Jesse Johnson, who he'd only known for a few days, and the two joined forces with Flyte Tyme to become the Time. Jerome Benton also joined, but played no musical instrument; he was originally used as a comic prop on stage, bringing out a mirror so Morris could comb his hair in the middle of a song.

Ironically, unsubstantiated rumors suggest that Prince secretly wrote and/or produced the songs, and played all or most of the instruments on the Time's 1981 self-titled debut album, though he was never a member of the band's line-up; officially, the group simply signed on with his production company. The Time did actually perform live later, though, and even backed Vanity 6, a Prince-concocted female vocal trio. The members of the Time did play on their second album, *What Time Is It?*, in 1982.

Harris and Lewis began producing other acts on the side, including the S. O. S. Band and Cheryl Lynn, and later, Change and Cherrelle. One night in 1982, while in Atlanta producing tracks for the S. O. S. Band, a freak snowstorm grounded them, forcing them to miss a Time concert. Prince fired the duo. Monte Moir then reportedly left to join Lewis and

Harris, who resumed production activities and also formed a band called the Secrets. Morale within the Time began to fall.

A reconstituted Time was featured in Prince's 1984 feature film, *Purple Rain*, and released a third Time album, *Ice Cream Castle*. Although all of the new Time appeared in the hit film, Day and Benton had major supporting roles; as a result of his growing popularity, Benton was listed as a band member for the first time. Day received terrific notices for his role in *Purple Rain*. Shortly after the reviews were out, Day announced he would move to Los Angeles to further his acting career, and that he would quit the Time to eventually form a new band—without input from Prince, who appeared to have controlled Day's career until then. About the same time, Jesse Johnson also decided to leave the Time in order to pursue a solo career.

The two remaining members of the original Time concept, Jellybean Johnson and Jerome Benton, along with members of the latter-day Time, evolved into another group, both physically and musically, and so were renamed the Family. Consequently, the Time ceased to exist in 1984.

January	1982	1. COOL	Warner Bros.
October	1982	2. 777-9311	Warner Bros.
October	1984	3. JUNGLE LOVE	Warner Bros.
February	1985	4. THE BIRD	Warner Bros.

TOBY BEAU

Members:
>   Balde Silver—vocals, guitar, harmonica—born: 1954
>   Danny McKenna—guitar, vocals (left group in 1979)
>   Ron Rose—guitar, banjo, mandolin, vocals
>   Steve "Zip" Zipper—bass, vocals
>   Rob Young—drums, percussion

Hometown: Texas

Toby Beau, which formed in 1975, was named after a shrimp boat spotted by guitarist Danny McKenna in the Gulf of Mexico, and the group played cover material on the Texas bar-band circuit. One night in 1977, a roadie for the rock band Starz heard Toby Beau playing in San Antonio and told his brother, Sean Delaney, about that performance. Sean inspired the group to write original songs and then produced the band's 1978 self-titled debut album. McKenna left the band midway through the recording of the second album, *More Than A Love Song*, and by Toby Beau's third album in 1980, *If You Believe*, the only remaining original member was Balde Silver.

June	1978	MY ANGEL BABY	RCA
August	1979	THEN YOU CAN TELL ME GOODBYE	RCA
July	1980	IF I WERE YOU	RCA

TOM TOM CLUB

Hometown: New York, New York

Tom Tom Club is a studio project by the husband-and-wife team of drummer Chris Frantz and bassist Tina Weymouth, both founding members of Talking Heads. The name Tom Tom Club came from the name of the place in the Bahamas where their first jams took place.

January	1982	GENIUS OF LOVE	Sire

TOMMY TUTONE

Members:
    Tommy Heath—vocals, guitar, piano
    Jim Keller—guitar, vocals
    Jon Lyons—bass—replaced (1983) by Greg Sutton
    Victor Carberry—drums—replaced (1983) by Jerry Angel
    Steve LeGassick—keyboards, synthesizer—added in 1983
Hometown: Los Angeles, California

Tommy Tutone's two principal members, Tommy Heath and Jim Keller, first teamed up in San Francisco in 1978, three years after Keller had moved west from New Jersey. While Heath had been playing in bands all over northern California, Keller had worked as a carpenter renovating old buildings, only occasionally playing his acoustic guitar. Both had already made demo tapes of original songs when they met, and when Heath heard Keller's guitar style (Keller had no training) he said this was the guitar sound he needed. Tommy Tutone's first album was released in 1980, and the group toured that year as opening act for Tom Petty & the Heartbreakers.

May	1980	ANGEL SAY NO	Columbia
January	1982	867-5309	Columbia

TORONTO

Members:
    Holly Woods—vocals
    Sharon Alton—guitar
    Brian Allen—guitar
    Scott Kreyer—keyboards
    Gary Allonde—bass (replaced Nick Costello in 1981)—replaced (1983) by
      Mike Gingrich
    Barry Connors—drums (replaced Jimmy Fox in 1981)
Hometown: Toronto, Ontario, Canada

Although the six original members of this group came from different parts of the world, they wound up working together several times in different combinations (the group's direct predecessor was Brian Allen's group, Rose) before settling in Toronto, the city, to form Toronto, the band (even though only one member is Canadian). The group's original rhythm section—Nick Costello and Jimmy Fox—left in 1981 and was replaced by two musicians, Gary Allonde and Barry Connors, who did not formally become members of Toronto.

| August | 1982 | YOUR DADDY DON'T KNOW | Network |

PETER TOSH

Born: October 19, 1944
Hometown: Jamaica

Peter Tosh is a legend in his native Jamaica, since he, Bob Marley, and Neville Livingston (aka Bunny Wailer) came from different parts of the island to form the Wailers. After years of scuffling in the street ghettoes of West Kingston, of livid dealings with quick-buck promoters, of government harassment, and of spiritual redemption in the Rastafarian religion, the Wailers became the most popular and most important band in reggae music.

In 1974, the original trio split up. Marley continued as Bob Marley & the Wailers, Livingston continued making records but stopped touring, and Tosh launched a solo career singing increasingly controversial songs. In early 1975, he was badly beaten by the police, reportedly without provocation, prompting him to write and record "Mark of the Beast," which was immediately banned on Jamaican radio. This was followed by his marijuana anthem, "Legalize It," which was also banned but became a big seller nevertheless. Eventually, the bans were lifted, and Tosh continued recording songs with overt socio-political and religious messages.

In 1978, Tosh became the first artist signed to Rolling Stones Records besides the Stones, and that summer, he opened many concerts on the Stones' tour of America. This led to a duet with the Stones' Mick Jagger on a Temptations classic written by Smokey Robinson and Ronald White of the Miracles, "Don't Look Back."

| November | 1978 | (YOU GOT TO WALK AND) DON'T LOOK BACK (with Mick Jagger) | Rolling Stones |
| July | 1983 | JOHNNY B. GOODE | EMI-America |

TOTO

Members:
    Bobby Kimball—vocals—born: March 29, 1947—replaced (1984) by Dennis "Fergie" Frederiksen—born: May 15, 1951
    Steve Lukather—guitar, vocals—born: October 21, 1957

Toto. *Left to right:* (*back row*) Mike Porcaro, Dave Paich, Steve Lukather, Bobby Kimball; (*front row*) Jeff Porcaro, Steve Porcaro.

David Paich—keyboards, vocals—born: June 25, 1954
Steve Porcaro—keyboards, vocals—born: September 2, 1957
David Hungate—bass—replaced (1984) by Mike Porcaro—born: May 29, 1955
Jeff Porcaro—drums, percussion—born: April 1, 1954
Hometown: Los Angeles, California

The members of Toto represent a collective of some of Los Angeles's most in-demand session musicians. In addition to working separately and together on a number of outside productions, the members of Toto have committed themselves to this self-contained sextet, a rare dedication among the ranks of studio musicians.

David Paich and Jeff Porcaro have known each other since they were 13, and their fathers Marty and Joe worked together on a Glen Campbell TV project. Jeff's brother Steve and Steve Lukather jammed together at Grant High School in San Fernando Valley. These four had known David Hungate, and met Bobby Kimball when he left his hometown of Vinton, Louisiana, to sing with S. S. Fools in Los Angeles. Toto was born in 1978 and started a string of hits with its first single "Hold The Line." Over the years, Toto became a very popular group, even though studio commitments prevented them from touring extensively. Toto has won gold and platinum records and Grammy Awards.

| October | 1978 | 1. HOLD THE LINE | Columbia |
| February | 1979 | 2. I'LL SUPPLY THE LOVE | Columbia |

April	1979	3. GEORGY PORGY	Columbia
December	1979	4. 99	Columbia
April	1982	5. ROSANNA	Columbia
August	1982	6. MAKE BELIEVE	Columbia
October	1982	★ 7. AFRICA	Columbia
March	1983	8. I WON'T HOLD BACK	Columbia
July	1983	9. WAITING FOR LOVE	Columbia
October	1984	10. STRANGER IN TOWN	Columbia
February	1985	11. HOLYANNA	Columbia

THE TOURISTS

Members:
Ann Lennox—vocals, keyboards—born: December 25, 1953
Peet Coombes—vocals, guitar
Dave Stewart—guitar—born: September 9, 1952
Eddie Chin—bass
Jim "Do It" Toomey—drums, percussion
Hometown: London, England

In 1977 Dave Stewart, who'd been a member of Longdancer, and Peet Coombes, both from the north of England, got together in London and began writing music. In London, they met Ann Lennox, who'd spent three years at the Royal Academy of Music learning flute and composition. Early in 1978, the trio called on drummer Jim Toomey and bassist Eddie Chin to help them with studio demos, and a working quintet was born. The group began working clubs around London. When they played the well-known Hope and Anchor to favorable reception, a record contract quickly followed. The Tourists broke up in 1981, and Lennox and Stewart formed the Eurythmics. (See *EURYTHMICS*).

May	1980	I ONLY WANT TO BE WITH YOU	Epic

PETE TOWNSHEND

Born: May 19, 1945
Hometown: Chiswick, England

As its principal composer and guitarist, Pete Townshend has guided the Who by writing hits from "My Generation" through "Won't Be Fooled Again" and more, as well as two rock operas, *Tommy* and *Quadrophenia*, which evolved from recordings to feature films. Townshend lives in Twickenham, England. He used the name Peter for his debut solo album, *Who Came First*, and Pete afterwards.

June	1980	LET MY LOVE OPEN THE DOOR	Atco
October	1980	A LITTLE IS ENOUGH	Atco
November	1980	ROUGH BOYS	Atco

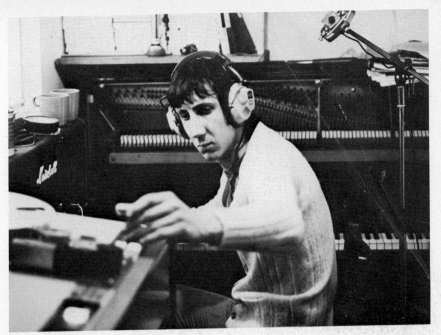

Pete Townshend

PAT TRAVERS

Born: 1954
Hometown: Toronto, Canada

Pumping the Canadian club circuit in early 1975, Pat Travers was thrilling the north country when he caught the ears of Ritchie Yorke, Canada's foremost pop music critic. They became friends, and Yorke convinced Travers to go to England and make it big. A couple of weeks after landing at Heathrow Airport, Pat bought two British music weeklies and began calling musicians who'd advertised in the classifieds. He found a drummer and a bassist on the same day, and that very day, the trio got together to rehearse. The next day, they cut five tracks at a recording studio. Demo tape in hand, Travers barged into the offices of a top British manager, and shortly the young guitarist had management, publishing, and recording contracts. Travers quickly became a guitar hero in the United Kingdom, but in 1978, the public's snowballing interest in the punk music scene rendered his hard-rock approach unfashionable, so he moved to the United States. Travers and his English setter, Gimble McGee, now live in a house in Orlando, Florida.

| September | 1979 | BOOM BOOM | Polydor |
| May | 1980 | IS THIS LOVE | Polydor |

JOEY TRAVOLTA

Hometown: Teaneck, New Jersey

Joey Travolta's artistic development came via a show business family. Joey started singing at age three. Although he has been in two films, *Sunnyside* and *The Warning*, Joey's movie and singing career have moved slowly. Perhaps it's because he has had to live in the shadow of his superstar brother John.

June   1978   I DON'T WANNA GO   Millennium

TRIUMPH

Members:

    Rik "The Rocket" Emmett—guitar, vocals—born: July 10, 1953
    Mike Levine—keyboards, bass—born: June 1, 1949
    Gil "the Bird" Moore—drums, vocals—born: February 12, 1951
Hometown: Toronto, Ontario, Canada

Mike Levine and Gil Moore, both already well-respected musicians on the Canadian rock scene, first got together to jam in the fall of 1975. Before long, they began searching for a guitarist with whom to form a high-energy, hard-rock power trio. They found what they wanted in a young virtuoso named Rik Emmett of a band called Act III. Emmett had

Triumph. *Left to right:* Rik Emmett, Mike Levine, Gil Moore.

been playing the guitar since age 14, spending the greater part of his youth studying classical and jazz guitar. The three musicians initially met in the office of a Canadian manager, and after a five-hour jam, Triumph was born.

Triumph worked the local clubs before headlining concert halls. Although the group was not well-known when it toured the United States for the first time in 1978, their elaborate stage show required Triumph to headline each American concert date.

Rik Emmett has worked as a cartoonist for *Hit Parader* magazine and as a columnist for *Guitar Player* magazine, and Gil Moore was named official pyrotechnic consultant to the Canadian Clearwater Festival fireworks display.

June	1979	1. HOLD ON	RCA
November	1979	2. LAY IT ON THE LINE	RCA
June	1980	3. I CAN SURVIVE	RCA
October	1981	4. MAGIC POWER	RCA
March	1985	5. FOLLOW YOUR HEART	MCA

THE TUBES

Members:
    Fee Waybill—vocals—born: September 17, 1950
    Bill Spooner—guitar, vocals—born: August 16, 1949
    Roger Steen—guitar, vocals—born: November 13, 1949
    Vince Walnick—keyboards—born: February 21, 1951
    Michael Cotten—synthesizer—born: January 25, 1950
    Rick Anderson—bass—born: August 1, 1947
    Prairie Prince—drums, percussion—born: May 7, 1950
    Re Styles—vocals, dancer—born: March 3, 1950
Hometown: Phoenix, Arizona

The members of the Tubes weren't all born in Arizona, but somehow they all ended up there at the same time. The group traces its history to Phoenix in the mid-sixties, when various individuals now in the Tubes played in various bands with musicians who would become Three Dog Night and Alice Cooper. They banded together in the late sixties—Fee Waybill joined because he was the only one with a car that could drag all the instruments to a gig; it wasn't until later that they discovered he could sing.

When Prairie Prince and Michael Cotten, friends since kindergarten and the Tubes' only native Arizonans, decided in the early seventies to attend San Francisco Art Institute, member by member, the Tubes moved to San Francisco, where they became the Bay area's most infamous nonhippie band. The Tubes developed an outrageous rock-theater presentation, including songs with skits and props. Even before the group had hits, it drew SRO crowds around the country thanks to its spectacular stage shows.

The Tubes

Prince and Cotten are also visual artists; their work has been displayed on the Charlie Chaplin soundstage on the A & M Records lot in Hollywood, on four murals in the Chemical Bank building at New York's Rockefeller Center, and on the five-story set at Tokyo's Budokan Theater.

July	1976	1. DON'T TOUCH ME THERE	A & M
June	1981	2. DON'T WANT TO WAIT ANYMORE	Capitol
April	1983	3. SHE'S A BEAUTY	Capitol
July	1983	4. TIP OF MY TONGUE	Capitol
October	1983	5. THE MONKEY TIME	Capitol
March	1985	6. PIECE BY PIECE	Capitol

LOUISE TUCKER

Born: 1958

Louise Tucker has always been steered toward a career in music; her father was a member of the BBC choir and her mother appeared in musicals and television plays. Louise took singing lessons at the Dartington College of Arts, then studied at the Guildhall School of Music. Some years later, she met producer/songwriters Tim Smit and Charlie Skarbek, who came up with the idea of doing a Christmas album with Tucker. At the first session, they realized that a combination of Louise's voice and modern instrumentation could lead to something special, so they began experimenting with an idea that had never been used in pop music before—the use of synthesizers on classical and classical-sounding melodies for which contemporary lyrics were written. The result led to "Midnight Blue," an adaptation of Beethoven's "Sonata Pathetique." The combination of Tucker's soprano, Skarbek's contrasting pop voice, the modern arrangement, and Beethoven's composition produced an international hit.

| June | 1983 | MIDNIGHT BLUE | Arista |

TANYA TUCKER

Born: October 10, 1958
Hometown: Wilcox, Arizona

Tanya Tucker's father, Beau, drove for miles to take young Tanya to local fairs where they'd watch famous country music singers perform. More often than not, Tanya managed to get herself onstage to perform with the stars. Beau was inspired enough to move the family to the nearest show-business center, Las Vegas, and to save $400 for Tanya to record a demo tape at a local studio. Beau mailed the tape to anyone he could think of in the music business, and though countless letters of rejection came back, Tanya eventually burst into the country music field as a 13-year-old powerhouse singer with the song "Delta Dawn." As a teenager, she had a string of country hits including "Blood Red And Goin' Down," "What's Your Mama's Name," "Would You Lay With Me (In A Field Of Stone)," and "Texas (When I Die)" before turning to rock 'n' roll on her 20th birthday.

An avid animal lover, Tucker has been an outspoken leader of the Save the Seals movement. She also advocated solar energy with the Campaign For Economic Democracy.

July	1972	1. DELTA DAWN	Columbia
May	1973	2. WHAT'S YOUR MAMA'S NAME	Columbia
August	1973	3. BLOOD RED AND GOIN' DOWN	Columbia
February	1974	4. WOULD YOU LAY WITH ME (IN A FIELD OF STONE)	Columbia
August	1974	5. THE MAN THAT TURNED MY MAMA ON	Columbia
May	1975	6. LIZZIE AND THE RAINMAN	MCA
October	1976	7. HERE'S SOME LOVE	MCA
January	1979	8. NOT FADE AWAY	MCA

TINA TURNER

Real Name: Anna Mae Bullock
Born: November 26, 1938
Hometown: Nutbush, Tennessee

Ike & Tina Turner had 20 hits together, including a top-10 song called "Proud Mary" in 1971. They went their separate ways and Tina became a major star. 1984 was her year: Tina made one of the most spectacular comebacks in rock history and she deservedly won several Grammies, among other awards. Her success continues in 1985.
See *Ike & Tina TURNER, Rock On: The Solid Gold Years.*

Tina Turner

January	1984	1. LET'S STAY TOGETHER	Capitol
May	1984	★ 2. WHAT'S LOVE GOT TO DO WITH IT	Capitol
September	1984	3. BETTER BE GOOD TO ME	Capitol
January	1985	4. PRIVATE DANCER	Capitol
May	1985	5. SHOW SOME RESPECT	Capitol

TUXEDO JUNCTION

Members:
  Jamie Edlin—vocals
  Marilyn Jackson—vocals
  Sue Allen—vocals
  Marti McCall—vocals
  Jane Scheckter—vocals—added in 1977
  Jeannie Kaufman—vocals—added in 1977
  Leisha—vocals—added in 1979
  Midge Barnett—vocals—added in 1979
  Caryn Richman—vocals—added in 1979

Although disco versions of seven swing-era classics were released under
the name of Tuxedo Junction, just who made up the group was puzzling.
Vocal group Tuxedo Junction's self-titled debut album listed its members
as Jamie Edlin, Marilyn Jackson, Sue Allen, and Marti McCall. A publicity
photo sent out about the same time showed Tuxedo Junction to be a trio,
identified as Jamie Edlin, Jane Scheckter, and Jeannie Kaufman. A follow-

up album of seven more disco-ized big band numbers listed Tuxedo Junction as Leisha, Midge Barnett, Caryn Richman, Marilyn Jackson, Marti McCall, and Sue Allen. We can only assume that Tuxedo Junction was really Laurin Rinder and W. Michael Lewis, who produced both albums.

April   1978   CHATTANOOGA CHOO CHOO   Butterfly

TWENNYNINE

Members:
   Nick Moroch—guitar, glockenspiel—replaced (1981) by Steve Williams
   Eddie Martinez—guitar—replaced (1981) by Steve "City" Horton
   Donald Blackman—keyboards, synthesizer, vocals (left group in 1981)
   Denzil Miller—keyboards
   Barry "Sonjohn" Johnson—bass, vocals
   Lenny White—drums, percussion, synthesizer—born: December 19, 1949
   John "Skip" Anderson—keyboards, vocals—added in 1980
   Carla Vaughn—vocals—added in 1981
   Jocelyn Smith—vocals—added in 1981
Hometown: New York, New York

After the break-up of the pioneer jazz-rock fusion band Return To Forever, Lenny White and the others all pursued solo careers. Over the course of four solo albums, White began putting together a band that in 1979 would be christened Twennynine, a name he said wouldn't lock the group into any particular musical style or styles. As a group, Twennynine is also a softball team.

February   1980   PEANUT BUTTER (featuring Lenny White)   Elektra

TWILIGHT 22

Real Name: Gordon Bahary
Born: 1960
Hometown: New York, New York

Twilight 22 is Gordon Bahary and his synthesizers. Bahary's interest in synthesizers began in 1974. A year later, at age 15, he coproduced the music for Harry Chapin's off-Broadway production called *Zinger*. At age 16, Bahary met Stevie Wonder, who was recording his *Songs in the Key of Life* album, and it was at these sessions that Bahary learned and refined the skills of record production. Wonder later asked him to program synthesizers for his *Journey Through the Secret Life of Plants* album. Bahary did the same for Herbie Hancock's *Feets Don't Fail Me Now* LP. Twilight 22 marks the start of Bahary's own musical adventures.

December   1983   ELECTRIC KINGDOM   Vanguard

DWIGHT TWILLEY

Born: June 6, 1951
Hometown: Tulsa, Oklahoma

Although originally inspired by the Beatles, by the late sixties, Dwight Twilley was more drawn to fellow-Okie Leon Russell's brand of gospel-oriented rock. From 1971 to 1973, Dwight and his sidekick, Phil Seymour, worked in rock bands, connecting with guitarist Bill Pitcock IV, who would be another sidekick. Twilley's first recording contract coincidentally proved to be with Leon Russell's Shelter Records, but by this time, Twilley's music no longer showed any of that influence, but rather consisted of cute pop tunes. Seymour eventually went off to try his own solo career, and Twilley bounced around to a few record labels before establishing himself with a pop hit, "Girls."

April	1975	I'M ON FIRE	Shelter
February	1984	GIRLS	EMI-America
May	1984	LITTLE BIT OF LOVE	EMI-America

TWISTED SISTER

Members:
    Dee Snider—vocals—Massapequa, Long Island—born: March 15, 1955
    Jay Jay French—guitar—New York, New York—born: July 20, 1954

Twisted Sister. *Left to right:* A. J. Pero, Jay Jay French, Dee Snider, Mark Mendoza, Eddie Ojeda.

Eddie "Fingers" Ojeda—guitar—Bronx, New York—born: August 5, 1954
Mark "the Animal" Mendoza—bass—born: July 13, 1956
A. J. Pero—drums—Staten Island, New York—born: October 14, 1959
Hometown: Massapequa, New York

In 1976, Dee, Jay Jay, and Eddie formed Twisted Sister and began playing clubs wearing shocking outfits like dresses and lingerie, startling their audiences with their wild attire and hard-rock sound. However, word about the group spread throughout the New York area, and in a short time they were filling theaters like the Palladium in Manhattan.

In 1978, bassist Mark Mendoza joined the group when the other bass player left, and in 1982 drummer A. J. Pero joined the group. By 1982 Twisted Sister had a fan club totaling 20,000 members. It was at this time they went to England for a series of concerts including an appearance on the television show "The Tube," an appearance that led to a recording contract with Atlantic Records.

During the summer of 1983, they released their debut album for the label, *You Can't Stop Rock 'N' Roll*, after which came the album *Stay Hungry*, which produced their first charted single, "We're Not Gonna Take It."

Dee Snider and his outrageous group have become one of the most talked about heavy-metal groups of the eighties.

| July | 1984 | WE'RE NOT GONNA TAKE IT | Atlantic |
| October | 1984 | I WANNA ROCK | Atlantic |

TYCOON

Members:
    Norman Mershon—vocals
    Jon Gordon—guitar, synthesizer, strings, vocals
    Michael Fonfara—keyboards, synthesizer, vocals—replaced (1980) by Keith Taylor
    Mark Rivera—saxophone, percussion, vocals (left group in 1980)
    Mark Kreider—bass, percussion, strings, vocals
    Richard Steinberg—drums—replaced (1980) by Michael Braun
    Bobby Messano—guitar—added in 1980
Hometown: New York, New York

On November 1, 1977, two well-seasoned session men, Mark Kreider and Norman Mershon, met and decided to form their own band rather than continuing to work for other musicians. Soon they recruited other session musicians to join Tycoon. But studio musicians do jump from job to job, and the group went through extensive personnel changes in a short time.

| March | 1979 | SUCH A WOMAN | Arista |

BONNIE TYLER

Real Name: Gaynor Hopkins
Born: June 8, 1953
Hometown: Swansea, Wales

Bonnie Tyler spent eight years singing with bands in cabaret rooms, night-clubs, and at rugby club socials, often struggling to be heard above the clink of glasses and the babble of conversation, before she was spotted by a talent scout for songwriter Ronnie Scott at the Townsman Club in Tyler's hometown. She auditioned and got to record one of his songs, "Lost In France." Tyler assumed the song would not be a hit and she'd be back playing clubs, but she was wrong, the tune became a hit throughout Europe. A follow-up, "More Than A Lover," was also a multinational smash, but it was "It's A Heartache" that hit number one in six countries, made the top five in eight other countries, and established her in the United States. Part of the song's charm was Tyler's raspy vocals, made possible by a delicate operation in 1976 to remove nodes from her vocal chords.

Bonnie lives in Skewen, a tiny village outside Swansea, with her husband Bobby Sullivan, a black-belt judo expert who represented Great Britain in the Olympics. The couple owns a pub, a restaurant, and two discos in Wales. Tyler can be heard on the soundtracks to *Footloose* ("Holding Out For A Hero") and *Metropolis*.

March	1978	1. IT'S A HEARTACHE	RCA
July	1983	★ 2. TOTAL ECLIPSE OF THE HEART	Columbia
December	1983	3. TAKE ME BACK	Columbia
February	1984	4. HOLDING OUT FOR A HERO	Columbia
August	1984	5. HERE SHE COMES	Columbia

UB40

Members:
    Ali Campbell—vocals, guitar
    Robin Campbell—guitar, vocals
    Michael Virtue—keyboards—added in 1979
    Brian Travers—saxophone
    Earl Falconer—bass
    James Brown—drums
    Norman Hassan—percussion, vocals
    Astro—percussion, trumpet—added in 1979
Hometown: Birmingham, England

In the summer of 1978, most of the members of what would become UB40 were unemployed, and only a few could play instruments. Nevertheless, they came together with the idea of playing reggae music, and took their name from the reference number on a British unemployment-benefits card. Shortly after the group's first gig in February 1979, UB40 became a popular attraction in Birmingham. By the early eighties, the UBs, as the fans call the group, were known internationally. Their first hit, "Red, Red Wine," was written and first recorded by Neil Diamond in early 1968.

January	1984	RED, RED WINE	A & M

TRACEY ULLMAN

Born: December 30, 1959
Hometown: Buckinghamshire, England

After a lengthy career as an actress in the United Kingdom, Tracey Ullman was inspired to become a singer when she met Rosemary Robinson (wife of Stiff Records head Dave Robinson) at their local hairdresser's salon in early 1983. Before the end of the year, Ullman had three hit singles back home. The video of her first American hit, "They Don't Know," features Paul McCartney in a cameo role. In turn, Ullman has a featured role in Paul McCartney's film, *Give My Regards To Broadstreet.*

February	1984	THEY DON'T KNOW	MCA
June	1984	BREAK-A-WAY	MCA/Stiff

375

Tracey Ullman

ULTIMATE

Members:
 Barbara Hernandez—vocals
 Riti Saunders—vocals
 Deborah McGriff—vocals

Ultimate began as a studio project of producers Juliano Salerni and Bruce Weeden. When the album produced a disco hit, "Touch Me Baby," three vocalists were selected to be Ultimate for a follow-up album, but that one produced no major hit.

April   1979   TOUCH ME BABY   Casablanca

ULTRAVOX

Members:
 Midge Ure—guitar, keyboards, vocals, synthesizer (replaced John Foxx—
    vocals, Robin Simon—guitar, and Stevie Shears—guitar in 1979)
 Billy Currie—keyboards, violin, viola, synthesizers
 Chris Cross—bass, guitar, synthesizers, vocals
 Warren Cann—drums, electronic percussion, vocals
Hometown: London, England

John Foxx formed Ultravox! (the exclamation point has since been deleted) in the mid-seventies and at first supported the band with the grant he'd received to attend art college in London; after six months, he dropped out of school altogether. The group achieved some notoriety and released several records, but in late 1978 found itself without a record contract. John quit, as did Robin Simon, who had replaced the group's original guitarist, Stevie Shears. Gary Numan, who had named Ultravox as his major musical influence, persuaded Billy Currie to leave the group and tour with him, and Chris Cross turned to photography for a living. Simon went on to play in Magazine, and Foxx founded a record company called Metrobeat.

After the Numan tour, Currie was approached by Midge Ure, then of the Rich Kids, and the two began playing music together. They ultimately recruited Cross and Cann, and a re-formed Ultravox set off for a tour of America. Once back in England, the group secured a record contract, toured the world, and became far more popular than the original group.

| April | 1983 | REAP THE WILD WIND | Chrysalis |

UTOPIA

Members:
  Todd Rundgren—guitar, harmonica, vocals—born: June 22, 1948
  Roger Powell—keyboards, guitar, vocals, synthesizer
  Kasim Sulton—bass, guitar, vocals
  John "Willie" Wilcox—drums, percussion, vocals
Hometown: Woodstock, New York

Although Todd Rundgren had a successful solo career, he also formed a band that would not be "Todd and the Back-ups" but a democratic collective of musicians. The formation of Utopia in 1974 did not preclude any of the members pursuing outside endeavors, so Todd's cohorts have worked on solo projects and played other gigs as well. (After the release of his solo album, however, Kasim Sulton was temporarily replaced by Doug Howard, formerly of Touch.) The group is heavily involved in technology, and some members were involved in the creation of a computer graphics program called the Utopia Tablet, which has been marketed by Apple Computers. Roger Powell also invented the Probe, an eight-pound synthesizer keyboard which hangs from the neck.

February	1980	SET ME FREE	Bearsville
June	1980	THE VERY LAST TIME	Bearsville
January	1983	FEET DON'T FAIL ME NOW	Network

U2

Members:
  Bono Vox (Paul Hewson)—vocals, guitar—born: May 10, 1960
  The Edge (Dave Evans)—guitar, piano—born: August 8, 1961
  Adam Clayton—bass—born: March 13, 1960
  Larry Mullen—drums—born: October 31, 1961
Hometown: Dublin, Ireland

In 1976, Larry Mullen was expelled from a local marching band because of his long hair, so he pinned a message to the notice board at Mount Temple Comprehensive School, looking for other musicians to form a band. The four who answered—Paul Hewson, Adam Clayton, Dave Evans, and his brother Dick—had no musical experience, but they became a band anyway, although Dick soon dropped out to attend university (he has since re-emerged as a member of the Virgin Prunes). Dave took the nickname given him (which reportedly had something to do with the shape of his head), and Paul took his from a fractured Latin translation of *good voice*. The group initially practiced in a garden shed behind the Edge's house in the Dublin suburb of Malahide Village. Later they took the name U2 and began playing local clubs. U2's popularity grew gradually until they were known the world over.

April	1983	NEW YEARS DAY	Island
January	1984	I WILL FOLLOW	Island
October	1984	(PRIDE) IN THE NAME OF LOVE	Island

VANDENBERG

Members:
Bert Heerink—vocals—born: January 26, 1953
Adrian Vandenberg—guitar, keyboards, vocals—born: January 31, 1954
Dick Kemper—bass, vocals—born: May 5, 1956
Jos Zoomer—drums, vocals—born: July 14, 1954
Hometown: Amsterdam, Holland

Adrian Vandenberg had been a session guitarist on 25 albums in Holland and had been in a locally popular band called Teaser when he found himself at a crossroads—should he continue a steady living as a graphic artist or should he form another band? He remembered seeing a vocalist in another band doing Led Zeppelin and Uriah Heep numbers. Adrian (Adje to his countrymen) contacted the singer, Bert Heerink, and found he hadn't sung in four years but was making a living repairing vacuum cleaners, TV sets, and the like. Adrian convinced him to form a band, and recruited a rhythm section in Dick Kemper and Jos Zoomer.

January   1983   BURNING HEART   Atlantic

Vandenberg. Adrian Vandenberg (*second from left*).

LUTHER VANDROSS

Born: April 20, 1951
Hometown: New York, New York

When Luther Vandross was three years old, his mother encouraged his interest in music by starting him on piano. While his brother might get a bicycle for Christmas, Luther would receive Aretha Franklin records. He attended Taft High School in the Bronx, and was a B-plus student for three years. Then in his senior year his grades dropped to a C-minus. Luther explains this by saying he couldn't study due to his distress about Diana Ross leaving the Supremes.

Luther's abilities in music were first recognized when he worked on some vocal arrangements in a Philadelphia recording studio where David Bowie was recording. Bowie liked Luther's suggestions, and hired him as a backing vocalist and vocal arranger. After an album (*Young Americans*) and tour with Bowie, Luther was hired in various capacities by Bette Midler, Carly Simon, Roberta Flack, Ringo Starr, Todd Rundgren, and Cat Stevens. Meanwhile, he formed a little-noticed band called Luther, but soon found that session work on jingles was more lucrative. In those years, Vandross also wrote a song for *The Wiz* and was the vocal arranger for the Barbra Streisand/Donna Sommer duet, "Enough Is Enough."

Vandross's credits go on and on, but the start of his solo career came through several hits he sang fronting two then-fictitious studio groups, Bionic Boogie and Change. Through these successes, for which he turned out stellar performances, Vandross was able to negotiate a contract as a solo recording artist and producer. This solo career, which began in 1971 with his *Never Too Much* album, has led to one platinum award after another.

Vandross has also produced albums for Cheryl Lynn, Aretha Franklin, Dionne Warwick, and Teddy Pendergrass, and was named celebrity chairman for the March of Dimes in 1982. In his spare time, he likes to watch wrestling matches at Madison Square Garden (while listening to Aretha Franklin tapes on his Walkman) and the CBS-TV daytime drama, "The Guiding Light."

October	1981	1. NEVER TOO MUCH	Epic
October	1982	2. BAD BOY/HAVING A PARTY	Epic
October	1983	3. HOW MANY TIMES CAN WE SAY GOODBYE (with Dionne Warwick)	Arista
May	1984	4. SUPERSTAR/UNTIL YOU COME BACK TO ME	Epic
March	1985	5. TILL MY BABY COMES HOME	Epic

VANGELIS

Real Name: Evangelos Papathanassiou
Hometown: Greece

In the early sixties, Vangelis Papathanassiou brought pop music to Greece with the group Formynx, composed of friends. Upon receiving massive recognition in Greece, Vangelis moved to Paris and formed the band Aphrodite's Child, another highly successful international unit. While in France, Vangelis began his career in soundtracks with a television program, but then moved to London in 1977, where he constructed his own sound laboratory and began recording his own albums.

Vangelis was asked to replace Rick Wakeman in Yes, but instead began a musical relationship with Jon Anderson, lead vocalist with that British progressive rock band. The two have released several albums as Jon and Vangelis, but the Greek composer/synthesizer player is perhaps best known for his film soundtracks for *Chariots Of Fire, The Bounty* and *Blade Runner*. (See *JON AND VANGELIS*.)

December	1981	★ TITLES (CHARIOTS OF FIRE)	Polydor

VAN HALEN

Members:
    David Lee Roth—vocals—born: October 10, 1955
    Edward Van Halen—guitar—born: January 26, 1957
    Michael Anthony—bass—born: January 20, 1955
    Alex Van Halen—drums—born: May 8, 1955
Hometown: Los Angeles, California

The two Van Halen brothers (both natives of the Netherlands and trained in classical piano), Mike Anthony, and the ever-outspoken Dave Lee Roth had all been playing in bands since high school days, but in 1974, when they grouped together, the chemistry was magical. Originally called Mammoth, then Rat Salad before becoming Van Halen, the quartet quickly became a top attraction at Gazzarri's, a rock club on Hollywood's Sunset Strip. Gene Simmons of Kiss was so knocked out by the group that he offered to fly them to New York and pay for demo tape sessions. Van Halen's debut album was released in 1978, and quickly became an international success.

Van Halen has been known for extremes. At the group's first major show, the four members made their entrance by skydiving from a plane into Anaheim Stadium. On stage, they wear flamboyant outfits (to date, no other act has outdone Roth's leather pants with the behind cut away). Meanwhile, Eddie Van Halen has won numerous awards for his innovative guitar techniques.

VAN HALEN

January	1978	1. YOU REALLY GOT ME	Warner Bros.
May	1978	2. RUNNIN' WITH THE DEVIL	Warner Bros.
April	1979	3. DANCE THE NIGHT AWAY	Warner Bros.
September	1979	4. BEAUTIFUL GIRLS	Warner Bros.
May	1980	5. AND THE CRADLE WILL ROCK	Warner Bros.
February	1982	6. PRETTY WOMAN	Warner Bros.
May	1982	7. DANCING IN THE STREET	Warner Bros.

Van Halen. *Left to right:* Alex Van Halen, David Lee Roth, Edward Van Halen, Michael Anthony.

January	1984	★ 8. JUMP	Warner Bros.
April	1984	9. I'LL WAIT	Warner Bros.
June	1984	10. PANAMA	Warner Bros.
October	1984	11. HOT FOR TEACHER	Warner Bros.
DAVID LEE ROTH			
January	1985	CALIFORNIA GIRLS	Warner Bros.
March	1985	JUST A GIGOLO/I AIN'T GOT NOBODY	Warner Bros.

GINO VANNELLI

Born: June 16, 1952
Hometown: Montreal, Canada

The first music Gino Vannelli ever enjoyed was jazz; as a boy, he'd bang on pots and pans to music by all the jazz greats. When he was about 10 years old, Gino decided he would be a drummer, so his brother Joe constructed a set out of pots and pans, and a family friend donated a real snare drum and a cymbal. Gino continued to play along with jazz tunes on the radio, but when the Beatles came out, he switched to pop, and then later, to soul music. In all, Gino spent his adolescence playing a

Gino Vannelli

variety of music with a variety of bands, and developed his skill as a songwriter.

Vannelli was one of the first Caucasian acts ever to appear on the syndicated "Soul Train" TV show, and the first major magazine to write about him was *Soul*. He was also one of the first pop artists to record and perform rock music with no guitars or bass. His first album, *Crazy Life*, featured only him on drums and his brother Joe on keyboards, but for most of his music, his band consisted of two keyboard players, three percussionists, and five synthesizer players. At one point, his band did include a guitarist and a bassist, as well as two backing vocalists, but they were overshadowed by 20 keyboards and 15 synthesizers.

October	1974	1. PEOPLE GOTTA MOVE	A & M
September	1976	2. LOVE OF MY LIFE	A & M
September	1978	3. I JUST WANNA STOP	A & M
February	1979	4. WHEELS OF LIFE	A & M
March	1981	5. LIVING INSIDE MYSELF	Arista
July	1981	6. NIGHTWALKER	Arista
March	1982	7. THE LONGER YOU WAIT	Arista

RANDY VANWARMER

Born: March 30, 1955
Hometown: Denver, Colorado

Indian Hills, Colorado, where Randy Vanwarmer grew up, consists of a gas station, a post office, a trading post, a population of 2000, and very little else that is man-made. Randy Vanwarmer was raised there as a Fundamentalist, which meant being around people who were not afraid to sing about their feelings. For a long time, his life in Indian Hills was gospel music, mountains, family, and friends. Though Fundamentalists are not permitted to listen to secular music, Randy's parents were not so strict that his older brother couldn't play rock 'n' roll on the radio; Randy was nine years old when he first heard pop songs.

When Randy was 12 years old, his father died in an auto crash; two years later, his mother moved the family to her father's homeland in Looe, a fishing village and seaside resort near Cornwall in the south of England. There, Randy learned to play guitar; a demo tape he crudely recorded in his bedroom was sporadically hampered by the sounds of seagulls and the like. Randy soon began playing clubs, occasionally commuting back to Colorado. Vanwarmer moved to Woodstock, New York, in 1979.

Vanwarmer's first hit, "Just When I Needed You Most," has been covered by a variety of pop and country music acts.

March	1979	JUST WHEN I NEEDED YOU MOST	Bearsville
August	1980	WHATEVER YOU DECIDE	Bearsville
June	1981	SUZI	Bearsville

VILLAGE PEOPLE

Members:
   Victor Willis—vocals—replaced (1980) by Ray Simpson
   Randy Jones—vocals—replaced (1980) by Jeff Olson
   David (Scar) Hodo—vocals
   Felipe Rose—vocals
   Glenn Hughes—vocals
   Alexander Briley—vocals
Hometown: New York, New York

The first Village People album in 1977 did so well in the discos that producers Jacques Morali and Henri Belolo quickly put together a permanent group and stage show to go under the name Village People. While the material and group image was designed to capitalize on buzz words and stereotypes within the gay community, Village People's hot dance tunes and flashy image rapidly crossed over to the masses. At the peak of its career, the group headlined two nights at New York's Madison Square Garden, and signed to star in a disco film called *Can't Stop The Music*. Disco had already peaked by the time the film was released, however, and it was a major investment failure. The group later tried to stay alive by adapting the "new romantic" look that was trendy at the time in England, but the look died an even quicker death in America than it did in England, and Village People went back to their established image as "macho men." Village People had no band and always performed with backing tapes, and until this day, no one outside the group knows if anyone in Village People except the lead singers actually sang on any of the records or in the concerts. Even some of the *spoken* parts in *Can't Stop The Music* appeared to be dubbed.

Nevertheless, the world will always remember Village People for their outrageous "macho" stage costumes—the cowboy, the construction worker, the military man, the leather biker, the motorcycle cop, and the Indian—and for their witty songs.

June	1978	1. MACHO MAN	Casablanca
October	1978	2. Y. M. C. A.	Casablanca
March	1979	3. IN THE NAVY	Casablanca
May	1979	4. GO WEST	Casablanca
November	1979	5. READY FOR THE 80'S	Casablanca

ROGER VOUDOURIS

Born: December 29, 1954
Hometown: Sacramento, California

Roger Voudouris began playing guitar at age four and composing songs at age eight. In high school, he fronted his first band, called Roger Voudouris's Loud as Hell Rockers, and later, a more mainstream Roger Voudouris

Band toured as an opening act for Stephen Stills, Lou Rawls, John Mayall, Boz Scaggs, Peter Frampton, the Doobie Brothers, and others. At home in northern California, Voudouris subsists on a purely vegetarian diet and runs 10 miles a day.

March   1979   GET USED TO IT   Warner Bros.

VOYAGE

Members:
    Marc Chantereau—vocals, keyboards, percussion
    Slim Pezin—vocals, bass, guitar
    Pierre-Alain Dahan—vocals, drums
Hometown: Paris, France

In 1978, three of France's star studio musicians teamed up to record disco music targeted for dances around the world. Several Voyage tunes became international hits, and in 1980, the group traveled to New York City to accept a special year-end award from *Billboard* magazine.

February   1979   SOUVENIRS   Marlin

JOHN WAITE

Born: July 4, 1955

A former lead singer of the group the Babys, John Waite is now a solo performer whose first solo hit was "Missing You."

June	1984	★ 1. MISSING YOU	EMI-America
October	1984	2. TEARS	EMI-America
January	1985	3. RESTLESS HEART	EMI-America
March	1985	4. CHANGE	Chrysalis

THE WAITRESSES

Members:
    Patty Donahue—vocals—replaced (1983) by Holly Beth Vincent
    Ariel Warner—vocals (left group in 1982)
    Chris Butler—guitar (left group in 1983)
    Dan Klayman—keyboards
    Mars Williams—reeds
    David Hofstra—bass—replaced (1982) by Tracy Wormworth
    Billy Ficca—drums
Hometown: Akron, Ohio

After leaving a bizarre art-rock band called Tin Huey, Chris Butler met a new challenge as a male writing lyrics to fit the persona of a female lead singer in the Waitresses. The band quickly became known for their deadpan delivery of witty lyrics. Patty Donahue appeared on Alice Cooper's *Zipper Catches Skin* LP, and the Waitresses provided the theme song to the CBS-TV sitcom "Square Pegs." The band appeared on both "Square Pegs" and the CBS-TV daytime drama "The Guiding Light" before Patty Donahue left in 1983 and was replaced by Holly Beth Vincent, formerly of Holly & the Italians. Shortly thereafter, Butler left, and Donahue returned. Holly then left, leaving Patty to lead a re-formed Waitresses.

| May | 1982 | I KNOW WHAT BOYS LIKE | Polydor |

NARADA MICHAEL WALDEN

Born: April 23, 1952
Hometown: Kalamazoo, Michigan

Narada Michael Walden

Narada Michael Walden says one of his earliest recollections is beating on the crib, adding that "drumming was always part of my soul." When Walden was 10, his family moved to rural Plainwell and he started lessons on the new $100 drum kit his grandfather had bought him. At age 12, he had his first official group, the Ambassadors, in which he played drums and his 10-year-old friend played organ. As a teenager, Walden played drums with various then-local hard-rock bands, including Ted Nugent & the Amboy Dukes, the MC5, and the Bob Seger System, until, when he was in college, a member of an all-white funk band, Deacon Williams & the Soul Revival, knocked on his dormitory room door and convinced Walden to go to California in the band's tour bus as their new drummer.

In 1972, Walden was drawn to guru Sri Chinmoy and one of his disciples, John McLaughlin, of the jazz-rock fusion group called the Mahavishnu Orchestra. Through McLaughlin, Walden met Chinmoy, who accepted him as a disciple and gave him the name Narada, which means "he whose soul brings light, delight, and compassion from heaven to earth and takes back to heaven from earth all her sufferings." Within a few months, Walden was asked to join McLaughlin's revamped Mahavishnu Orchestra with Jean-Luc Ponty, Gayle Moran, Walden's friend Ralphe Armstrong, and a string section. Walden remained with the group until they broke up in 1976, after which Walden became both a solo artist (starting with the *Garden of Love Light* LP) and a session musician (for Rick James, Jeff Beck, Carlos Santana, Weather Report, Roy Buchanan, Alan Holdsworth, Tommy Bolin, Alphonso Johnson, and others). Walden has also produced albums for Stacey Lattisaw, Johnny Gill, Phyllis Hyman, Angela Bofill, Don Cherry, Sister Sledge, and Wanda Walden. His songs have been recorded by virtually all of the above artists as well as by Amii Stewart, Ray Gomez and High Inergy.

| March | 1979 | I DON'T WANT NOBODY ELSE | Atlantic |
| February | 1980 | I SHOULDA LOVED YA | Atlantic |

WENDY WALDMAN

Hometown: Los Angeles, California

Wendy Waldman's musical background started with her dad, Fred Steiner, who composed soundtrack music for television and motion pictures, and her mom, who had been concertmistress for the New Haven Symphony. Wendy grew up listening to classical music, but at age 15 formed her first rock band, a trio which included Peter Bernstein and Andrew Gold, themselves the sons of film composers Elmer Bernstein and Ernest Gold. After a brief stint studying at the University of California at Berkeley, Wendy returned to Los Angeles, and her house became the home base for Bryndle, the group Wendy formed in 1969 with Andrew Gold, Karla Bonoff, and Kenny Edwards. The group recorded one single before disbanding. Wendy recorded her first album, *Love Has Got Me*, in 1973. Her songs have been recorded by Linda Ronstadt, Melissa Manchester, Kim Carnes, Judy Collins, Patti Austin, Maria Muldaur, and ex-Eagle Randy Meisner. Waldman and Ronstadt also cowrote and sang "I Want A Horse" for the *In Harmony* children's album.

| August | 1978 | LONG HOT SUMMER NIGHTS | Warner Bros. |

WALL OF VOODOO

Members:
    Stanard Ridgway—vocals, harmonica, keyboards
    Marc Moreland—guitar
    Chas T. Gray—synthesizer, bass, vocals—added in 1979
    Oliver "Joe" Nanini—percussion, drums—added in 1979
Hometown: Los Angeles, California

Stanard Ridgway and Marc Moreland met in 1977 at the Masque, a basement punk club under the Pussycat Theater in Hollywood. In no time, the two formed a company, Wall of Voodoo, Inc., and began collaborating on unsolicited scores for science fiction and horror films. Few scores were ever accepted, and soon the duo was reduced to selling mail-order giant telescopes and packets of "amazing sea monkeys" to survive. Ultimately drawn back to music, the two recruited Marc's brother Bruce and a rhythm machine they called Ace Kalamazoo, and using the company's name, Wall of Voodoo, made their band debut in December 1978, when offered a paltry wage to play their unsold film scores at Immaculate Hearts Girls School in Hollywood. Stanard made up lyrics on the spot, and Marc tripped over the main power cable, blowing the fuse and plunging the entire audience into darkness. Chas T. Gray and Oliver "Joe" Nanini soon joined the group, and the revamped line-up became popular on the Los Angeles club circuit. Wall of Voodoo released its self-titled EP in September 1980, and the *Dark Continent* LP in August 1981. Bassist/keyboardist Bruce Moreland left the group in May 1982, reportedly to join a traveling circus as a calliope player and part-time strong man. Ridgway also collaborated with Stewart Copeland of the Police on a song for the film *Rumblefish* called "Don't Box Me In."

March   1983   MEXICAN RADIO   I.R.S.

WANG CHUNG

Members:
  Jack Hues—vocals, guitar
  Nick Feldman—bass
  Darren Costin—drums
Hometown: Gillingham, Kent, England

Wang Chung. *Left to right:* Nick Feldman, Jack Hues, Darren Costin.

Founded in 1981, this English trio, whose Chinese appellation means "perfect pitch," holds views about harmonic progressions that are as high-minded as the band's name. Jack Hues, the group's only classically trained musician, would like to see a "branching out away from the traditional harmonies of jazz and rock, into a whole new area of architectural harmony." Hues feels that the group's first single, "Don't Let Go," from their debut album *Points On A Curve,* reveals little of their musical sophistication.

February	1984	DON'T LET GO	Geffen
April	1984	DANCE HALL DAYS	Geffen
September	1984	DON'T BE MY ENEMY	Geffen

ANITA WARD

Hometown: Philadelphia, Pennsylvania

This onetime school teacher cashed in on the disco craze of the seventies with her number-one national hit called "Ring My Bell" in 1979. The song had a nice moderate beat, but it was the novel "pinging" sound that was heard throughout the recording that made it so catchy it became a top-selling smash that summer.

May	1979	★ RING MY BELL	TK
November	1979	DON'T DROP MY LOVE	Juana

GROVER WASHINGTON, JR.

Born: December 12, 1943
Hometown: Buffalo, New York

While Grover Washington, Jr. has played all forms of contemporary American music since he was 12 years old, his first love is jazz. He was an established jazz sax player by age 25, but crossed over to pop in 1981 on the strength of "Just the Two of Us," a composition he included on his *Winelight* album. While that song, sung by Bill Withers, was a towering success, Washington continued a low profile at Temple University in Philadelphia—as a student! In 1980 Washington enrolled in a five-year program to get his doctorate degree in composition, and in 1981 he produced a young Philadelphia-based jazz trio, Pieces of a Dream. He also coaches the elementary school basketball team at Friends Central Lower School.

Washington works out every day with the Philadelphia 76ers and plays the national anthem at many 76ers and Philadelphia Eagles games. Julius "Dr. J" Erving of the 76ers and Washington are good friends, and in spring 1981, Erving was present when Washington was awarded with Philadelphia's prestigious Liberty Bell, the equivalent of the key to the city.

Grover and his wife Christine have two children, Grover III and Shana.

May	1975	MISTER MAGIC	Kudu
February	1981	JUST THE TWO OF US (with Bill Withers)	Elektra
February	1982	BE MINE (with Grady Tate)	Elektra

THE WEATHER GIRLS

Members:
  Martha Wash—vocals
  Izora Armstead—vocals
Hometown: San Francisco, California

Martha Wash once studied opera, and her singing range covers three octaves. Izora Armstead had scholarships to various music schools in the Bay area, majoring in piano. Both sang in gospel choirs, but began to appeal to secular crowds when Sylvester added the duo to his group and named them Two Tons o' Fun. Later, Wash and Armstead went off on their own as the Two Tons. Even though the two large singers lost none of their "tonnage," they were renamed the Weather Girls when they sang "It's Raining Men" on a Paul Jabara album, *Paul Jabara And Friends.*

| January | 1983 | IT'S RAINING MEN | Columbia |

BOB WEIR

Real Name: Robert Hall Weir
Born: October 16, 1947
Hometown: San Francisco, California

Bob Weir is a member of the Grateful Dead, but sporadically records solo albums and plays in other bands. In the early seventies he led Bobby & the Midnites between Grateful Dead commitments, and in the mid-seventies he played in a band called Kingfish, also between Dead tours. (See *THE GRATEFUL DEAD, Rock On: The Years of Change.*)

| March | 1978 | BOMBS AWAY | Arista |

TIM WEISBERG

Born: 1943
Hometown: Hollywood, California

Since Tim Weisberg's surname starts with one of the last letters of the alphabet, he was among the last in his seventh grade class to select an instrument for music class. With few instruments left to choose from, he picked the flute, and his love affair with music quickly began.

Early in his adolescence, Weisberg joined the Robin Hood Band, a marching and concert band that featured some of Los Angeles's finest young musicians. After years of playing only classical flute, he learned to improvise. He began jamming with rock bands wherever he could, ultimately securing a record deal. Because the majority of his work is instrumental, Weisberg has appealed to jazz fans, although his music is more pop-oriented.

October 1978 POWER OF GOLD (with Dan Fogelberg) Full Moon

DOTTIE WEST

Maiden Name: Dottie Marsh
Born: October 11, 1932
Hometown: Nashville, Tennessee

Dottie Marie is one of 10 children in her family born in an 11-year period in McMinnville, Tennessee, 70 miles south of Nashville. A music major at Tennessee Tech, Dottie first appeared at the Grand Ole Opry in 1959. Soon thereafter she moved with her husband Bill West to Cleveland, Ohio, where he got a job as an engineer. They stayed there until 1964, during which time Dottie got a job singing on the country TV show "Landmark Jamboree" and built up a sizeable following.

Upon their return to Nashville, Dottie became a regular at the Grand Ole Opry and began gaining recognition as a songwriter. One of her compositions, "Is This Me," was recorded by Jim Reeves, who brought her to Chet Atkins, who signed her to RCA. At that label she recorded 36 albums and released more than 100 singles. Dottie left the label in

Dottie West

1975, and a year later signed with United Artists Records, now known as Liberty Records. In 1978, she met Kenny Rogers in a recording studio. The two soon recorded the smash country hit "Every Time Two Fools Collide." Since that time they have recorded several songs together, including the hit "What Are We Doin' In Love."

January	1973	1. IF IT'S ALL RIGHT WITH YOU	RCA
September	1973	2. COUNTRY SUNSHINE	RCA
March	1980	3. A LESSON IN LEAVIN'	United Artists
March	1981	4. WHAT ARE WE DOIN' IN LOVE (with Kenny Rogers)	Liberty

WHAM!

Members:
    George Michael—born: June 25, 1963—Radlett, Hertfordshire, England
    Andrew Ridgeley—born: January 26, 1963—Bushey, Hertfordshire, England
Hometown: Watford, England

George Michael and Andrew Ridgeley have known each other since childhood. While still of school age, the two banged around on various instruments at Andrew's house, and eventually played in local bands. In January 1982, they came up with a song and went into a recording studio

Wham! Andrew Ridgeley (*left*), George Michael.

to make a demo; George sang lead and played bass, Andrew played guitar and a drum machine, and the rhythm and session musicians did the rest. The song, "Wham Rap (Enjoy What You Do)," was a success in England, and quickly led to "Young Guns," a successful follow-up single. When Wham! came to the States they added *U.K.* to their name to differentiate themselves from an American group called Wham. They have since dropped the U.K. and gone back to simply Wham!

August	1983	1. BAD BOYS	Columbia
September	1984	★ 2. WAKE ME UP BEFORE YOU GO-GO	Columbia
December	1984	★ 3. CARELESS WHISPER (with George Michael)	Columbia
March	1985	★ 4. EVERYTHING SHE WANTS	Columbia

THE WHISPERS

Members:
   Wallace (Scotty) Scott—lead tenor—born: September 23, 1943
   Walter Scott—lead tenor—born: September 23, 1943
   Marcus Hutson—baritone—born: January 8, 1943
   Leaveil Degree—first tenor—born: July 31, 1948 (replaced Gordy Harmon in 1973)
   Nicholas Caldwell—second tenor—born: April 5, 1944
Hometown: Los Angeles, California

As adolescents, identical twins Wallace and Walter Scott called themselves the Scott Brothers and took their well-practiced harmonies out in public. With the addition of Marcus Hutson, Nicholas Caldwell and Gordy Harmon, they became the Whispers. When Harmon left the group in 1973, Leaveil Degree, a long time Whispers fan, took his place. The Whispers played an instrumental part in launching the now annual Donny Hathaway Scholarship Fund by donating to the fund all proceeds from the group's single, "A Song For Donny."

September	1970	1. SEEMS LIKE I GOTTA DO WRONG	Soul Clock
May	1971	2. YOUR LOVE IS SO DOGGONE GOOD	Janus
January	1973	3. SOMEBODY LOVES YOU	Janus
February	1974	4. A MOTHER FOR MY CHILDREN	Janus
September	1976	5. ONE FOR THE MONEY	Soul Train
August	1977	6. MAKE IT WITH YOU	Soul Train
February	1980	7. AND THE BEAT GOES ON	Solar
April	1980	8. LADY	Solar
February	1981	9. IT'S A LOVE THING	Solar
April	1983	10. TONIGHT	Solar

WHITESNAKE

Members:
   David Coverdale—vocals—born: September 22, 1951
   Micky Moody—guitarist
   Bernie Marsden—guitarist
   Jon Lord—keyboards—added in 1979

Neil Murray—bass
Ian Paice—drums (replaced David Dowell in 1980)
Hometown: England

When David Coverdale launched a solo career in 1976, he was best known as the vocalist in Deep Purple's final line-up. His first solo album, released only in England, was titled *Whitesnake*, and that became the name of the band he would front. A short time after forming the band, Coverdale was reunited with two former Deep Purple members, Jon Lord and then Ian Paice, who both joined the group. (Between Deep Purple and Whitesnake gigs, Lord and Paice had also worked with Whitesnake's Bernie Marsden in a short-lived band called Paice, Ashton & Lord.) Since its inception, Whitesnake has been a super attraction in Japan, Great Britain, and Europe.

August   1980   FOOL FOR YOUR LOVING   Mirage

KIM WILDE

Born: November 18, 1960
Hometown: London, England

Kim's parents, Marty Wilde, a solo performer, and Joyce, a member of the Vernons Girls, were both very popular recording artists throughout

Kim Wilde

Great Britain during the fifties and early sixties. This family tradition is one of the reasons Kim wanted to get into show business.

Kim's younger brother Ricky attempted a career as a pop singer, but decided to follow his talents as a songwriter instead. Ricky, along with his father, wrote a song called "Kids In America" and asked Kim if she would sing the demo. Legendary British producer Micky Most was asked to produce the single and after a few tries, it was released in 1981, becoming a hit throughout Great Britain.

The song was released on EMI-America records in May 1982, and went into the top thirty on the national charts.

| May | 1982 | KIDS IN AMERICA | EMI-America |
| January | 1985 | GO FOR IT | MCA |

MATTHEW WILDER

Hometown: New York, New York

Matthew Wilder studied classical piano early on, but at age 15 took up guitar and became a street musician in Greenwich Village. In the late seventies, he moved to Los Angeles, where he began working as a background vocalist (for Rickie Lee Jones, Robbie Dupree, and Bette Midler) and songwriter (for Bette Midler and Eddie Kendricks). His debut album, *I Don't Speak The Language*, was released in 1983.

September	1983	BREAK MY STRIDE	Private
February	1984	THE KID'S AMERICAN	Private
September	1984	BOUNCING OFF THE WALL	Private

DENIECE WILLIAMS

Born: June 3, 1951
Hometown: Gary, Indiana

In 1968, the owner of a record shop in which Deniece Williams worked after classes heard the high school student singing along with the current hits and brought in some talent scouts from Chicago to listen. In a short time, she recorded her first single, "Love Is Tears," for a local record company and achieved regional success. Two years later, Stevie Wonder heard the single and brought her to Detroit to join his back-up group, Wonderlove. In 1975, Deniece left Stevie to pursue a career in acting and writing. She sent Maurice White a tape of songs she hoped Earth, Wind & Fire would record, but he was so impressed with her singing on the demo tape that he convinced her to record her own songs. Since then, she's had many successful records, and at one point was so popular in England that she gave a command performance for Prince Charles. She's

Deniece Williams

also done several duets with Johnny Mathis, including the theme song for NBC-TV's "Family Ties." Williams's songs have been recorded by Frankie Valli, the Whispers, the Emotions, Stanley Turrentine, Nancy Wilson, Freda Payne, and others. She has two sons, Ken and Kevin.

January	1977	1. FREE	Columbia
April	1978	★ 2. TOO MUCH, TOO LITTLE, TOO LATE (with Johnny Mathis)	Columbia
July	1978	3. YOU'RE ALL I NEED TO GET BY (with Johnny Mathis)	Columbia
August	1979	4. I'VE GOT THE NEXT DANCE	ARC
August	1981	5. SILLY	ARC/Columbia
April	1982	6. IT'S GONNA TAKE A MIRACLE	ARC/Columbia
April	1984	★ 7. LET'S HEAR IT FOR THE BOY	Columbia
August	1984	8. NEXT LOVE	Columbia

DON WILLIAMS

Born: May 27, 1939
Hometown: Floydada, Texas

When Don Williams was three years old, he sang in a local talent contest and won the first prize, an alarm clock. In 1957, while in high school, Don and a group of friends got their first paid job in music; they performed for the opening of the Billups Service Station in Taft, Texas, and were paid $25. Don later worked as a bill collector, drove a bread truck, worked in the Texas oil fields, in the furniture business, in a smelting plant, and for Pittsburgh Plate Glass before forming the Pozo Seco Singers in Corpus Christi in 1964. The folk/pop vocal trio did well, but disbanded in 1971. Don's first solo single, "Don't You Believe," launched a solo career in 1972. He's now well-known in the country-music field, touring constantly with just a quartet of musicians. Williams's songs have been recorded by Eric Clapton, Kenny Rogers, Charley Pride, Lobo, the Who's Pete Townshend, Johnny Cash, and others. He costarred with Burt Reynolds in *W. W. & the Dixie Dancekings* and appeared in *Smokey & the Bandit II.* He lives outside Nashville with his wife Joy Bucher and two sons, Gary and Timmy.

September   1980   I BELIEVE IN YOU   MCA

JOHN WILLIAMS

Born: February 8, 1932
Hometown: New York, New York

John Williams studied piano at UCLA and at Julliard. In 1955, he moved to California to work in film studios, and shortly thereafter signed a two-year contract as pianist with the Columbia Pictures Orchestra. At home, he plays chamber music with friends, but his best-known work is on movie soundtracks, of which he's done more than 50. Among his better-known film scores are *Superman, Star Wars, Close Encounters of the Third Kind, Jaws, The Poseidon Adventure, The Towering Inferno, Earthquake, Fiddler on the Roof, 1941, Raiders of the Lost Ark, Return of the Jedi,* and *E. T. The Extra-Terrestrial.*

August	1975	1. THEME FROM JAWS	MCA
July	1977	2. STAR WARS	20th Century
January	1978	3. THEME FROM CLOSE ENCOUNTERS OF THE THIRD KIND	Arista
January	1979	4. SUPERMAN	Warner Bros.

CARL WILSON

Born: December 21, 1946
Hometown: Hawthorne, California

After 20 years with the Beach Boys, Carl Wilson took time between the group's commitments to record a self-titled solo album with Myrna Smith of the Sweet Inspirations and producer Jim Guercio. At the time, he insisted he was not leaving the Beach Boys, but after coinciding the release of the *Carl Wilson* album with his own band opening concerts for the Doobie Brothers in 1981, Carl took a sabbatical from the veteran band. Carl announced, "I haven't quit the Beach boys, but I do not plan on touring with them until they decide that 1981 means as much to them as 1961." He also said that he wanted the Beach Boys to record an album of new songs instead of relying on old hits, he wanted the group to rehearse thoroughly before a tour, and he didn't want a major thrust of Beach Boys concerts to be multi-night engagements in places like Lake Tahoe and Las Vegas. He rejoined the Beach Boys a year later, although it's not clear if his demands were met, and released another solo album in April 1983, *Young Blood*.

| May | 1983 | WHAT YOU DO TO ME | Caribou |

JESSE WINCHESTER

Real Name: James R. Winchester
Born: May 17, 1948
Hometown: Memphis, Tennessee

Jesse Winchester's family can be traced back to blood ties with General Robert E. Lee, but faced with the draft during the height of the Vietnam War in 1967, Winchester moved to Canada. Crossing the 49th parallel with just an electric guitar, a suitcase, and $200, he became a citizen of Canada and started a new life. In 1969, he was discovered by the Band's Robbie Robertson, who produced Winchester's self-titled debut album released a year later. Winchester became somewhat of a political culture hero, but record sales were minimal since he couldn't enter the States to promote his music. Following President Carter's 1977 pardon of the 10,000 or so draft resisters who fled the States, Winchester was finally able to return to Memphis (where he grew up) and tour the States with his band. He and his wife live in Montreal and have two children, James and Alice.

| August | 1977 | NOTHING BUT A BREEZE | Bearsville |
| April | 1981 | SAY WHAT | Bearsville |

STEVE WINWOOD

Born: May 12, 1948
Hometown: Birmingham, England

In 1963, 15-year-old Stevie Winwood joined his brother Muff's band, the Muff Woody Jazz Band. Spencer Davis heard Stevie sing at Digbeth Civic Hall, and persuaded the two brothers to join his Spencer Davis Group. After a few hits, the group split; Muff became a record producer and Stevie teamed up with Eric Clapton and other stars-to-be in a short-lived group called Powerhouse. Stevie formed Traffic in 1967, but the group's long and prosperous career was briefly interrupted in 1969, when Winwood, Clapton, Ginger Baker, and Rick Grech formed the first British supergroup, Blind Faith. Traffic finally split in 1975. Winwood did studio work with many varied artists before starting a sporadic career as a solo artist in 1977.

February	1981	1. WHILE YOU SEE A CHANCE	Island
May	1981	2. ARC OF A DIVER	Island
July	1982	3. STILL IN THE GAME	Island
November	1982	4. VALERIE	Island

PETER WOLF

Born: March 7, 1946
Hometown: Boston, Massachusetts

From the late sixties until early 1984, Peter sang as the lead vocalist for the legendary J. Geils Band, charting fifteen national singles, including the 1982 number-one song, "Centerfold." Wolf decided to pursue a solo career and had his first hit in the summer of 1984.

July	1984	LIGHTS OUT	EMI-America
October	1984	I NEED YOU TONIGHT	EMI-America
May	1985	OO-EEDIDDLEY-BOP	EMI-America

THE WONDER BAND

Members:
Silvio Tancredi—guitars, percussion
Neil Jason—bass
Al Izzo—drums, percussion
Jeff Schoen—keyboards
Teddy Coletti—keyboards
Victor Salazar—congas, bongos, tablas, percussion
Armando Noriega—sax, flute, percussion
Allen Schwartzberg—electronic percussion
Bob Miller—electronic percussion
Ray Gomez—guitar
Gil Robbins—tympani
Tony Pennisi—synthesizer
Suzanne Cianni—synthesizer

Although all the above members are listed as members of the Wonder Band on its one and only album, *Stairway To Love*, the project was conceived by three producers and a vocal arranger, and performed by session musicians. Ironically, not listed as a member of the Wonder Band was its lead singer/vocal arranger Phil Anastasi, who recorded in the sixties under the fictitious name Dean Parrish. The premise of *Stairway To Love* was to record an orchestrated disco medley of two popular Led Zeppelin songs, "Stairway To Heaven" and "Whole Lotta Love."

| March | 1979 | WHOLE LOTTA LOVE | Atco |

LAUREN WOOD

Hometown: Pittsburgh, Pennsylvania

Lauren Wood was bribed by her parents when she was five—if she practiced her piano, they'd buy her the rock 'n' roll and musical comedy records she'd requested. Lauren wrote her first song at age 10 and began playing guitar at age 15, learning her chops in the hopes of attracting the attention of her favorite Beatle, Paul McCartney, so they'd marry and write songs together for the rest of their lives. As teenagers, she and her cousin Novi Novog sang in a group called Rebecca and the Sunnybrook Farmers, which recorded one album, *Birth*, and toured. When that group broke up, the creative core, Lauren (renamed Chunky), Novi, and Ernie Eremita became a trio called Chunky, Novi & Ernie, and recorded two albums. Lauren, that group's principal writer, went on as a solo act, but continued to use assistance from Novi and Ernie. Her first hit, "Please Don't Leave," featured vocals by Michael McDonald, then of the Doobie Brothers. Lauren's songs have been recorded by Cher, Maxine Nightingale, Nicolette Larson, Lani Hall, Montrose, and others. She lives in Hollywood's Laurel Canyon in a house that features a larger-than-life-size robot named Igor.

September	1979	PLEASE DON'T LEAVE	Warner Bros.

STEVIE WOODS

Hometown: Columbus, Ohio

Stevie Woods left home at age 17 to front a touring band, but after six years he quit the road and settled in Austin, Texas, where he sang at nightclubs and wrote songs in the day. By late 1979, he realized he needed greater exposure, and packed up his car and drove to Los Angeles. Eight months later, a German producer hired a talent scout to comb Los Angeles for a singer for his first American production. That scout discovered Stevie singing in a nightclub. Stevie's first album, *Take Me to Your Heaven*, was released in August 1981, and spawned three charted singles.

September,	1981	STEAL THE NIGHT	Cotillion
January	1982	JUST CAN'T WIN 'EM ALL	Cotillion
May	1982	FLY AWAY	Cotillion

BILL WRAY

Hometown: Louisiana

While attending Louisiana State University, Bill Wray organized his first band. During summer vacations, he and the band took off for Hawaii, where they became very popular. In the summer of 1974, a Canadian-based manager heard them play at a rained-out bikini contest there, and invited them to Vancouver. Wray's first album was released in the spring of 1976.

Sometime later, Wray wrote and sang seven songs for a Brooke Shields movie called *Tilt*, and six songs for Michael (*Hair*) Butler's Broadway musical *Reggae*. Wray also appeared on NBC's music show, "Midnight Special." Fred Silverman, then a key figure at NBC, was reportedly so excited about Wray's stage presence and singing and writing talents that he approached Wray about doing his own TV special. Wray declined, saying he wasn't ready for such a career move.

May   1979   PINBALL THAT'S ALL   MCA

"WEIRD AL" YANKOVIC

Born: 1960
Hometown: Los Angeles, California

A long-time contributor to the nationally syndicated "Dr. Demento Radio Show," "Weird Al" Yankovic had his first major success in 1979 with his parody of the Knack's "My Sharona." He retitled it "My Bologna" and recorded it in the bathroom across the hall from the radio station at Cal Poly-San Luis Obispo, where he hosted a weekly comedy show while working toward a degree in architecture. The following year, the comic accordian player performed "Another One Rides The Bus," his parody of Queen's "Another One Bites The Dust," on Dr. Demento's live Sunday show on KMET in Los Angeles. The immediate audience response was overwhelming, and a tape of the song was added to the playlists of radio stations nationwide. Soon there was "Ricky," on which, as Lucy and Ricky

"Weird Al" Yankovic

Ricardo, he parodied Toni Basil's "Mickey," and then "Eat It," which parodied Michael Jackson's "Beat It," in both record and video formats.

April	1983	1. RICKY	Rock 'N' Roll
March	1984	2. EAT IT	Rock 'N' Roll
May	1984	3. KING OF SUEDE	Rock 'N' Roll
June	1984	4. I LOST ON JEOPARDY	Rock 'N' Roll

YARBROUGH & PEOPLES

Members:
    Cavin Yarbrough—vocals
    Alisa Peoples—vocals
Hometown: Dallas, Texas

Music has linked Cavin Yarbrough and Alisa Peoples since preschool days. Both from musical families, Cavin and Alisa were sent to the same piano teachers at a very early age. As they matured, both joined a church choir, where ultimately Cavin became the male lead singer and Alisa the female lead singer. They later led separate lives, but always looked forward to getting together at the church's annual meetings. Cavin joined a local band called Grand Theft, and would invite Alisa on stage whenever she was spotted in the audience. The two became Yarbrough & Peoples in 1977 and were discovered singing in a club by the Gap Band. The duo signed with the Gap Band's management and record companies and quickly had a hit record.

| February | 1981 | DON'T STOP THE MUSIC | Mercury |
| April | 1984 | DON'T WASTE YOUR TIME | RCA |

YAZ

Members:
    Genevieve Alison Moyet—vocals—Basildon, Essex, England
    Vince Clarke—synthesizers—Basildon, Essex, England
Hometown: England

Fresh out of a popular electronic band in England called Depeche Mode, Vince Clarke considered a solo career until he met Genevieve Alison Moyet. Nicknamed Alf by her French father, Moyet had been connected with countless rhythm and blues bands in the Southend/South Essex area. Fed up with not getting onto the London circuit, she advertised for "a rootsy blues band," but instead got Vince Clarke and his extensive collection of synthesizers. The duo, known as Yazoo in Great Britain but Yaz in the States (where another band coined the name Yazoo), immediately scored a big hit in their native country, where one music newspaper proclaimed Yazoo the most successful duo since Simon & Garfunkel. 1985 found Alf as a major solo act.

| September | 1982 | SITUATION | Sire |
| February | 1983 | ONLY YOU | Sire |

YELLOW MAGIC ORCHESTRA

Members:
  Haroumi Hosono—synthesizers—born: July 9, 1947
  Ryuichi Sakamoto—synthesizers—born: January 17, 1952
  Yukihiro Yakahashi—synthesizers—born: June 6, 1952
Hometown: Tokyo, Japan

Haroumi Hosono leads and produces the trio of Japanese musicians who are collectively known as Yellow Magic Orchestra, or Y.M.O. Fellow member Ryuichi Sakamoto is a classically trained musician and a graduate of Japan's best music and art school, where he is now an assistant professor. His lyrical piano playing is highly acclaimed in his native country, and so he is in steady demand as a studio musician. In 1983, he costarred with David Bowie in the film *Merry Christmas, Mr. Lawrence.* Yukihiro Takahashi, formerly the drummer in the Sadistic Miki Band, once opened on a long Roxy Music tour. He is Y.M.O.'s firmest bridge to the rhythms of rock.

Y.M.O. came together in early 1978, while "Harry" Hosono was working on "futuristic" concepts on his fourth solo album, *Paraiso.* He met Sakamoto and Takahashi at those sessions, a friendship materialized, and Y.M.O. became a working entity almost on the spot. In short time, the trio became a supergroup in Japan.

February   1980   COMPUTER GAMES   Horizon

YIPES!

Members:
  Pat McCurdy—vocals, keyboards
  Andy Bartel—guitar, vocals
  Michael Hoffman—guitar, vocals, percussion
  Pete Strand—bass, vocals
  Teddy Freese—drums
Hometown: Milwaukee, Wisconsin

Pat McCurdy, Pete Strand, and Michael Hoffman formed Yipes! in 1976. Many were called to audition for the group, but only Andy Bartel and Teddy Freese passed. The band's brand of humor made their performances popular, and the group was able to get over 250 gigs a year even before an album was recorded. Then, in a local battle of the bands contest, Yipes! won 12 hours of sessions at a local recording studio. With that time, Yipes! was able to record the demo tape that led to an album deal.

August   1980   DARLIN'   Millennium

PAUL YOUNG

Born: January 17, 1956
Hometown: Luton, Bedfordshire, England

Paul Young acknowledges that his leanings toward black American dance and soul music flew in the face of friends and fellow musicians in England, causing him to reluctantly suppress those inclinations during his first professional role as lead singer with Streetband, a short-lived heavy-metal band. From the ashes of Streetband came the Q-Tips, and at last Paul was able to explore his penchant for soul music. Even without a hit record, the Q-Tips became the highest paid, biggest-drawing act in the United Kingdom club circuit, playing some 700 gigs in the two and a half years the group remained together. When the Q-tips folded in 1982, Paul began writing songs for what would become his debut album in 1984, *No Parlez*. His backing group, the Royal Family, consists of ex-Q-Tip keyboardist Ian Kewley, guitarist Steve Bolton, bassist Pino Palladino, drummer Mark Pinder, and backing vocalists the Fabulous Wealthy Tarts (Maz Roberts and Kim Leslie).

October	1983	WHEREVER I LAY MY HAT	Columbia
February	1984	COME BACK AND STAY	Columbia
May	1984	LOVE OF THE COMMON PEOPLE	Columbia

YUTAKA

Hometown: Tokyo, Japan

Yutaka Yokokura and his band had just won the Yamaha Light Festival when his music came to the attention of Tats Nagashima, the well-known concert promoter who first brought the Beatles to Japan. Yutaka gave Tats a cassette, and Tats responded to the music by signing Yutaka to his publishing company and sending him to America to study. Once in the States, Yutaka sought out arranger/producer David Grusin, who agreed to produce Yutaka's debut jazz/pop album. That album, originally available only in Japan, became a much-in-demand import album in America, and was finally licensed to an American record firm.

July	1981	LOVE LIGHT	Alfa

Z

PIA ZADORA

Born: 1955
Hometown: New York, New York

Pia Zadora received national attention as a media personality, but has often been ridiculed in her attempts to become a singer, actress, nightclub entertainer, and film star. Pia is the daughter of "Skip" Schipani, one of Broadway's most distinguished first violinists, and Nina Zadora Schipani, a theatrical wardrobe supervisor and consultant, and following in her parents' line, Pia has appeared in Broadway shows. Pia is married to a real estate tycoon 30 years her senior.

March	1982	I'M IN LOVE AGAIN	Elektra/Curb
December	1982	THE CLAPPING SONG	Elektra
February	1985	WHEN THE RAIN BEGINS TO FALL (with Jermaine Jackson)	MCA/Curb

THE MICHAEL ZAGER BAND

Michael Zager grew up in New Jersey and spent time in several local bands there through the sixties before organizing one of New York City's

Michael Zager

Zapp. Roger Troutman (*middle, top row*).

landmark jazz-rock bands, Ten Wheel Drive, featuring Genya Ravan. (See *Genya RAVAN.*) Along with coleader Aram Schefrim, he led the band through four years and four albums. A few years later, Zager dove into disco music, arranging or producing music for Peabo Bryson, the Spinners, Dr. Hook, Cissy Houston, Fontella Bass, Paul Davis, and Ronnie Dyson. In 1977, he doubled his career by beginning to release records under his own name, the first as the Michael Zager Moon Band, which turns out to be Zager and a variety of session musicians.

| March | 1976 | DO IT WITH FEELING | Bang |
| March | 1978 | LET'S ALL CHANT | Private Stock |

ZAPP

Members:
>   Zapp Troutman—vocals, bass
>   Bobby Glover—vocals
>   Gregory Jackson—vocals, keyboards
>   Jerome Derrickson—horns
>   Eddie Barber—horns
>   Sherman Fleetwood—keyboards
>   Jannetta Boyce—vocals
>   Michael Warren—horns

Lester Troutman—percussion, drums
Larry Troutman—percussion
Roger Troutman—vocals, guitars, keyboards, talk box, bass, harmonica, vibes
Hometown: Hamilton, Ohio

Although Zapp's line-up is flexible, it is basically a flagship created by the four Troutman brothers, Roger, Lester, Larry, and "Zapp" (for whom the band is named). Roger Troutman, the leader of the group and also a solo artist who goes by the name Roger only, was friendly with another Ohio-based funk musician, William "Bootsy" Collins, who arranged sessions in a recording studio owned by his associate, George Clinton, of Parliament-Funkadelic. Bootsy played on and produced those tracks, which ultimately became Zapp's self-titled debut album. Zapp has since worked separately from Bootsy and Clinton.
See *ROGER*.

October   1980   MORE BOUNCE TO THE OUNCE   Warner Bros.

ZEBRA

Members:
Randy Jackson—vocals, guitar, piano, mellotron, synthesizers, percussion—born: February 28, 1955
Felix Hanemann—bass, keyboards, strings, synthesizers, vocals—born: May 1, 1953
Guy Gelso—drums, percussion, vocals—born: October 29, 1951
Hometown: New Orleans, Louisiana

Zebra. *Left to right:* Felix Hanemann, Guy Gelso, Randy Jackson.

As teenagers in New Orleans, Randy Jackson and Felix Hanemann first played together in a band called Shepherd's Bush before going on as an acoustic duo. Randy then met Guy Gelso, and with a keyboard player, Randy, Felix, and Guy formed Maelstrom, which lasted two months. Three months later, in 1975, the trio reunited and Zebra was born. (The name was picked while sitting in a bar one night trying to come up with a name; they noticed a Vogue magazine cover tacked to the wall depicting a beautiful woman riding a zebra, and the image appealed to the three.) The group slowly developed a following on the local club circuit, but knowing they needed to avoid overexposure, they started spending several months a year working the lucrative Long Island, New York, rock circuit. Zebra simultaneously became a very popular act in both regions. By the time the group's self-titled debut album was released, other parts of the country were beginning to respond favorably as well.

| July | 1983 | WHO'S BEHIND THE DOOR? | Atlantic |

WARREN ZEVON

Born: January 24, 1947
Hometown: Chicago, Illinois

Warren Zevon was born in Chicago and raised in California and Arizona. From his earliest years, he intended to be a serious composer, but wound up writing commercials for Ernest and Julio Gallo as well as songs, one of which appeared on the soundtrack of the film *Midnight Cowboy*. Zevon then toured with the Everly Brothers as pianist and bandleader, and following that duo's breakup, played alternately with Phil or Don. Zevon headed for Spain in 1975, but was urged by his old friend Jackson Browne to return to Los Angeles. Once back in the States, Zevon landed a record deal; Browne produced Zevon's self-titled debut album, and coproduced the second LP, *Excitable Boy*. Zevon's songs have been recorded by Boulder (which later became his touring band) and Linda Ronstadt. Zevon is divorced, has two children, Jordan and Ariel, and lives in Los Angeles with Kim Lankford of TV's "Knot's Landing."

| March | 1978 | WEREWOLVES OF LONDON | Asylum |
| March | 1980 | A CERTAIN GIRL | Asylum |

APPENDIX

These Too Made It

ADDRISI BROTHERS
April	1977	1. SLOW DANCIN' DON'T TURN ME ON	Buddah
September	1977	2. DOES SHE DO IT LIKE SHE DANCES	Buddah
December	1977	3. NEVER MY LOVE	Buddah
August	1979	4. GHOST DANCER	Scotti Bros.

AIRWAVES
| June | 1978 | SO HARD LIVING WITHOUT YOU | A & M |

THE AMERICAN COMEDY
| February | 1984 | BREAKING UP IS HARD ON YOU | Critique |

ARPEGGIO
| March | 1979 | LOVE & DESIRE | Polydor |

CHRISTOPHER ATKINS
| August | 1982 | HOW CAN I LIVE WITHOUT HER | Polydor |

AURRA
| March | 1982 | MAKE UP YOUR MIND | Salsoul |

BAND AID
| December | 1984 | DO THEY KNOW IT'S CHRISTMAS | Columbia |

BANDIT
| March | 1979 | ONE WAY LOVE | Ariola |

LONG JOHN BALDRY
| August | 1979 | YOU'VE LOST THAT LOVIN' FEELIN' | EMI-America |

THE FRANK BARBER ORCHESTRA
| May | 1982 | HOOKED ON THE BIG BANDS | Victory |

CHERYL BARNES
| April | 1979 | EASY TO BE HARD (HAIR SOUNDTRACK) | RCA |

THE BARRON KNIGHTS
| August | 1979 | THE TOPICAL SONG | Epic |

BECKMEIER BROTHERS
| July | 1979 | ROCK AND ROLL DANCIN' | Casablanca |

THE BLEND
| December | 1978 | I'M GONNA MAKE YOU LOVE ME | MCA |

BONNIE BOYER

July   1979   GOT TO GIVE INTO LOVE   Columbia

BREATHLESS

January   1980   TAKIN' IT BACK   EMI-America

NANCY BROOKS

March   1979   I'M NOT GONNA CRY ANYMORE   Arista

CHUCK BROWN & THE SOUL SEARCHERS

February   1979   BUSTIN' LOOSE   Source

JOCELYN BROWN

June   1984   SOMEBODY ELSE'S GUY   Vinyl Dreams

RANDY BROWN

March   1979   YOU SAYS IT ALL   Parachute

BUCKEYE

August   1979   WHERE WILL YOUR HEART TAKE YOU   Polydor

GARY BURBANK WITH BAND McNALLY

June   1980   WHO SHOT J. R.   Ovation

TANE CAIN

August   1982   HOLDIN' ON   RCA

THE CALL

May   1983   THE WALLS CAME DOWN   Mercury

CAMEO

April   1984   SHE'S STRANGE   Atlanta Artists

THE CANTINA BAND

July   1981   SUMMER 81 (BEACH BOY'S MEDLEY)   Millennium

DAVID CASTLE

September   1977   TEN TO EIGHT   Parachute
January   1978   THE LONELIEST MAN ON THE MOON   Parachute

CHANSON

November   1978   DON'T HOLD BACK   Ariola America

THE JOE CHEMAY BAND

February   1981   PROUD   Unicorn

CHRIS CHRISTIAN

October   1981   I WANT YOU, I NEED YOU   Boardwalk
August   1982   AIN'T NOTHIN' LIKE THE REAL THING/YOU'RE ALL I NEED   Boardwalk
                  TO GET BY

CLUB HOUSE

August   1983   DO IT AGAIN BILLIE JEAN MEDLEY   Atlantic

JOYCE COBB

| November | 1979 | DIG THE GOLD | Cream |

CONDUCTOR

| January | 1982 | VOICE ON THE RADIO | Montage |

COOPER BROTHERS

| October | 1978 | THE DREAM NEVER DIES | Capricorn |
| June | 1979 | I'LL KNOW HER WHEN I SEE HER | Capricorn |

MARSHALL CRENSHAW

| July | 1982 | SOMEDAY, SOMEWAY | Warner Bros. |

CUGINI

| December | 1979 | LET ME SLEEP ALONE | Scotti Bros. |

MICHAEL DAMIAN

| May | 1981 | SHE DID IT | Leg |

DANDY & THE DOOLITTLE BAND

| October | 1980 | WHO WERE YOU THINKIN' OF | Columbia |

DELIVERANCE

| August | 1980 | LEAVING L. A. | Columbia |

THE DILLMAN BAND

| May | 1981 | LOVIN' THE NIGHT AWAY | RCA |

DOLLAR

| December | 1979 | SHOOTING STAR | Atco |

DOUBLE IMAGE

| July | 1983 | NIGHT PULSE | Curb |

J. D. DREWS

| December | 1980 | DON'T WANT NOBODY | Unicorn |

EDDIE AND THE CRUISERS

| October | 1983 | ON THE DARK SIDE | Scotti Bros. |

EL COCO

October	1976	LET'S GET IT TOGETHER	Avi
November	1977	LOCOMOTION	Avi
October	1978	DANCING IN PARADISE	Avi

JACKIE ENGLISH

| December | 1980 | ONCE A NIGHT | Venture |

ERUPTION

| March | 1978 | I CAN'T STAND THE RAIN | Ariola |

JOE FAGIN

| July | 1982 | YOUNGER DAYS | Millennium |

FAITH BAND

December	1978	DANCIN' SHOES	Mercury
June	1979	YOU'RE MY WEAKNESS	Mercury

CEE FARROW

September	1983	SHOULD I LOVE YOU	Rocshire

FESTIVAL

March	1980	DON'T CRY FOR ME ARGENTINA	RSO

FIRE INC.

June	1984	TONIGHT IS WHAT IT MEANS TO BE YOUNG	MCA

JOHN FOGERTY

December	1984	THE OLD MAN DOWN THE ROAD	Warner Bros.

CHARLES FOX

January	1981	SEASONS	Handshake

FOXY

July	1978	GET OFF	Dash
March	1979	HOT NUMBER	Dash

ANDY FRASER

March	1984	DO YOU LOVE ME	Island

FUNKY COMMUNICATION COMMITTEE

July	1979	BABY I WANT YOU	Free Flight

GABRIEL

October	1978	MARTHA	Epic

GAMMA

January	1980	I'M ALIVE	Elektra
April	1982	RIGHT THE FIRST TIME	Elektra

GARY O.

July	1981	PAY YOU BACK WITH INTEREST	Capitol

GENTLE PERSUASION

February	1983	PLEASE MR. POSTMAN	Capitol

GET WET

April	1981	JUST SO LONELY	Boardwalk

THE GIBSON BROTHERS

June	1979	CUBA	Island

GIDEA PARK FEATURING ADRIAN BAKER

January	1982	SEASONS OF GOLD	Profile

JOHNNY GILL

March	1984	PERFECT COMBINATION (with Stacy Lattisaw)	Cotillion

GLASS MOON
March   1982   ON A CAROUSEL   Radio Records

GOANNA
June   1983   SOLID ROCK   Atco

GONZALES
January   1979   HAVEN'T STOPPED DANCING YET   Capitol

GOODY GOODY
November   1978   #1 D. J.   Atlantic

MICHAEL GORE
April   1984   TERMS OF ENDEARMENT   Capitol

G. Q.
March   1979   DISCO NIGHTS   Arista
June   1979   I DO LOVE YOU   Arista
March   1982   SAD GIRL   Arista

GRAND MASTER FLASH & THE FURIOUS FIVE
October   1982   THE MESSAGE   Sugar Hill

GREY & HANKS
March   1979   DANCIN'   RCA

GREG GUIDRY
February   1982   GOIN' DOWN   Columbia
July   1982   INTO MY LOVE   Columbia

HAGAR, SCHON, AARONSON, SHRIEVE
May   1984   WHITER SHADE OF PALE   Warner Bros.

HAIRCUT ONE HUNDRED
May   1982   LOVE PLUS ONE   Arista

LANI HALL
March   1981   WHERE'S YOUR ANGEL   A & M

COREY HART
May   1984   SUNGLASSES AT NIGHT   EMI-America
September   1984   IT AIN'T ENOUGH   EMI-America

HAWKS
March   1981   RIGHT AWAY   Columbia

HAYSI FANTAYZEE
July   1983   SHINY SHINY   RCA

THE HEADBOYS
November   1979   THE SHAPE OF THINGS TO COME   RSO

HEAD EAST

October	1975	NEVER BEEN ANY REASON	A & M
February	1976	LOVE ME TONIGHT	A & M
April	1978	SINCE YOU'VE BEEN GONE	A & M

HEADPINS

December	1983	JUST ONE MORE TIME	Solid Gold/MCA

MICHAEL HENDERSON

October	1978	TAKE ME I'M YOURS	Buddah

KEITH HERMAN

October	1979	SHE'S GOT A WHOLE NUMBER	Radio

HIGH ENERGY

September	1977	YOU CAN'T TURN ME OFF	Gordy
March	1978	LOVE IS ALL YOU NEED	Gordy
May	1983	HE'S A PRETENDER	Gordy

ERIC HINE

August	1981	NOT FADE AWAY	Montage

ROMAN HOLIDAY

June	1983	STAND BY	Jive/Arista
October	1983	DON'T TRY TO STOP IT	Jive/Arista

AMY HOLLAND

August	1980	HOW DO I SURVIVE	Capitol

LOLEATTA HOLLOWAY

March	1975	CRY TO ME	Aware
February	1977	DREAMIN'	Gold Mine
November	1978	ONLY YOU (with Bunny Sigler)	Gold Mine

JIMMY "BO" HORNE

April	1978	DANCE ACROSS THE FLOOR	Sunshine Sound

DAVID HUDSON

June	1980	HONEY, HONEY	Alston

HUGHES/THRALL

December	1982	BEG, BORROW OR STEAL	Boulevard

JOHN HUNTER

December	1984	TRAGEDY	Private

JIM HURT

October	1980	I LOVE WOMEN	Scotti Bros.

ICEHOUSE

August	1981	WE CAN GET TOGETHER	Chrysalis

INDUSTRY

November	1983	STATE OF THE NATION	Capitol

THE INMATES

December	1979	DIRTY WATER	Polydor

INSTANT FUNK

February	1979	I GOT MY MIND MADE UP	Salsoul

THE INVISIBLE MAN'S BAND

May	1980	ALL NIGHT THING	Mango

LaTOYA JACKSON

May	1984	HEART DON'T LIE	Private

MICK JACKSON

August	1978	BLAME IT ON THE BOOGIE	Atco

DEBBIE JACOBS

March	1980	HIGH ON YOUR LOVE	MCA

JO BOXERS

September	1983	JUST GOT LUCKY	RCA

THE JOHNNY AVERAGE BAND

February	1981	CH CH CHERLE	Bearsville

MICHAEL JOHNSON

April	1978	1. BLUER THAN BLUE	EMI-America
August	1978	2. ALMOST LIKE BEING IN LOVE	EMI-America
August	1979	3. THIS NIGHT WON'T LAST FOREVER	EMI-America
August	1980	4. YOU CAN CALL ME BLUE	EMI-America

HOWARD JONES

January	1984	NEW SONG	Elektra
April	1984	WHAT IS LOVE	Elektra

THE JONES GIRLS

June	1979	YOU GONNA MAKE ME LOVE SOMEONE ELSE	P.I.R.

JUNIOR

February	1982	MAMA USED TO SAY	Mercury

MADLEEN KANE

February	1982	YOU CAN	Chalet

KANO

December	1981	CAN'T HOLD BACK	Mirage

RAY KENNEDY

May	1980	JUST FOR THE MOMENT	Arc/Columbia

NIK KERSHAW
March   1984   WOULDN'T IT BE GOOD   MCA

FERN KINNEY
August   1979   GROOVE ME   Malaco

JIM KIRK & THE TM SINGERS
February   1980   VOICE OF FREEDOM   Capitol

KISSING THE PINK
August   1983   MAYBE THIS DAY   Atlantic

KLIQUE
October   1983   STOP DOGGIN' ME AROUND   MCA

KONGAS
April   1978   GIMME SOME LOVIN'   Polydor

KORONA
March   1980   LET ME BE   United Artists

KRAFTWERK
March   1975   AUTOBAHN   Vertigo
June   1978   TRANS-EUROPE EXPRESS   Capitol

LA FLAVOUR
June   1980   ONLY THE LONELY   Sweet City

LAID BACK
February   1984   WHITE HORSE   Sire

LAKESIDE
January   1981   FANTASTIC VOYAGE   Solar

KEVIN LAMB
June   1978   ON THE WRONG TRACK   Arista

LANIER AND COMPANY
December   1982   AFTER I CRY TONIGHT   Larc

DENISE LaSALLE
August   1971   1. TRAPPED BY A THING CALLED LOVE   Westbound
February   1972   2. NOW RUN AND TELL THAT   Westbound
October   1972   3. MAN SIZED JOB   Westbound
January   1978   4. LOVE ME RIGHT   ABC

DAVID LASLEY
March   1982   IF I HAD MY WISH TONIGHT   EMI-America

JAMES LAST BAND
January   1972   MUSIC FROM ACROSS THE WAY   Polydor
March   1980   THE SEDUCTION   Polydor

DEBRA LAWS

| August | 1981 | VERY SPECIAL (with Ronnie Laws) | Elektra |

LAZY RACER

| July | 1979 | KEEP ON RUNNING AWAY | A & M |

MARCY LEVY

| November | 1980 | HELP ME (with Robin Gibb) | RSO |

ORSA LIA

| March | 1979 | I NEVER SAID I LOVE YOU | Infinity |

LINDISFARNE

| September | 1972 | LADY ELEANOR | Elektra |
| September | 1978 | RUN FOR HOME | Atco |

LINER

| March | 1979 | YOU AND ME | Atco |

LIQUID GOLD

| April | 1979 | MY BABY'S BABY | Parachute |
| September | 1983 | WHAT SHE'S GOT | Critique |

MACHINE

| March | 1979 | THERE BUT FOR THE GRACE OF GOD GO I | Hologram |

BENNY MARDONES

| June | 1980 | INTO THE NIGHT | Polydor |

MARSHALL HAIN

| December | 1978 | DANCIN' IN THE CITY | Capitol |

WAYNE MASSEY

| October | 1980 | ONE LIFE TO LIVE | Polydor |

ALTON McCLAIN & DESTINY

| April | 1979 | IT MUST BE LOVE | Polydor |

McCRARY'S

| August | 1978 | YOU | Portrait |

McFADDEN, McLARTY

| October | 1980 | I COULD BE GOOD FOR YOU | Casablanca |

PETER McIAN

| April | 1980 | SOLITAIRE | Arc/Columbia |

GERARD McMAHON

| April | 1983 | COUNT ON ME | Warner Bros. |

LARRY JOHN McNALLY

| August | 1981 | JUST LIKE PARADISE | Arc/Columbia |

SHAMUS M'COOL

| July | 1981 | AMERICAN MEMORIES | Perspective |

MEN WITHOUT HATS

| June | 1983 | THE SAFETY DANCE | Backstreet |
| November | 1983 | I LIKE | MCA |

FRANK MILLS

January	1972	LOVE ME, LOVE ME LOVE	Sunflower
January	1979	MUSIC BOX DANCER	Polydor
November	1979	PETER PIPER	Polydor

MINOR DETAIL

| September | 1983 | CANVAS OF LIFE | Polydor |

MISTRESS

| November | 1979 | MISTRUSTED LOVE | RSO |

MODERN ENGLISH

| April | 1983 | I MELT WITH YOU | Sire |
| April | 1984 | HANDS ACROSS THE SEA | Sire |

T. S. MONK

| February | 1981 | BON BON VIE | Mirage |

THE MONROES

| May | 1982 | WHAT DO ALL THE PEOPLE KNOW | Alfa |

GIORGIO MORODER

March	1972	SON OF MY FATHER	Dunhill
January	1979	THE CHASE	Casablanca
July	1984	REACH OUT (with Paul Engeman)	Columbia

THE MOTORS

| May | 1980 | LOVE AND LONELINESS | Virgin |

MOVING PICTURES

| September | 1982 | WHAT ABOUT ME | Network |

MUSIQUE

| October | 1978 | IN THE BUSH | Prelude |

NATURE'S DIVINE

| November | 1979 | I JUST CAN'T CONTROL MYSELF | Infinity |

LOZ NETTO

| June | 1983 | FADE AWAY | 21 Records |

NEWCLEUS
June   1984   JAM ON IT   Sunnyview

NEW ENGLAND
May   1979   DON'T EVER WANNA LOSE YOU   Infinity
September   1979   HELLO, HELLO, HELLO   Infinity

NIELSEN/PEARSON
September   1980   IF YOU SHOULD SAIL   Capitol
August   1981   THE SUN AIN'T GONNA SHINE ANYMORE   Capitol

NIGHT
June   1979   HOT SUMMER NIGHTS   Planet
February   1981   LOVE ON THE AIRWAVES   Planet

NITEFLYTE
September   1979   IF YOU WANT IT   Ariola

CHRIS NORMAN
January   1979   STUMBLIN' IN (with Suzie Quatro)   RSO

JOHN O'BANION
March   1981   LOVE YOU LIKE I NEVER LOVED BEFORE   Elektra

O'BRYAN
March   1982   THE GIGOLO   Capitol

RIC OCASEK
February   1983   SOMETHING TO GRAB FOR   Geffen

OFF BROADWAY
March   1980   STAY IN TIME   Atlantic

JANE OLIVOR
September   1977   SOME ENCHANTED EVENING   Columbia
May   1978   HE'S SO FINE   Columbia

OLLIE AND JERRY
June   1984   BREAKIN' . . . THERE'S NO STOPPING US   Polydor

LENORE O'MALLEY
July   1980   FIRST BE A WOMAN   Polydor

ONE WAY
May   1982   CUTIE PIE   MCA

YOKO ONO
March   1981   WALKING ON THIN ICE   Geffen

ORION THE HUNTER
June   1984   SO YOU RAN   Portrait

ROBERT ELLIS ORRAL

March	1983	I COULDN'T SAY NO (with Carlene Carter)	RCA

OXO

February	1983	WHIRLY GIRL	Geffen

ROBBIE PATTON

July	1981	DON'T GIVE IT UP	Liberty
March	1983	SMILING ISLANDS	Atlantic

HENRY PAUL BAND

December	1981	KEEPING OUR LOVE ALIVE	Atlantic

PENDULUM

November	1980	GYPSY SPIRIT	Venture

PHILLY CREME

June	1979	MOTOWN REVIEW	Fantasy/WMOT

PHOTOGLO

PHOTOGLOW

March	1980	WE WERE MEANT TO BE LOVERS	20th Century

JIM PHOTOGLO

April	1981	FOOL IN LOVE WITH YOU	20th Century

PINK LADY

June	1979	KISS IN THE DARK	Elektra/Curb

PLANET P

April	1983	WHY ME	Geffen

PLEASURE

December	1979	GLIDE	Fantasy

THE PLIMSOULS

July	1983	A MILLION MILES AWAY	Geffen

POUSETTE-DART BAND

September	1979	FOR LOVE	Capitol

DON RAY

September	1978	GOT TO HAVE LOVIN'	Polydor

RCR

April	1980	SCANDEL	Radio Records

DANN ROGERS

December	1979	LOOKS LIKE LOVE AGAIN	International Artists

SAVOY BROWN

December	1969	I'M TIRED	Parrot
November	1971	TELL MAMA	Parrot
October	1981	RUN TO ME	Townhouse

PHIL SEYMOUR

| January | 1981 | PRECIOUS TO ME | Boardwalk |

TOMMY SHAW

| September | 1984 | GIRLS WITH GUNS | A & M |
| December | 1984 | LONELY SCHOOL | A & M |

SHOT IN THE DARK

| April | 1981 | PLAYING WITH LIGHTNING | RSO |

SILVERADO

| July | 1981 | READY FOR LOVE | Pavillion |

ERROL SOBER

| March | 1979 | HEART TO HEART | Number One |

THE STAR WARS INTERGALACTIC DROID CHOIR & CHORALE

| December | 1980 | WHAT CAN YOU GET A WOOKIEE FOR CHRISTMAS | RSO |

DAVE STEWART

| December | 1981 | IT'S MY PARTY (with Barbra Gaskin) | Platinum |

THE STOMPERS

| June | 1983 | NEVER TELL AN ANGEL | Boardwalk |

STONEBOLT

| August | 1978 | I WILL STILL LOVE YOU | Parachute |
| February | 1979 | LOVE STRUCK | Parachute |

THE STYLE COUNCIL

| April | 1984 | MY EVER CHANGING MOODS | Geffen |
| July | 1984 | YOU'RE THE BEST THING | Geffen |

SUGAR HILL GANG

November	1979	RAPPER'S DELIGHT	Sugar Hill
February	1981	8TH WONDER	Sugar Hill
February	1982	APACHE	Sugar Hill

GLENN SUTTON

| January | 1979 | THE FOOTBALL CARD | Mercury |

TAKA BOOM

| May | 1979 | NIGHT DANCIN' | Ariola |

TALK TALK

October	1982	TALK TALK	EMI-America
March	1984	IT'S MY LIFE	EMI-America
June	1984	SUCH A SHAME	EMI-America

GARY TANNER

May	1978	SOMEWHERE OVER THE RAINBOW	20th Century

TASHA THOMAS

January	1979	SHOOT ME	Atlantic

TIGHT FIT

October	1981	BACK TO THE 60'S	Arista

TMG

March	1979	LAZY EYES	Atco

TOTAL COELLO

April	1983	I EAT CANNIBALS	Chrysalis

TOUCH

July	1980	WHEN THE SPIRIT MOVES YOU	Atco
January	1981	DON'T YOU KNOW WHAT LOVE IS	Atco

TROOPER

August	1978	RAISE A LITTLE HELL	MCA

ERIC TROYER

July	1980	MIRAGE	Chrysalis

UNIPOP

December	1982	WHAT IF I SAID I LOVE YOU	Kat Family

USA FOR AFRICA

March	1985	★ WE ARE THE WORLD	Columbia

DANA VALERY

June	1976	WILL YOU LOVE ME TOMORROW	Phantom
January	1980	I DON'T WANT TO BE LONELY	Scotti Bros.

THE VAPORS

September	1980	TURNING JAPANESE	United Artists

VAUGH MASON AND CREWE

March	1980	BOUNCE, ROCK, SKATE, ROLL	Brunswick

WILLIS VIGORISH

December	1980	MERRY CHRISTMAS IN THE NFL	Handshake

JACK WAGNER

October	1984	ALL I NEED	Qwest

JAMES WALSH GYPSY BAND

October   1978   CUZ IT'S YOU GIRL   RCA

MAX WERNER

May   1981   RAIN IN MAY   Radio Records

WEST STREET MOB

September   1981   (LET'S DANCE) MAKE YOUR BODY MOVE   Sugarhill
April   1982   SING A SIMPLE SONG   Sugarhill

WILSON BROTHERS

October   1979   ANOTHER NIGHT   Atco

WITCH QUEEN

April   1979   BANG A GONG   Roadshow

BOB WOLFER

December   1982   PAPA WAS A ROLLING STONE   Constellation

JOHN PAUL YOUNG

January   1976   YESTERDAY'S HERO   Ariola American
July   1978   LOVE IS IN THE AIR   Scotti Brothers
December   1978   LOST IN YOUR LOVE   Scotti Brothers

KAREN YOUNG

September   1978   HOT SHOT   West End

ZWOL

September   1978   NEW YORK CITY   EMI-America
February   1979   CALL OUT MY NAME   EMI-America

INDEX OF SONG TITLES

PHOTO CREDITS